RECORDS OF THE
LIFE OF JESUS

RECORDS OF THE LIFE OF JESUS

Book I: *The Record of Mt-Mk-Lk*
Book II: *The Record of John*

By
HENRY BURTON SHARMAN, PH.D.
Honorary Lecturer in the Department of History
Yenching University, Peking, China

SEQUOIA SEMINAR FOUNDATION

PALO ALTO

Printed in the
United States of America

RECORDS OF THE LIFE OF JESUS

THE PURPOSE

The purpose of the book is to present the records of the life of Jesus in that form which will make most fully available the contributions of the several sources, both individual and collective, to an understanding of the actual career of Jesus. It has been the aim so to set forth the material as to provide primarily for an historical rather than a critical knowledge of the records. Stated in another way, the foremost intention has been to produce, in the language and in the order of the original records, a Life of Jesus. But it is thought also that, in the pursuance of that aim, the literary phenomena of the records have been so exhibited as to provide the basis for somewhat thorough critical study of the source relationships of these records.

THE METHOD

At no point throughout the work has any theory or hypothesis as to any literary or other relation of these records to one another had any part in the determination of the arrangement or the showing forth of the material. Mark is placed in the order of Mark; Luke is placed in the order of Luke, and John in its own order. In the case of Matthew only has any departure in order been made, and there for three chapters only (8–9–10) of the twenty-eight of that record. The departure made in that case was not based on any theory as to the source relations of the records, but resulted simply from the decision to conform Matthew in these chapters (8–9–10), as Matthew of itself is conformed throughout the rest of its structure, to that order of events on which Mark and Luke are in complete agreement. It will be evident, therefore, that not only has no theory of the relations of these records had any place in the work but also that the book cannot be regarded as a harmony of the records.

THE FORM

Those portions of the text that appear in roman type represent each record in its own chronological order, except that chapters 8–9–10 of Matthew, though in roman type, are not in the Matthew order,[1] but are conformed to the order of Mark-Luke. Those portions of the text that appear in italic type are not in the sequence of the records from which they come, but are placed where they stand in order that they may be studied there in relation to the record that does stand chronologically at that point. If, therefore, the reader will pass over what stands in italic type, the book may be used for the independent consecutive study of any one of the four individual records.[2]

[1] It should be observed that even within these chapters the Matthew order of events corresponds in considerable measure to that of Mark-Luke, for example, the consecution of §§ 50–52 and of §§ 29–31.

[2] In the case of the apparent (though not real) confusion in the Matthew order resulting from the conforming of Matthew 8–9–10 to the order of Mark-Luke, guidance is given by indicating in parts of Matthew the place of the succeeding portion by means of the notation (+§ 26) and the like at the end of the section, and for backward reference (§ 23+) and the like at the head of the section.

THE FEATURES

It has been the intention throughout to show on each page all related material from all parts of the records—either by direct parallelism or by attached references to footnotes. When the related material has chronological agreement, all the reports stand in parallelism in roman type. When the relation is one of event or of thought only and not also of chronology, the report out of its own chronological order stands in parallelism in italic type, with a cross-reference to the section where it may be found in its own order and therefore in roman type. When the related material from distant places in the records has such bond with, or relationship in, those other places as cannot be properly or adequately shown by immediate parallelism, these related portions are set forth as attached footnotes. It should be true, therefore, that on any page of the book one may find the account of every occurrence within the records of those events or sayings that appear on that page—subject only to the general reservation that in the record of Matt-Mark-Luke no references forward are given to the record of John,[1] though every effort has been made to give completeness to the references that are shown throughout John to the related material in Matt-Mark-Luke.

THE SUBDIVISIONS

The subdivisions of the paragraphs,[2] made by the simple expedient of opening the text without any change of form or order, have been determined (a) by what it was thought would best contribute to comparative study and to ease of cross-reference, and (b) by what seemed the natural subdivisions of the thought. In general, the former consideration controlled the subdivisions in Matt-Mark-Luke; while in much of John, where cross-references and comparisons are fewer, the subdivisions of paragraphs were made with the purpose of possibly facilitating at some points the grasp and memory of the complex thought.

THE ORDER

It has been believed that the clearest and soundest results could not be reached, in any serious effort to understand Jesus, by an endeavor to reconstruct the history through the direct combination of the record of Matt-Mark-Luke with the record of John. Rather it has been thought that one should first be enabled to acquire the contributions of Matt-Mark-Luke, without taking any account of the chronological or other elements of John—not necessarily because of any judgment as to the relative historical worth of these sources, but solely on the basis of the fundamental difference in the method of their approach to the theme. When one has attained some adequate knowledge of the record of Matt-Mark-Luke, the immeasurable values in the record of John will be both better understood and more justly used in coming to the fulness of the knowledge of the stature of Jesus.

EASTER, 1917

[1] The references forward from the record of Mt-Mk-Lk to the record of John are shown completely and in order on page 235.

[2] The paragraphing of the text in roman type does not depart from the Revised Version of 1881, except that not always (though usually) does that version show a paragraph where this book begins a section and therefore starts another paragraph.

RECORDS OF THE LIFE OF JESUS

BOOK I: THE RECORD OF MT-MK-LK

CHAPTER I

STATEMENTS ABOUT ORIGINS

CHAPTER II

EARLY LIFE OF JOHN AND OF JESUS

CHAPTER III

ACTIVITY OF JOHN AND ITS RELATION TO JESUS

CHAPTER IV

BEGINNINGS OF THE PUBLIC ACTIVITY OF JESUS

CHAPTER X

TOUR OF THE DISCIPLES AND RESULTANT EVENTS

CHAPTER XI

DEMAND BY PHARISEES FOR CONFORMITY AND CREDENTIALS

CHAPTER XII

FORECASTS OF CONFLICT WITH THE JERUSALEM AUTHORITIES

CHAPTER XIII

DEPARTURE FROM GALILEE FOR JERUSALEM

CHAPTER XIV

CONDEMNATION FOR OPPONENTS AND CONCERN FOR DISCIPLES

CHAPTER XV

DEEP FEELING AND DIRECT TEACHING

CHAPTER XVI

MANY TRUTHS TAUGHT IN PARABLES

CHAPTER XVII

TEACHING AND JOURNEYING ON TO JERUSALEM

CHAPTER XXIV

EVENTS SUBSEQUENT TO THE DEATH OF JESUS

BOOK II: THE RECORD OF JOHN

CHAPTER I

PROLOGUE TO THE RECORD OF JOHN

CHAPTER II

IN BETHANY BEYOND JORDAN

CHAPTER III

IN THE PROVINCE OF GALILEE

CHAPTER IV

IN JERUSALEM AT THE PASSOVER

CHAPTER V

IN THE LAND OF JUDÆA

CHAPTER VI

IN THE PROVINCE OF SAMARIA

CHAPTER VII

IN THE PROVINCE OF GALILEE

CHAPTER VIII

IN JERUSALEM AT A FEAST

CHAPTER IX

ABOUT THE SEA OF GALILEE

CHAPTER X

AT THE FEAST OF TABERNACLES

CHAPTER XI

AT THE FEAST OF THE DEDICATION

CHAPTER XII

IN THE REGION OF JERUSALEM

CHAPTER XIII

CHALLENGE TO THE JERUSALEM LEADERS

CHAPTER XIV

FINAL HOURS WITH DISCIPLES

CHAPTER XV

JUDICIAL TRIALS AND CRUCIFIXION

CHAPTER XVI

SUBSEQUENT TO THE DEATH OF JESUS

BOOK I

THE RECORD OF MT-MK-LK

RECORDS OF THE LIFE OF JESUS

BOOK I

THE RECORD OF MT-MK-LK

CHAPTER I

STATEMENTS ABOUT ORIGINS

§1 ORIGIN OF THE RECORDS

LUKE 1:1-4

Forasmuch as many have taken in hand to 1 draw up a narrative concerning those matters which have been [1]fulfilled among us, even as 2 they delivered them unto us, which from the beginning were eyewitnesses and ministers of the word, it seemed good to me also, having 3 traced the course of all things accurately from the first, to write unto thee in order, most excellent Theophilus; that thou mightest know the 4 certainty concerning the [2]things [3]wherein thou wast instructed.

§2 THE GENEALOGY OF JESUS

MATT 1:1-17	LUKE 3:23-38	
1 [4]The book of the [5]generation of Jesus Christ, the son of David, the son of Abraham.	23 And Jesus himself, when he began to teach, was about thirty years of age, being the son (as was supposed) of Joseph,	
2 Abraham begat Isaac; and Isaac begat Jacob; and Jacob begat Judah and his brethren;	the son of Heli,	the son of Levi,
3 and Judah begat Perez and Zerah of Tamar;	24the son of Matthat, the son of Levi, the son of Melchi, the son of Jannai,	30the son of Symeon, the son of Judas, the son of Joseph, the son of Jonam,
and Perez begat Hezron; and Hezron begat [6]Ram;	the son of Joseph, 25the son of Mattathias,	the son of Eliakim, 31the son of Melea,
4 and [6]Ram begat Amminadab; and Amminadab begat Nahshon; and Nahshon begat Salmon;	the son of Amos, the son of Nahum, the son of Esli, the son of Naggai,	the son of Menna, the son of Mattatha, the son of Nathan, the son of David,
5 and Salmon begat Boaz of Rahab; and Boaz begat Obed of Ruth; and Obed begat Jesse;	26the son of Maath, the son of Mattathias, the son of Semein, the son of Josech,	32the son of Jesse, the son of Obed, the son of Boaz, the son of [10]Salmon,
6 and Jesse begat David the king.	the son of Joda,	the son of Nahshon,
And David begat Solomon of her that had been the wife of Uriah;	27the son of Joanan, the son of Rhesa, the son of Zerubbabel,	33the son of Amminadab, [11]the son of [12]Arni,
7 and Solomon begat Rehoboam; and Rehoboam begat Abijah; and Abijah begat [7]Asa;	the son of [9]Shealtiel, the son of Neri,	the son of Hezron, the son of Perez,
8 and [7]Asa begat Jehoshaphat; and Jehoshaphat begat Joram; and Joram begat Uzziah;	28the son of Melchi, the son of Addi, the son of Cosam, the son of Elmadam,	the son of Judah, 34the son of Jacob, the son of Isaac, the son of Abraham,
9 and Uzziah begat Jotham; and Jotham begat Ahaz; and Ahaz begat Hezekiah;	the son of Er, 29the son of Jesus, the son of Eliezer,	the son of Terah, the son of Nahor, 35the son of Serug,
10and Hezekiah begat Manasseh; and Manasseh begat [8]Amon; and [8]Amon begat Josiah;	the son of Jorim, the son of Matthat,	the son of Reu, the son of Peleg,

ERV margin: 1 Or fully established   2 Greek words   3 Or which thou wast taught by word of mouth   4 Or The genealogy of Jesus Christ   5 Or birth: as in verse 18   6 Greek Aram   7 Greek Asaph   8 Greek Amos   9 Greek Salathiel   10 Some ancient authorities write Sala and one writes Admin for Amminadab   12 Some ancient authorities write Aram   11 Many ancient authorities insert the son of Admin:

OT references: Mt 1:2-6 and Lk 3:31-34 = 1 Chronicles 2:1-15   Mt 1:3-6 and Lk 3:32-33 = Ruth 4:18-22
Mt 1:7-12 = 1 Chronicles 3:10-17   Lk 3:27 = 1 Chronicles 3:17   Lk 3:34-36 = 1 Chronicles 1:24-28

MATT 1

[11]and Josiah begat Jechoniah and his brethren, at the time of the [1]carrying away to Babylon.

[12] And after the [1]carrying away to Babylon, Jechoniah begat [2]Shealtiel;
  and [2]Shealtiel begat Zerubbabel;
[13]and Zerubbabel begat Abiud;
  and Abiud begat Eliakim;
  and Eliakim begat Azor;
[14]and Azor begat Sadoc;
  and Sadoc begat Achim;
  and Achim begat Eliud;
[15]and Eliud begat Eleazar;
  and Eleazar begat Matthan;
  and Matthan begat Jacob;
[16]and Jacob begat Joseph the husband of Mary, of whom was born Jesus, who is called Christ.

[17] So all the generations from Abraham unto David are fourteen generations; and from David unto the [1]carrying away to Babylon fourteen generations; and from the [1]carrying away to Babylon unto the Christ fourteen generations.

LUKE 3

the son of Eber,
the son of Shelah,
[36]the son of Cainan,
the son of Arphaxad,
the son of Shem,
the son of Noah,
the son of Lamech,
[37]the son of Methuselah,
the son of Enoch,

the son of Jared,
the son of Mahalaleel,
the son of Cainan,
[38]the son of Enos,
the son of Seth,
the son of Adam,
the son of God.
(§19)

§ 3 FORECAST TO THE FATHER OF JOHN

MATTHEW

A   *In the days of Herod the king.* (§11 A) = 2:1

D   *With verse 17b, compare §17 EF and §41 E*

LUKE 1:5-25

A   There was in the days of Herod, king of [5] Judæa, a certain priest named Zacharias, of the course of Abijah: and he had a wife of the daughters of Aaron, and her name was Elisabeth. And they were both righteous before [6] God, walking in all the commandments and ordinances of the Lord blameless. And they [7] had no child, because that Elisabeth was barren, and they both were *now* [3]well stricken in years.
B   Now it came to pass, while he executed the [8] priest's office before God in the order of his course, according to the custom of the priest's [9] office, his lot was to enter into the [4]temple of the Lord and burn incense. And the whole[10] multitude of the people were praying without at the hour of incense.
C   And there appeared[11] unto him an angel of the Lord standing on the right side of the altar of incense. And Zacha-[12] rias was troubled when he saw *him,* and fear fell upon him. But the angel said unto him, Fear[13] not, Zacharias: because thy supplication is heard, and thy wife Elisabeth shall bear thee a son, and thou shalt call his name John.
D   And[14] thou shalt have joy and gladness; and many shall rejoice at his birth. For he shall be great[15] in the sight of the Lord, and he shall drink no wine nor [5]strong drink; and he shall be filled with the [6]Holy Ghost, even from his mother's womb. And many of the children of Israel[16]

ERV margin: 1 Or *removal to Babylon*   2 Greek *Salathiel*   3 Greek *advanced in their days*   4 Or *sanctuary*
5 Greek *sikera*   6 Or *Holy Spirit:* and so throughout this book

OT references: Lk 3:36-38 = 1 Chronicles 1:1-4   Lk 1:5 = 1 Chronicles 24:10   Lk 1:15 = Numbers 6:3 and Judges 13:4-5

LUKE I

shall he turn unto the Lord their God. And he[17] shall [1]go before his face in the spirit and power of Elijah, to turn the hearts of the fathers to the children, and the disobedient *to walk* in the wisdom of the just; to make ready for the Lord a people prepared *for him*.

E And Zacharias said[18] unto the angel, Whereby shall I know this? for I am an old man, and my wife [2]well stricken in years. And the angel answering said unto him,[19] I am Gabriel, that stand in the presence of God; and I was sent to speak unto thee, and to bring thee these good tidings. And behold, thou[20] shalt be silent and not able to speak, until the day that these things shall come to pass, because thou believedst not my words, which shall be fulfilled in their season.

F And the people were[21] waiting for Zacharias, and they marvelled [3]while he tarried in the [4]temple. And when he[22] came out, he could not speak unto them: and they perceived that he had seen a vision in the [4]temple: and he continued making signs unto them, and remained dumb. And it came to[23] pass, when the days of his ministration were fulfilled, he departed unto his house.

G And after these days Elisabeth his wife con-[24]ceived; and she hid herself five months, saying, Thus hath the Lord done unto me in the days[25] wherein he looked upon *me*, to take away my reproach among men.

§ 4 FORECAST TO THE MOTHER OF JESUS

MATTHEW	LUKE 1:26-38

A *Mary had been betrothed to Joseph.* (§6 A) = 1:18

Joseph, thou son of David. (§6 B) = 1:20

A Now in the sixth month the angel Gabriel[26] was sent from God unto a city of Galilee, named Nazareth, to a virgin betrothed to a man whose[27] name was Joseph, of the house of David; and the virgin's name was Mary. And he came in[28] unto her, and said, Hail, thou that art [5]highly favoured, the Lord *is* with thee.[6] But she was[29] greatly troubled at the saying, and cast in her mind what manner of salutation this might be. And the angel said unto her, Fear not, Mary:[30] for thou hast found [7]favour with God.

B *And she shall bring forth a son; and thou shalt call his name* JESUS. (§6 C) = 1:21

B And be-[31]hold, thou shalt conceive in thy womb, and bring forth a son, and shalt call his name JESUS.

C [8]*Where is he that is born King of the Jews?* (§11 B) = 2:2

C He shall be great, and shall be called[32] the Son of the Most High: and the Lord God shall give unto him the throne of his father David: and he shall reign over the house of[33] Jacob [9]for ever; and of his kingdom there shall be no end.

D *She was found with child of the* [10]*Holy Ghost.* (§6 A) = 1:18

That which is [11]*conceived in her is of the Holy Ghost.* (§6 B) = 1:20

D And Mary said unto the angel,[34] How shall this be, seeing I know not a man? And the angel answered and said unto her, The[35] Holy Ghost shall come upon thee, and the

---

ERV margin: [1] Some ancient authorities read *come nigh before his face* [2] Greek *advanced in her days* [3] Or *at his tarrying* [4] Or *sanctuary* [5] Or *endued with grace* [6] Many ancient authorities add *blessed* art *thou among women:* see verse 42 [7] Or *grace* [8] Or *Where is the King of the Jews that is born?* [9] Greek *unto the ages* [10] Or *Holy Spirit:* and so throughout this book [11] Greek *begotten*

OT references: Lk 1:17 = Malachi 4:5-6   Lk 1:19 = Daniel 8:16 and 9:21   Lk 1:31 = Isaiah 7:14   Lk 1:32-33 = 2 Samuel 7:12-17   Mt 2:2 = Numbers 24:17   Lk 1:35 = Exodus 13:12

LUKE 1

power of the Most High shall overshadow thee: wherefore also [1]that which [2]is to be born[3] shall be called holy, the Son of God.

E   And behold,36 Elisabeth thy kinswoman, she also hath conceived a son in her old age: and this is the sixth month with her that [4]was called barren. For37 no word from God shall be void of power. And38 Mary said, Behold, the [5]handmaid of the Lord; be it unto me according to thy word. And the angel departed from her.

§ 5 FORECAST BY THE MOTHER OF JOHN

LUKE 1:39-56

A   And Mary arose in these days and went into30 the hill country with haste, into a city of Judah; and entered into the house of Zacharias and40 saluted Elisabeth. And it came to pass, when41 Elisabeth heard the salutation of Mary, the babe leaped in her womb; and Elisabeth was filled with the Holy Ghost; and she lifted up42 her voice with a loud cry, and said,

B   Blessed *art* thou among women, and blessed *is* the fruit of thy womb. And whence is this to me, that the43 mother of my Lord should come unto me? For44 behold, when the voice of thy salutation came into mine ears, the babe leaped in my womb for joy. And blessed *is* she that [6]believed; for45 there shall be a fulfilment of the things which have been spoken to her from the Lord.

C   And46 Mary said,

My soul doth magnify the Lord,
And my spirit hath rejoiced in God my47 Saviour.
For he hath looked upon the low estate of his48 [7]handmaiden:
For behold, from henceforth all generations shall call me blessed.
For he that is mighty hath done to me great49 things;
And holy is his name.
And his mercy is unto generations and gen-50 erations
On them that fear him.
He hath shewed strength with his arm;   51
He hath scattered the proud [8]in the imagination of their heart.
He hath put down princes from *their* thrones,52
And hath exalted them of low degree.
The hungry he hath filled with good things; 53
And the rich he hath sent empty away.
He hath holpen Israel his servant,   54
That he might remember mercy
(As he spake unto our fathers)   55
Toward Abraham and his seed for ever.

D   And Mary abode with her about three56 months, and returned unto her house.

ERV margin: 1 Or *the holy thing which is to be born shall be called the Son of God*   2 Or *is begotten*   3 Some ancient authorities insert *of thee*   4 Or *is*   5 Greek *bondmaid*   6 Or *believed that there shall be*   7 Greek *bond-maiden*   8 Or *by*

OT references: Lk 1:37 = Genesis 18:14   Lk 1:46-47 = 1 Samuel 2:1   Lk 1:48 = 1 Samuel 1:11   Lk 1:50 = Psalm 103:17   Lk 1:51 = Psalm 89:10   Lk 1:52 = 1 Samuel 2:7-8 and Job 5:11 and 12:19   Lk 1:53 = 1 Samuel 2:5 and Psalm 107:9   Lk 1:54-55 = Isaiah 41:8-9   Lk 1:55 = Genesis 17:7 and Micah 7:20

§ 6 FORECAST TO JOSEPH OF NAZARETH

MATT 1:18–25	LUKE
A Now the [1]birth [2]of Jesus Christ was on this[18] wise: When his mother Mary had been betrothed to Joseph, before they came together she was found with child of the [3]Holy Ghost. And Joseph her husband, being a righteous[19] man, and not willing to make her a public example, was minded to put her away privily.	**A** *A virgin betrothed to a man whose name was Joseph . . . . and the virgin's name was Mary.* (§4A)=1:27
	Mary, who was betrothed to him. (§8B)=2:5 *Compare the passage from §4D under B below*
B But when he thought on these things, behold,[20] an angel of the Lord appeared unto him in a dream, saying, Joseph, thou son of David, fear not to take unto thee Mary thy wife: for that which is [4]conceived in her is of the Holy Ghost.	**B** *Joseph, of the house of David.* (§4A)=1:27 *The Holy Ghost shall come upon thee, and the power of the Most High shall overshadow thee: wherefore also [5]that which [6]is to be born[7] shall be called holy, the Son of God.* (§4D)=1:35
C And she shall bring forth a son; and thou[21] shalt call his name JESUS; for it is he that shall save his people from their sins.	**C** *And behold, thou shalt conceive in thy womb, and bring forth a son, and shalt call his name* JESUS. (§4B)=1:31
D Now all this is[22] come to pass, that it might be fulfilled which was spoken by the Lord through the prophet, saying, Behold, the virgin shall be with child, and[23] shall bring forth a son, And they shall call his name [8]Immanuel; which is, being interpreted, God with us.	
E And[24] Joseph arose from his sleep, and did as the angel of the Lord commanded him, and took unto him his wife; and knew her not till she had brought[25] forth a son: and he called his name JESUS.	**E** *And she brought forth her firstborn son.* (§8C)=2:7 *His name was called* JESUS, *which was so called by the angel.* (§10A)=2:21

ERV margin: 1 Or *generation:* as in verse 1   2 Some ancient authorities read *of the Christ*   3 Or *Holy Spirit:* and so throughout this book   4 Greek *begotten*   5 Or *the holy thing which is to be born shall be called the Son of God* 6 Or *is begotten*   7 Some ancient authorities insert *of thee*   8 Greek *Emmanuel*

OT references: Lk 1:31=Isaiah 7:14   Lk 1:35=Exodus 13:12   Lk 2:21=Genesis 17:12   Mt 1:23= Isaiah 7:14

CHAPTER II

EARLY LIFE OF JOHN AND OF JESUS

---

§7 BIRTH OF JOHN THE BAPTIST

A Now Elisabeth's time was fulfilled that she[57] should be delivered; and she brought forth a son. And her neighbours and her kinsfolk[58] heard that the Lord had magnified his mercy towards her; and they rejoiced with her. And[59] it came to pass on the eighth day, that they came to circumcise the child;

B   and they would have called him Zacharias, after the name of his father. And his mother answered and said,[60] Not so; but he shall be called John. And they[61] said unto her, There is none of thy kindred that is called by this name. And they made signs[62] to his father, what he would have him called. And he asked for a writing tablet, and wrote,[63] saying, His name is John. And they marvelled all. And his mouth was opened immediately,[64] and his tongue *loosed*, and he spake, blessing God.

C   And fear came on all that dwelt round[65] about them: and all these sayings were noised abroad throughout all the hill country of Judæa. And all that heard them laid them up in their[66] heart, saying, What then shall this child be? For the hand of the Lord was with him.

D And his father Zacharias was filled with the[67] Holy Ghost, and prophesied, saying,

Blessed *be* the Lord, the God of Israel;   68
For he hath visited and wrought redemption
    for his people,
And hath raised up a horn of salvation for us[69]
In the house of his servant David
(As he spake by the mouth of his holy[70]
    prophets which have been since the world
    began),
Salvation from our enemies, and from the[71]
    hand of all that hate us;
To shew mercy towards our fathers,   72
And to remember his holy covenant;
The oath which he sware unto Abraham our[73]
    father,
To grant unto us that we being delivered out[74]
    of the hand of our enemies
Should serve him without fear,
In holiness and righteousness before him all[75]
    our days.

E Yea and thou, child, shalt be called the[76]
    prophet of the Most High:
For thou shalt go before the face of the Lord
    to make ready his ways;
To give knowledge of salvation unto his[77]
    people

E *With verse 76b, compare §17 EF and §41 E*
With verse 77b, compare §17 portion H

OT references: Lk 1:59=Leviticus 12:3   Lk 1:68=Psalm 72:18 and 111:9   Lk 1:69=1 Samuel 2:10
Lk 1:71=Psalm 106:10   Lk 1:72-73=Genesis 17:7 and 22:16-18 and Leviticus 26:42 and Psalm 105:8-9 and
Micah 7:20   Lk 1:76-77=Malachi 3:1

9

LUKE I

In the remission of their sins,
Because of the [1]tender mercy of our God,   78
[2]Whereby the dayspring from on high [3]shall
     visit us,
To shine upon them that sit in darkness and 79
     the shadow of death;
To guide our feet into the way of peace.

F   And the child grew, and waxed strong in 80
spirit, and was in the deserts till the day of his
shewing unto Israel.

§ 8   BIRTH OF JESUS AT BETHLEHEM

MATTHEW

LUKE 2:1-7

A   Now it came to pass in those days, there 1
went out a decree from Cæsar Augustus, that
all [4]the world should be enrolled.   This was the 2
first enrolment made when Quirinius was governor of Syria.   And all went to enrol them- 3
selves, every one to his own city.

B   *Jesus was born in Bethlehem of Judæa.*
(§11 A)=2:1

    Mary had been betrothed to Joseph.
(§6 A)=1:18

B   And Joseph 4
also went up from Galilee, out of the city of
Nazareth, into Judæa, to the city of David,
which is called Bethlehem, because he was of
the house and family of David; to enrol himself 5
with Mary, who was betrothed to him, being
great with child.

C   *And knew her not till she had brought forth a*
son.   (§6 E)=1:25

C   And it came to pass, while 6
they were there, the days were fulfilled that she
should be delivered.   And she brought forth 7
her firstborn son; and she wrapped him in
swaddling clothes, and laid him in a manger,
because there was no room for them in the inn.

§9   THANKSGIVINGS FOR THE BIRTH OF JESUS

LUKE 2:8-20

A   And there were shepherds in the same coun- 8
try abiding in the field, and keeping [5]watch by
night over their flock.   And an angel of the 9
Lord stood by them, and the glory of the Lord
shone round about them: and they were sore
afraid.   And the angel said unto them, Be not 10
afraid; for behold, I bring you good tidings of
great joy which shall be to all the people: for 11
there is born to you this day in the city of David
a Saviour, which is [6]Christ the Lord.   And this 12
is the sign unto you; Ye shall find a babe
wrapped in swaddling clothes, and lying in a
manger.

B   And suddenly there was with the 13
angel a multitude of the heavenly host praising
God, and saying,
    Glory to God in the highest,   14
And on earth [7]peace among [8]men in whom he
     is well pleased.

C   And it came to pass, when the angels went 15
away from them into heaven, the shepherds
said one to another, Let us now go even unto
Bethlehem, and see this [9]thing that is come to
pass, which the Lord hath made known unto us.

ERV margin: 1 Or *heart of mercy*   2 Or *Wherein*   3 Many ancient authorities read *hath visited us*   4 Greek
the inhabited earth   5 Or *night-watches*   6 Or *Anointed Lord*   7 Many ancient authorities read *peace, good pleasure*
among men   8 Greek *men of good pleasure*   9 Or *saying*

OT references: Lk 1:79=Isaiah 9:2

LUKE 2

And they came with haste, and found both[16] Mary and Joseph, and the babe lying in the manger.

D   And when they saw it, they made[17] known concerning the saying which was spoken to them about this child.   And all that heard[18] it wondered at the things which were spoken unto them by the shepherds.   But Mary kept[19] all these ¹sayings, pondering them in her heart. And the shepherds returned, glorifying and[20] praising God for all the things that they had heard and seen, even as it was spoken unto them.

§ 10   THE DEDICATION AT JERUSALEM

MATTHEW

A *And he called his name* JESUS.   (§6 E) = 1:25

LUKE 2:21–39

A And when eight days were fulfilled for cir-[21] cumcising him, his name was called JESUS, which was so called by the angel before he was conceived in the womb.

B And when the days of their purification[22] according to the law of Moses were fulfilled, they brought him up to Jerusalem, to present him to the Lord (as it is written in the law of the[23] Lord, Every male that openeth the womb shall be called holy to the Lord), and to offer a sacri-[24] fice according to that which is said in the law of the Lord, A pair of turtledoves, or two young pigeons.

C   And behold, there was a man in Jeru-[25] salem, whose name was Simeon; and this man was righteous and devout, looking for the consolation of Israel: and the Holy Spirit was upon him.   And it had been revealed unto him by[26] the Holy Spirit, that he should not see death, before he had seen the Lord's Christ.   And he[27] came in the Spirit into the temple: and when the parents brought in the child Jesus, that they might do concerning him after the custom of the law, then he received him into his arms, and[28] blessed God, and said,

Now lettest thou thy ²servant depart, O ³Lord,
    According to thy word, in peace;
For mine eyes have seen thy salvation,   30
Which thou hast prepared before the face of[31]
    all peoples;
A light for ⁴revelation to the Gentiles,   32
And the glory of thy people Israel.

And his father and his mother were marvelling[33] at the things which were spoken concerning him; and Simeon blessed them, and said unto[34] Mary his mother, Behold, this *child* is set for the falling and rising up of many in Israel; and for a sign which is spoken against; yea and a sword[35] shall pierce through thine own soul; that thoughts out of many hearts may be revealed.

D And there was one Anna, a prophetess, the[36] daughter of Phanuel, of the tribe of Asher (she was ⁵of a great age, having lived with a hus-

---

ERV margin: 1 Or *things*   2 Greek *bondservant*   3 Greek *Master*   4 Or *the unveiling of the Gentiles*
5 Greek *advanced in many days*

OT references: Lk 2:21 = Genesis 17:12 and Leviticus 12:3   Lk 2:22–24 = Leviticus 12:1–8   Lk 2:23 =
Exodus 13:2, 12, 15   Lk 2:30–31 = Isaiah 52:10   Lk 2:32 = Isaiah 42:6 and 49:6

LUKE 2

band seven years from her virginity, and she37 had been a widow even for fourscore and four years), which departed not from the temple, worshipping with fastings and supplications night and day. And coming up at that very38 hour she gave thanks unto God, and spake of him to all them that were looking for the redemption of Jerusalem.

E   And when they had39 accomplished all things that were according to the law of the Lord, they returned into Galilee, to their own city Nazareth.

§ 11   JESUS AS KING OF THE JEWS

MATT 2:1–12

A   Now when Jesus was born in Bethlehem of 1 Judæa in the days of Herod the king, behold, 1wise men from the east came to Jerusalem.

B   saying, 2Where is he that is born King of the 2 Jews? for we saw his star in the east, and are come to worship him.

C   And when Herod the 3 king heard it, he was troubled, and all Jerusalem with him. And gathering together all 4 the chief priests and scribes of the people, he inquired of them where the Christ should be born. And they said unto him, In Bethlehem 5 of Judæa: for thus it is written 4by the prophet,

And thou Bethlehem, land of Judah,   6
Art in no wise least among the princes of
    Judah:
For out of thee shall come forth a governor,
Which shall be shepherd of my people Israel.

D   Then Herod privily called the 1wise men, 7 and learned of them carefully 5what time the star appeared. And he sent them to Bethle- 8 hem, and said, Go and search out carefully concerning the young child; and when ye have found *him*, bring me word, that I also may come and worship him.

E   And they, having heard the 9 king, went their way; and lo, the star, which they saw in the east, went before them, till it came and stood over where the young child was. And when they saw the star, they rejoiced with10 exceeding great joy. And they came into the11 house and saw the young child with Mary his mother; and they fell down and worshipped him; and opening their treasures they offered unto him gifts, gold and frankincense and myrrh.

F   And being warned *of God* in a dream12 that they should not return to Herod, they departed into their own country another way.

LUKE

A   *In the days of Herod, king of Judæa.* (§3 A)=1:5

And Joseph also went up . . . into Judæa . . . to Bethlehem . . . with Mary . . . and she brought forth her firstborn son. (§8 BC)=2:4–7

B   *The Lord God shall give unto him the throne of his father David: and he shall reign over the house of Jacob 3for ever; and of his kingdom there shall be no end.* (§4 C)=1:32–33

ERV margin: 1 Greek *Magi:* compare Esther 1:13 and Daniel 2:12   2 Or *Where is the King of the Jews that is born?*   3 Greek *unto the ages*   4 Or *through*   5 Or *the time of the star that appeared*

OT references: Mt 2:2=Numbers 24:17   Mt 2:6=Micah 5:2   Lk 1:32–33=2 Samuel 7:12–17

§ 12 ROMAN RULE IN RELATION TO JESUS

MATT 2:13–23

A Now when they were departed, behold, an[13] angel of the Lord appeareth to Joseph in a dream, saying, Arise and take the young child and his mother, and flee into Egypt, and be thou there until I tell thee: for Herod will seek the young child to destroy him.   And he arose[14] and took the young child and his mother by night, and departed into Egypt; and was there[15] until the death of Herod: that it might be fulfilled which was spoken by the Lord through the prophet, saying, Out of Egypt did I call my son.

B Then Herod, when he saw that he was[16] mocked of the [1]wise men, was exceeding wroth, and sent forth, and slew all the male children that were in Bethlehem, and in all the borders thereof, from two years old and under, according to the time which he had carefully learned of the [1]wise men.   Then was fulfilled that[17] which was spoken [2]by Jeremiah the prophet, saying,

> A voice was heard in Ramah,   [18]
> Weeping and great mourning,
> Rachel weeping for her children;
> And she would not be comforted, because
>   they are not.

C But when Herod was dead, behold, an[19] angel of the Lord appeareth in a dream to Joseph in Egypt, saying, Arise and take the[20] young child and his mother, and go into the land of Israel: for they are dead that sought the young child's life.   And he arose and took[21] the young child and his mother, and came into the land of Israel.

D   But when he heard that[22] Archelaus was reigning over Judæa in the room of his father Herod, he was afraid to go thither; and being warned *of God* in a dream, he withdrew into the parts of Galilee, and came and[23] dwelt in a city called Nazareth: that it might be fulfilled which was spoken [2]by the prophets, that he should be called a Nazarene.

§ 13 THE YOUTH OF JOHN

LUKE 1:80

And the child grew, and waxed strong in spirit,[80] and was in the deserts till the day of his shewing unto Israel.   (§7 F)

§ 14 THE YOUTH OF JESUS

MATT 2:22–23

But when he heard that Archelaus was reigning[22] over Judæa in the room of his father Herod, he was afraid to go thither; and being warned of God in a dream, he withdrew into the parts of Galilee, and came and dwelt in a city called[23] Nazareth: that it might be fulfilled which was spoken [2]by the prophets, that he should be called a Nazarene.   (§12 D)

LUKE 2:39–40

And when they had accomplished all things[39] that were according to the law of the Lord, they returned into Galilee, to their own city Nazareth. (§10 E)

And the child grew, and waxed strong, [3]filled[40] with wisdom: and the grace of God was upon him.

ERR margin: [1] Greek *Magi:* compare Esther 1:13 and Daniel 2:12   [2] Or *through*   [3] Greek *becoming full of wisdom*

OT references: Mt 2:15 = Hosea 11:1   Mt 2:18 = Jeremiah 31:15   Mt 2:23 = Isaiah 11:1 (?)

§ 15 JESUS THE YOUTH AT JERUSALEM

LUKE 2:41–50

A And his parents went every year to Jeru-41
salem at the feast of the passover. And when42
he was twelve years old, they went up after the
custom of the feast; and when they had fulfilled43
the days, as they were returning, the boy Jesus
tarried behind in Jerusalem; and his parents
knew it not; but supposing him to be in the44
company, they went a day's journey; and they
sought for him among their kinsfolk and
acquaintance: and when they found him not,45
they returned to Jerusalem, seeking for him.

B And it came to pass, after three days they46
found him in the temple, sitting in the midst of
the ¹doctors, both hearing them, and asking
them questions: and all that heard him were47
amazed at his understanding and his answers.
And when they saw him, they were astonished:48
and his mother said unto him, ²Son, why hast
thou thus dealt with us? behold, thy father
and I sought thee sorrowing. And he said unto49
them, How is it that ye sought me? wist ye
not that I must be ³in my Father's house?
And they understood not the saying which he50
spake unto them.

§ 16 DEVELOPMENT OF JESUS

LUKE 2:51–52

And he went down with them, and came to51
Nazareth; and he was subject unto them: and
his mother kept all *these* ⁴sayings in her heart.

And Jesus advanced in wisdom and ⁵stature,52
and in ⁶favour with God and men.

ERV margin: 1 Or *teachers*   2 Greek *Child*   3 Or *about my Father's business:* Greek *in the things of my Father*
4 Or *things*   5 Or *age*   6 Or *grace*

OT references: Lk 2:41 = Exodus 23:14–17 and Deuteronomy 16:1–8   Lk 2:52 = 1 Samuel 2:26

CHAPTER III

ACTIVITY OF JOHN AND ITS RELATION TO JESUS

§ 17 STATEMENT OF THE WORK OF JOHN

MATT 3:1-12	MARK 1:1-8	LUKE 3:1-20
	A The beginning of the gos-¹ pel of Jesus Christ, ¹the Son of God.	
		B Now in the fifteenth year¹ of the reign of Tiberius Cæsar, Pontius Pilate being governor of Judæa, and Herod being tetrarch of Galilee, and his brother Philip tetrarch of the region of Ituræa and Tracho-nitis, and Lysanias tetrarch of Abilene, in the high-priesthood² of Annas and Caiaphas,
cc And in those days cometh¹ John the Baptist, preaching in the wilderness of Judæa, saying, Repent ye; for the² kingdom of heaven is at hand.	cc *Compare portion H below*	cc the word of God came unto John the son of Zacharias in the wilderness. And he came into³ all the region round about Jor-dan, preaching the baptism of repentance unto remission of sins;
D For this is he that was³ spoken of ²by Isaiah the prophet, saying,	D Even as it is written ³in² Isaiah the prophet,	D as it is written in the⁴ book of the words of Isaiah the prophet,
E *Compare §41 portion E*	E Behold, I send my messen-ger before thy face, Who shall prepare thy way;	E *Compare §41 portion E*
F The voice of one crying in the wilderness, Make ye ready the way of the Lord, Make his paths straight.	F The voice of one crying in³ the wilderness, Make ye ready the way of the Lord, Make his paths straight;	F The voice of one crying in the wilderness, Make ye ready the way of the Lord, Make his paths straight.
		G Every valley shall be filled,⁵ And every mountain and hill shall be brought low; And the crooked shall be-come straight, And the rough ways smooth; And all flesh shall see the⁶ salvation of God.
H *Compare portion C above*	H John came, who baptized⁴ in the wilderness and preached the baptism of repentance unto remission of sins.	H *Compare portion C above*

ERV margin: ı Some ancient authorities omit *the Son of God*   2 Or *through*   3 Some ancient authorities read *in the prophets*

OT references: Mk 1:2=Malachi 3:1   Mt 3:3 and Mk 1:3 and Lk 3:4=Isaiah 40:3   Lk 3:5-6=Isaiah 40:4-5

c With the saying of John in Matt 3:2, compare the saying of Jesus in §21 c (Mt)
c With Luke 3:3ᵃ of portion c, compare Matt 3:5ᵇ in portion J below

MATT 3

1 Now John himself had his 4 raiment of camel's hair, and a leathern girdle about his loins; and his food was locusts and wild honey.

JJ   Then went out 5 unto him Jerusalem, and all Judæa, and all the region round about Jordan; and 6 they were baptized of him in the river Jordan, confessing their sins.

K *Compare portion I above*

L   But when he saw 7 many of the Pharisees and Sadducees coming to his baptism, he said unto them,

MM   Ye offspring of vipers, who warned you to flee from the wrath to come? Bring forth therefore 8 fruit worthy of [1]repentance: and think not to say within 9 yourselves, We have Abraham to our father: for I say unto you, that God is able of these stones to raise up children unto Abraham. And even 10 now is the axe laid unto the root of the trees: every tree therefore that bringeth not forth good fruit is hewn down, and cast into the fire.

MARK 1

1 *Compare portion K below*

JJ   And 5 there went out unto him all the country of Judæa, and all they of Jerusalem; and they were baptized of him in the river Jordan, confessing their sins.

K   And John was clothed 6 with camel's hair, and *had* a leathern girdle about his loins, and did eat locusts and wild honey.

LUKE 3

L He said therefore to the 7 multitudes that went out to be baptized of him,

MM   Ye offspring of vipers, who warned you to flee from the wrath to come? Bring forth therefore 8 fruits worthy of [1]repentance, and begin not to say within yourselves, We have Abraham to our father: for I say unto you, that God is able of these stones to raise up children unto Abraham. And even 9 now is the axe also laid unto the root of the trees: every tree therefore that bringeth not forth good fruit is hewn down, and cast into the fire.

N And the multitudes asked 10 him, saying, What then must we do? And he answered 11 and said unto them, He that hath two coats, let him impart to him that hath none; and he that hath food, let him do likewise. And there came 12 also [2]publicans to be baptized, and they said unto him, [3]Master, what must we do? And 13 he said unto them, Extort no more than that which is appointed you. And [4]soldiers 14 also asked him, saying, And we, what must we do? And he said unto them, Do violence to no man, neither [5]exact *anything* wrongfully; and be content with your wages.

O And as the people were in 15 expectation, and all men reasoned in their hearts concern-

---

ERV margin: 1 Or *your repentance*   2 That is *collectors or renters of Roman taxes:* and so elsewhere   3 Or
Teacher   4 Greek *soldiers on service*   5 Or *accuse* any one

J With Matt 3:5b of portion J, compare Luke 3:3a in portion C above
M With the first sentence of portion M, compare §45 N and §132 P. With the last sentence of portion M, compare §38 T

MATT 3	MARK 1	LUKE 3
		ing John, whether haply he were the Christ; John an-[16] swered, saying unto them all,
P I in-[11] deed baptize you [1]with water unto repentance: but he that cometh after me is mightier than I, whose shoes I am not [2]worthy to bear: he shall baptize you [1]with the Holy Ghost and *with* fire:	P And he preached, say-[7] ing, There cometh after me he that is mightier than I, the latchet of whose shoes I am not [2]worthy to stoop down and unloose. I baptized you [8] [1]with water; but he shall baptize you [1]with the [3]Holy Ghost.	P I indeed baptize you with water; but there cometh he that is mightier than I, the latchet of whose shoes I am not [2]worthy to unloose: he shall baptize you [1]with the Holy Ghost and *with* fire:
Q whose[12] fan is in his hand, and he will throughly cleanse his threshing-floor; and he will gather his wheat into the gar-ner, but the chaff he will burn up with unquenchable fire.		Q whose fan is in his hand,[17] throughly to cleanse his threshing-floor, and to gather the wheat into his garner; but the chaff he will burn up with unquenchable fire.
R *Compare §58 portion D*	R *Compare §58 portion D*	R With many other exhorta-[18] tions therefore preached he [4]good tidings unto the people; but Herod the tetrarch, being[19] reproved by him for Herodias his brother's wife, and for all the evil things which Herod had done, added yet this[20] above all, that he shut up John in prison.

§ 18 THE BAPTISM OF JESUS BY JOHN

MATT 3:13–17	MARK 1:9–11	LUKE 3:21–22
A Then cometh Jesus from[13] Galilee to the Jordan unto John, to be baptized of him.	A And it came to pass in[9] those days, that Jesus came from Nazareth of Galilee, and was baptized of John [5]in the Jordan.	A Now it came to pass, when[21] all the people were baptized, that, Jesus also having been baptized,
B But John would have hin-[14] dered him, saying, I have need to be baptized of thee, and comest thou to me? But[15] Jesus answering said unto him, Suffer [6]*it* now: for thus it becometh us to fulfil all righteousness. Then he suf-fereth him.		
c And Jesus, when[16] he was baptized, went up straightway from the water: and lo, the heavens were opened [7]unto him, and he saw the Spirit of God descending as a dove, and coming upon him; and lo, a voice out of[17] the heavens, saying,	c And straightway[10] coming up out of the water, he saw the heavens rent asun-der, and the Spirit as a dove descending upon him: and a[11] voice came out of the heavens,	c and praying, the heaven was opened, and the[22] Holy Ghost descended in a bodily form, as a dove, upon him, and a voice came out of heaven,
D[D] [8]This is my beloved Son, in whom I am well pleased.	D[D] Thou art my beloved Son, in thee I am well pleased.	D[D] Thou art my beloved Son; in thee I am well pleased.

ERV margin: 1 Or *in*   2 Greek *sufficient*   3 Or *Holy Spirit:* and so throughout this book   4 Or *the gospel*
5 Greek *into*   6 Or, me   7 Some ancient authorities omit *unto him*   8 Or *This is my Son; my beloved in whom I am
well pleased:* see Matt 12:18 (§34)

OT references: Mt 3:17 and Mk 1:11 and Lk 3:22 = Psalm 2:7 and Isaiah 42:1

D Compare §74 portion E

§ 19 THE GENEALOGY OF JESUS

MATT 1:1–17

1 ¹*The book of the ²generation of Jesus Christ, the son of David, the son of Abraham.*

2 *Abraham begat Isaac;*
    and Isaac begat Jacob;
    and Jacob begat Judah and his
       brethren;
3 *and Judah begat Perez and Zerah*
       of Tamar;
    and Perez begat Hezron;
    and Hezron begat ³Ram;
4 *and ³Ram begat Amminadab;*
    and Amminadab begat Nahshon;
    and Nahshon begat Salmon;
5 *and Salmon begat Boaz of Rahab;*
    and Boaz begat Obed of Ruth;
    and Obed begat Jesse;
6 *and Jesse begat David the king.*

And David begat Solomon of her that had been the wife *of Uriah;*
7 *and Solomon begat Rehoboam;*
    and Rehoboam begat Abijah;
    and Abijah begat ⁴Asa;
8 *and ⁴Asa begat Jehoshaphat;*
    and Jehoshaphat begat Joram;
    and Joram begat Uzziah;
9 *and Uzziah begat Jotham;*
    and Jotham begat Ahaz;
    and Ahaz begat Hezekiah;
10*and Hezekiah begat Manasseh;*
    and Manasseh begat ⁵Amon;
    and ⁵Amon begat Josiah;
11*and Josiah begat Jechoniah and his*
    brethren, at the time of the ⁶carrying
    away to Babylon.

12 *And after the ⁶carrying away to Babylon,* *Jechoniah begat ⁷Shealtiel;*
    and ⁷Shealtiel begat Zerubbabel;
13*and Zerubbabel begat Abiud;*
    and Abiud begat Eliakim;
    and Eliakim begat Azor;
14*and Azor begat Sadoc;*
    and Sadoc begat Achim;
    and Achim begat Eliud;
15*and Eliud begat Eleazar;*
    and Eleazar begat Matthan;
    and Matthan begat Jacob;
16*and Jacob begat Joseph the husband*
    of Mary, of whom was born Jesus,
    who is called Christ.

17 *So all the generations from Abraham unto David are fourteen generations; and from David unto the ⁶carrying away to Babylon fourteen generations; and from the ⁶carrying away to Babylon unto the Christ fourteen generations.* (§2)

LUKE 3:23–38

23 And Jesus himself, when he began *to teach,* was about thirty years of age, being the son (as was supposed) of Joseph,
the *son* of Heli,
24the *son* of Matthat,
the *son* of Levi,
the *son* of Melchi,
the *son* of Jannai,
the *son* of Joseph,
25the *son* of Mattathias,
the *son* of Amos,
the *son* of Nahum,
the *son* of Esli,
the *son* of Naggai,
26the *son* of Maath,
the *son* of Mattathias,
the *son* of Semein,
the *son* of Josech,
the *son* of Joda,
27the *son* of Joanan,
the *son* of Rhesa,
the *son* of Zerubbabel,
the *son* of ⁷Shealtiel,
the *son* of Neri,
28the *son* of Melchi,
the *son* of Addi,
the *son* of Cosam,
the *son* of Elmadam,
the *son* of Er,
29the *son* of Jesus,
the *son* of Eliezer,
the *son* of Jorim,
the *son* of Matthat,
the *son* of Levi,
30the *son* of Symeon,
the *son* of Judas,
the *son* of Joseph,
the *son* of Jonam,
the *son* of Eliakim,
31the *son* of Melea,
the *son* of Menna,
the *son* of Mattatha,

the *son* of Nathan,
the *son* of David,
32the *son* of Jesse,
the *son* of Obed,
the *son* of Boaz,
the *son* of ⁸Salmon,
the *son* of Nahshon,
33the *son* of Amminadab
the *son* of ¹⁰Arni,
the *son* of Hezron,
the *son* of Perez,
the *son* of Judah,
34the *son* of Jacob,
the *son* of Isaac,
the *son* of Abraham,
the *son* of Terah,
the *son* of Nahor,
35the *son* of Serug,
the *son* of Reu,
the *son* of Peleg,
the *son* of Eber,
the *son* of Shelah,
36the *son* of Cainan,
the *son* of Arphaxad,
the *son* of Shem,
the *son* of Noah,
the *son* of Lamech,
37the *son* of Methuselah,
the *son* of Enoch,
the *son* of Jared,
the *son* of Mahalaleel
the *son* of Cainan,
38the *son* of Enos,
the *son* of Seth,
the *son* of Adam,
the *son* of God.

ERV margin: 1 Or *The genealogy of Jesus Christ*   2 Or *birth:* as in Matt 1:18   3 Greek *Aram*   4 Greek *Asaph*   5 Greek *Amos*   6 Or *removal to Babylon*   7 Greek *Salathiel*   8 Some ancient authorities write *Sala* 9 Many ancient authorities insert *the* son *of Admin:* and one writes *Admin* for *Amminadab*   10 Some ancient authorities write *Aram*

OT references: Mt 1:2–6 and Lk 3:31–34 = 1 Chronicles 2:1–15   Mt 1:3–6 and Lk 3:32–33 = Ruth 4:18–22 Mt 1:7–12 = 1 Chronicles 3:10–17   Lk 3:27 = 1 Chronicles 3:17   Lk 3:34–36 = 1 Chronicles 1:24–28   Lk 3:36–38 = 1 Chronicles 1:1–4

§ 20 WITHDRAWAL OF JESUS TO THE WILDERNESS

MATT 4:1-11	MARK 1:12-13	LUKE 4:1-13
A Then was Jesus led up of [1] the Spirit into the wilderness to be tempted of the devil. And when he had fasted forty [2] days and forty nights, he afterward hungered.	A And straightway the Spirit [12] driveth him forth into the wilderness. And he was in the [13] wilderness forty days tempted of Satan;	A And Jesus, full of the Holy [1] Spirit, returned from the Jordan, and was led [1]by the Spirit in the wilderness during forty days, being tempted [2] of the devil. And he did eat nothing in those days: and when they were completed, he hungered.
B And the [3] tempter came and said unto him, If thou art the Son of God, command that these stones become [2]bread. But [4] he answered and said, It is written, Man shall not live by bread alone, but by every word that proceedeth out of the mouth of God.		B And the devil said [3] unto him, If thou art the Son of God, command this stone that it become [3]bread. And [4] Jesus answered unto him, It is written, Man shall not live by bread alone.

C Then the [5] devil taketh him into the holy city; and he set him on the [4]pinnacle of the temple, and [6] saith unto him, If thou art the Son of God, cast thyself down: for it is written,
He shall give his angels
  charge concerning thee:
And on their hands they
  shall bear thee up,
Lest haply thou dash thy
  foot against a stone.
Jesus said unto him, Again [7] it is written, Thou shalt not tempt the Lord thy God.
		C *Compare portion E below*

D Again, the devil taketh him [8] unto an exceeding high mountain, and sheweth him all the kingdoms of the world, and the glory of them; and he said [9] unto him, All these things will I give thee, if thou wilt fall down and worship me. Then[10] saith Jesus unto him, Get thee hence, Satan: for it is written, Thou shalt worship the Lord thy God, and him only shalt thou serve.		D And he led [5] him up, and shewed him all the kingdoms of [5]the world in a moment of time. And the [6] devil said unto him, To thee will I give all this authority, and the glory of them: for it hath been delivered unto me; and to whomsoever I will I give it. If thou therefore wilt [7] worship before me, it shall all be thine. And Jesus answered [8] and said unto him, It is written, Thou shalt worship the Lord thy God, and him only shalt thou serve.
E *Compare portion C above*		E And he led [9] him to Jerusalem, and set him on the [4]pinnacle of the temple, and said unto him, If thou art the Son of God, cast thyself down from hence: for it is[10] written,

---

ERV margin: 1 Or *in*   2 Greek *loaves*   3 Or *a loaf*   4 Greek *wing*   5 Greek *the inhabited earth*

OT references: Mt 4:4 and Lk 4:4 = Deuteronomy 8:3   Mt 4:6 and Lk 4:10-11 = Psalm 91:11-12   Mt 4:7 and Lk 4:12 = Deuteronomy 6:16   Mt 4:10 and Lk 4:8 = Deuteronomy 6:13

MATT 4	MARK 1	LUKE 4
		He shall give his angels charge concerning thee, to guard thee:
		and,
		On their hands they shall bear thee up, Lest haply thou dash thy foot against a stone.
		And Jesus answering said unto[12] him, It is said, Thou shalt not tempt the Lord thy God.
F Then the devil[11] leaveth him;		F And when the devil had[13] completed every temptation, he departed from him [1]for a season.
G and behold, angels came and ministered unto him.	G and he was with the wild beasts; and the angels ministered unto him.	

ERV margin: 1 Or *until*

OT references: Lk 4:12 and Mt 4:7 = Deuteronomy 6:16

CHAPTER IV

BEGINNINGS OF THE PUBLIC ACTIVITY OF JESUS

---

§ 21 GENERAL STATEMENT OF THE WORK OF JESUS

MATT 4:12-17	MARK 1:14-15	LUKE 4:14-15

A Now when he heard that[12] John was delivered up, he withdrew into Galilee;
 B and[13] leaving Nazareth, he came and dwelt in Capernaum, which is by the sea, in the borders of Zebulun and Naphtali: that it might be fulfilled[14] which was spoken [1]by Isaiah the prophet, saying,
  The land of Zebulun and[15] the land of Naphtali,
  [2]Toward the sea, beyond Jordan,
  Galilee of the [3]Gentiles,
  The people which sat in[16] darkness
  Saw a great light,
  And to them which sat in the region and shadow of death,
  To them did light spring up.
	A Now after that John was[14] delivered up, Jesus came into Galilee,
	 B *Compare §24 portion A*
		A And Jesus returned in the[14] power of the Spirit into Galilee:
		 B *Compare §24 portion A*

C[c] From that time began[17] Jesus to preach, and to say, Repent ye; for the kingdom of heaven is at hand.	C[c] preaching the gospel of God, and saying, The time[15] is fulfilled, and the kingdom of God is at hand: repent ye, and believe in the gospel.	C[c] and a fame went out concerning him through all the region round about. And[15] he taught in their synagogues, being glorified of all.

§ 22 JESUS BEGINS AT NAZARETH

MATT 13:54-58	MARK 6:1-6	LUKE 4:16-30
A *And coming into his own[54] country he taught them in their synagogue,*	A *And he went out from[1] thence; and he cometh into his own country; and his disciples follow him. And when[2] the sabbath was come, he began to teach in the synagogue:*	A And he came to Nazareth,[16] where he had been brought up: and he entered, as his custom was, into the synagogue on the sabbath day, and stood up to read. B And[17] there was delivered unto him [4]the book of the prophet Isaiah. And he opened the [5]book, and found the place where it was written, The Spirit of the Lord is[18] upon me,

---

ERV margin: 1 Or *through*   2 Greek *The way of the sea*   3 Greek *nations:* and so elsewhere   4 Or *a roll*
5 Or *roll*

OT references: Mt 4:15-16 = Isaiah 9:1-2   Lk 4:18-19 = Isaiah 61:1-2

c With the saying of Jesus in Matt 4:17, compare the saying of John in §17 c (Mt)

MATT 13	MARK 6	LUKE 4

[Luke 4]

¹Because he anointed me to preach ²good tidings to the poor:
He hath sent me to proclaim release to the captives,
And recovering of sight to the blind,
To set at liberty them that are bruised,
To proclaim the acceptable¹⁹ year of the Lord.
And he closed the ³book, and²⁰ gave it back to the attendant, and sat down: and the eyes of all in the synagogue were fastened on him. And he be-²¹ gan to say unto them, To-day hath this scripture been fulfilled in your ears.

c   *insomuch that they were astonished, and said, Whence hath this man this wisdom, and these ⁴mighty works?*

     Compare portion E below

c   *and ⁵many hearing him were astonished, saying, Whence hath this man these things? and, What is the wisdom that is given unto this man, and what mean such ⁴mighty works wrought by his hands?*

c   And all²² bare him witness, and wondered at the words of grace which proceeded out of his mouth:

D   *Is not this the car-55 penter's son? is not his mother called Mary? and his brethren, James, and Joseph, and Simon, and Judas? And his⁵⁶ sisters, are they not all with us?*

E *Whence then hath this man all these things?*

F   *And they⁵⁷ were ⁶offended in him.*

D   *Is not 3 this the carpenter, the son of Mary, and brother of James, and Joses, and Judas, and Simon? and are not his sisters here with us?*

E *Compare portion C above*

F   *And they were ⁶offended in him.*

D   and they said, Is not this Joseph's son?

F *Compare portion K below*

G   And he²³ said unto them, Doubtless ye will say unto me this parable, Physician, heal thyself: whatsoever we have heard done at Capernaum, do also here in thine own country.

H   *But Jesus said unto them, A prophet is not without honour, save in his own country, and in his own house.*

H   *And Jesus 4 said unto them, A prophet is not without honour, save in his own country, and among his own kin, and in his own house.*

H   And he²⁴ said, Verily I say unto you, No prophet is acceptable in his own country.

I   But of a²⁵ truth I say unto you, There were many widows in Israel in the days of Elijah, when the heaven was shut up three years and six months, when there came a great famine over all the land; and unto²⁶ none of them was Elijah sent, but only to ⁷Zarephath, in the land of Sidon, unto a woman that was a widow. And²⁷ there were many lepers in

---

ERV margin: 1 Or *Wherefore*   2 Or *the gospel*   3 Or *roll*   4 Greek *powers*   5 Some ancient authorities insert *the*   6 Greek *caused to stumble*   7 Greek *Sarepta*

OT references: Lk 4:25 = 1 Kings 17:1 and 18:1–2   Lk 4:26 = 1 Kings 17:8–9   Lk 4:27 = 2 Kings 5:1, 14

MATT 13	MARK 6	LUKE 4
		Israel in the time of Elisha the prophet; and none of them was cleansed, but only Naaman the Syrian.
J *And he did⁵⁸ not many ¹mighty works there because of their unbelief.* (§54 A–J)	J *And he could there do no 5 ²mighty work, save that he laid his hands upon a few sick folk, and healed them. And he 6 marvelled because of their unbelief.* (§54 A–J)	
K *Compare portion F above*	K *Compare portion F above*	K And²⁸ they were all filled with wrath in the synagogue, as they heard these things; and they²⁹ rose up, and cast him forth out of the city, and led him unto the brow of the hill whereon their city was built, that they might throw him down headlong. But he pass-³⁰ ing through the midst of them went his way.

§ 23   JESUS WINS FISHERMAN FOLLOWERS

MATT 4:18–22	MARK 1:16–20	LUKE 5:1–11
A And walking by the sea of¹⁸ Galilee, he saw two brethren, Simon who is called Peter, and Andrew his brother, casting a net into the sea; for they were fishers. B And he saith unto¹⁹ them, Come ye after me, and I will make you fishers of men. And they straightway left the²⁰ nets, and followed him. C And²¹ going on from thence he saw other two brethren, ³James the *son* of Zebedee, and John his brother, in the boat with Zebedee their father, mending their nets; D and he called them. And they straight-²² way left the boat and their father, and followed him. (+ §26)	A And passing along by the¹⁶ sea of Galilee, he saw Simon and Andrew the brother of Simon casting a net in the sea: for they were fishers. B And¹⁷ Jesus said unto them, Come ye after me, and I will make you to become fishers of men. And straightway they left¹⁸ the nets, and followed him. C And going on a little fur-¹⁹ ther, he saw James the *son* of Zebedee, and John his brother, who also were in the boat mending the nets. D And²⁰ straightway he called them: and they left their father Zebedee in the boat with the hired servants, and went after him.	*Now it came to pass, while 1 the multitude pressed upon him and heard the word of God, that he was standing by the lake of Gennesaret; and 2 he saw two boats standing by the lake: but the fishermen had gone out of them, and were washing their nets. And 3 he entered into one of the boats, which was Simon's, and asked him to put out a little from the land. And he sat down and taught the multitudes out of the boat. And when he had left 4 speaking, he said unto Simon, Put out into the deep, and let down your nets for a draught. And Simon answered and said, 5 Master, we toiled all night, and took nothing: but at thy word I will let down the nets. And 6 when they had this done, they inclosed a great multitude of fishes; and their nets were breaking; and they beckoned 7 unto their partners in the other boat, that they should come and help them. And they came, and filled both the boats, so that they began to sink. But Simon Peter, when he 8 saw it, fell down at Jesus' knees, saying, Depart from me; for I am a sinful man, O Lord. For he was amazed, 9 and all that were with him, at the draught of the fishes which*

ERV margin :   1 Greek *powers*   2 Greek *power*   3 Or *Jacob:* and so elsewhere

LUKE 5

they had taken; and so were[10] also James and John, sons of Zebedee, which were partners with Simon. And Jesus said unto Simon, Fear not; from henceforth thou shalt [1]catch men. And when they had[11] brought their boats to land, they left all, and followed him. (§27)

§ 24 EARLY POPULAR OPINIONS ABOUT JESUS

MATTHEW	MARK 1:21–28	LUKE 4:31–37
A *Compare §21 portion B*	A And they go into Caper-[21] naum;	A And he came down to[31] Capernaum, a city of Galilee.
B *Compare §38 portion X*	B and straightway on the sabbath day he entered into the synagogue and taught. And they were astonished at his[22] teaching: for he taught them as having authority, and not as the scribes.	B And he was teaching them on the sabbath day: and they[32] were astonished at his teaching; for his word was with authority.
	C And straight-[23] way there was in their synagogue a man with an unclean spirit; and he cried out, say-[24] ing, What have we to do with thee, thou Jesus of Nazareth? art thou come to destroy us? I know thee who thou art, the Holy One of God.	C And in the syna-[33] gogue there was a man, which had a spirit of an unclean [2]devil; and he cried out with a loud voice, [3]Ah! what have[34] we to do with thee, thou Jesus of Nazareth? art thou come to destroy us? I know thee who thou art, the Holy One of God.
	D And Jesus[25] rebuked [4]him, saying, Hold thy peace, and come out of him. And the unclean spirit,[26] [5]tearing him and crying with a loud voice, came out of him.	D And Jesus rebuked[35] him, saying, Hold thy peace, and come out of him. And when the [2]devil had thrown him down in the midst, he came out of him, having done him no hurt.
	E And they were all amazed,[27] insomuch that they questioned among themselves, saying, What is this? a new teaching! with authority he commandeth even the unclean spirits, and they obey him.	E And amaze-[36] ment came upon all, and they spake together, one with another, saying, What is [6]this word? for with authority and power he commandeth the unclean spirits, and they come out.
	F And the report of him went[28] out straightway everywhere into all the region of Galilee round about.	F And there went forth a[37] rumour concerning him into every place of the region round about.

§ 25 THE HEALING POWER OF JESUS

(§39+) MATT 8:14–17	MARK 1:29–34	LUKE 4:38–41
A And when Jesus was come[14] into Peter's house,	A And straightway, [7]when[29] they were come out of the synagogue, they came into the house of Simon and Andrew, with James and John.	A And he rose up from the[38] synagogue, and entered into the house of Simon.

ERV margin: 1 Greek *take alive word, that with authority . . . come out?*   2 Greek *demon*   3 Or *Let alone*   4 Or *it*   5 Or *convulsing*   6 Or *this*   7 Some ancient authorities read *when he was come out of the synagogue, he came etc.*

MATT 8	MARK 1	LUKE 4
B he saw his wife's mother lying sick of a fever. And he touched her[15] hand,	B Now[30] Simon's wife's mother lay sick of a fever; and straightway they tell him of her: and he[31] came and took her by the hand, and raised her up;	B And Simon's wife's mother was holden with a great fever; and they besought him for her. And he stood over her, and[39] rebuked the fever;
C and the fever left her; and she arose, and ministered unto him.	C and the fever left her, and she ministered unto them.	C and it left her: and immediately she rose up and ministered unto them.
D And when even[16] was come, they brought unto him many 'possessed with devils:	D And at even, when the sun[32] did set, they brought unto him all that were sick, and them that were 'possessed with devils. And all the city[33] was gathered together at the door.	D And when the sun was set-[40]ting, all they that had any sick with divers diseases brought them unto him;
E and he cast out the spirits with a word, and healed all that were sick:	E And he healed many[34] that were sick with divers diseases, and cast out many ²devils; *Compare §34 portion E*	E and he laid his hands on every one of them, and healed them. And ²devils also came out[41] from many, crying out, and saying, Thou art the Son of God.
	F and he suffered not the ²devils to speak, because they knew him.³	F And rebuking them, he suffered them not to speak, because they knew that he was the Christ.
G that it[17] might be fulfilled which was spoken ⁴by Isaiah the prophet, saying, Himself took our infirmities, and bare our diseases. (+ §50)		

§ 26 JESUS TEACHES THROUGHOUT GALILEE

(§23+) MATT 4:23	MARK 1:35-39	LUKE 4:42-44
	A And in the morning, a[35] great while before day, he rose up and went out, and departed into a desert place, and there prayed.	A And when it was day, he[42] came out and went into a desert place:
	B And Simon[36] and they that were with him followed after him; and they[37] found him, and say unto him, All are seeking thee.	B and the multitudes sought after him, and came unto him, and would have stayed him, that he should not go from them.
	C And[38] he saith unto them, Let us go elsewhere into the next towns, that I may preach there also; for to this end came I forth.	c But he said unto them, I[43] must preach the ⁵good tidings of the kingdom of God to the other cities also: for therefore was I sent.
DD And ⁶Jesus went about in[23] all Galilee, teaching in their synagogues, and preaching the ⁷gospel of the kingdom, and healing all manner of disease and all manner of sickness among the people. (+ §34)	DD And he went into their[39] synagogues throughout all Galilee, preaching and casting out ²devils.	DD And he was preaching in[44] the synagogues of ⁸Galilee.

ERV margin: 1 Or *demoniacs*   2 Greek *demons*   3 Many ancient authorities add *to be Christ:* see Luke 4:41   4 Or *through*   5 Or *gospel*   6 Some ancient authorities read *he*   7 Or *good tidings:* and so elsewhere   8 Very many ancient authorities read *Judæa*

OT references: Mt 8:17 = Isaiah 53:4

D   With the latter half of the Matthew record, compare §55 portion B

§ 27   JESUS WINS FISHERMAN FOLLOWERS

MATT 4:18–22	MARK 1:16–20	LUKE 5:1–11
A *And walking by the sea of* [18] *Galilee, he saw two brethren, Simon who is called Peter, and Andrew his brother, casting a net into the sea; for they were fishers.* B *And he saith unto* [19] *them, Come ye after me, and I will make you fishers of men. And they straightway left the* [20] *nets, and followed him.* C *And* [21] *going on from thence he saw other two brethren,* [1]*James the son of Zebedee, and John his brother, in the boat with Zebedee their father, mending their nets;* D *and he called them. And* [22] *they straightway left the boat and their father, and followed him.* (§23 A–D)	A *And passing along by the* [16] *sea of Galilee, he saw Simon and Andrew the brother of Simon casting a net in the sea: for they were fishers.* B *And* [17] *Jesus said unto them, Come ye after me, and I will make you to become fishers of men. And* [18] *straightway they left the nets, and followed him.* C *And going* [19] *on a little further, he saw James the son of Zebedee, and John his brother, who also were in the boat mending the nets.* D *And straightway he* [20] *called them: and they left their father Zebedee in the boat with the hired servants, and went after him.* (§23 A–D)	Now it came to pass, while [1] the multitude pressed upon him and heard the word of God, that he was standing by the lake of Gennesaret; and [2] he saw two boats standing by the lake: but the fishermen had gone out of them, and were washing their nets. And he entered into one of [3] the boats, which was Simon's, and asked him to put out a little from the land. And he sat down and taught the multitudes out of the boat. And [4] when he had left speaking, he said unto Simon, Put out into the deep, and let down your nets for a draught. And [5] Simon answered and said, Master, we toiled all night, and took nothing: but at thy word I will let down the nets. And when they had this done, [6] they inclosed a great multitude of fishes; and their nets were breaking; and they [7] beckoned unto their partners in the other boat, that they should come and help them. And they came, and filled both the boats, so that they began to sink. But Simon [8] Peter, when he saw it, fell down at Jesus' knees, saying, Depart from me; for I am a sinful man, O Lord. For he [9] was amazed, and all that were with him, at the draught of the fishes which they had taken; and so were also [10] James and John, sons of Zebedee, which were partners with Simon. And Jesus said unto Simon, Fear not; from henceforth thou shalt [2]catch men. And when they had [11] brought their boats to land, they left all, and followed him.

§ 28   GROWTH IN FAME OF JESUS

(§38+) MATT 8:2–4	MARK 1:40–45	LUKE 5:12–16
A And behold, there came to [2] him a leper and worshipped him, saying, Lord, if thou wilt, thou canst make me clean. B And he stretched forth his [3] hand, and touched him, say-	A And there cometh to him [40] a leper, beseeching him, [3]and kneeling down to him, and saying unto him, If thou wilt, thou canst make me clean. B And being moved with [41] compassion, he stretched	A And it came to pass, while [12] he was in one of the cities, behold, a man full of leprosy: and when he saw Jesus, he fell on his face, and besought him, saying, Lord, if thou wilt, thou canst make me clean. B And he stretched forth his [13] hand, and touched him, say-

---

ERV margin: [1] Or *Jacob:* and so elsewhere   [2] Greek *take alive*   [3] Some ancient authorities omit *and kneeling down to him*

MATT 8	MARK 1	LUKE 5
ing, I will; be thou made clean. And straightway his leprosy was cleansed.	forth his hand, and touched him, and saith unto him, I will; be thou made clean. And straightway the leprosy42 departed from him, and he was made clean.	ing, I will; be thou made clean. And straightway the leprosy departed from him.
c And 4 Jesus saith unto him, See thou tell no man; but go thy way, shew thyself to the priest, and offer the gift that Moses commanded, for a testimony unto them. (+ §39)	c And he43 ¹strictly charged him, and straightway sent him out, and saith unto him, See thou44 say nothing to any man: but go thy way, shew thyself to the priest, and offer for thy cleansing the things which Moses commanded, for a testimony unto them.	c And he charged him to tell14 no man: but go thy way, and shew thyself to the priest, and offer for thy cleansing, according as Moses commanded, for a testimony unto them.
	D But45 he went out, and began to publish it much, and to spread abroad the ²matter, insomuch that ³Jesus could no more openly enter into ⁴a city, but was without in desert places: and they came to him from every quarter.	D But15 so much the more went abroad the report concerning him: and great multitudes came together to hear, and to be healed of their infirmities. But he withdrew himself in16 the deserts, and prayed.

ERV margin: 1 Or *sternly*   2 Greek *word*   3 Greek *he*   4 Or *the city*

OT references: Mt 8:4 and Mk 1:44 and Lk 5:14 = Leviticus 13:49 and 14:2

CHAPTER V

DEVELOPMENT OF OPPOSITION TO JESUS

§ 29 CRITICISM OF FREE FORGIVENESS FOR SIN

(§52A+) MATT 9:2–8 | MARK 2:1–12 | LUKE 5:17–26

B And behold, they brought 2 to him a man sick of the palsy, lying on a bed:

A And when he entered 1 again into Capernaum after some days, it was noised that he was 1in the house. And 2 many were gathered together, so that there was no longer room *for them*, no, not even about the door: and he spake the word unto them.

A And it came to pass on one17 of those days, that he was teaching; and there were Pharisees and doctors of the law sitting by, which were come out of every village of Galilee and Judæa and Jerusalem: and the power of the Lord was with him 2to heal.

B And 3 they come, bringing unto him a man sick of the palsy, borne of four.

B And behold, men bring on18 a bed a man that was palsied: and they sought to bring him in, and to lay him before him.

C And when they 4 could not 3come nigh unto him for the crowd, they uncovered the roof where he was: and when they had broken it up, they let down the bed whereon the sick of the palsy lay.

C And not finding by what19 *way* they might bring him in because of the multitude, they went up to the housetop, and let him down through the tiles with his couch into the midst before Jesus.

D and Jesus seeing their faith said unto the sick of the palsy, 4Son, be of good cheer; thy sins are forgiven.

D And Jesus seeing their 5 faith saith unto the sick of the palsy, 4Son, thy sins are forgiven.

D And seeing20 their faith, he said, Man, thy sins are forgiven thee.

E And be- 3 hold, certain of the scribes said within themselves, This man blasphemeth.

E But there were cer- 6 tain of the scribes sitting there, and reasoning in their hearts, Why doth this man 7 thus speak? he blasphemeth: who can forgive sins but one, *even* God?

E And the scribes and the21 Pharisees began to reason, saying, Who is this that speaketh blasphemies? Who can forgive sins, but God alone?

F And Jesus 4 5knowing their thoughts said, Wherefore think ye evil in your hearts? For whether 5 is easier, to say, Thy sins are forgiven; or to say, Arise, and walk?

F And straightway 8 Jesus, perceiving in his spirit that they so reasoned within themselves, saith unto them, Why reason ye these things in your hearts? Whether is 9 easier, to say to the sick of the palsy, Thy sins are forgiven; or to say, Arise, and take up thy bed, and walk?

F But Jesus perceiving22 their reasonings, answered and said unto them, 6What reason ye in your hearts? Whether is easier, to say,23 Thy sins are forgiven thee; or to say, Arise and walk?

G But that ye may 6 know that the Son of man hath 7power on earth to forgive sins (then saith he to the sick of the palsy), Arise, and take up thy bed, and go unto thy house.

G But that10 ye may know that the Son of man hath 7power on earth to forgive sins (he saith to the sick of the palsy), I say unto11 thee, Arise, take up thy bed, and go unto thy house.

G But that ye may know24 that the Son of man hath 7power on earth to forgive sins (he said unto him that was palsied), I say unto thee, Arise, and take up thy couch, and go unto thy house.

ERV margin: 1 Or *at home*   2 Greek *that he should heal:* many ancient authorities read *that he should heal them*   3 Many ancient authorities read *bring him unto him*   4 Greek *Child*   5 Many ancient authorities read *seeing*   6 Or *Why*   7 Or *authority*

MATT 9	MARK 2	LUKE 5
H And he arose, and 7 departed to his house. But 8 when the multitudes saw it, they were afraid, and glorified God, which had given such 'power unto men.	H And[12] he arose, and straightway took up the bed, and went forth before them all; insomuch that they were all amazed, and glorified God, saying, We never saw it on this fashion.	H And[25] immediately he rose up before them, and took up that whereon he lay, and departed to his house, glorifying God. And[26] amazement took hold on all, and they glorified God; and they were filled with fear, saying, We have seen strange things to-day.

§ 30   CRITICISM FOR ASSOCIATION WITH SINNERS

MATT 9:9–13	MARK 2:13–17	LUKE 5:27–32
	A And he went forth again[13] by the sea side; and all the multitude resorted unto him, and he taught them.	A And after these things he[27] went forth,
B And as Jesus passed by 9 from thence, he saw a man, called Matthew, sitting at the place of toll: and he saith unto him, Follow me. And he arose, and followed him.	B And as[14] he passed by, he saw Levi the *son* of Alphæus sitting at the place of toll, and he saith unto him, Follow me. And he arose and followed him.	B and beheld a publican, named Levi, sitting at the place of toll, and said unto him, Follow me. And he for-[28] sook all, and rose up and followed him.
c And it came to pass, as he[10] ²sat at meat in the house, behold, many publicans and sinners came and sat down with Jesus and his disciples.	c And it came to pass, that[15] he was sitting at meat in his house, and many ³publicans and sinners sat down with Jesus and his disciples: for there were many, and they followed him.	c And Levi made[29] him a great feast in his house: and there was a great multitude of publicans and of others that were sitting at meat with them.
D And[11] when the Pharisees saw it, they said unto his disciples, Why eateth your ⁸Master with the publicans and sinners?	D And the scribes[16] ⁴of the Pharisees, when they saw that he was eating with the sinners and publicans, said unto his disciples, ⁶He eateth ⁷and drinketh with publicans and sinners.	D And ⁵the[30] Pharisees and their scribes murmured against his disciples, saying, Why do ye eat and drink with the publicans and sinners?
E But when he heard it,[12] he said, They that are ⁹whole have no need of a physician, but they that are sick.	E And[17] when Jesus heard it, he saith unto them, They that are ⁹whole have no need of a physician, but they that are sick:	E And Jesus an-[31] swering said unto them, They that are whole have no need of a physician; but they that are sick.
F[F] But[13] go ye and learn what *this* meaneth, I desire mercy, and not sacrifice:		
G for I came not to call the righteous, but sinners.	G I came not to call the righteous, but sinners.	G I am not come to[32] call the righteous but sinners to repentance.

§ 31   CRITICISM OF ATTITUDE TOWARD FASTING

MATT 9:14–17	MARK 2:18–22	LUKE 5:33–39
A Then come to him the dis-[14] ciples of John, saying, Why do we and the Pharisees fast ¹⁰oft, but thy disciples fast not?	A And John's disciples and[18] the Pharisees were fasting: and they come and say unto him, Why do John's disciples	A And they said unto him,[33] The disciples of John fast often, and make supplications; likewise also the *dis-*

ERV margin: 1 Or *authority*   2 Greek *reclined:* and so always   3 That is, *collectors or renters of Roman taxes:* and so elsewhere   4 Some ancient authorities read *and the Pharisees*   5 Or *the Pharisees and the scribes among them*   6 Or, How is it *that he eateth . . . sinners?*   7 Some ancient authorities omit *and drinketh*   8 Or *Teacher*   9 Greek *strong*   10 Some ancient authorities omit *oft*

OT references: Mt 9:13 = Hosea 6:6

F   Compare §32 portion E

MATT 9	MARK 2	LUKE 5
	and the disciples of the Pharisees fast, but thy disciples fast not?	*ciples* of the Pharisees; but thine eat and drink.
B And Jesus said unto them,[15] Can the sons of the bride-chamber mourn, as long as the bridegroom is with them? but the days will come, when the bridegroom shall be taken away from them, and then will they fast.	B And Jesus said[19] unto them, Can the sons of the bride-chamber fast, while the bridegroom is with them? as long as they have the bridegroom with them, they cannot fast. But the days will come,[20] when the bridegroom shall be taken away from them, and then will they fast in that day.	B And[34] Jesus said unto them, Can ye make the sons of the bride-chamber fast, while the bridegroom is with them? But[35] the days will come; and when the bridegroom shall be taken away from them, then will they fast in those days.
c And no man[16] putteth a piece of undressed cloth upon an old garment; for that which should fill it up taketh from the garment, and a worse rent is made.	c No man seweth a piece of[21] undressed cloth on an old garment: else that which should fill it up taketh from it, the new from the old, and a worse rent is made.	c And[36] he spake also a parable unto them; No man rendeth a piece from a new garment and putteth it upon an old garment; else he will rend the new, and also the piece from the new will not agree with the old.
D Neither do *men* put new[17] wine into old ¹wine-skins: else the skins burst, and the wine is spilled, and the skins perish: but they put new wine into fresh wine-skins, and both are preserved. (+§52 B)	D And no[22] man putteth new wine into old ¹wine-skins: else the wine will burst the skins, and the wine perisheth, and the skins: but *they put* new wine into fresh wine-skins.	D And no man putteth new[37] wine into old ¹wine-skins; else the new wine will burst the skins, and itself will be spilled, and the skins will perish. But new wine must be put[38] into fresh wine-skins. E And[39] no man having drunk old *wine* desireth new: for he saith, The old is ²good.

§ 32 CRITICISM FOR WORKING ON THE SABBATH

(§41+) MATT 12:1-8	MARK 2:23-28	LUKE 6:1-5
A At that season Jesus went[1] on the sabbath day through the cornfields; and his disciples were an hungred, and began to pluck ears of corn, and to eat.	A And it came to pass, that[23] he was going on the sabbath day through the cornfields; and his disciples ⁴began, as they went, to pluck the ears of corn.	A Now it came to pass on a[1] ³sabbath, that he was going through the cornfields; and his disciples plucked the ears of corn, and did eat, rubbing them in their hands.
B But the Phari-[2] sees, when they saw it, said unto him, Behold, thy disciples do that which it is not lawful to do upon the sabbath.	B And the Pharisees[24] said unto him, Behold, why do they on the sabbath day that which is not lawful?	B But[2] certain of the Pharisees said, Why do ye that which it is not lawful to do on the sabbath day?
c But he said unto them,[3] Have ye not read what David did, when he was an hungred, and they that were with him; how he entered[4] into the house of God, and ⁶did eat the shewbread, which it was not lawful for him to eat, neither for them that were with him, but only for the priests?	c And he said unto them, Did[25] ye never read what David did, when he had need, and was an hungred, he, and they that were with him? How he[26] entered into the house of God ⁵when Abiathar was high priest, and did eat the shewbread, which it is not lawful to eat save for the priests, and gave also to them that were with him?	c And Jesus[3] answering them said, Have ye not read even this, what David did, when he was an hungred, he, and they that were with him; how he[4] entered into the house of God, and did take and eat the shewbread, and gave also to them that were with him; which it is not lawful to eat save for the priests alone?

ERV margin: 1 That is, *skins used as bottles*   2 Many ancient authorities read *better*   3 Many ancient authorities insert *second-first*   4 Greek *began to make their way plucking*   5 Some ancient authorities read *in the days of Abiathar the high priest*   6 Some ancient authorities read *they did eat*

OT references: Mt 12:1 and Mk 2:23 and Lk 6:1=Deuteronomy 23:25   Mt 12:2 and Mk 2:24 and Lk 6:2=Exodus 20:10 and Deuteronomy 5:14   Mt 12:3-4 and Mk 2:25-26 and Lk 6:3-4=1 Samuel 21:1-6 and Leviticus 24:9

MATT 12	MARK 2	LUKE 6
D Or have ye 5 not read in the law, how that on the sabbath day the priests in the temple profane the sabbath, and are guiltless? But I say unto you, that 'one 6 greater than the temple is here.		
E^E But if ye had known 7 what this meaneth, I desire mercy, and not sacrifice, ye would not have condemned the guiltless.		
	F And he said unto 27 them, The sabbath was made for man, and not man for the sabbath:	F And he said unto them, 5
G For the Son of 8 man is lord of the sabbath.	G so that the Son of 28 man is lord even of the sabbath.	G The Son of man is lord of the sabbath.

§ 33   CRITICISM OF HEALING ON THE SABBATH

MATT 12:9–14	MARK 3:1–6	LUKE 6:6–11
A And he departed thence, 9 and went into their synagogue: and behold, a man 10 having a withered hand.	A And he entered again into 1 the synagogue; and there was a man there which had his hand withered.	A And it came to pass on 6 another sabbath, that he entered into the synagogue and taught: and there was a man there, and his right hand was withered.
B And they asked him, saying, Is it lawful to heal on the sabbath day? that they might accuse him.	B And they 2 watched him, whether he would heal him on the sabbath day; that they might accuse him.	B And the 7 scribes and the Pharisees watched him, whether he would heal on the sabbath; that they might find how to accuse him.
	c And he saith 3 unto the man that had his hand withered, ²Stand forth.	c But he knew 8 their thoughts; and he said to the man that had his hand withered, Rise up, and stand forth in the midst. And he arose and stood forth.
D And he 11 said unto them, What man shall there be of you, that shall have one sheep, and if this fall into a pit on the sabbath day, will he not lay hold on it, and lift it out? How 12 much then is a man of more value than a sheep!		D *And he said unto them,* 14: *Which of you shall have* ³*an* 5 *ass or an ox fallen into a well, and will not straightway draw him up on a sabbath day?* (§102 D)
E^E Wherefore it is lawful to do good on the sabbath day.	E^E And he saith unto them, 4 Is it lawful on the sabbath day to do good, or to do harm? to save a life, or to kill? But they held their peace.	E^E And 9 Jesus said unto them, I ask you, Is it lawful on the sabbath to do good, or to do harm? to save a life, or to destroy it?
F Then saith 13 he to the man, Stretch forth	F And when he had 5 looked round about on them	F And he looked 10 round about on them all, and

ERV margin: 1 Greek *a greater thing*   2 Greek *Arise into the midst*   3 Many ancient authorities read *a son:* see Luke 13:15

OT references: Mt 12:5 = Numbers 28:9-10   Mt 12:7 = Hosea 6:6

E   Compare §30 portion F

E And Jesus answering spake unto the lawyers and Pharisees, saying, Is it lawful to heal on the sabbath, or not? But they held their peace. (§102 B = Lk 14:3-4)

MATT 12	MARK 3	LUKE 6
thy hand. And he stretched it forth; and it was restored whole, as the other.	with anger, being grieved at the hardening of their heart, he saith unto the man, Stretch forth thy hand. And he stretched it forth: and his hand was restored.	said unto him, Stretch forth thy hand. And he did *so:* and his hand was restored.
G But the[14] Pharisees went out, and took counsel against him, how they might destroy him. (+§34C)	G And the 6 Pharisees went out, and straightway with the Herodians took counsel against him, how they might destroy him.	G But they were filled with[1] [1]madness; and communed one with another what they might do to Jesus.

ERV margin: 1 Or *foolishness*

CHAPTER VI

DEFINITION OF STANDARDS OF RIGHTEOUSNESS BY JESUS

§ 34 WIDESPREAD FAME OF JESUS

(§26+) MATT 4:24–25
(§33+) MATT 12:15–21

A *Compare portion C below*

B And the report of him went 4:
forth into all Syria: and they24
brought unto him all that were
sick, holden with divers diseases and torments, [1]possessed
with devils, and epileptic, and
palsied; and he healed them.
And there followed him great25
multitudes from Galilee and
Decapolis and Jerusalem and
Judæa and *from* beyond Jordan. (+ § 36)
c And Jesus perceiving it[12]:
withdrew from thence: 15
D   and
many followed him; and he
healed them all,

F   and charged[16]
them that they should not
make him known:
G   that it[17]
might be fulfilled which was
spoken [5]by Isaiah the prophet,
saying,
Behold, my servant whom[18]
  I have chosen;
My beloved in whom my
  soul is well pleased:
I will put my Spirit upon
  him,
And he shall declare judgement to the Gentiles.
He shall not strive, nor cry[19]
  aloud:

MARK 3:7–12

A And Jesus with his disciples 7
withdrew to the sea:
B   and a
great multitude from Galilee
followed: and from Judæa,
and from Jerusalem, and from 8
Idumæa, and beyond Jordan,
and about Tyre and Sidon, a
great multitude, hearing [2]what
great things he did, came unto
him.

c *Compare portion A above*

D   And he spake to his dis- 9
ciples, that a little boat should
wait on him because of the
crowd, lest they should throng
him: for he had healed many;[10]
insomuch that as many as had
[3]plagues [4]pressed upon him
that they might touch him.

E And the unclean spirits,[11]
whensoever they beheld him,
fell down before him, and
cried, saying, Thou art the
Son of God.
F   And he charged[12]
them much that they should
not make him known.

LUKE

B *Compare §35 portion E*

D *Compare §35 portion G*

E *Compare §35 portion F*
   Compare §25 portion E

ERV margin: 1 Or *demoniacs*   2 Or *all the things that he did*   3 Greek *scourges*   4 Greek *fell*   5 Or *through*

OT references: Mt 12:18–21 = Isaiah 42:1–4

MATT 12

Neither shall any one hear
his voice in the streets.
A bruised reed shall he not[20]
break,
And smoking flax shall he
not quench,
Till he send forth judge-
ment unto victory.
And in his name shall the[21]
Gentiles hope.　(+ §45)

§ 35　APPOINTMENT OF TWELVE ASSOCIATES

MATT 10:1–4	MARK 3:13–19[a]	LUKE 6:12–19
A　*Compare §36 portion A*	A And he goeth up into the[13] mountain,	A And it came to pass in these[12] days, that he went out into the mountain to pray; and he continued all night in prayer to God.
B *And he called unto him his* [1] *twelve disciples, and gave them authority over unclean spirits, to cast them out, and to heal all manner of disease and all manner of sickness.*	B 　　　　and calleth unto him whom he himself would: and they went unto him. And[14] he appointed twelve,[1] that they might be with him, and that he might send them forth to preach, and to have author-[15] ity to cast out [2]devils:	B 　　　　And when it was[13] day, he called his disciples: and he chose from them twelve, whom also he named apostles;
C *Now the names of the twelve* [2] *apostles are these: The first, Simon, who is called Peter, and Andrew his brother; James the son of Zebedee, and John his brother; Philip, and Bartholo-* [3] *mew; Thomas, and Matthew the publican; James the son of Alphæus, and Thaddæus; Simon the* [4]*Cananæan, and Judas Iscariot, who also* [6]*betrayed him.　(§56 CD)*	C 　　　　[3]and[16] Simon he surnamed Peter; and[17] James the *son* of Zebedee, and John the brother of James; and them he surnamed Boanerges, which is, Sons of thunder: and Andrew, and Philip,[18] and Bartholomew, and Matthew, and Thomas, and James the *son* of Alphæus, and Thaddæus, and Simon the [4]Cananæan, and Judas Iscariot,[19a] which also betrayed him.	C 　　　　Simon, whom he also[14] named Peter, and Andrew his brother, and James and John, and Philip and Bartholomew, and Matthew and Thomas, and[15] James *the son* of Alphæus, and Simon which was called the Zealot, and Judas *the* [5]*son* of[16] James, and Judas Iscariot, which was the traitor;
D　*Compare §36 portion A* 　*Compare §38 portion Y*		D 　　　　and[17] he came down with them, and stood on a level place,
E　*Compare §34 portion B* 　*Compare §38 portion Y*	E 　*Compare §34 portion B*	E 　　　　and a great multitude of his disciples, and a great number of the people from all Judæa and Jerusalem, and the sea coast of Tyre and Sidon, which came to hear him, and to be healed of their diseases;
F　*Compare §34 portion B*	F 　*Compare §34 portion E*	F 　　　　and[18] they that were troubled with unclean spirits were healed.
	G 　*Compare §34 portion D*	G And all the multitude sought[19] to touch him: for power came forth from him, and healed *them* all.

ERV margin:　1 Some ancient authorities add *whom also he named apostles:* see Luke 6:13　2 Greek *demons*
3 Some ancient authorities insert *and he appointed twelve*　4 Or *Zealot:* see Luke 6:15 and Acts 1:13　5 Or, *brother:*
see Jude 1　6 Or *delivered him up:* and so always

§36 DISCOURSE ON STANDARDS OF RIGHTEOUSNESS

(§34 B+) MATT 5:1—8:1

A And seeing the multitudes, he went up into [1] the mountain: and when he had sat down, his disciples came unto him:
B   and he opened his [2] mouth and taught them, saying,
  Blessed are the poor in spirit: for theirs is [3] the kingdom of heaven.
C [1]Blessed are they that mourn: for they shall [4] be comforted.
D Blessed are the meek: for they shall inherit [5] the earth.
E Blessed are they that hunger and thirst after [6] righteousness: for they shall be filled.
F *Compare portion C above*

G Blessed are the merciful: for they shall [7] obtain mercy.
  Blessed are the pure in heart: for they shall [8] see God.
  Blessed are the peacemakers: for they shall [9] be called sons of God.
H Blessed are they that have been persecuted[10] for righteousness' sake: for theirs is the kingdom of heaven.
I Blessed are ye when *men* shall reproach you,[11] and persecute you, and say all manner of evil against you falsely, for my sake. Rejoice, and[12] be exceeding glad: for great is your reward in heaven: for so persecuted they the prophets which were before you.

K Ye are the salt of the earth: [13]
L^L   but if the salt have lost its savour, wherewith shall it be salted? it is thenceforth good for nothing, but to be cast out and trodden under foot of men.
M Ye are the light of the world.   [14]
N^N   A city set on a hill cannot be hid. Neither do *men* light a[15] lamp, and put it under the bushel, but on the stand; and it shineth unto all that are in the house.
O   Even so let your light shine before[16] men, that they may see your good works, and glorify your Father which is in heaven.

LUKE 6:20—49

A *Compare §35 portion A*
  Compare §35 portion D

B And he lifted up his eyes on his disciples,[20] and said,
  Blessed *are* ye poor: for yours is the kingdom of God.
C *Compare portion F below*

E Blessed *are* ye that hunger now: for ye shall[21] be filled.
F Blessed *are* ye that weep now: for ye shall laugh.

H *Compare portion I below*

I Blessed are ye, when men shall hate you,[22] and when they shall separate you *from their company*, and reproach you, and cast out your name as evil, for the Son of man's sake. Re-[23]joice in that day, and leap *for joy:* for behold, your reward is great in heaven: for in the same manner did their fathers unto the prophets.
J But woe unto you that are rich! for ye have[24] received your consolation.
  Woe unto you, ye that are full now! for ye[25] shall hunger.
  Woe *unto you*, ye that laugh now! for ye shall mourn and weep.
  Woe *unto you*, when all men shall speak well[26] of you! for in the same manner did their fathers to the false prophets.

L^L *Salt therefore is good: but if even the salt*[14:] *have lost its savour, wherewith shall it be sea-34 soned? It is fit neither for the land nor for the*35 *dunghill: men cast it out.* (§104E)

N^N *No man, when he hath lighted a lamp, putteth*[11:] *it in a cellar, neither under the bushel, but on the*33 *stand, that they which enter in may see the light.* (§89A)

ERV margin: [1] Some ancient authorities transpose verses 4 and 5

OT references: Mt 5:5 = Psalm 37:11

L Salt is good: but if the salt have lost its saltness, wherewith will ye season it? Have salt in yourselves, and be at **peace** one with another. (§78 O = Mk 9:50)

N Is the lamp brought to be put under the bushel, or under the bed, *and* not to be put on the stand? (§47 Q = Mk 4:21)

N And no man, when he hath lighted a lamp, covereth it with a vessel, or putteth it under a bed; but putteth it on a stand, that they which enter in may see the light. (§47 Q = Lk 8:16)

MATT 5   LUKE

P Think not that I came to destroy the law[17] or the prophets: I came not to destroy, but to fulfil.

Q   For verily I say unto you, Till heaven[18] and earth pass away, one jot or one tittle shall in no wise pass away from the law, till all things be accomplished.

Q *But it is easier for heaven and earth to pass[16]: away, than for one tittle of the law to fall.* (§107 D)[17]

R   Whosoever therefore shall[19] break one of these least commandments, and shall teach men so, shall be called least in the kingdom of heaven: but whosoever shall do and teach them, he shall be called great in the kingdom of heaven.

S   For I say unto you, that[20] except your righteousness shall exceed *the righteousness* of the scribes and Pharisees, ye shall in no wise enter into the kingdom of heaven.

§37 DISCOURSE ON STANDARDS OF RIGHTEOUSNESS (*continued*)

A Ye have heard that it was said to them of old[21] time, Thou shalt not kill; and whosoever shall kill shall be in danger of the judgement: but I[22] say unto you, that every one who is angry with his brother[1] shall be in danger of the judgement; and whosoever shall say to his brother, [2]Raca, shall be in danger of the council; and whosoever shall say, [3]Thou fool, shall be in danger [4]of the [5]hell of fire.   If therefore thou art offer-[23] ing thy gift at the altar, and there rememberest that thy brother hath aught against thee, leave[24] there thy gift before the altar, and go thy way, first be reconciled to thy brother, and then come and offer thy gift.

B   Agree with thine adversary[25] quickly, whiles thou art with him in the way; lest haply the adversary deliver thee to the judge, and the judge [6]deliver thee to the officer, and thou be cast into prison.   Verily I say unto[26] thee, Thou shalt by no means come out thence, till thou have paid the last farthing.

B *For as thou art going with thine adversary be-[12]: fore the magistrate, on the way give diligence to[58] be quit of him; lest haply he hale thee unto the judge, and the judge shall deliver thee to the [7]officer, and the [7]officer shall cast thee into prison. I say unto thee, Thou shalt by no means come[59] out thence, till thou have paid the very last mite.* (§96 C)

C[C] Ye have heard that it was said, Thou shalt[27] not commit adultery: but I say unto you, that[28] every one that looketh on a woman to lust after her hath committed adultery with her already in his heart.   And if thy right eye causeth thee[29] to stumble, pluck it out, and cast it from thee: for it is profitable for thee that one of thy members should perish, and not thy whole body be

---

ERV margin: 1 Many ancient authorities insert *without cause*   2 An expression of contempt   3 Or *Moreh*, a Hebrew expression of condemnation   4 Greek *unto* or *into*   5 Greek *Gehenna of fire*   6 Some ancient authorities omit *deliver thee*   7 Greek *exactor*

OT references: Mt 5:21 = Exodus 20:13 and Deuteronomy 5:17; also Exodus 21:12 and Leviticus 24:17 and Deuteronomy 17:8-9   Mt 5:27 = Exodus 20:14 and Deuteronomy 5:18

C And if thy hand or thy foot causeth thee to stumble, cut it off, and cast it from thee: it is good for thee to enter into life maimed or halt, rather than having two hands or two feet to be cast into the eternal fire.   And if thine eye causeth thee to stumble, pluck it out, and cast it from thee: it is good for thee to enter into life with one eye, rather than having two eyes to be cast into the hell of fire. (§78 M = Mt 18:8-9)

C And if thy hand cause thee to stumble, cut it off: it is good for thee to enter into life maimed, rather than having thy two hands to go into hell, into the unquenchable fire.   And if thy foot cause thee to stumble, cut it off: it is good for thee to enter into life halt, rather than having thy two feet to be cast into hell.   And if thine eye cause thee to stumble, cast it out: it is good for thee to enter into the kingdom of God with one eye, rather than having two eyes to be cast into hell. (§78 M = Mk 9:43-47)

| MATT 5 | LUKE 6 |

cast into [1]hell. And if thy right hand causeth[30] thee to stumble, cut it off, and cast it from thee: for it is profitable for thee that one of thy members should perish, and not thy whole body go into [1]hell.

D It was said also, Whosoever shall[31] put away his wife, let him give her a writing of divorcement:

E[E] but I say unto you, that every[32] one that putteth away his wife, saving for the cause of fornication, maketh her an adulteress: and whosoever shall marry her when she is put away committeth adultery.

E[E] *Every one that putteth away his wife, and*[16:] *marrieth another, committeth adultery: and he*[8] *that marrieth one that is put away from a husband committeth adultery.* (§107 E)

F Again, ye have heard that it was said to them[33] of old time, Thou shalt not forswear thyself, but shalt perform unto the Lord thine oaths: but I say unto you, Swear not at all; neither[34] by the heaven, for it is the throne of God; nor[35] by the earth, for it is the footstool of his feet; nor [2]by Jerusalem, for it is the city of the great King. Neither shalt thou swear by thy head,[36] for thou canst not make one hair white or black. [3]But let your speech be, Yea, yea; Nay, nay:[37] and whatsoever is more than these is of [4]the evil *one*.

G Ye have heard that it was said, An eye for[38] an eye, and a tooth for a tooth:

H *Compare portion N below*

H But I say unto you which hear, Love your[27] enemies, do good to them that hate you, bless[28] them that curse you, pray for them that despitefully use you.

I To him that smiteth thee[29] on the *one* cheek offer also the other; and from him that taketh away thy cloke withhold not thy coat also.

I but I say[39] unto you, Resist not [5]him that is evil: but whosoever smiteth thee on thy right cheek, turn to him the other also. And if any man would[40] go to law with thee, and take away thy coat, let him have thy cloke also. And whosoever[41] shall [6]compel thee to go one mile, go with him twain.

J Give to him that asketh thee, and from[42] him that would borrow of thee turn not thou away.

K *Compare §38 portion L*

J Give to every one that asketh[30] thee; and of him that taketh away thy goods ask them not again.

K And as ye would that[31] men should do to you, do ye also to them likewise.

L Ye have heard that it was said, Thou shalt[43] love thy neighbour, and hate thine enemy:

M *Compare portion Q below*

M And if ye love them that love you, what[32] thank have ye? for even sinners love those that love them. And if ye do good to them that do[33] good to you, what thank have ye? for even sinners do the same. And if ye lend to them of[34] whom ye hope to receive, what thank have ye? even sinners lend to sinners, to receive again as much.

ERV margin: 1 Greek *Gehenna* 2 Or *toward* 3 Some ancient authorities read *But your speech shall be* 4 Or *evil:* as in verse 39 and 6:13 5 Or *evil* 6 Greek *impress*

OT references: Mt 5:31=Deuteronomy 24:1 Mt 5:33=Leviticus 19:12 and Numbers 30:2 and Deuteronomy 23:21; also Exodus 20:7 and Deuteronomy 5:11 Mt 5:34-35ª=Isaiah 66:1 Mt 5:35ᵇ=Psalm 48:2 Mt 5:38=Exodus 21:24 and Leviticus 24:20 and Deuteronomy 19:21 Mt 5:43ª=Leviticus 19:18 Mt 5:43ᵇ= Deuteronomy 23:6 and 25:19

E And I say unto you, Whosoever shall put away his wife, except for fornication, and shall marry another, committeth adultery: and he that marrieth her when she is put away committeth adultery. (§115 F=Mt 19:9)

E And he saith unto them, Whosoever shall put away his wife, and marry another, committeth adultery against her: and if she herself shall put away her husband, and marry another, she committeth adultery. (§115 F=Mk 10:11-12)

MATT 5–6

N   but44
I say unto you, Love your enemies, and pray
for them that persecute you;
O   *Compare portion J above*

P   that ye may be45
sons of your Father which is in heaven: for he
maketh his sun to rise on the evil and the good,
and sendeth rain on the just and the unjust.

Q For if ye love them that love you, what re-46
ward have ye? do not even the ²publicans the
same? And if ye salute your brethren only,47
what do ye more *than others?* do not even the
Gentiles the same?

R   Ye therefore shall be per-48
fect, as your heavenly Father is perfect.

S Take heed that ye do not your righteousness 6:
before men, to be seen of them: else ye have 1
no reward with your Father which is in heaven.

T When therefore thou doest alms, sound not a 2
trumpet before thee, as the hypocrites do in
the synagogues and in the streets, that they
may have glory of men. Verily I say unto you,
They have received their reward. But when 3
thou doest alms, let not thy left hand know
what thy right hand doeth: that thine alms 4
may be in secret: and thy Father which seeth
in secret shall recompense thee.

U And when ye pray, ye shall not be as the 5
hypocrites: for they love to stand and pray in
the synagogues and in the corners of the streets,
that they may be seen of men. Verily I say
unto you, They have received their reward.
But thou, when thou prayest, enter into thine 6
inner chamber, and having shut thy door, pray
to thy Father which is in secret, and thy Father
which seeth in secret shall recompense thee.

V^V And in praying use not vain repetitions, as 7
the Gentiles do: for they think that they shall
be heard for their much speaking. Be not 8
therefore like unto them: for ³your Father
knoweth what things ye have need of, before
ye ask him.

W   After this manner therefore pray 9
ye: Our Father which art in heaven, Hallowed
be thy name. Thy kingdom come. Thy will10
be done, as in heaven, so on earth. Give us11
this day ⁴our daily bread. And forgive us our12
debts, as we also have forgiven our debtors.
And bring us not into temptation, but deliver13
us from ⁵the evil *one*.⁶

X^X For if ye forgive men14
their trespasses, your heavenly Father will also
forgive you. But if ye forgive not men their15
trespasses, neither will your Father forgive your
trespasses.

LUKE 6

N   But love your enemies, and do *them*35
good,   *Compare portion H above*

O   and lend, ¹never despairing; and your reward shall be great,

P   and ye shall be sons of the
Most High: for he is kind toward the unthank-
ful and evil.

Q   *Compare portion M above*

R   Be ye merciful, even as your36
Father is merciful.

W   *When ye pray, say, ⁷Father, Hallowed be thy*11:
*name. Thy kingdom come.*⁸ *Give us day by* 2
day ⁴*our daily bread. And forgive us our sins;* 3
for we ourselves also forgive every one that is in- 4
*debted to us. And bring us not into temptation.*⁹
(§85 B)

ERV margin: 1 Some ancient authorities read *despairing of no man*   2 That is, *collectors or renters of Roman taxes:* and so elsewhere   3 Some ancient authorities read *God your Father*   4. Greek *our bread for the coming day* 5 Or *evil*   6 Many authorities, some ancient, but with variations, add *For thine is the kingdom, and the power, and the glory, for ever. Amen.*   7 Many ancient authorities read *Our Father, which art in heaven:* see Matt 6:9   8 Many ancient authorities add *Thy will be done, as in heaven, so on earth:* see Matt 6:10   9 Many ancient authorities add *but deliver us from the evil* one (or *from evil*): see Matt 6:13

v   With Matt 6:8 above, compare Matt 6:32=Luke 12:30 in §38 D
x   And whensoever ye stand praying, forgive, if ye have aught against any one; that your Father also which is in heaven may forgive you your trespasses. (§127 E=Mk 11:25)
x   So shall also my heavenly Father do unto you, if ye forgive not every one his brother from your hearts. (§78 x=Mt 18:35)

MATT 6	LUKE

Y Moreover when ye fast, be not, as the hypo-[16] crites, of a sad countenance: for they disfigure their faces, that they may be seen of men to fast. Verily I say unto you, They have received their reward. But thou, when thou[17] fastest, anoint thy head, and wash thy face; that thou be not seen of men to fast, but of thy[18] Father which is in secret: and thy Father, which seeth in secret, shall recompense thee.

§38 DISCOURSE ON STANDARDS OF RIGHTEOUSNESS (*concluded*)

A Lay not up for yourselves treasures upon the[19] earth, where moth and rust doth consume, and where thieves ¹break through and steal: but[20] lay up for yourselves treasures in heaven, where neither moth nor rust doth consume, and where thieves do not ¹break through nor steal: for[21] where thy treasure is, there will thy heart be also.

B The lamp of the body is the eye: if[22] therefore thine eye be single, thy whole body shall be full of light. But if thine eye be evil,[23] thy whole body shall be full of darkness. If therefore the light that is in thee be darkness, how great is the darkness!

C   No man can serve[24] two masters: for either he will hate the one, and love the other; or else he will hold to one, and despise the other. Ye cannot serve God and mammon.

D[D]   Therefore I say unto you, Be[25] not anxious for your life, what ye shall eat, or what ye shall drink; nor yet for your body, what ye shall put on. Is not the life more than the food, and the body than the raiment? Be-[26] hold the birds of the heaven, that they sow not, neither do they reap, nor gather into barns; and your heavenly Father feedeth them. Are not ye of much more value than they? And[27] which of you by being anxious can add one cubit unto his ³stature? And why are ye[28] anxious concerning raiment? Consider the lilies of the field, how they grow; they toil not, neither do they spin: yet I say unto you, that[29] even Solomon in all his glory was not arrayed like one of these. But if God doth so clothe[30] the grass of the field, which to-day is, and to-morrow is cast into the oven, *shall he* not much more *clothe* you, O ye of little faith? Be not[31] therefore anxious, saying, What shall we eat? or, What shall we drink? or, Wherewithal shall we be clothed? For after all these things do[32] the Gentiles seek; for your heavenly Father knoweth that ye have need of all these things. But seek ye first his kingdom, and his right-[33] eousness; and all these things shall be added unto you.

E   Be not therefore anxious for the[34] morrow: for the morrow will be anxious for itself. Sufficient unto the day is the evil thereof.

A *Sell that ye have, and give alms; make for*[12]*: yourselves purses which wax not old, a treasure*[33] *in the heavens that faileth not, where no thief draweth near, neither moth destroyeth. For*[34] *where your treasure is, there will your heart be also.* (§93 *I–K*)

B *The lamp of thy body is thine eye: when thine*[11]*: eye is single, thy whole body also is full of light;*[34] *but when it is evil, thy body also is full of darkness. Look therefore whether the light that is in thee be*[35] *not darkness.* (§89 *BC*)

C *No ²servant can serve two masters: for either*[16]*: he will hate the one, and love the other; or else*[13] *he will hold to one, and despise the other. Ye cannot serve God and mammon.* (§107 *A*)

D[D] *Therefore I say unto you, Be not anxious for*[12]*: your ⁴life, what ye shall eat; nor yet for your*[22] *body, what ye shall put on. For the ⁴life is more*[23] *than the food, and the body than the raiment. Consider the ravens, that they sow not, neither*[24] *reap; which have no store-chamber nor barn; and God feedeth them: of how much more value are ye than the birds! And which of you by being*[25] *anxious can add a cubit unto his ³stature? If*[26] *then ye are not able to do even that which is least, why are ye anxious concerning the rest? Con-*[27] *sider the lilies, how they grow: they toil not, neither do they spin; yet I say unto you, Even Solomon in all his glory was not arrayed like one of these. But if God doth so clothe the grass in*[28] *the field, which to-day is, and to-morrow is cast into the oven; how much more shall he clothe you, O ye of little faith? And seek not ye what ye*[29] *shall eat, and what ye shall drink, neither be ye of doubtful mind. For all these things do the*[30] *nations of the world seek after: but your Father knoweth that ye have need of these things. How-*[31] *beit seek ye ⁵his kingdom, and these things shall be added unto you.*

E   *Fear not, little flock; for it is*[32] *your Father's good pleasure to give you the king-dom.* (§93 *B–H*)

ERV margin: ¹ Greek *dig through*   ² Greek *household-servant*   ³ Or *age*   ⁴ Or *soul*   ⁵ Many ancient authorities read *the kingdom of God*

D With Matt 6:32=Luke 12:30 above, compare Matt 6:8 in §37 V

MATT 7

Fᶠ Judge not, that ye be not judged. For [1] with what judgement ye judge, ye shall be [2] judged: and with what measure ye mete, it shall be measured unto you.

G *Let them alone: they are blind guides. And* [15:] *if the blind guide the blind, both shall fall into a* [14] *pit.* (§63J)
H *A disciple is not above his* [1]*master, nor a* [10:] [2]*servant above his lord. It is enough for the* [24] *disciple that he be as his* [1]*master, and the* [2]*serv-* [25] *ant as his lord.* (§57G)
I   And why be- [3] holdest thou the mote that is in thy brother's eye, but considerest not the beam that is in thine own eye? Or how wilt thou say to thy [4] brother, Let me cast out the mote out of thine eye; and lo, the beam is in thine own eye? Thou hypocrite, cast out first the beam out of [5] thine own eye; and then shalt thou see clearly to cast out the mote out of thy brother's eye.

J Give not that which is holy unto the dogs, [6] neither cast your pearls before the swine, lest haply they trample them under their feet, and turn and rend you.
K Ask, and it shall be given you; seek, and ye [7] shall find; knock, and it shall be opened unto you: for every one that asketh receiveth; and [8] he that seeketh findeth; and to him that knocketh it shall be opened. Or what man is [9] there of you, who, if his son shall ask him for a loaf, will give him a stone; or if he shall ask [10] for a fish, will give him a serpent? If ye then, [11] being evil, know how to give good gifts unto your children, how much more shall your Father which is in heaven give good things to them that ask him?
Lᴸ   All things therefore whatso- [12] ever ye would that men should do unto you, even so do ye also unto them: for this is the law and the prophets.
M Enter ye in by the narrow gate: for wide [13] [4]is the gate, and broad is the way, that leadeth to destruction, and many be they that enter in thereby. [5]For narrow is the gate, and [14] straitened the way, that leadeth unto life, and few be they that find it.
N Beware of false prophets, which come to [15] you in sheep's clothing, but inwardly are ravening wolves.
Oᵒ *Compare portion S below*

Pᴾ   By their fruits ye shall know [16] them. Do *men* gather grapes of thorns, or figs of thistles?

LUKE 6

Fᶠ And judge not, and ye shall not be judged: [37] and condemn not, and ye shall not be condemned: release, and ye shall be released: give, and it shall be given unto you; good [38] measure, pressed down, shaken together, running over, shall they give into your bosom. For with what measure ye mete it shall be measured to you again.
G And he spake also a parable unto them, Can [39] the blind guide the blind? shall they not both fall into a pit?
H   The disciple is not above his [40] [1]master: but every one when he is perfected shall be as his [1]master.

I   And why beholdest [41] thou the mote that is in thy brother's eye, but considerest not the beam that is in thine own eye? Or how canst thou say to thy brother, [42] Brother, let me cast out the mote that is in thine eye, when thou thyself beholdest not the beam that is in thine own eye? Thou hypocrite, cast out first the beam out of thine own eye, and then shalt thou see clearly to cast out the mote that is in thy brother's eye.

K *Ask, and it shall be given you; seek, and ye* [11:] *shall find; knock, and it shall be opened unto* [9] *you. For every one that asketh receiveth; and he* [10] *that seeketh findeth; and to him that knocketh it shall be opened. And of which of you that is a* [11] *father shall his son ask* [3]*a loaf, and he give him a stone? or a fish, and he for a fish give him a serpent? Or if he shall ask an egg, will he give* [12] *him a scorpion? If ye then, being evil, know* [13] *how to give good gifts unto your children, how much more shall your heavenly Father give the Holy Spirit to them that ask him?* (§85D)
Lᴸ *Compare §37 portion K*

M *Strive to enter in by the narrow door: for* [13:] *many, I say unto you, shall seek to enter in, and* [24] *shall not be able.* (§100C)

Oᵒ   For there is [43] no good tree that bringeth forth corrupt fruit; nor again a corrupt tree that bringeth forth good fruit.
Pᴾ   For each tree is known by its own [44] fruit. For of thorns men do not gather figs, nor of a bramble bush gather they grapes.

ERV margin: [1] Or *teacher* [2] Greek *bondservant* [3] Some ancient authorities omit *a loaf, and he give him a stone?* or [4] Some ancient authorities omit *is the gate* [5] Many ancient authorities read *How narrow is the gate, etc.*

F With what measure ye mete it shall be measured unto you: and more shall be given unto you. (§47 U = Mk 4:24)
L On these two commandments hangeth the whole law, and the prophets. (§130 N = Mt 22:40)
OP With portions OP above, compare §45 LM. With the first half of portion P above, compare the second half of portion T below

MATT 7	LUKE 6

Q   Even so every good tree bringeth[17] forth good fruit; but the corrupt tree bringeth forth evil fruit.

R *For out of the abundance of the heart the*[12]: *mouth speaketh. The good man out of his good*[34] *treasure bringeth forth good things: and the evil*[35] *man out of his evil treasure bringeth forth evil things.* (§45 O)

R   The good[45] man out of the good treasure of his heart bring-eth forth that which is good; and the evil *man* out of the evil *treasure* bringeth forth that which is evil: for out of the abundance of the heart his mouth speaketh.

s *Compare portion O above*

s   A good tree cannot bring forth[18] evil fruit, neither can a corrupt tree bring forth good fruit.

T[T]   Every tree that bringeth not forth[19] good fruit is hewn down, and cast into the fire. Therefore by their fruits ye shall know them.[20]

U Not every one that saith unto me, Lord, Lord,[21] shall enter into the kingdom of heaven; but he that doeth the will of my Father which is in heaven.

U And why call ye me, Lord, Lord, and do not[46] the things which I say?

V   Many will say to me in that day, Lord,[22] Lord, did we not prophesy by thy name, and by thy name cast out [1]devils, and by thy name do many [2]mighty works? And then will I profess[23] unto them, I never knew you: depart from me, ye that work iniquity.

V *Then shall ye begin to say, We did eat and*[13]: *drink in thy presence, and thou didst teach in*[26] *our streets; and he shall say, I tell you, I know*[27] *not whence ye are; depart from me, all ye workers of iniquity.* (§100 EF)

W   Every one therefore[24] which heareth these words of mine, and doeth them, shall be likened unto a wise man, which built his house upon the rock: and the rain de-[25] scended, and the floods came, and the winds blew, and beat upon that house; and it fell not: for it was founded upon the rock. And every[26] one that heareth these words of mine, and doeth them not, shall be likened unto a foolish man, which built his house upon the sand: and the[27] rain descended, and the floods came, and the winds blew, and smote upon that house; and it fell: and great was the fall thereof.

W   Every one that[47] cometh unto me, and heareth my words, and doeth them, I will shew you to whom he is like: he is like a man building a house, who digged[48] and went deep, and laid a foundation upon the rock: and when a flood arose, the stream brake against that house, and could not shake it: [3]because it had been well builded. But he[49] that heareth, and doeth not, is like a man that built a house upon the earth without a founda-tion; against which the stream brake, and straightway it fell in; and the ruin of that house was great.

X And it came to pass, when Jesus ended these[28] words, the multitudes were astonished at his teaching: for he taught them as *one* having[29] authority, and not as their scribes.

X *Compare §24 portion B*

Y And when he was come down from the moun-[8]: tain, great multitudes followed him. (+§ 28) [1]

Y *Compare §35 portions DE*

ERV margin: 1 Greek *demons*   2 Greek *powers*   3 Many ancient authorities read *for it had been founded upon the rock:* as in Matt 7:25

OT references: Mt 7:23 and Lk 13:27 = Psalm 6.?

---

[1] For a saying by John the Baptist similar to verse 19, compare §17 M end.   With verse 20 compare portion P above

CHAPTER VII

CONTEMPORARY OPINIONS ABOUT THE WORTH OF JESUS

§ 39 OPINION OF A ROMAN CENTURION

(§28+) MATT 8:5-13

A And when he was entered into Capernaum, 5 there came unto him a centurion, beseeching him, and saying, Lord, my [1]servant lieth in the 6 house sick of the palsy, grievously tormented. And he saith unto him, I will come and heal 7 him.

B And the centurion answered and said, 8 Lord, I am not [4]worthy that thou shouldest come under my roof: but only say [5]the word, and my [1]servant shall be healed. For I also 9 am a man [6]under authority, having under myself soldiers: and I say to this one, Go, and he goeth; and to another, Come, and he cometh; and to my [2]servant, Do this, and he doeth it.

c And when Jesus heard it, he marvelled, and[10] said to them that followed, Verily I say unto you, [8]I have not found so great faith, no, not in Israel.

D[D] And I say unto you, that many shall[11] come from the east and the west, and shall [9]sit down with Abraham, and Isaac, and Jacob, in the kingdom of heaven: but the sons of the[12] kingdom shall be cast forth into the outer darkness: there shall be the weeping and gnashing of teeth.

E And Jesus said unto the centurion,[13] Go thy way; as thou hast believed, so be it done unto thee. And the [1]servant was healed in that hour. (+§25)

LUKE 7:1-10

A After he had ended all his sayings in the ears [1] of the people, he entered into Capernaum.

And a certain centurion's [2]servant, who was [2] [3]dear unto him, was sick and at the point of death. And when he heard concerning Jesus, 3 he sent unto him elders of the Jews, asking him that he would come and save his [2]servant. And they, when they came to Jesus, besought 4 him earnestly, saying, He is worthy that thou shouldest do this for him: for he loveth our 5 nation, and himself built us our synagogue. And Jesus went with them. 6

B And when he was now not far from the house, the centurion sent friends to him, saying unto him, Lord, trouble not thyself: for I am not [4]worthy that thou shouldest come under my roof: wherefore 7 neither thought I myself worthy to come unto thee: but [7]say the word, and my [1]servant shall be healed. For I also am a man set under 8 authority, having under myself soldiers: and I say to this one, Go, and he goeth; and to another, Come, and he cometh; and to my [2]servant, Do this, and he doeth it.

c And when 9 Jesus heard these things, he marvelled at him, and turned and said unto the multitude that followed him, I say unto you, I have not found so great faith, no, not in Israel.

D[D] *There shall be the weeping and gnashing*[13]: *of teeth, when ye shall see Abraham, and Isaac,*[28] *and Jacob, and all the prophets, in the kingdom of God, and yourselves cast forth without. And*[29] *they shall come from the east and west, and from the north and south, and shall* [9]sit *down in the kingdom of God.* (§100 G)

E And they that[10] were sent, returning to the house, found the [2]servant whole.

ERV margin: 1 Or *boy*   2 Greek *bondservant*   3 Or *precious to him* or *honourable with him*   4 Greek *sufficient*   5 Greek *with a word*   6 Some ancient authorities insert *set:* as in Luke 7:8   7 Greek *say with a word*   8 Many ancient authorities read *With no man in Israel have I found so great faith*   9 Greek *recline*

OT references: Mt 8:11 and Lk 13:29=Psalm 107:3 and Isaiah 49:12

D And shall cast them into the furnace of fire: there shall be the weeping and gnashing of teeth. (§48 L=Mt 13:42)
D And shall cast them into the furnace of fire: there shall be the weeping and gnashing of teeth. (§48 Q=Mt 13:50)
D And cast him out into the outer darkness; there shall be the weeping and gnashing of teeth. (§129 P=Mt 22:13)
D And shall cut him asunder, and appoint his portion with the hypocrites: there shall be the weeping and gnashing of teeth. (§136 D=Mt 24:51)   D And shall cut him asunder, and appoint his portion with the unfaithful. (§94 E=Lk 12:46)
D And cast ye out the unprofitable servant into the outer darkness: there shall be the weeping and gnashing of teeth. (§136 Q=Mt 25:30)

§ 40   OPINION OF THE COMMON PEOPLE

LUKE 7:11-17

And it came to pass [1]soon afterwards, that[11] he went to a city called Nain; and his disciples went with him, and a great multitude. Now[12] when he drew near to the gate of the city, behold, there was carried out one that was dead, the only son of his mother, and she was a widow: and much people of the city was with her. And when the Lord saw her, he had[13] compassion on her, and said unto her, Weep not. And he came nigh and touched the bier:[14] and the bearers stood still. And he said, Young man, I say unto thee, Arise. And he[15] that was dead sat up, and began to speak. And he gave him to his mother. And fear took[16] hold on all: and they glorified God, saying, A great prophet is arisen among us: and, God hath visited his people. And this report went[17] forth concerning him in the whole of Judæa, and all the region round about.

§ 41   OPINION OF JOHN THE BAPTIST

(§ 57+) MATT 11:2-30

A   Now when John heard in the prison the [2] works of the Christ, he sent by his disciples, [3] and said unto him, Art thou he that cometh, or look we for another?

C   And Jesus answered [4] and said unto them, Go your way and tell John the things which ye do hear and see: the [5] blind receive their sight, and the lame walk, the lepers are cleansed, and the deaf hear, and the dead are raised up, and the poor have [4]good tidings preached to them. And blessed [6] is he, whosoever shall find none occasion of stumbling in me.

D   And as these went their [7] way, Jesus began to say unto the multitudes concerning John, What went ye out into the wilderness to behold? a reed shaken with the wind? But what went ye out for to see? [8] a man clothed in soft *raiment*? Behold, they that wear soft *raiment* are in kings' houses. [5]But wherefore went ye out? to see a prophet? [9] Yea, I say unto you, and much more than a prophet.

E[E]   This is he, of whom it is written,   10

Behold, I send my messenger before thy face,
Who shall prepare thy way before thee.
Verily I say unto you, Among them that are[11] born of women there hath not arisen a greater

LUKE 7:18-35

A   And the disciples of John told him of all[18] these things. And John calling unto him [2]two[19] of his disciples sent them to the Lord, saying, Art thou he that cometh, or look we for another?

B   And when the men were come unto[20] him, they said, John the Baptist hath sent us unto thee, saying, Art thou he that cometh, or look we for another? In that hour he cured[21] many of diseases and [3]plagues and evil spirits; and on many that were blind he bestowed sight.

C   And he answered and said unto them,[22] Go your way, and tell John what things ye have seen and heard; the blind receive their sight, the lame walk, the lepers are cleansed, and the deaf hear, the dead are raised up, the poor have [4]good tidings preached to them. And blessed is he, whosoever shall find none[23] occasion of stumbling in me.

D   And when the messengers of John were[24] departed, he began to say unto the multitudes concerning John, What went ye out into the wilderness to behold? a reed shaken with the wind? But what went ye out to see? a[25] man clothed in soft raiment? Behold, they which are gorgeously apparelled, and live delicately, are in kings' courts. But what went[26] ye out to see? a prophet? Yea, I say unto you, and much more than a prophet.

E[E]   This is[27] he of whom it is written,

Behold, I send my messenger before thy face,
Who shall prepare thy way before thee.
I say unto you, Among them that are born of[28] women there is none greater than John: yet

---

ERV margin: 1 Many ancient authorities read *on the next day*   2 Greek *certain two*   3 Greek *scourges*
4 Or *the gospel*   5 Many ancient authorities read *But what went ye out to see? a prophet?*

OT references: Mt 11:5 and Lk 7:22=Isaiah 29:18-19 and 35:5-6 and 61:1   Mt 11:10 and Lk 7:27=
Malachi 3:1

E   Compare the record of Mark in § 17 portion E

MATT 11	LUKE 7
than John the Baptist: yet he that is [1]but little in the kingdom of heaven is greater than he.	he that is [1]but little in the kingdom of God is greater than he.
F And from the days of John the Baptist until[12] now the kingdom of heaven suffereth violence, and men of violence take it by force. For all[13] the prophets and the law prophesied until John.	F *The law and the prophets* were *until John:*[16]: *from that time the gospel of the kingdom of God*[16] *is preached, and every man entereth violently into it.* (§*107 C*)
G[G] And if ye are willing to receive [2]*it*, this is[14] Elijah, which is to come.	
H[H] He that hath ears[15] [3]to hear, let him hear.	H[H] *He that hath ears to hear, let him hear.*[14]: (§*104 F*) *35*
I *Jesus saith unto them, Verily I say unto you,*[21]: *that the publicans and the harlots go into the*[31] *kingdom of God before you. For John came*[32] *unto you in the way of righteousness, and ye believed him not: but the publicans and the harlots believed him: and ye, when ye saw it, did not even repent yourselves afterward, that ye might believe him.* (§*129 B*)	I And all the people when[29] they heard, and the publicans, justified God, [4]being baptized with the baptism of John. But the Pharisees and the lawyers rejected for[30] themselves the counsel of God, [5]being not baptized of him.
J But whereunto shall[16] I liken this generation? It is like unto children sitting in the marketplaces, which call unto their fellows, and say, We piped unto[17] you, and ye did not dance; we wailed, and ye did not [6]mourn. For John came neither[18] eating nor drinking, and they say, He hath a [7]devil. The Son of man came eating and[19] drinking, and they say, Behold, a gluttonous man, and a winebibber, a friend of publicans and sinners! And wisdom [8]is justified by her [9]works.	J Whereunto then shall I liken[31] the men of this generation, and to what are they like? They are like unto children that[32] sit in the marketplace, and call one to another; which say, We piped unto you, and ye did not dance; we wailed, and ye did not weep. For[33] John the Baptist is come eating no bread nor drinking wine; and ye say, He hath a [7]devil. The Son of man is come eating and drinking;[34] and ye say, Behold, a gluttonous man, and a winebibber, a friend of publicans and sinners! And wisdom [8]is justified of all her children. 35
K Then began he to upbraid the cities wherein[20] most of his [10]mighty works were done, because they repented not.	
L *Compare portion O below*	L *I say unto you, It shall be more tolerable in*[10]:
Compare §56 portion L	*that day for Sodom, than for that city.* *12*
M Woe unto thee, Chorazin![21] woe unto thee, Bethsaida! for if the [10]mighty works had been done in Tyre and Sidon which were done in you, they would have repented long ago in sackcloth and ashes. Howbeit I[22] say unto you, it shall be more tolerable for Tyre and Sidon in the day of judgement, than for you. And thou, Capernaum, shalt thou be[23] exalted unto heaven? thou shalt [11]go down unto Hades:	M *Woe unto*[13] *thee, Chorazin! woe unto thee, Bethsaida! for if the* [10]*mighty works had been done in Tyre and Sidon, which were done in you, they would have repented long ago, sitting in sackcloth and ashes. Howbeit it shall be more tolerable for Tyre and*[14] *Sidon in the judgement, than for you. And thou,*[15] *Capernaum, shalt thou be exalted unto heaven? thou shalt be brought down unto Hades.* (§*82 L–P*)
N for if the [10]mighty works had been done in Sodom which were done in thee, it would have remained until this day.	
O Howbeit I say[24] unto you, that it shall be more tolerable for the land of Sodom in the day of judgement, than for thee. *Compare §56 portion L*	O *Compare portion L above*
P At that season Jesus answered and said,[25] I [13]thank thee, O Father, Lord of heaven	P *In that same hour he rejoiced* [12]*in the Holy*[10]: *Spirit, and said, I* [13]*thank thee, O Father, Lord*[21]

ERV margin: 1 Greek *lesser*   2 Or, him   3 Some ancient authorities omit *to hear*   4 Or *having been* 5 Or *not having been*   6 Greek *beat the breast*   7 Greek *demon*   8 Or *was*   9 Many ancient authorities read *children*: as in Luke 7:35   10 Greek *powers*   11 Many ancient authorities read *be brought down*   12 Or *by* 13 Or *praise*

OT references: Mt 11:14 = Malachi 4:5   Mt 11:23[a] and Lk 10:15 = Isaiah 14:13-15   Mt 11:23[b]-24 and Lk 10:12 = Genesis 19:24

G   For another record of the identification of John the Baptist with Elijah by Jesus, compare §74 K–O H   He that hath ears, let him hear.   H   Who hath ears to hear, let him   H   He that hath ears to hear, let him (§47 F = Mt 13:9)   hear.   (§47 F = Mk 4:9)   hear.   (§47 F = Lk 8:8) H   If any man hath ears to hear, let him hear.   (§47 S = Mk 4:23) H   He that hath ears, let him hear.   (§48 M = Mt 13:43)

MATT 11	LUKE
and earth, that thou didst hide these things from the wise and understanding, and didst reveal them unto babes: yea, Father, [1]for[26] so it was well-pleasing in thy sight. Q[Q] 　　　　　　　　　All[27] things have been delivered unto me of my Father: and no one knoweth the Son, save the Father; neither doth any know the Father, save the Son, and he to whomsoever the Son willeth to reveal *him*.	*of heaven and earth, that thou didst hide these things from the wise and understanding, and didst reveal them unto babes: yea, Father; [1]for so it was well-pleasing in thy sight.* Q[Q] 　　　　　　　　　*All things[22] have been delivered unto me of my Father: and no one knoweth who the Son is, save the Father; and who the Father is, save the Son, and he to whomsoever the Son willeth to reveal him.* (§*82 ST*)

R 　　　　　　Come unto me, all ye[28] that labour and are heavy laden, and I will give you rest. Take my yoke upon you, and[29] learn of me; for I am meek and lowly in heart: and ye shall find rest unto your souls. For my[30] yoke is easy, and my burden is light. (+§32)

§ 42　OPINION OF A SINNER *vs* OPINION OF A PHARISEE

LUKE 7:36–50

A　*For an account in Matt–Mark having some elements in common with the narrative here recorded by Luke, compare* §*137 B*

A　And one of the Pharisees desired him that[36] he would eat with him. And he entered into the Pharisee's house, and sat down to meat. And behold, a woman which was in the city, a[37] sinner; and when she knew that he was sitting at meat in the Pharisee's house, she brought [2]an alabaster cruse of ointment, and standing be-[38] hind at his feet, weeping, she began to wet his feet with her tears, and wiped them with the hair of her head, and [3]kissed his feet, and anointed them with the ointment.

B·　　　　　　　　　　Now when[39] the Pharisee which had bidden him saw it, he spake within himself, saying, This man, if he were [4]a prophet, would have perceived who and what manner of woman this is which toucheth him, that she is a sinner.

C　　　　　　And Jesus answering[40] said unto him, Simon, I have somewhat to say unto thee. And he saith, [5]Master, say on. A[41] certain lender had two debtors: the one owed five hundred [6]pence, and the other fifty. When they had not *wherewith* to pay, he for-[42] gave them both. Which of them therefore will love him most? Simon answered and[43] said, He, I suppose, to whom he forgave the most. And he said unto him, Thou hast rightly judged.

D　　　　　And turning to the woman,[44] he said unto Simon, Seest thou this woman? I entered into thine house, thou gavest me no water for my feet: but she hath wetted my feet with her tears, and wiped them with her hair. Thou gavest me no kiss: but she, since the[45] time I came in, hath not ceased to [7]kiss my feet. My head with oil thou didst not anoint: but[46] she hath anointed my feet with ointment. Wherefore I say unto thee, Her sins, which are[47] many, are forgiven; for she loved much: but to whom little is forgiven, *the same* loveth little.

ERV margin:　1 Or *that*　2 Or *a flask*　3 Greek *kissed much*　4 Some ancient authorities read *the prophet:* see John 1:21,25　5 Or *Teacher*　6 The word in the Greek denotes a coin worth about eight pence halfpenny 7 Greek *kiss much*

OT references:　Mt 11:29 = Jeremiah 6:16

Q　All authority hath been given unto me in heaven and on earth. (§151 B = Mt 28:18)

LUKE 7

E And he said unto her, Thy sins are forgiven.48
And they that sat at meat with him began to49
say ¹within themselves, Who is this that even
forgiveth sins? And he said unto the woman,50
Thy faith hath saved thee; go in peace.

§ 43 ON A TOUR IN GALILEE

LUKE 8:1-3

And it came to pass soon afterwards, that he ¹
went about through cities and villages, preaching and bringing the ²good tidings of the kingdom of God, and with him the twelve, and ²
certain women which had been healed of evil
spirits and infirmities, Mary that was called
Magdalene, from whom seven ³devils had gone
out, and Joanna the wife of Chuza Herod's ³
steward, and Susanna, and many others, which
ministered unto ⁴them of their substance.

§ 44 OPINION OF THE FRIENDS OF JESUS

MARK 3:19ᵇ-21

And he cometh ⁵into a19ᵇ
house. And the multitude20
cometh together again, so that
they could not so much as
eat bread. And when his21
friends heard it, they went out
to lay hold on him: for they
said, He is beside himself.

§ 45 OPINION OF THE RELIGIOUS LEADERS

(§34+) MATT 12:22-45

AᴬA Then was brought unto22
him ⁶one possessed with a
devil, blind and dumb: and
he healed him, insomuch that
the dumb man spake and saw.

Bᴮ And all the multitudes were23
amazed, and said, Is this the
son of David?

Cᶜ But when the24
Pharisees heard it, they said,
This man doth not cast out
³devils, but ⁸by Beelzebub the
prince of the ³devils.

D *Compare portion Q below*

E And25
knowing their thoughts he
said unto them, Every kingdom divided against itself is
brought to desolation; and
every city or house divided
against itself shall not stand:
and if Satan casteth out26

MARK 3:22-30

Cᶜ And the scribes which22
came down from Jerusalem
said, He hath Beelzebub, and,
⁹By the prince of the ³devils
casteth he out the ³devils.

E And he called them unto23
him, and said unto them in
parables, How can Satan
cast out Satan? And if a24
kingdom be divided against
itself, that kingdom cannot
stand. And if a house be25
divided against itself, that

LUKE 11:14-32

Aᴬ *And he was casting out a14
⁷devil which was dumb. And
it came to pass, when the ⁷devil
was gone out, the dumb man
spake;*

Bᴮ *and the multitudes marvelled.*

Cᶜ *But some of them said,15
⁹By Beelzebub the prince of
the ³devils casteth he out
³devils.*

D *And others, tempting16
him, sought of him a sign from
heaven.*

E *But he, knowing their17
thoughts, said unto them, Every
kingdom divided against itself
is brought to desolation; ¹⁰and
a house divided against itself a
house falleth. And if Satan18
also is divided against himself,
how shall his kingdom stand?*

ERV margin: ı Or *among*   2 Or *gospel*   3 Greek *demons*   4 Many ancient authorities read *him*   5 Or
home   6 Or *a demoniac*   7 Greek *demon*   8 Or *in*   9 Or *In*   10 Or *and house falleth upon house*

ᴀʙᴄ   For another Matthew account covering portions ᴀʙᴄ, compare §53 ʙ

MATT 12	MARK 3	LUKE 11
Satan, he is divided against himself; how then shall his kingdom stand?	house will not be able to stand. And if Satan hath[26] risen up against himself, and is divided, he cannot stand, but hath an end.	*because ye say that I cast out* [1]*devils* [2]*by Beelzebub.*

F   And if I [2]by[27] Beelzebub cast out [1]devils, [2]by whom do your sons cast them out? therefore shall they be your judges. But if I[28] [2]by the Spirit of God cast out [1]devils, then is the kingdom of God come upon you.

G   Or[29] how can one enter into the house of the strong *man*, and spoil his goods, except he first bind the strong *man*? and then he will spoil his house.

[Mark:] But no[27] one can enter into the house of the strong *man*, and spoil his goods, except he first bind the strong *man;* and then he will spoil his house.

[Luke:]
F   *And*[19] *if I* [2]*by Beelzebub cast out* [1]*devils, by whom do your sons cast them out? therefore shall they be your judges. But if*[20] *I by the finger of God cast out* [1]*devils, then is the kingdom of God come upon you.*
G   *When*[21] *the strong* man *fully armed guardeth his own court, his goods are in peace: but when a*[22] *stronger than he shall come upon him, and overcome him, he taketh from him his whole armour wherein he trusted, and divideth his spoils.*

H[H]   He[30] that is not with me is against me; and he that gathereth not with me scattereth.

H[H]   *He*[23] *that is not with me is against me; and he that gathereth not with me scattereth.* (§86 A–H)

I   There-[31] fore I say unto you, Every sin and blasphemy shall be forgiven [3]unto men; but the blasphemy against the Spirit shall not be forgiven.

I   Verily[28] I say unto you, All their sins shall be forgiven unto the sons of men, and their blasphemies wherewith soever they shall blaspheme: but[29] whosoever shall blaspheme against the Holy Spirit hath never forgiveness,

I   *Compare portion J below*

J   And[32] whosoever shall speak a word against the Son of man, it shall be forgiven him; but whosoever shall speak against the Holy Spirit, it shall not be forgiven him,
K   neither in this [4]world, nor in that which is to come.

J   *Compare portion I above*

K   but is guilty of an eternal sin: because they said, He hath[30] an unclean spirit.

J   *And every one who shall*[12] *speak a word against the Son*[10] *of man, it shall be forgiven him: but unto him that blasphemeth against the Holy Spirit it shall not be forgiven.* (§91 H)

L[L]   Either make the[33] tree good, and its fruit good; or make the tree corrupt, and its fruit corrupt:
M[M]   for the tree is known by its fruit.

L[L]   *For there is no good tree* [6]: *that bringeth forth corrupt fruit;*[43] *nor again a corrupt tree that bringeth forth good fruit.*
M[M]   *For*[44] *each tree is known by its own fruit. For of thorns men do not gather figs, nor of a bramble bush gather they grapes.*

N[N]   Ye[34] offspring of vipers, how can ye, being evil, speak good things?

ERV margin: 1 Greek *demons*   2 Or *in*   3 Some ancient authorities read *unto you men*   4 Or *age*

H   With the first half of this saying, compare the last verse of §78 portion I
L   A good tree cannot bring forth evil fruit, neither can   L   *Luke parallel is shown above under portion L*
a corrupt tree bring forth good fruit. (§38 s = Mt 7:18)
M   By their fruits ye shall know them. Do *men* gather   M   *Luke parallel is shown above under portion M*
grapes of thorns, or figs of thistles? (§38 P = Mt 7:16)
M   Therefore by their fruits ye shall know them. (§38 T = Mt 7:20)
N   For another record of these terms as from Jesus, compare §132 P. For the record of the use of them by John the Baptist, compare §17 M

MATT 12

o   for out of the abundance of the heart the mouth speaketh. The good35 man out of his good treasure bringeth forth good things: and the evil man out of his evil treasure bringeth forth evil things.

P   And I say unto36 you, that every idle word that men shall speak, they shall give account thereof in the day of judgement. For by37 thy words thou shalt be justified, and by thy words thou shalt be condemned.

Q^Q Then certain of the scribes38 and Pharisees answered him, saying, ¹Master, we would see a sign from thee.

R^R But he answered and said39 unto them, An evil and adulterous generation seeketh after a sign; and there shall no sign be given to it but the sign of Jonah the prophet:

s for as Jonah was three days40 and three nights in the belly of the ²whale; so shall the Son of man be three days and three nights in the heart of the earth.

T   *Compare portion V below*

U   The men of41 Nineveh shall stand up in the judgement with this generation, and shall condemn it: for they repented at the preaching of Jonah; and behold, ³a greater than Jonah is here.

V   The queen42 of the south shall rise up in

LUKE

o   *The45 good man out of the good treasure of his heart bringeth forth that which is good; and the evil* man *out of the evil* treasure *bringeth forth that which is evil: for out of the abundance of the heart his mouth speaketh.* (§380–S)

Q^Q *Compare portion D above*

LUKE 11

R^R *And when the multitudes29 were gathering together unto him, he began to say, This generation is an evil generation: it seeketh after a sign; and there shall no sign be given to it but the sign of Jonah.*

s *For even as Jonah became a30 sign unto the Ninevites, so shall also the Son of man be to this generation.*

T   *The queen of the31 south shall rise up in the judgement with the men of this generation, and shall condemn them: for she came from the ends of the earth to hear the wisdom of Solomon; and behold, ³a greater than Solomon is here.*

U   *The men of Nineveh32 shall stand up in the judgement with this generation, and shall condemn it: for they repented at the preaching of Jonah; and behold, ³a greater than Jonah is here.* (§88 A–F)

V   *Compare portion T above*

ERV margin: 1 Or *Teacher*   2 Greek *sea-monster*   3 Greek *more than*

OT references: Mt 12:39 and Lk 11:29 = Jonah 3:1–4   Mt 12:40 = Jonah 1:17   Mt 12:41 and Lk 11:32 =
Jonah 3:5–10   Mt 12:42 and Lk 11:31 = 1 Kings 10:1–3

Q And the Pharisees and Sadducees came, and tempting him asked him to shew them a sign from heaven.
R   But he answered and said unto them, ... An evil and adulterous generation seeketh after a sign; and there shall no sign be given unto it, but the sign of Jonah. And he left them, and departed. (§68 A–D = Mt 16:1–4)

Q And the Pharisees came forth, and began to question with him, seeking of him a sign from heaven, tempting him.
R   And he sighed deeply in his spirit, and saith, Why doth this generation seek a sign? verily I say unto you, There shall no sign be given unto this generation. And he left them, and again entering into *the boat* departed to the other side. (§68 A–D = Mk 8:11–13)

MATT 12

the judgement with this generation, and shall condemn it: for she came from the ends of the earth to hear the wisdom of Solomon; and behold, [1]a greater than Solomon is here.

w   But the unclean spirit,43 when [2]he is gone out of the man, passeth through waterless places, seeking rest, and findeth it not. Then [2]he44 saith, I will return into my house whence I came out; and when [2]he is come, [2]he findeth it empty, swept, and garnished. Then goeth [2]he, and45 taketh with [3]himself seven other spirits more evil than [3]himself, and they enter in and dwell there: and the last state of that man becometh worse than the first.

x   Even so shall it be also unto this evil generation.

LUKE 11

w   *The unclean spirit when*24 *[2]he is gone out of the man, passeth through waterless places, seeking rest; and finding none, [2]he saith, I will turn back unto my house whence I came out. And when [2]he is come, [2]he*25 *findeth it swept and garnished. Then goeth [2]he, and taketh to*26 *him seven other spirits more evil than [3]himself; and they enter in and dwell there: and the last state of that man becometh worse than the first.* (§86*1*)

ERV margin: 1 Greek *more than*   2 Or *it*   3 Or *itself*

CHAPTER VIII

THE MYSTERY OF THE KINGDOM OF GOD

§ 46 BASIS OF REAL RELATIONSHIP TO JESUS*

MATT 12:46-50	MARK 3:31-35	LUKE 8:19-21
A While he was yet speaking46 to the multitudes, behold, his mother and his brethren stood without, seeking to speak to him.	A And there come his mother31 and his brethren; and, standing without, they sent unto him, calling him. And a32 multitude was sitting about him;	A *And there came to him his19 mother and brethren, and they could not come at him for the crowd.*
B 1And one said unto him,47 Behold, thy mother and thy brethren stand without, seeking to speak to thee.	B and they say unto him, Behold, thy mother and thy brethren without seek for thee.	B *And it was told him,20 Thy mother and thy brethren stand without, desiring to see thee.*
c But he48 answered and said unto him that told him,	c And he answereth33 them, and saith,	c *But he answered and21 said unto them,*
D Who is my mother? and who are my brethren? And he stretched49 forth his hand towards his disciples, and said, Behold, my mother and my brethren!	D Who is my mother and my brethren? And looking round on them34 which sat round about him, he saith, Behold, my mother and my brethren!	
E For whosoever shall do the50 will of my Father which is in heaven, he is my brother, and sister, and mother.	E For who-35 soever shall do the will of God, the same is my brother, and sister, and mother.	E *My mother and my brethren are these which hear the word of God, and do it.* (§49 A–E)

§ 47 DISCOURSE ON THE KINGDOM OF GOD

MATT 13:1-53	MARK 4:1-34	LUKE 8:4-18
A On that day went Jesus 1 out of the house, and sat by the sea side. And there were 2 gathered unto him great multitudes, so that he entered into a boat, and sat; and all the multitude stood on the beach. And he spake to them 3 many things in parables, saying,	A And again he began to 1 teach by the sea side. And there is gathered unto him a very great multitude, so that he entered into a boat, and sat in the sea; and all the multitude were by the sea on the land. And he taught 2 them many things in parables, and said unto them in his teaching,	A And when a great multi- 4 tude came together, and they of every city resorted unto him, he spake by a parable: *Compare §27 verses 1–3*
B Behold, the sower went forth to sow; and as he sowed, 4 some *seeds* fell by the way side, and the birds came and devoured them:	B Hearken: Behold, 3 the sower went forth to sow: and it came to pass, as he 4 sowed, some *seed* fell by the way side, and the birds came and devoured it.	B The sower went forth to 5 sow his seed: and as he sowed, some fell by the way side; and it was trodden under foot, and the birds of the heaven devoured it.
c and others 5 fell upon the rocky places, where they had not much earth: and straightway they sprang up, because they had	c And other 5 fell on the rocky *ground*, where it had not much earth; and straightway it sprang up, because it had no deepness of	c And other fell 6 on the rock; and as soon as it grew, it withered away, because it had no moisture.

ERV margin: 1 Some ancient authorities omit verse 47

* With these accounts compare the record in §87

MATT 13	MARK 4	LUKE 8

no deepness of earth: and [6] when the sun was risen, they were scorched; and because they had no root, they withered away.

D   And others [7] fell upon the thorns; and the thorns grew up, and choked them:

E   and others fell upon [8] the good ground, and yielded fruit, some a hundredfold, some sixty, some thirty.

F[F]   He [9] that hath ears,[1] let him hear.

G And the disciples came,[10] and said unto him, Why speakest thou unto them in parables? And he answered[11] and said unto them, Unto you it is given to know the mysteries of the kingdom of heaven, but to them it is not given.

H   For whosoever[12] hath, to him shall be given, and he shall have abundance: but whosoever hath not, from him shall be taken away even that which he hath.

I   There-[13] fore speak I to them in par-ables; because seeing they see not, and hearing they hear not, neither do they understand.

J   And unto them is ful-[14] filled the prophecy of Isaiah, which saith,

By hearing ye shall hear, and shall in no wise understand;
And seeing ye shall see, and shall in no wise perceive:
For this people's heart is[15] waxed gross,
And their ears are dull of hearing,
And their eyes they have closed;
Lest haply they should perceive with their eyes,
And hear with their ears,
And understand with their heart,
And should turn again,
And I should heal them.

---

earth: and when the sun was [6] risen, it was scorched; and because it had no root, it withered away.

D   And other [7] fell among the thorns, and the thorns grew up, and choked it, and it yielded no fruit.

E   And others fell into [8] the good ground, and yielded fruit, growing up and increasing; and brought forth, thirtyfold, and sixtyfold, and a hundredfold.

F[F]   And he said, [9] Who hath ears to hear, let him hear.

G And when he was alone,[10] they that were about him with the twelve asked of him the parables. And he said unto[11] them, Unto you is given the mystery of the kingdom of God: but unto them that are without, all things are done in parables:

H   *Compare portion V below*

I   that seeing they[12] may see, and not perceive; and hearing they may hear, and not understand;

J   lest haply they should turn again, and it should be forgiven them.

D And other fell amidst the [7] thorns; and the thorns grew with it, and choked it.

E   And [8] other fell into the good ground, and grew, and brought forth fruit a hundredfold.

F[F]   As he said these things, he cried, He that hath ears to hear, let him hear.

G And his disciples asked [9] him what this parable might be. And he said, Unto you[10] it is given to know the mysteries of the kingdom of God: but to the rest in parables;

H   *Compare portion V below*

I that seeing they may not see, and hearing they may not understand.

ERV margin: 1 Some ancient authorities add here, and in verse 43, *to hear:* as in Mark 4:9 and Luke 8:8

OT references: Mt 13:13–15 and Mk 4:12 and Lk 8:10 = Isaiah 6:9–10

F   He that hath ears to hear, let him hear. (§41 H = Mt 11:15)
F   Compare portion s below and §48 M

F   He that hath ears to hear, let him hear. (§104 F = Lk 14:35)

MATT 13	MARK 4	LUKE 8
K But blessed are your eyes,[16] for they see; and your ears, for they hear. For verily I[17] say unto you, that many prophets and righteous men desired to see the things which ye see, and saw them not; and to hear the things which ye hear, and heard them not.		K *Blessed* are *the eyes which*[10:] *see the things that ye see: for I*[23] *say unto you, that many*[24] *prophets and kings desired to see the things which ye see, and saw them not; and to hear the things which ye hear, and heard them not.* (*§82 U*)
L Hear then ye the parable[18] of the sower.	L And he saith unto them,[13] Know ye not this parable? and how shall ye know all the parables?	L Now the par-[11] able is this:
M When any one[19] heareth the word of the kingdom, and understandeth it not, *then* cometh the evil *one*, and snatcheth away that which hath been sown in his heart. This is he that was sown by the way side.	M The sower soweth[14] the word. And these are[15] they by the way side, where the word is sown; and when they have heard, straightway cometh Satan, and taketh away the word which hath been sown in them.	M The seed is the word of God. And those by[12] the way side are they that have heard; then cometh the devil, and taketh away the word from their heart, that they may not believe and be saved.
N And[20] he that was sown upon the rocky places, this is he that heareth the word, and straightway with joy receiveth it; yet hath he not[21] root in himself, but endureth for a while; and when tribulation or persecution ariseth because of the word, straightway he stumbleth.	N And[16] these in like manner are they that are sown upon the rocky *places*, who, when they have heard the word, straightway receive it with joy; and they[17] have no root in themselves, but endure for a while; then, when tribulation or persecution ariseth because of the word, straightway they stumble.	N And those on the rock[13] *are* they which, when they have heard, receive the word with joy; and these have no root, which for a while believe, and in time of temptation fall away.
O And he[22] that was sown among the thorns, this is he that heareth the word; and the care of the [1]world, and the deceitfulness of riches, choke the word, and he becometh unfruitful.	O And others are they[18] that are sown among the thorns; these are they that have heard the word, and the[19] cares of the [1]world, and the deceitfulness of riches, and the lusts of other things entering in, choke the word, and it becometh unfruitful.	O And that[14] which fell among the thorns, these are they that have heard, and as they go on their way they are choked with cares and riches and pleasures of *this* life, and bring no fruit to perfection.
P And[23] he that was sown upon the good ground, this is he that heareth the word, and understandeth it; who verily beareth fruit, and bringeth forth, some a hundredfold, some sixty, some thirty.	P And[20] those are they that were sown upon the good ground; such as hear the word, and accept it, and bear fruit, thirtyfold, and sixtyfold, and a hundredfold.	P And that in the good[15] ground, these are such as in an honest and good heart, having heard the word, hold it fast, and bring forth fruit with patience.
	Q[Q] And he said unto them,[21] Is the lamp brought to be put under the bushel, or under the bed, *and* not to be put on the stand?	Q[Q] And no man, when he[16] hath lighted a lamp, covereth it with a vessel, or putteth it under a bed; but putteth it on a stand, that they which enter in may see the light.
	R[R] For there is[22] nothing hid, save that it should be manifested; neither	R[R] For nothing is hid, that[17] shall not be made manifest; nor *anything* secret, that shall

ERV margin: 1 Or *age*

Q Neither do *men* light a lamp, and put it under the bushel, but on the stand; and it shineth unto all that are in the house. (§36 N =Mt 5:15)

R For there is nothing covered, that shall not be revealed; and hid, that shall not be known. (§57 H =Mt 10:26)

Q No man, when he hath lighted a lamp, putteth it in a cellar, neither under the bushel, but on the stand, that they which enter in may see the light. (§89 A =Lk 11:33)

R But there is nothing covered up, that shall not be revealed: and hid, that shall not be known. (§91 C = Lk 12:2)

MATT 13	MARK 4	LUKE 8
	was *anything* made secret, but that it should come to light.	not be known and come to light.
	s^s If any man hath ears[23] to hear, let him hear.	
	T And he[24] said unto them, Take heed what ye hear:	T Take heed therefore[18] how ye hear:
	u^u with what measure ye mete it shall be measured unto you: and more shall be given unto you.	
v^v *Compare portion H above*	v^v For[25] he that hath, to him shall be given: and he that hath not, from him shall be taken away even that which he hath.	v^v for whosoever hath, to him shall be given; and whosoever hath not, from him shall be taken away even that which he [1]thinketh he hath.

§ 48   DISCOURSE ON THE KINGDOM OF GOD (*concluded*)

A Another parable set he be-[24] fore them, saying, The kingdom of heaven is likened unto a man that sowed good seed in his field: but while men[25] slept, his enemy came and sowed [2]tares also among the wheat, and went away. But[26] when the blade sprang up, and brought forth fruit, then appeared the tares also.

B   And[27] the [3]servants of the householder came and said unto him, Sir, didst thou not sow good seed in thy field? whence then hath it tares? And he[28] said unto them, [4]An enemy hath done this. And the [3]servants say unto him, Wilt thou then that we go and gather them up? But he[29] saith, Nay; lest haply while ye gather up the tares, ye root up the wheat with them. Let both grow together until[30] the harvest:

C   and in the time of the harvest I will say to the reapers, Gather up first the tares, and bind them in bundles to burn them: but gather the wheat into my barn.

D And he said, So is the[26] kingdom of God, as if a man should cast seed upon the earth; and should sleep and[27] rise night and day, and the

---

ERV margin: 1 Or *seemeth to have*   2 Or *darnel*   3 Greek *bondservants*   4 Greek *A man* that is *an enemy*

s Compare portion F above and attached references

u And with what measure ye mete, it shall be measured unto you. (§38 F=Mt 7:2)

v For unto every one that hath shall be given, and he shall have abundance: but from him that hath not, even that which he hath shall be taken away. (§136 P=Mt 25:29)

u For with what measure ye mete it shall be measured to you again. (§38 F=Lk 6:38)

v I say unto you, that unto every one that hath shall be given; but from him that hath not, even that which he hath shall be taken away from him. (§123 J=Lk 19:26)

MATT 13	MARK 4	LUKE

MARK 4

seed should spring up and grow, he knoweth not how. The earth [1]beareth fruit of[28] herself; first the blade, then the ear, then the full corn in the ear. But when the[29] fruit [2]is ripe, straightway he [3]putteth forth the sickle, because the harvest is come.

MATT 13

E Another parable set he be-[31] fore them, saying, The kingdom of heaven is like unto a grain of mustard seed, which a man took, and sowed in his field: which indeed is less[32] than all seeds; but when it is grown, it is greater than the herbs, and becometh a tree, so that the birds of the heaven come and lodge in the branches thereof.

MARK 4

E And he said, How shall we[30] liken the kingdom of God? or in what parable shall we set it forth? [4]It is like a[31] grain of mustard seed, which, when it is sown upon the earth, though it be less than all the seeds that are upon the earth, yet when it is sown,[32] groweth up, and becometh greater than all the herbs, and putteth out great branches; so that the birds of the heaven can lodge under the shadow thereof.

LUKE

E *He said therefore, Unto*[23] *what is the kingdom of God*[18] *like? and whereunto shall I liken it? It is like unto a*[19] *grain of mustard seed, which a man took, and cast into his own garden; and it grew, and became a tree; and the birds of the heaven lodged in the branches thereof.*

MATT 13

F Another parable spake he[33] unto them; The kingdom of heaven is like unto leaven, which a woman took, and hid in three [5]measures of meal, till it was all leavened.

LUKE

F   *And again*[20] *he said, Whereunto shall I liken the kingdom of God? It is like unto leaven, which*[21] *a woman took and hid in three [5]measures of meal, till it was all leavened.* (§99 AB)

MATT 13

G All these things spake[34] Jesus in parables unto the multitudes; and without a parable spake he nothing unto them:

MARK 4

G And with many such par-[33] ables spake he the word unto them, as they were able to hear it: and without a parable[34] spake he not unto them: H   but privately to his own disciples he expounded all things.

MATT 13

I   that it might be ful-[35] filled which was spoken [6]by the prophet, saying,
  I will open my mouth in parables;
  I will utter things hidden from the foundation [7]of the world.
J Then he left the multi-[36] tudes, and went into the house: and his disciples came unto him, saying, Explain unto us the parable of the tares of the field.
K   And he[37] answered and said, He that soweth the good seed is the Son of man; and the field is[38] the world; and the good seed, these are the sons of the kingdom; and the tares are the sons of the evil *one;* and[39]

ERV margin: 1 Or *yieldeth*   2 Or *alloweth*   3 Or *sendeth forth*   4 Greek *As unto*   5 The word in the Greek denotes the Hebrew seah, a measure containing nearly a peck and a half   6 Or *through*   7 Many ancient authorities omit *of the world*

OT references: Mk 4:29 = Joel 3:13   Mt 13:32 and Mk 4:32 and Lk 13:19 = Daniel 4:12, 21   Mt 13:35 = Psalm 78:2

MATT 13

the enemy that sowed them is the devil:

L[L]　　　　　and the harvest is [1]the end of the world; and the reapers are angels. As[40] therefore the tares are gathered up and burned with fire; so shall it be in [1]the end of the world. The Son of[41] man shall send forth his angels, and they shall gather out of his kingdom all things that cause stumbling, and them that do iniquity, and[42] shall cast them into the furnace of fire: there shall be the weeping and gnashing of teeth. Then shall the right-[43] eous shine forth as the sun in the kingdom of their Father.

M[M] He that hath ears, let him hear.

N　The kingdom of heaven is[44] like unto a treasure hidden in the field; which a man found, and hid; and [2]in his joy he goeth and selleth all that he hath, and buyeth that field.

O　Again, the kingdom of[45] heaven is like unto a man that is a merchant seeking goodly pearls: and having found one[46] pearl of great price, he went and sold all that he had, and bought it.

P　Again, the kingdom of[47] heaven is like unto a [3]net, that was cast into the sea, and gathered of every kind: which,[48] when it was filled, they drew up on the beach; and they sat down, and gathered the good into vessels, but the bad they cast away.

Q[Q]　　　　　So shall it be in[49] [1]the end of the world: the angels shall come forth, and sever the wicked from among the righteous, and shall cast[50] them into the furnace of fire:

ERV margin:	1 Or *the consummation of the age*	2 Or *for joy thereof*	3 Greek *drag-net*

OT references:	Mt 13:43 = Daniel 12:3

L And I say unto you, that many shall come from the east and the west, and shall sit down with Abraham, and Isaac, and Jacob, in the kingdom of heaven: but the sons of the kingdom shall be cast forth into the outer darkness: there shall be the weeping and gnashing of teeth. (§39 D = Mt 8:11-12)

L And shall cast them into the furnace of fire: there shall be the weeping and gnashing of teeth. (§48 Q = Mt 13:50)

L And cast him out into the outer darkness: there shall be the weeping and gnashing of teeth. (§129 P = Mt 22:13)

L And shall cut him asunder, and appoint his portion with the hypocrites: there shall be the weeping and gnashing of teeth. (§136 D = Mt 24:51)

L And cast ye out the unprofitable servant into the outer darkness: there shall be the weeping and gnashing of teeth. (§136 Q = Mt 25:30)

M Compare §47 F and attached references

Q Compare portion L above and attached references

L There shall be the weeping and gnashing of teeth, when ye shall see Abraham, and Isaac, and Jacob, and all the prophets, in the kingdom of God, and yourselves cast forth without. And they shall come from the east and west, and from the north and south, and shall sit down in the kingdom of God. (§100 G = Lk 13:28-29)

L And shall cut him asunder, and appoint his portion with the unfaithful. (§94 E = Lk 12:46)

MATT 13

there shall be the weeping and gnashing of teeth.

R Have ye understood all[51] these things? They say unto him, Yea. And he said unto[52] them, Therefore every scribe who hath been made a disciple to the kingdom of heaven is like unto a man that is a householder, which bringeth forth out of his treasure things new and old.

S And it came to pass,[53] when Jesus had finished these parables, he departed thence. (+§54)

§49 BASIS OF REAL RELATIONSHIP TO JESUS*

MATT 12:46–50	MARK 3:31–35	LUKE 8:19–21
A *While he was yet speaking*[46] *to the multitudes, behold, his mother and his brethren stood without, seeking to speak to him.*	A *And there come his mother*[31] *and his brethren; and, standing without, they sent unto him, calling him. And a multitude*[32] *was sitting about him;*	A And there came to him his[19] mother and brethren, and they could not come at him for the crowd.
B [1]*And one said unto him,*[47] *Behold, thy mother and thy brethren stand without, seeking to speak to thee.*	B and *they say unto him, Behold, thy mother and thy brethren without seek for thee.*	B And it was[20] told him, Thy mother and thy brethren stand without, desiring to see thee.
C *But he*[48] *answered and said unto him that told him.*	C *And he*[33] *answereth them, and saith,*	C But he[21] answered and said unto them,
D *Who is my mother? and who are my brethren? And he stretched*[49] *forth his hand towards his disciples, and said, Behold, my mother and my brethren!*	D *Who is my mother and my brethren? And looking round*[34] *on them which sat round about him, he saith, Behold, my mother and my brethren!*	
E *For*[50] *whosoever shall do the will of my Father which is in heaven, he is my brother, and sister, and mother.* (§46 *A–E*)	E *For whosoever shall do the*[35] *will of God, the same is my brother, and sister, and mother.* (§46 *A–E*)	E My mother and my brethren are these which hear the word of God, and do it.

ERV margin: [1] Some ancient authorities omit verse 47

* With these accounts compare the record in §87

CHAPTER IX

THE PLACE OF FAITH IN THE WORK OF JESUS

§ 50 "HAVE YE NOT YET FAITH?"

(§25+) MATT 8:18-27

A Now when Jesus saw great[18] multitudes about him, he gave commandment to depart unto the other side.

B And there[19] came [1]a scribe, and said unto him, [2]Master, I will follow thee whithersoever thou goest. And Jesus saith unto him,[20] The foxes have holes, and the birds of the heaven *have* [3]nests; but the Son of man hath not where to lay his head. And another of the[21] disciples said unto him, Lord, suffer me first to go and bury my father. But Jesus saith[22] unto him, Follow me; and leave the dead to bury their own dead.

C And when he was entered[23] into a boat, his disciples followed him.

D And behold,[24] there arose a great tempest in the sea, insomuch that the boat was covered with the waves: but he was asleep. And they came to him, and[25] awoke him, saying, Save, Lord; we perish.

E And he[26] saith unto them, Why are ye fearful, O ye of little faith?

F Then he arose, and rebuked the winds and the sea; and there was a great calm.

G *Compare portion E above*

H And[27] the men marvelled, saying, What manner of man is this,

MARK 4:35-41

A And on that day, when[35] even was come, he said unto them, Let us go over unto the other side.

C And leaving the[36] multitude, they take him with them, even as he was, in the boat. And other boats were with him.

D And there ariseth[37] a great storm of wind, and the waves beat into the boat, insomuch that the boat was now filling. And he himself was in[38] the stern, asleep on the cushion: and they awake him, and say unto him, [2]Master, carest thou not that we perish?

E *Compare portion G below*

F And he awoke, and rebuked[39] the wind, and said unto the sea, Peace, be still. And the wind ceased, and there was a great calm.

G And he said[40] unto them, Why are ye fearful? have ye not yet faith?

H And they feared exceed-[41] ingly, and said one to another, Who then is this, that even

LUKE 8:22-25

A Now it came to pass on one[22] of those days, that he entered into a boat, himself and his disciples; and he said unto them, Let us go over unto the other side of the lake:

B *And as they went in the* 9 *way, a certain man said unto[57] him, I will follow thee whithersoever thou goest. And Jesus[58] said unto him, The foxes have holes, and the birds of the heaven have* [3]*nests; but the Son of man hath not where to lay his head. And he said unto[59] another, Follow me. But he said, Lord, suffer me first to go and bury my father. But[60] he said unto him, Leave the dead to bury their own dead; but go thou and publish abroad the kingdom of God. (§81 AB)*

C and they launched forth.

D But as[23] they sailed he fell asleep: and there came down a storm of wind on the lake; and they were filling *with water*, and were in jeopardy. And they[24] came to him, and awoke him, saying, Master, master, we perish.

E *Compare portion G below*

F And he awoke, and rebuked the wind and the raging of the water: and they ceased, and there was a calm.

G And he said unto them,[25] Where is your faith?

H And being afraid they marvelled, saying one to another, Who

---

ERV margin: 1 Greek *one scribe* 2 Or *Teacher* 3 Greek *lodging-places*

MATT 8	MARK 4	LUKE 8
that even the winds and the sea obey him?	the wind and the sea obey him?	then is this, that he commandeth even the winds and the water, and they obey him?

§ 51   ATTITUDE OF THE GERASENES

MATT 8:28–34	MARK 5:1–20	LUKE 8:26–39
A And when he was come to²⁸ the other side into the country of the Gadarenes,	A And they came to the ¹ other side of the sea, into the country of the Gerasenes.	A And they arrived at the²⁶ country of the ²Gerasenes, which is over against Galilee.
B there met him two ¹possessed with devils, coming forth out of the tombs,	B And when he was come out ² of the boat, straightway there met him out of the tombs a man with an unclean spirit, who had his dwelling in the ³ tombs:	B And when he was come²⁷ forth upon the land, there met him a certain man out of the city, who had ³devils; and for a long time he had worn no clothes, and abode not in *any* house, but in the tombs.
C exceeding fierce, so that no man could pass by that way.	C and no man could any more bind him, no, not with a chain; because that he ⁴ had been often bound with fetters and chains, and the chains had been rent asunder by him, and the fetters broken in pieces: and no man had strength to tame him. And ⁵ always, night and day, in the tombs and in the mountains, he was crying out, and cutting himself with stones.	C *Compare portion F below*
D And behold, they²⁹ cried out, saying, What have we to do with thee, thou Son of God? art thou come hither to torment us before the time?	D And ⁶ when he saw Jesus from afar, he ran and worshipped him; and crying out with a loud ⁷ voice, he saith, What have I to do with thee, Jesus, thou Son of the Most High God? I adjure thee by God, torment me not.	D And when he saw Jesus, he²⁸ cried out, and fell down before him, and with a loud voice said, What have I to do with thee, Jesus, thou Son of the Most High God? I beseech thee, torment me not.
	E For he said unto ⁸ him, Come forth, thou unclean spirit, out of the man.	E For²⁹ he commanded the unclean spirit to come out from the man.
F *Compare portion C above*	F *Compare portion C above*	F For ⁴oftentimes it had seized him: and he was kept under guard, and bound with chains and fetters; and breaking the bands asunder, he was driven of the ⁵devil into the deserts.
	G And he asked him, What ⁹ is thy name? And he saith unto him, My name is Legion; for we are many. And he be-¹⁰ sought him much that he would not send them away out of the country.	G And Jesus asked³⁰ him, What is thy name? And he said, Legion; for many ³devils were entered into him. And they intreated³¹ him that he would not command them to depart into the abyss.
H Now there was afar off from³⁰ them a herd of many swine feeding. And the ³devils³¹ besought him, saying, If thou	H Now¹¹ there was there on the mountain side a great herd of swine feeding. And they besought¹²	H Now there was there³² a herd of many swine feeding on the mountain: and they intreated him that he would

ERV margin: ¹ Or *demoniacs*   ² Many ancient authorities read *Gergesenes;* others, *Gadarenes:* and so in verse 37   ³ Greek *demons*   ⁴ Or *of a long time*   ⁵ Greek *demon*

MATT 8	MARK 5	LUKE 8
cast us out, send us away into the herd of swine. And[32] he said unto them, Go.	him, saying, Send us into the swine, that we may enter into them. And he gave them[13] leave.	give them leave to enter into them. And he gave them leave.
I And they came out, and went into the swine: and behold, the whole herd rushed down the steep into the sea, and perished in the waters.	I And the unclean spirits came out, and entered into the swine: and the herd rushed down the steep into the sea, *in number* about two thousand; and they were choked in the sea.	I And the [2]devils came[33] out from the man, and entered into the swine: and the herd rushed down the steep into the lake, and were choked.
J And[33] they that fed them fled, and went away into the city, and told everything, and what was befallen to them that were [1]possessed with devils. And[34] behold, all the city came out to meet Jesus:	J And they[14] that fed them fled, and told it in the city, and in the country. And they came to see what it was that had come to pass.	J And[34] when they that fed them saw what had come to pass, they fled, and told it in the city and in the country. And they[35] went out to see what had come to pass;
	K And they come to[15] Jesus, and behold [3]him that was possessed with devils sitting, clothed and in his right mind, *even* him that had the legion: and they were afraid. And they that saw[16] it declared unto them how it befell [3]him that was possessed with devils, and concerning the swine.	K and they came to Jesus, and found the man, from whom the [2]devils were gone out, sitting, clothed and in his right mind, at the feet of Jesus: and they were afraid. And they that saw[36] it told them how he that was possessed with [2]devils was [4]made whole.
L and when they saw him, they besought *him* that he would depart from their borders.	L And they began[17] to beseech him to depart from their borders.	L And all the[37] people of the country of the Gerasenes round about asked him to depart from them; for they were holden with great fear:
	M And as he was[18] entering into the boat, he that had been possessed with [2]devils besought him that he might be with him. And he[19] suffered him not, but saith unto him, Go to thy house unto thy friends, and tell them how great things the Lord hath done for thee, and *how* he had mercy on thee. And[20] he went his way, and began to publish in Decapolis how great things Jesus had done for him: and all men did marvel.	M and he entered into a boat, and returned. But the[38] man from whom the [2]devils were gone out prayed him that he might be with him: but he sent him away, saying, Re-[39] turn to thy house, and declare how great things God hath done for thee. And he went his way, publishing throughout the whole city how great things Jesus had done for him.

§ 52 "FEAR NOT, ONLY BELIEVE"

MATT 9:1,(§31+)18–26	MARK 5:21–43	LUKE 8:40–56
A And he entered into a [1] boat, and crossed over, and came into his own city. (+§ 29)	A And when Jesus had[21] crossed over again in the boat unto the other side, a great multitude was gathered unto him: and he was by the sea.	A And as Jesus returned, the[40] multitude welcomed him; for they were all waiting for him.
B While he spake these[18] things unto them, behold, there came [5]a ruler, and wor-	B And there cometh one of[22] the rulers of the synagogue, Jaïrus by name; and seeing	B And behold, there came a[4] man named Jaïrus, and he was a ruler of the synagogue: and

ERV margin: 1 Or *demoniacs*   2 Greek *demons*   3 Or *the demoniac*   4 Or *saved*   5 Greek *one ruler*

MATT 9	MARK 5	LUKE 8
shipped him, saying, My daughter is even now dead: but come and lay thy hand upon her, and she shall live.	him, he falleth at his feet, and[23] beseecheth him much, saying, My little daughter is at the point of death: *I pray thee,* that thou come and lay thy hands on her, that she may be [1]made whole, and live.	he fell down at Jesus' feet, and besought him to come into his house; for he had an only[42] daughter, about twelve years of age, and she lay a dying.
c And Jesus arose, and fol-[19] lowed him, and *so did* his disciples.	c And[24] he went with him; and a great multitude followed him, and they thronged him.	c But as he went the multitudes thronged him.
d And behold, a wo-[20] man, who had an issue of blood twelve years, came behind him, and touched the border of his garment: for she[21] said within herself, If I do but touch his garment, I shall be [1]made whole.	d And a woman, which had[25] an issue of blood twelve years, and had suffered many things[26] of many physicians, and had spent all that she had, and was nothing bettered, but rather grew worse, having[27] heard the things concerning Jesus, came in the crowd behind, and touched his garment. For she said, If I[28] touch but his garments, I shall be [1]made whole.	d And a woman having an[43] issue of blood twelve years, which [2]had spent all her living upon physicians, and could not be healed of any, came behind him, and touched[44] the border of his garment:
e *Compare portion K below*	e And[29] straightway the fountain of her blood was dried up; and she felt in her body that she was healed of her [3]plague.	e and immediately the issue of her blood stanched.
	f And straightway Jesus, per-[30] ceiving in himself that the power *proceeding* from him had gone forth, turned him about in the crowd, and said, Who touched my garments?	f And[45] Jesus said, Who is it that touched me? *Compare portion H below*
	g And his disciples said unto[31] him, Thou seest the multitude thronging thee, and sayest thou, Who touched me?	g And when all denied, Peter said, [4]and they that were with him, Master, the multitudes press thee and crush *thee.*
	h *Compare portion F above*	h But Jesus said,[46] Some one did touch me: for I perceived that power had gone forth from me.
	i And he looked round about[32] to see her that had done this thing. But the woman fear-[33] ing and trembling, knowing what had been done to her, came and fell down before him, and told him all the truth.	i And[47] when the woman saw that she was not hid, she came trembling, and falling down before him declared in the presence of all the people for what cause she touched him, and how she was healed immediately.
j But Jesus[22] turning and seeing her said, Daughter, be of good cheer; thy faith hath [5]made thee whole.	j And he said unto her,[34] Daughter, thy faith hath [5]made thee whole; go in peace, and be whole of thy [3]plague.	j And he said unto[48] her, Daughter, thy faith hath [5]made thee whole; go in peace.
k And the woman was [2]made whole from that hour.	k *Compare portion E above*	k *Compare portion E above*
	l While he yet spake, they[35] come from the ruler of the synagogue's *house,* saying,	l While he yet spake, there[49] cometh one from the ruler of the synagogue's *house,* saying,

---

ERV margin: 1 Or *saved*   2 Some ancient authorities omit *had spent all her living upon physicians, and*
2 Greek *scourge*   4 Some ancient authorities omit *and they that were with him*   5 Or *saved thee*

MATT 9	MARK 5	LUKE 8
	Thy daughter is dead: why troublest thou the ¹Master any further?	Thy daughter is dead; trouble not the ¹Master.

MARK 5

M   But Jesus ²not³⁶ heeding the word spoken, saith unto the ruler of the synagogue, Fear not, only believe.

N   And he suffered no³⁷ man to follow with him, save Peter, and James, and John the brother of James.

O   *Compare portion Q below*

LUKE 8

M   But Jesus⁵⁰ hearing it, answered him, Fear not: only believe, and she shall be ³made whole.

N And when he came to the⁵¹ house, he suffered not any man to enter in with him, save Peter, and John, and James,

O and the father of the maiden and her mother.

MATT 9

P And when Jesus came into²³ the ruler's house, and saw the flute-players, and the crowd making a tumult, he said,²⁴ Give place: for the damsel is not dead, but sleepeth. And they laughed him to scorn.

MARK 5

P   And³⁸ they come to the house of the ruler of the synagogue; and he beholdeth a tumult, and *many* weeping and wailing greatly. And when he³⁹ was entered in, he saith unto them, Why make ye a tumult, and weep? the child is not dead, but sleepeth. And they⁴⁰ laughed him to scorn.

LUKE 8

P And all were weeping, and⁵² bewailing her: but he said, Weep not; for she is not dead, but sleepeth. And they⁵³ laughed him to scorn, knowing that she was dead.

MATT 9

Q But when the crowd was²⁵ put forth, he entered in, and took her by the hand; and the damsel arose.

MARK 5

Q   But he, having put them all forth, taketh the father of the child and her mother and them that were with him, and goeth in where the child was. And⁴¹ taking the child by the hand, he saith unto her, Talitha cumi; which is, being interpreted, Damsel, I say unto thee, Arise. And straight-⁴² way the damsel rose up, and walked;

R   for she was twelve years old.

S   *Compare portion U below*

LUKE 8

Q   But⁵⁴ he, taking her by the hand, called, saying, Maiden, arise. And her spirit returned, and⁵⁵ she rose up immediately:

Compare portion O above

R   *Compare portion B above*

S   and he commanded that *something* be given her to eat.

MATT 9

T   And ⁴the fame²⁶ hereof went forth into all that land.

MARK 5

T   And they were amazed straightway with a great amazement. And he⁴³ charged them much that no man should know this:

U   and he commanded that *something* should be given her to eat.

LUKE 8

T   And her⁵⁶ parents were amazed: but he charged them to tell no man what had been done.

U   *Compare portion S above*

---

§ 53   "BELIEVE YE THAT I AM ABLE?"

MATT 9:27-34

A   And as Jesus passed by from thence, two²⁷ blind men followed him, crying out, and saying, Have mercy on us, thou son of David. And²⁸ when he was come into the house, the blind men came to him: and Jesus saith unto them, Believe ye that I am able to do this? They say unto him, Yea, Lord. Then touched he²⁹ their eyes, saying, According to your faith be it done unto you. And their eyes were opened.³⁰

A   *For an account in Matt–Mark–Luke of similar general content, compare §121*

ERV margin: ı Or *Teacher*   2 Or *overhearing*   3 Or *saved*   4 Greek *this fame*

MATT 9

And Jesus [1]strictly charged them, saying, See that no man know it. But they went forth,[31] and spread abroad his fame in all that land.

B   And as they went forth, behold, there was[32] brought to him a dumb man possessed with a [2]devil. And when the [2]devil was cast out, the[33] dumb man spake: and the multitudes marvelled, saying, It was never so seen in Israel. But the Pharisees said, [3]By the prince of the[34] [4]devils casteth he out [4]devils. (+§55)

B   *For an account in Matt-Mark-Luke of similar general content, compare §45 ABC*

§ 54   "BECAUSE OF THEIR UNBELIEF"

(§48+)MATT 13:54-58

A   And coming into his own[54] country he taught them in their synagogue,

MARK 6:1-6[a]

A   And he went out from [1] thence; and he cometh into his own country; and his disciples follow him. And when [2] the sabbath was come, he began to teach in the synagogue:

LUKE 4:16-30

A   *And he came to Nazareth,[16] where he had been brought up: and he entered, as his custom was, into the synagogue on the sabbath day, and stood up to read.*

B   *And there[17] was delivered unto him [5]the book of the prophet Isaiah. And he opened the [6]book, and found the place where it was written,*

The Spirit of the Lord is[18] upon me,
[7]Because he anointed me to preach [8]good tidings to the poor:
He hath sent me to proclaim release to the captives,
And recovering of sight to the blind,
To set at liberty them that are bruised,
To proclaim the acceptable[19] year of the Lord.

And he closed the [6]book,[20] and gave it back to the attendant, and sat down: and the eyes of all in the synagogue were fastened on him. And he began to say unto[21] them, To-day hath this scripture been fulfilled in your ears.

C   insomuch that they were astonished, and said, Whence hath this man this wisdom, and these [9]mighty works?
Compare portion E below

C and [10]many hearing him were astonished, saying, Whence hath this man these things? and, What is the wisdom that is given unto this man, and *what mean* such [9]mighty works wrought by his hands?

C *And all bare him witness,[22] and wondered at the words of grace which proceeded out of his mouth:*

D   Is not this[55] the carpenter's son? is not his mother called Mary? and his brethren, James, and Joseph, and Simon, and Judas? And his sisters, are[56]

D   Is not this the car- [3] penter, the son of Mary, and brother of James, and Joses, and Judas, and Simon? and are not his sisters here with us?

D   *and they said, Is not this Joseph's son?*

ERV margin: 1 Or *sternly*   2 Greek *demon*   3 Or *In*   4 Greek *demons*   5 Or *a roll*   6 Or *roll*   7 Or *Wherefore*   8 Or *the gospel*   9 Greek *powers*   10 Some ancient authorities insert *the*

OT references: Lk 4:18-19 = Isaiah 61:1-2

MATT 13	MARK 6	LUKE 4

MATT 13

they not all with us?

E Whence then hath this man all these things?

F And[57] they were [1]offended in him.

H But Jesus said unto them, A prophet is not without honour, save in his own country, and in his own house.

J And he did not many[58] [3]mighty works there because of their unbelief. (+§ 58)

K *Compare portion F above*

MARK 6

E *Compare portion C above*

F And they were [1]offended in him.

H And Jesus said unto 4 them, A prophet is not without honour, save in his own country, and among his own kin, and in his own house.

J And he could there do no 5 [4]mighty work, save that he laid his hands upon a few sick folk, and healed them. And [6a] he marvelled because of their unbelief.

K *Compare portion F above*

LUKE 4

F *Compare portion K below*

G And he[23] said unto them, Doubtless ye will say unto me this parable, Physician, heal thyself: whatsoever we have heard done at Capernaum, do also here in thine own country.

H And he[24] said, Verily I say unto you, No prophet is acceptable in his own country.

I But of a truth I[25] say unto you, There were many widows in Israel in the days of Elijah, when the heaven was shut up three years and six months, when there came a great famine over all the land; and unto none of them was[26] Elijah sent, but only to [2]Zarephath, in the land of Sidon, unto a woman that was a widow. And there were many lepers[27] in Israel in the time of Elisha the prophet; and none of them was cleansed, but only Naaman the Syrian.

K And they were all[28] filled with wrath in the synagogue, as they heard these things; and they rose up, and[29] cast him forth out of the city, and led him unto the brow of the hill whereon their city was built, that they might throw him down headlong. But he[30] passing through the midst of them went his way. (§22 A–K)

ERV margin: 1 Greek *caused to stumble*   2 Greek *Sarepta*   3 Greek *powers*   4 Greek *power*

OT references: Lk 4:25 = 1 Kings 17:1 and 18:1–2   Lk 4:26 = 1 Kings 17:8–9   Lk 4:27 = 2 Kings 5:1, 14

CHAPTER X

TOUR OF THE DISCIPLES AND RESULTANT EVENTS

§ 55 JESUS TOURS IN GALILEE

(§53+) MATT 9:35	MARK 6:6ᵇ
A And Jesus went about all35 the cities and the villages, teaching in their synagogues, BB and preaching the gospel of the kingdom, and healing all manner of disease and all manner of sickness.	A And he went round about 6ᵇ the villages teaching.

§ 56 DISCOURSE ON THE MISSION OF THE DISCIPLES

MATT 9:36—11:1	MARK 6:7-13	LUKE 9:1-6
A But when he saw the mul-36 titudes, he was moved with compassion for them, because they were distressed and scattered, as sheep not having a shepherd.	A *And he came forth and saw* 6: *a great multitude, and he had34 compassion on them, because they were as sheep not having a shepherd.* (§60B)	
B Then saith he unto37 his disciples, The harvest truly is plenteous, but the labourers are few. Pray ye therefore38 the Lord of the harvest, that he send forth labourers into his harvest.		B *And he said unto them, The*10: *harvest is plenteous, but the la-* 2 *bourers are few: pray ye therefore the Lord of the harvest, that he send forth labourers into his harvest.* (§82B)
Cᶜ And he called un-10: to him his twelve disciples, and 1 gave them authority over unclean spirits, to cast them out, and to heal all manner of disease and all manner of sickness.	Cᶜ And he called unto him the 7 twelve, and began to send them forth by two and two; and he gave them authority over the unclean spirits;	Cᶜ And he called the twelve 1 together, and gave them power and authority over all ¹devils, and to cure diseases.
D Now the names of the 2 twelve apostles are these: The first, Simon, who is called Peter, and Andrew his brother; James the *son* of Zebedee, and John his brother; Philip, and 3 Bartholomew; Thomas, and Matthew the publican; James the *son* of Alphæus, and Thaddæus; Simon the ⁴Cananæan, 4 and Judas Iscariot, who also ⁶betrayed him.	D *And he appointed twelve,*² 3: *. . . ³and Simon he surnamed*16 *Peter; and James the son of*17 *Zebedee, and John the brother of James; and them he surnamed Boanerges, which is, Sons of thunder: and Andrew, and*18 *Philip, and Bartholomew, and Matthew, and Thomas, and James the son of Alphæus, and Thaddæus, and Simon the* ⁴*Cananæan, and Judas Iscariot,*19 *which also betrayed him.* (§35C)	D *He called his disciples: and* 6: *he chose from them twelve,*13 *whom also he named apostles; Simon, whom he also named*14 *Peter, and Andrew his brother, and James and John, and Philip and Bartholomew, and*15 *Matthew and Thomas, and James* the son of *Alphæus, and Simon which was called the Zealot, and Judas the* ⁵son of¹⁶ *James, and Judas Iscariot, which was the traitor.* (§35 BC)

ERV margin: 1 Greek *demons* 2 Some ancient authorities add *whom also he named apostles:* see Luke 6:13 3 Some ancient authorities insert *and he appointed twelve* 4 Or *Zealot:* see Luke 6:15 and Acts 1:13 5 Or, brother: see Jude 1 6 Or *delivered him up:* and so always

OT references: Mt 9:36 and Mk 6:34 = Numbers 27:17 and Ezekiel 34:5

B Compare the latter half of the Matthew record in §26 D
C Now after these things the Lord appointed seventy others, and sent them two and two before his face into every city and place, whither he himself was about to come. (§82 A = Lk 10:1)

MATT 10	MARK 6	LUKE 9

E^E   These twelve 5 Jesus sent forth, and charged them, saying,

Go not into *any* way of the Gentiles, and enter not into any city of the Samaritans: but go rather to the lost sheep 6 of the house of Israel.

F^F   And as 7 ye go, preach, saying, The kingdom of heaven is at hand. Heal the sick, raise the dead, 8 cleanse the lepers, cast out ^1devils: freely ye received, freely give.

G^G   Get you no gold, 9 nor silver, nor brass in your ^3purses; no wallet for *your*^10 journey, neither two coats, nor shoes, nor staff:

H   for the labourer is worthy of his food.

I^1 And into whatsoever city or^11 village ye shall enter, search out who in it is worthy; and there abide till ye go forth.

J And as ye enter into the^12 house, salute it. And if the^13 house be worthy, let your peace come upon it: but if it be not worthy, let your peace return to you.

K^K   And whoso-^14 ever shall not receive you, nor hear your words, as ye go forth out of that house or that city, shake off the dust of your feet.

L Verily I say unto you, It^15 shall be more tolerable for the land of Sodom and Gomorrah in the day of judgement, than for that city.

Howbeit I say unto you, that^11: *it shall be more tolerable for the*^24 *land of Sodom in the day of judgement, than for thee.* (§41O)

M Behold, I send you forth as^16 sheep in the midst of wolves: be ye therefore wise as serpents, and ^8harmless as doves.

G^G   and 8 he charged them that they should take nothing for *their* journey, save a staff only; no bread, no wallet, no ^4money in their ^5purse; but *to go* shod 9 with sandals: and, *said he,* put not on two coats.

I^1   And he^10 said unto them, Wheresoever ye enter into a house, there abide till ye depart thence.

K^K And whatsoever place shall^11 not receive you, and they hear you not, as ye go forth thence, shake off the dust that is under your feet for a testimony unto them.

F^F   And he 2 sent them forth to preach the kingdom of God, and to heal ^2the sick.

G^G   And he said unto 3 them, Take nothing for your journey, neither staff, nor wallet, nor bread, nor money; neither have two coats.

H *For the labourer is worthy*^10: *of his hire.* (§82H)   7

I^1   And 4 into whatsoever house ye enter, there abide, and thence depart.

J *And into whatsoever house ye* ^10: *shall* ^6*enter, first say, Peace be* 5 *to this house. And if a son of* 6 *peace be there, your peace shall rest upon* ^7*him: but if not, it shall turn to you again.* (§82G)

K^K   And as many as re- 5 ceive you not, when ye depart from that city, shake off the dust from your feet for a testimony against them.

L *I say unto you, It shall be*^10: *more tolerable in that day for*^12 *Sodom, than for that city.* (§82L)

M *Go your ways: behold, I*^10: *send you forth as lambs in the* 3 *midst of wolves.* (§82D)

ERV margin: 1 Greek *demons*   2 Some ancient authorities omit *the sick*   3 Greek *girdles*   4 Greek *brass*
5 Greek *girdle*   6 Or *enter first, say*   7 Or *it*   8 Or *simple*

E With the Matthew report here, compare the Matthew form of the record in §64 D
F And heal the sick that are therein, and say unto them, The kingdom of God is come nigh unto you. (§82 I=Lk 10:9)
F Howbeit know this, that the kingdom of God is come nigh.   (§82 K=Lk 10:11)
G Carry no purse, no wallet, no shoes: and salute no man on the way.   (§82 E=Lk 10:4)
I And in that same house remain, eating and drinking such things as they give . . . . Go not from house to house. And into whatsoever city ye enter, and they receive you, eat such things as are set before you.   (§82 H=Lk 10:7-8)
K But into whatsoever city ye shall enter, and they receive you not, go out into the streets thereof and say, Even the dust from your city, that cleaveth to our feet, we do wipe off against you. (§82 J=Lk 10:10-11)

§ 57 DISCOURSE ON THE MISSION OF THE DISCIPLES (*concluded*)

MATT 10	MARK	LUKE
A But beware of men: for they[17] will deliver you up to councils, and in their synagogues they will scourge you; yea[18] and before governors and kings shall ye be brought for my sake, for a testimony to them and to the Gentiles. *Then shall they deliver you*[24] *up unto tribulation,* (*§134G*) *9a*	A *But take ye heed to your-*[13]*: selves: for they shall deliver you 9 up to councils; and in syna- gogues shall ye be beaten; and before governors and kings shall ye stand for my sake, for a tes- timony unto them.*	A *But before all these things,*[21]*: they shall lay their hands on*[12] *you, and shall persecute you, delivering you up to the syna- gogues and prisons, [1]bringing you before kings and governors for my name's sake. It shall*[13] *turn unto you for a testimony.*
B *Compare portion F below Compare §134 portion N*	B *And the gos-*[10] *pel must first be preached unto all the nations.*	
C[c] But when they deliver you[19] up, be not anxious how or what ye shall speak: for it shall be given you in that hour what ye shall speak. For it[20] is not ye that speak, but the Spirit of your Father that speaketh in you.	C[c] *And when they*[11] *lead you to judgement, and deliver you up, be not anxious beforehand what ye shall speak: but whatsoever shall be given you in that hour, that speak ye: for it is not ye that speak, but the Holy Ghost.*	C[c] *Settle it therefore in your*[14] *hearts, not to meditate before- hand how to answer: for I will*[15] *give you a mouth and wisdom, which all your adversaries shall not be able to withstand or to gainsay.*
D And brother[21] shall deliver up brother to death, and the father his child: and children shall rise up against parents, and [2]cause them to be put to death. *and shall*[24]*: kill you:* (*§134J*) *9b*	D *And brother*[12] *shall deliver up brother to death, and the father his child; and children shall rise up against parents, and [2]cause them to be put to death.*	D *But ye shall be deliv-*[16] *ered up even by parents, and brethren, and kinsfolk, and friends; and some of you [3]shall they cause to be put to death.*
E And[22] ye shall be hated of all men for my name's sake: but he that endureth to the end, the same shall be saved. *and ye shall be hated*[24]*: of all the nations for my name's 9c sake. . . . . But he that en-*[13] *dureth to the end, the same shall be saved.* (*§134K–M*)	E *And ye shall be*[13] *hated of all men for my name's sake: but he that endureth to the end, the same shall be saved.* (*§134G–M*)	E *And ye shall be hated of all*[17] *men for my name's sake. And*[18] *not a hair of your head shall perish. In your patience ye*[19] *shall win your [4]souls.* (*§134G–M*)
F But when they[23] persecute you in this city, flee into the next: for verily I say unto you, Ye shall not have gone through the cities of Israel, till the Son of man be come.	F *Compare portion B above*	
G A disciple is not above[24] his [5]master, nor a [6]servant above his lord. It is enough[25] for the disciple that he be as his [5]master, and the [6]servant as his lord. If they have called the master of the house [7]Beelzebub, how much more *shall they call* them of his household!		G *The disciple is not above his* 6*: [5]master: but every one when he*[40] *is perfected shall be as his [5]mas- ter.* (*§38H*)

ERV margin: 1 Greek *you being brought*   2 Or *put them to death*   3 Or *shall they put to death*   4 Or *lives*
5 Or *teacher*   6 Greek *bondservant*   7 Greek *Beelzebul:* and so elsewhere

c And when they bring you before the synagogues, and the rulers, and the authorities, be not anxious how or what ye shall answer, or what ye shall say: for the Holy Spirit shall teach you in that very hour what ye ought to say. (§91 I = Lk 12:11–12)

MATT 10

H^H Fear them not therefore:26 for there is nothing covered, that shall not be revealed; and hid, that shall not be known. What I tell you in the dark-27 ness, speak ye in the light: and what ye hear in the ear, proclaim upon the housetops.

I And be not afraid of them28 which kill the body, but are not able to kill the soul: but rather fear him which is able to destroy both soul and body in ²hell.

J^J Are not two spar-29 rows sold for a farthing? and not one of them shall fall on the ground without your Father: but the very hairs of your30 head are all numbered. Fear31 not therefore; ye are of more value than many sparrows.

K^K Every one therefore who32 shall confess ³me before men, ⁴him will I also confess before my Father which is in heaven. But whosoever shall deny me33 before men, him will I also deny before my Father which is in heaven.

L Think not that I came to34 ⁵send peace on the earth: I came not to ⁵send peace, but a sword. For I came to set35 a man at variance against his father, and the daughter against her mother, and the daughter in law against her mother in law: and a man's36 foes *shall be* they of his own household.

M   He that loveth37 father or mother more than me is not worthy of me: and

MARK

LUKE

H^H *But there is nothing covered*12: *up, that shall not be revealed:* 2 *and hid, that shall not be known. Wherefore whatsoever ye have* 3 *said in the darkness shall be heard in the light; and what ye have spoken in the ear in the inner chambers shall be proclaimed upon the housetops.*

I *And I say unto you my* 4 *friends, Be not afraid of them which kill the body, and after that have no more that they can do. But I will warn you whom* 5 *ye shall fear: Fear him, which after he hath killed hath* ¹*power to cast into* ²*hell; yea, I say unto you, Fear him.*

J^J *Are not* 6 *five sparrows sold for two farthings? and not one of them is forgotten in the sight of God. But the very hairs of your* 7 *head are all numbered. Fear not: ye are of more value than many sparrows.*

K^K *And I say* 8 *unto you, Every one who shall confess* ³*me before men* ⁴*him shall the Son of man also confess before the angels of God: but he that denieth me in the* 9 *presence of men shall be denied in the presence of the angels of God.* (§91 C-G)

L *Think ye that I am come to*12: *give peace in the earth? I tell*51 *you, Nay; but rather division: for there shall be from hence-*52 *forth five in one house divided, three against two, and two against three. They shall be*53 *divided, father against son, and son against father; mother against daughter, and daughter against her mother; mother in law against her daughter in law, and daughter in law against her mother in law.* (§95 B)

M *If any man cometh unto me,*14: *and hateth not his own father,*26 *and mother, and wife, and chil-*

ERV margin: 1 Or *authority*   2 Greek *Gehenna*   3 Greek *in me*   4 Greek *in him*   5 Greek *cast*

OT references: Mt 10:35-36 and Lk 12:52-53 = Micah 7:6

H For there is nothing hid, save that it should be manifested; neither was *anything* made secret, but that it should come to light. (§47 R = Mk 4:22)

J And not a hair of your head shall perish. (§134 M = Lk 21:18)

K For the Son of man shall come in the glory of his Father with his angels; and then shall he render unto every man according to his deeds. (§73 C = Mt 16:27)

H For nothing is hid, that shall not be made manifest; nor *anything* secret, that shall not be known and come to light. (§47 R = Lk 8:17)

K For whosoever shall be ashamed of me and of my words in this adulterous and sinful generation, the Son of man also shall be ashamed of him, when he cometh in the glory of his Father with the holy angels. (§73 C = Mk 8:38)

K For whosoever shall be ashamed of me and of my words, of him shall the Son of man be ashamed, when he cometh in his own glory, and *the glory* of the Father, and of the holy angels. (§73 C = Lk 9:26)

MATT 10	MARK 6	LUKE 9

MATT 10:

he that loveth son or daughter more than me is not worthy of me.

N^N And he that doth not³⁸ take his cross and follow after me, is not worthy of me.

O^O He³⁹ that ¹findeth his ²life shall lose it; and he that ³loseth his ²life for my sake shall find it.

P He that receiveth you re-⁴⁰ ceiveth me, and he that receiveth me receiveth him that sent me. He that receiveth a⁴¹ prophet in the name of a prophet shall receive a prophet's reward; and he that receiveth a righteous man in the name of a righteous man shall receive a righteous man's reward.

Q And whosoever shall⁴² give to drink unto one of these little ones a cup of cold water only, in the name of a disciple, verily I say unto you, he shall in no wise lose his reward.

R And it came to pass, when¹¹: Jesus had made an end of ¹ commanding his twelve disciples, he departed thence to teach and preach in their cities. (+§41)

MARK 6:

P *And whosoever receiveth me,* 9: *receiveth not me, but him that*³⁷ *sent me.* (§78 G)

Q *For whosoever shall give you* 9: *a cup of water to drink,* ⁵be-⁴¹ *cause ye are Christ's, verily I say unto you, he shall in no wise lose his reward.* (§78 J)

R And they went out, and¹² preached that *men* should repent. And they cast out¹³ many ⁶devils, and anointed with oil many that were sick, and healed them.

LUKE 9:

dren, and brethren, and sisters, yea, and his own life also, he cannot be my disciple.

N^N Who-²⁷ soever doth not bear his own cross, and come after me, cannot be my disciple. (§104 BC)

O^O *Whosoever shall seek to gain*¹⁷ⁱ *his* ²*life shall lose it: but who-*³³ *soever shall lose his* ²*life shall* ⁴*preserve it.* (§112 J)

P *And whosoever shall receive* 9: *me receiveth him that sent me.*⁴⁸ (§78 G)

*He that heareth you heareth*¹⁰ *me; and he that rejecteth you re-*¹⁶ *jecteth me; and he that rejecteth me rejecteth him that sent me.* (§82 Q)

R And they departed, and ⁶ went throughout the villages, preaching the gospel, and healing everywhere.

§58 FATE OF JOHN THE BAPTIST

(§54+) MATT 14:1-12	MARK 6:14-29	LUKE 9:7-9

(§54+) MATT 14:1-12:

A At that season Herod the ¹ tetrarch heard the report concerning Jesus, and said unto ² his servants, This is John the Baptist; he is risen from the dead; and therefore do these powers work in him.

MARK 6:14-29:

A And king Herod heard¹⁴ *thereof;* for his name had become known: and ⁷he said, John ⁸the Baptist is risen from the dead, and therefore do these powers work in him.

B^B But others said, It is Elijah.¹⁵ And others said, *It is* a prophet, *even* as one of the prophets.

C^C But Herod, when¹⁶ he heard *thereof,* said, John, whom I beheaded, he is risen.

LUKE 9:7-9:

A Now Herod the tetrarch ⁷ heard of all that was done: and he was much perplexed, because that it was said by some, that John was risen from the dead;

B^B and by some, ⁸ that Elijah had appeared; and by others, that one of the old prophets was risen again.

C^C And ⁹ Herod said, John I beheaded: but who is this, about whom I hear such things? And he sought to see him.

N If any man would come after me, let him deny himself, and take up his cross, and follow me.

O For whosoever would save his life shall lose it: and whosoever shall lose his life for my sake shall find it. (§73 AB=Mt 16:24-25)

N If any man would come after me, let him deny himself, and take up his cross, and follow me.

O For whosoever would save his life shall lose it; and whosoever shall lose his life for my sake and the gospel's shall save it. (§73 AB=Mk 8:34-35)

N If any man would come after me, let him deny himself, and take up his cross daily, and follow me.

O For whosoever would save his life shall lose it; but whosoever shall lose his life for my sake, the same shall save it. (§73 AB=Lk 9:23-24)

BC For another record of these estimates of Jesus, compare §71 C

MATT 14	MARK 6	LUKE

D   For 3 Herod had laid hold on John, and bound him, and put him in prison for the sake of Herodías, his brother Philip's wife. For John said unto him, It is 4 not lawful for thee to have her.

D For Herod himself had sent[17] forth and laid hold upon John, and bound him in prison for the sake of Herodias, his brother Philip's wife: for he had married her. For John[18] said unto Herod, It is not lawful for thee to have thy brother's wife.

D *With many other exhorta-* 3: *tions therefore preached he*[18] *[1]good tidings unto the people; but Herod the tetrarch, being*[19] *reproved by him for Herodias his brother's wife, and for all the evil things which Herod had done, added yet this above all,*[20] *that he shut up John in prison.* (§ *17 R*)

E   And when he would have 5 put him to death, he feared the multitude, because they counted him as a prophet.

E   And Herodias[19] set herself against him, and desired to kill him; and she could not; for Herod feared[20] John, knowing that he was a righteous man and a holy, and kept him safe. And when he heard him, he [2]was much perplexed; and he heard him gladly.

F But when Herod's birthday 6 came, the daughter of Herodias danced in the midst, and pleased Herod. Whereupon 7 he promised with an oath to give her whatsoever she should ask.

F   And when a conven-[21] ient day was come, that Herod on his birthday made a supper to his lords, and the [3]high captains, and the chief men of Galilee; and when [4]the[22] daughter of Herodias herself came in and danced, [5]she pleased Herod and them that sat at meat with him; and the king said unto the damsel, Ask of me whatsoever thou wilt, and I will give it thee. And he sware unto her, What-[23] soever thou shalt ask of me, I will give it thee, unto the half of my kingdom.

G   And she, being 8 put forward by her mother, saith, Give me here in a charger the head of John the Baptist.

G   And she[24] went out, and said unto her mother, What shall I ask? And she said, The head of John [6]the Baptist. And she[25] came in straightway with haste unto the king, and asked, saying, I will that thou forthwith give me in a charger the head of John [6]the Baptist.

H   And the king was 9 grieved; but for the sake of his oaths, and of them which sat at meat with him, he commanded it to be given; and[10] he sent, and beheaded John in the prison. And his head was[11] brought in a charger, and given to the damsel: and she brought it to her mother.

H And the king was exceeding[26] sorry; but for the sake of his oaths, and of them that sat at meat, he would not reject her. And straightway the king sent[27] forth a soldier of his guard, and commanded to bring his head: and he went and beheaded him in the prison, and[28] brought his head in a charger, and gave it to the damsel; and the damsel gave it to her mother.

ERV margin: 1 Or *the gospel*   2 Many ancient authorities read *di d many things*   3 Or *military tribunes* Greek *chiliarchs*   4 Some ancient authorities read *his daughter Herodias*   5 Or *it*   6 Greek *the Baptizer*

OT references: Mt 14:4 and Mk 6:18 and Lk 3:19 = Leviticus 18:16 and 20:21

MATT 14	MARK 6
1 And[12] his disciples came, and took up the corpse, and buried him; and they went and told Jesus.	1 And when his dis-[29] ciples heard *thereof*, they came and took up his corpse, and laid it in a tomb.

§ 59 REPORT OF ASSOCIATES ON THEIR TOUR*

MARK 6:30–31	LUKE 9:10ᵃ
And the apostles gather[30] themselves together unto Jesus; and they told him all things, whatsoever they had done, and whatsoever they had taught. And he saith[31] unto them, Come ye yourselves apart into a desert place, and rest a while. For there were many coming and going, and they had no leisure so much as to eat.	And the apostles, when they[10ᵃ] were returned, declared unto him what things they had done.

§ 60 TEACHING AND FEEDING THE MULTITUDE

MATT 14:13–23ᵃ	MARK 6:32–46	LUKE 9:10ᵇ–17
A Now when Jesus heard *it*,[13] he withdrew from thence in a boat, to a desert place apart: and when the multitudes heard *thereof*, they followed him [1]on foot from the cities.	A And they went away in the[32] boat to a desert place apart. And *the people* saw them go-[33] ing, and many knew *them*, and they ran there together [1]on foot from all the cities, and outwent them.	A And he took them, and[10ᵇ] withdrew apart to a city called Bethsaida. But the multi-[11] tudes perceiving it followed him:
Bᴮ And he came forth, and[14] saw a great multitude, and he had compassion on them, and healed their sick.	Bᴮ And he came[34] forth and saw a great multitude, and he had compassion on them, because they were as sheep not having a shepherd: and he began to teach them many things.	Bᴮ and he welcomed them, and spake to them of the kingdom of God, and them that had need of healing he healed.
c And when[15] even was come, the disciples came to him, saying, The place is desert, and the time is already past; send the multitudes away, that they may go into the villages, and buy themselves food.	c And when the[35] day was now far spent, his disciples came unto him, and said, The place is desert, and the day is now far spent: send[36] them away, that they may go into the country and villages round about, and buy themselves somewhat to eat.	c And the day began to wear[12] away; and the twelve came, and said unto him, Send the multitude away, that they may go into the villages and country round about, and lodge, and get victuals: for we are here in a desert place.
D But Jesus[16] said unto them, They have no need to go away; give ye them to eat. And they say[17] unto him, We have here but five loaves, and two fishes. And he said, Bring them[18] hither to me.	D But[37] he answered and said unto them, Give ye them to eat. And they say unto him, Shall we go and buy two hundred [2]pennyworth of bread, and give them to eat? And he[38] saith unto them, How many loaves have ye? go *and* see. And when they knew, they say, Five, and two fishes.	D But he said unto them,[13] Give ye them to eat. And they said, We have no more than five loaves and two fishes; except we should go and buy food for all this people.

ERV margin: 1 Or *by land*   2 The word in the Greek denotes a coin worth about eight pence halfpenny

---

OT references: Mk 6:34 (Mt 9:36) = Numbers 27:17 and Ezekiel 34:5

B But when he saw the mulititudes, he was moved with compassion for them, because they were distressed and scattered, as sheep not having a shepherd. (§56 A = Mt 9:36)

---

* For another record of a report on a Tour, compare §82 R

MATT 14	MARK 6	LUKE 9
E　*Compare portion I below*	E　*Compare portion I below*	E　　　For they were about[14] five thousand men.
F　　　And he com-[19] manded the multitudes to [1]sit down on the grass;	F And he commanded them[39] that all should [1]sit down by companies upon the green grass. And they sat down in[40] ranks, by hundreds, and by fifties.	F　　　And he said unto his disciples, Make them [1]sit down in companies, about fifty each. And they[15] did so, and made them all [1]sit down.
G　　　and he took the five loaves, and the two fishes, and looking up to heaven, he blessed, and brake and gave the loaves to the disciples, and the disciples to the multitudes.	G　　And he took the five[41] loaves and the two fishes, and looking up to heaven, he blessed, and brake the loaves; and he gave to the disciples to set before them; and the two fishes divided he among them all.	G　　　And he took the five[16] loaves and the two fishes, and looking up to heaven, he blessed them, and brake; and gave to the disciples to set before the multitude.
H　　　And they did all[20] eat, and were filled: and they took up that which remained over of the broken pieces, twelve baskets full.	H　And they did all eat,[42] and were filled. And they[43] took up broken pieces, twelve basketfuls, and also of the fishes.	H　　　　　And[17] they did eat, and were all filled: and there was taken up that which remained over to them of broken pieces, twelve baskets.
I　　　And[21] they that did eat were about five thousand men, beside women and children.	I　　　And they that ate the[44] loaves were five thousand men.	I　*Compare portion E above*
J　And straightway he con-[22] strained the disciples to enter into the boat, and to go before him unto the other side, till he should send the multitudes away.	J　And straightway he con-[45] strained his disciples to enter into the boat, and to go before *him* unto the other side to Bethsaida, while he himself sendeth the multitude away.	
K　　　And after he had sent[23a] the multitudes away, he went up into the mountain apart to pray.	K And after he had taken[46] leave of them, he departed into the mountain to pray.	K　*Compare §71 portion A*

§ 61　ACROSS THE SEA OF GALILEE

MATT 14:23^b–33	MARK 6:47–52
A　And when even was come,[23b] he was there alone. But the[24] boat [2]was now in the midst of the sea, distressed by the waves; for the wind was contrary. And in the fourth[25] watch of the night he came unto them, walking upon the sea.	A　And when even was come,[47] the boat was in the midst of the sea, and he alone on the land. And seeing them dis-[48] tressed in rowing, for the wind was contrary unto them, about the fourth watch of the night he cometh unto them, walking on the sea;
B　　　And when the disciples[26] saw him walking on the sea, they were troubled, saying, It is an apparition; and they cried out for fear. But[27] straightway Jesus spake unto them, saying, Be of good cheer; it is I; be not afraid.	B　　　and he would have passed by them: but they, when they saw him[49] walking on the sea, supposed that it was an apparition, and cried out: for they all saw[50] him, and were troubled. But he straightway spake with them, and saith unto them, Be of good cheer: it is I; be not afraid.
c And Peter answered him[28] and said, Lord, if it be thou, bid me come unto thee upon the waters. And he said,[29]	

MATT 14

Come. And Peter went down from the boat, and walked upon the waters, [1]to come to Jesus. But when he saw the[30] wind,[2] he was afraid; and beginning to sink, he cried out, saying, Lord, save me. And[31] immediately Jesus stretched forth his hand, and took hold of him, and saith unto him, O thou of little faith, wherefore didst thou doubt?

D And when[32] they were gone up into the boat, the wind ceased. And[33] they that were in the boat worshipped him, saying, Of a truth thou art the Son of God.

MARK 6

D And he went up[51] unto them into the boat; and the wind ceased: and they were sore amazed in themselves; for they understood[52] not concerning the loaves, but their heart was hardened.

§ 62 MANY SICK BROUGHT TO JESUS

MATT 14:34–36

A And when they had crossed[34] over, they came to the land, unto Gennesaret. And when[35] the men of that place knew him, they sent into all that region round about, and brought unto him all that were sick;

C and they besought[36] him that they might only touch the border of his garment: and as many as touched were made whole.

MARK 6:53–56

A And when they had [3]crossed[53] over, they came to the land unto Gennesaret, and moored to the shore. And when they[54] were come out of the boat, straightway *the people* knew him, and ran round about that[55] whole region, and began to carry about on their beds those that were sick, where they heard he was.
B And[56] wheresoever he entered, into villages, or into cities, or into the country, they laid the sick in the marketplaces,
C and besought him that they might touch if it were but the border of his garment: and as many as touched [4]him were made whole.

ERV margin: 1 Some ancient authorities read *and came over to the land, they came unto Gennesaret* 4 Or *it* 2 Many ancient authorities add *strong* 3 Or *crossed*

CHAPTER XI

DEMAND BY PHARISEES FOR CONFORMITY AND CREDENTIALS

---

§ 63 CONCERNING TRADITIONS ABOUT DEFILEMENT

MATT 15:1-20	MARK 7:1-23	LUKE
A Then there come to Jesus 1 from Jerusalem Pharisees and scribes,	A And there are gathered to-1 gether unto him the Pharisees, and certain of the scribes, which had come from Jerusalem, and had seen that some 2 of his disciples ate their bread with 1defiled, that is, unwashen, hands.	A Compare §90 portion A
	B For the 3 Pharisees, and all the Jews, except they wash their hands 2diligently, eat not, holding the tradition of the elders: and when they come from the 4 marketplace, except they 3wash themselves, they eat not: and many other things there be, which they have received to hold, 4washings of cups, and pots, and brasen vessels.5	
C saying, Why do thy 2 disciples transgress the tradition of the elders? for they wash not their hands when they eat bread.	C And the Pharisees 5 and the scribes ask him, Why walk not thy disciples according to the tradition of the elders, but eat their bread with 1defiled hands?	
D And he 3 answered and said unto them, Why do ye also transgress the commandment of God because of your tradition? For 4 God said, Honour thy father and thy mother: and, He that speaketh evil of father or mother, let him 6die the death.	D Compare portion G below	
E But ye say, Whosoever 5 shall say to his father or his mother, That wherewith thou mightest have been profited by me is given to God; he shall 6 not honour his father.7 And ye have made void the 8word of God because of your tradition.	E Compare portion H below	
F Ye hypocrites, well did 7 Isaiah prophesy of you, saying,	F And he 6 said unto them, Well did Isaiah prophesy of you hypocrites, as it is written,	

ERV margin: 1 Or *common* 2 Or *up to the elbow:* Greek *with the fist* 3 Greek *baptize:* some ancient authorities read *sprinkle themselves* 4 Greek *baptizings* 5 Many ancient authorities add *and couches* 6 Or *surely die* 7 Some ancient authorities add *or his mother* 8 Some ancient authorities read *law*

OT references: Mt 15:4 and Mk 7:10=Exodus 20:12 and Deuteronomy 5:16 and Exodus 21:17 and Leviticus 20:9

MATT 15

This people honoureth me [8]
with their lips;
But their heart is far from
me.
But in vain do they wor- [9]
ship me,
Teaching *as their* doctrines
the precepts of men.

G *Compare portion D above*

H *Compare portion E above*

[1] And he called to him the [10]
multitude, and said unto
them, Hear, and understand:
Not that which entereth into [11]
the mouth defileth the man;
but that which proceedeth
out of the mouth, this defileth the man.

J   Then came [12]
the disciples, and said unto
him, Knowest thou that the
Pharisees were [3]offended,
when they heard this saying?
But he answered and said, [13]
Every [4]plant which my
heavenly Father planted not,
shall be rooted up. Let them [14]
alone: they are blind guides.
And if the blind guide the
blind, both shall fall into a
pit.

K   And Peter answered and [15]
said unto him, Declare unto
us the parable. And he said, [16]
Are ye also even yet without
understanding? Perceive ye [17]
not, that whatsoever goeth
into the mouth passeth into
the belly, and is cast out into
the draught?

MARK 7

This people honoureth me
with their lips,
But their heart is far from
me.
But in vain do they wor- [7]
ship me,
Teaching *as their* doctrines
the precepts of men.

G Ye leave the commandment [8]
of God, and hold fast the tradition of men. And he said [9]
unto them, Full well do ye
reject the commandment of
God, that ye may keep your
tradition. For Moses said, [10]
Honour thy father and thy
mother; and, He that speaketh evil of father or mother,
let him [1]die the death:

H   but [11]
ye say, If a man shall say to
his father or his mother, That
wherewith thou mightest have
been profited by me is Cor-
ban, that is to say, Given *to
God;* ye no longer suffer [12]
him to do aught for his father
or his mother; making void [13]
the word of God by your tradition, which ye have de-
livered: and many such like
things ye do.

[1]   And he called [14]
to him the multitude again,
and said unto them, Hear me
all of you, and understand:
there is nothing from without [15]
the man, that going into him
can defile him: but the things
which proceed out of the man
are those that defile the man. [2]

K And when he was entered [17]
into the house from the multitude, his disciples asked of
him the parable. And he [18]
saith unto them, Are ye so
without understanding also?
Perceive ye not, that whatsoever from without goeth
into the man, *it* cannot defile

LUKE

J *And he spake also a par-* [6:]
able unto them, Can the blind [39]
*guide the blind? shall they not
both fall into a pit?* (§38 G)

ERV margin: [1] Or *surely die*   [2] Many ancient authorities insert verse 16: *If any man hath ears to hear, let him
hear*   [3] Greek *caused to stumble*   [4] Greek *planting*

OT references: Mt 15:8-9 and Mk 7:6-7 = Isaiah 29:13   Mk 7:10 = compare page **79**

MATT 15	MARK 7
	him; because it goeth not into[19] his heart, but into his belly, and goeth out into the draught? *This he said*, making all meats clean.
L But the things[18] which proceed out of the mouth come forth out of the heart; and they defile the man. For out of the heart[19] come forth evil thoughts, murders, adulteries, fornications, thefts, false witness, railings: these are the things which de-[20] file the man: but to eat with unwashen hands defileth not the man.	L And he[20] said, That which proceedeth out of the man, that defileth the man. For from[21] within, out of the heart of men, [1]evil thoughts proceed, fornications, thefts, murders, adulteries, covetings, wicked-[22] nesses, deceit, lasciviousness, an evil eye, railing, pride, foolishness: all these evil[23] things proceed from within, and defile the man.

§64 WITHDRAWAL TOWARD TYRE AND SIDON

MATT 15:21-28	MARK 7:24-30
A And Jesus went out[21] thence, and withdrew into the parts of Tyre and Sidon.	A And from thence he arose,[24] and went away into the borders of Tyre [2]and Sidon. And he entered into a house, and would have no man know it: and he could not be hid.
B And behold, a Canaanitish[22] woman came out from those borders, and cried, saying, Have mercy on me, O Lord, thou son of David; my daughter is grievously vexed with a [4]devil.	B But[25] straightway a woman, whose little daughter had an unclean spirit, having heard of him, came and fell down at his feet. Now the woman was a [3]Greek,[26] a Syrophœnician by race. And she besought him that he would cast forth the [4]devil out of her daughter.
C But he an-[23] swered her not a word. And his disciples came and besought him, saying, Send her away; for she crieth after us.	
D[D] But he answered and said,[24] I was not sent but unto the lost sheep of the house of Israel.	D[D] And[27] he said unto her, Let the children first be filled:
E But she came and wor-[25] shipped him, saying, Lord, help me. And he answered[26] and said, It is not meet to take the children's [5]bread and cast it to the dogs. But she said,[27] Yea, Lord: for even the dogs eat of the crumbs which fall from their masters' table.	E for it is not meet to take the children's [5]bread and cast it to the dogs. But she answered[28] and saith unto him, Yea, Lord: even the dogs under the table eat of the children's crumbs.
F Then Jesus answered and[28] said unto her, O woman, great is thy faith: be it done unto thee even as thou wilt. And her daughter was healed from that hour.	F And he said unto[29] her, For this saying go thy way; the [4]devil is gone out of thy daughter. And she[30] went away unto her house, and found the child laid upon the bed, and the [4]devil gone out.

ERV margin: 1 Greek *thoughts that are evil* 2 Some ancient authorities omit *and Sidon* 3 Or *Gentile* 4 Greek *demon* 5 Or *loaf*

D With the Matthew form of the record here, compare the Matthew report in §55 E

81

§ 65 RETURN JOURNEY THROUGH DECAPOLIS

MATT 15:29ᵃ

And Jesus departed thence,²⁹ᵃ and came nigh unto the sea of Galilee.

MARK 7:31

And again he went out³¹ from the borders of Tyre, and came through Sidon unto the sea of Galilee, through the midst of the borders of Decapolis.

§ 66 THE DEAF AND DUMB MAN

MARK 7:32–37

A And they bring unto him³² one that was deaf, and had an impediment in his speech; and they beseech him to lay his hand upon him. And he³³ took him aside from the multitude privately, and put his fingers into his ears, and he spat, and touched his tongue; and looking up to heaven, he³⁴ sighed, and saith unto him, Ephphatha, that is, Be opened. And his ears were opened,³⁵ and the bond of his tongue was loosed, and he spake plain.

B   And he charged them³⁶ that they should tell no man: but the more he charged them, so much the more a great deal they published it.

C   And they³⁷ were beyond measure astonished, saying, He hath done all things well: he maketh even the deaf to hear, and the dumb to speak.

§ 67 HEALING AND FEEDING THE MULTITUDE

MATT 15:29ᵇ–39

A And he went up into the²⁹ᵇ mountain, and sat there. And there came unto him³⁰ great multitudes, having with them the lame, blind, dumb, maimed, and many others, and they cast them down at his feet; and he healed them:

B insomuch that the multi-³¹ tude wondered, when they saw the dumb speaking, the maimed whole, and the lame walking, and the blind seeing: and they glorified the God of Israel.

C And Jesus called unto him³² his disciples, and said, I have compassion on the multitude, because they continue with me now three days and have nothing to eat: and I would not send them away fasting,

MARK 8:1–10

A In those days, when there ¹ was again a great multitude, and they had nothing to eat,

B *Compare §66 portion C*

c he called unto him his disciples, and saith unto them, I ² have compassion on the multitude, because they continue with me now three days, and have nothing to eat: and ³ if I send them away fasting

MATT 15	MARK 8
lest haply they faint in the way.	to their home, they will faint in the way; and some of them are come from far.
D And the disciples say33 unto him, Whence should we have so many loaves in a desert place, as to fill so great a multitude? And Jesus34 saith unto them, How many loaves have ye? And they said, Seven, and a few small fishes.	D And his disciples answered 4 him, Whence shall one be able to fill these men with ¹bread here in a desert place? And 5 he asked them, How many loaves have ye? And they said, Seven. *Compare portion G below*
E And he commanded35 the multitude to sit down on the ground;	E And he com- 6 mandeth the multitude to sit down on the ground:
F and he took the36 seven loaves and the fishes; and he gave thanks and brake, and gave to the disciples, and the disciples to the multitudes.	F and he took the seven loaves, and having given thanks, he brake, and gave to his disciples, to set before them; and they set them before the multitude.
G *Compare portion D above*	G And they had a 7 few small fishes: and having blessed them, he commanded to set these also before them.
H And they did all eat,37 and were filled: and they took up that which remained over of the broken pieces, seven baskets full.	H And they did eat, and were 8 filled: and they took up, of broken pieces that remained over, seven baskets.
I And they that38 did eat were four thousand men, beside women and children.	I And 9 they were about four thousand:
J And he sent away the39 multitudes, and entered into the boat, and came into the borders of Magadan.	J and he sent them away. And straightway he entered10 into the boat with his disciples, and came into the parts of Dalmanutha.

§ 68 PHARISEES DEMAND SIGNS FROM JESUS

MATT 16:1-4	MARK 8:11-13	LUKE
Aᴬ And the Pharisees and 1 Sadducees came, and tempting him asked him to shew them a sign from heaven.	Aᴬ And the Pharisees came11 forth, and began to question with him, seeking of him a sign from heaven, tempting him.	
B But he answered and said 2 unto them, ²When it is evening, ye say, It will be fair weather: for the heaven is red. And in the morning, 3 It will be foul weather to-day: for the heaven is red and lowring. Ye know how to discern the face of the heaven; but ye cannot *discern* the signs of the times.		B *And he said to the multi-*12: *tudes also, When ye see a cloud*54 *rising in the west, straightway ye say, There cometh a shower; and so it cometh to pass. And*55 *when ye see a south wind blowing, ye say, There will be a* ³*scorching heat; and it cometh to pass. Ye hypocrites, ye*56 *know how to* ⁴*interpret the face of the earth and the heaven; but*

ERV margin: 1 Greek *loaves*   2 The following words, to the end of verse 3, are omitted by some of the most ancient and other important authorities   3 Or *hot wind*   4 Greek *prove*

A   Then certain of the scribes and Pharisees answered him, saying, Master, we would see a sign from thee. (§45 Q = Mt 12:38)

A   And others, tempting *him*, sought of him a sign from heaven. (§86 D = Lk 11:16)

MATT 16	MARK 8	LUKE
		how is it that ye know not how to [1]*interpret this time?* (§96 A)
c[C] An evil 4 and adulterous generation seeketh after a sign; and there shall no sign be given unto it, but the sign of Jonah.	c[C] And he sighed deeply[12] in his spirit, and saith, Why doth this generation seek a sign? verily I say unto you, There shall no sign be given unto this generation.	
D And he left them, and departed.	D And he[13] left them, and again entering into *the boat* departed to the other side.	

§ 69   THE LEAVEN OF THE PHARISEES

MATT 16:5–12	MARK 8:14–21	LUKE
A And the disciples came to 5 the other side and forgot to take [2]bread. And Jesus said 6 unto them, Take heed and beware of the leaven of the Pharisees and Sadducees.	A And they forgot to take[14] bread; and they had not in the boat with them more than one loaf. And he charged[15] them, saying, Take heed, beware of the leaven of the Pharisees and the leaven of Herod.	A *Compare portion D below*
B And they reasoned among 7 themselves, saying, [4]We took no [2]bread. And Jesus per- 8 ceiving it said, O ye of little faith, why reason ye among yourselves, because ye have no [2]bread?	B And they reasoned[16] one with another, [3]saying, [5]We have no bread. And[17] Jesus perceiving it saith unto them, Why reason ye, because ye have no bread?	
c Do ye not yet 9 perceive, neither remember the five loaves of the five thousand, and how many [6]baskets ye took up? Neither[10] the seven loaves of the four thousand, and how many [6]baskets ye took up? How is[11] it that ye do not perceive that I spake not to you concerning [2]bread?	c do ye not yet perceive, neither understand? have ye your heart hardened? Having[18] eyes, see ye not? and having ears, hear ye not? and do ye not remember? When I[19] brake the five loaves among the five thousand, how many [7]baskets full of broken pieces took ye up? They say unto him, Twelve. And when the[20] seven among the four thousand, how many [7]basketfuls of broken pieces took ye up? And they say unto him, Seven. And he said unto[21] them, Do ye not yet understand?	
D But beware of the leaven of the Pharisees and Sadducees. Then understood[12] they how that he bade them not beware of the leaven of [2]bread, but of the teaching of the Pharisees and Sadducees.	D *Compare portion A above*	D *Beware ye of the leaven of*[12]: *the Pharisees, which is hypoc-* [1] *risy.* (§91 B)

ERV margin: [1] Greek *prove*   [2] Greek *loaves*   [3] Some ancient authorities read *because they had no bread*   [4] Or, It is *because we took no bread*   [5] Or, It is *because we have no bread*   [6] *Basket* in verses 9 and 10 represents different Greek words   [7] *Basket* in verses 19 and 20 represents different Greek words

OT references: Mt 16:4 = Jonah 3:1–4   Mk 8:18 = Jeremiah 5:21 and Ezekiel 12:2

c   But he answered and said unto them, An evil and adulterous generation seeketh after a sign; and there shall no sign be given to it but the sign of Jonah the prophet. (§45 R = Mt 12·39)

c And when the multitudes were gathering together unto him, he began to say, This generation is an evil generation: it seeketh after a sign; and there shall no sign be given to it but the sign of Jonah. (§88 B = Lk 11:29)

§ 70 THE BLIND MAN OF BETHSAIDA

MARK 8:22–26

A   And they come unto Beth-[22]
saida.   And they bring to him
a blind man, and beseech him
to touch him.   And he took[23]
hold of the blind man by the
hand, and brought him out of
the village; and when he had
spit on his eyes, and laid his
hands upon him, he asked
him, Seest thou aught? And[24]
he looked up, and said, I see
men; for I behold *them* as
trees, walking.   Then again[25]
he laid his hands upon his
eyes; and he looked sted-
fastly, and was restored, and
saw all things clearly.
B   And[26]
he sent him away to his home,
saying, Do not even enter into
the village.

CHAPTER XII

FORECASTS OF CONFLICT WITH THE JERUSALEM AUTHORITIES

§ 71 OPINION OF DISCIPLES ABOUT JESUS

MATT 16:13–20	MARK 8:27–30	LUKE 9:18–21
A *Compare §60 portion K*	A *Compare §60 portion K*	A And it came to pass, as he[18] was praying alone,
B Now when Jesus came into[13] the parts of Cæsarea Philippi, he asked his disciples, saying, Who do men say [1]that the Son of man is?	B And Jesus went forth, and[27] his disciples, into the villages of Cæsarea Philippi: and in the way he asked his disciples, saying unto them, Who do men say that I am?	B the disciples were with him: and he asked them, saying, Who do the multitudes say that I am?
C[C] And they[14] said, Some *say* John the Baptist; some, Elijah: and others, Jeremiah, or one of the prophets.	C[C] And[28] they told him, saying, John the Baptist: and others, Elijah; but others, One of the prophets.	C[C] And they answering said,[19] John the Baptist; but others *say*, Elijah; and others, that one of the old prophets is risen again.
D He saith unto[15] them, But who say ye that I am? And Simon Peter an-[16]swered and said, Thou art the Christ, the Son of the living God.	D And he asked[29] them, But who say ye that I am? Peter answereth and saith unto him, Thou art the Christ.	D And he said unto[20] them, But who say ye that I am? And Peter answering said, The Christ of God.
E And Jesus an-[17]swered and said unto him, Blessed art thou, Simon Bar-Jonah: for flesh and blood hath not revealed it unto thee, but my Father which is in heaven. And I also say unto[18] thee, that thou art [2]Peter, and upon this [3]rock I will build my church; and the gates of Hades shall not prevail against it.		
F[F] I will give unto thee the[19] keys of the kingdom of heaven: and whatsoever thou shalt bind on earth shall be bound in heaven: and whatsoever thou shalt loose on earth shall be loosed in heaven.		
G Then charged he the[20] disciples that they should tell no man that he was the Christ.	G And he charged them[30] that they should tell no man of him.	G But[21] he charged them, and commanded *them* to tell this to no man;

ERV margin: 1 Many ancient authorities read *that I the Son of man am:* see Mark 8:27 and Luke 9:18   2 Greek *Petros*   3 Greek *petra*

c For another record of these estimates of Jesus, compare §58 BC

F Verily I say unto you, What things soever ye shall bind on earth shall be bound in heaven: and what things soever ye shall loose on earth shall be loosed in heaven. (§78 T=Mt 18:18)

§ 72   JESUS FORETELLS EVENTS AT JERUSALEM

MATT 16:21-23	MARK 8:31-33	LUKE 9:22
A^A From that time began[21] Jesus to shew unto his disciples, how that he must go unto Jerusalem, and suffer many things of the elders and chief priests and scribes, and be killed, and the third day be raised up.	A^A And he began to teach[31] them, that the Son of man must suffer many things, and be rejected by the elders, and the chief priests, and the scribes, and be killed, and after three days rise again. And he spake the saying[32] openly.	A^A saying, The Son of man[22] must suffer many things, and be rejected of the elders and chief priests and scribes, and be killed, and the third day be raised up.
B And Peter took[22] him, and began to rebuke him, saying, [2]Be it far from thee, Lord: this shall never be unto thee. But he turned,[23] and said unto Peter, Get thee behind me, Satan: thou art a stumblingblock unto me: for thou mindest not the things of God, but the things of men.	B And Peter took him, and began to rebuke him. But he turning about, and[33] seeing his disciples, rebuked Peter, and saith, Get thee behind me, Satan: for thou mindest not the things of God, but the things of men.	

§ 73   SOME COSTS OF DISCIPLESHIP

MATT 16:24-28	MARK 8:34—9:1	LUKE 9:23-27
A^A Then said Jesus unto his[24] disciples, If any man would come after me, let him deny himself, and take up his cross, and follow me.	A^A And he called unto him[34] the multitude with his disciples, and said unto them, If any man would come after me, let him deny himself, and take up his cross, and follow me.	A^A And he said unto all, If[23] any man would come after me, let him deny himself, and take up his cross daily, and follow me.
B^B For whoso-[25]ever would save his [3]life shall lose it: and whosoever shall lose his [3]life for my sake shall find it. For what shall a man[26] be profited, if he shall gain the whole world, and forfeit his [3]life? or what shall a man give in exchange for his [3]life?	B^B For whosoever would save[35] his [3]life shall lose it; and whosoever shall lose his [3]life for my sake and the gospel's shall save it. For what doth[36] it profit a man, to gain the whole world, and forfeit his [3]life? For what should a man[37] give in exchange for his [3]life?	B^B For whosoever would[24] save his [3]life shall lose it; but whosoever shall lose his [3]life for my sake, the same shall save it. For what is a man[25] profited, if he gain the whole world, and lose or forfeit his own self?
C^C For the Son of man shall[27] come in the glory of his	C^C For whosoever shall be[38] ashamed of me and of my	C^C For whosoever[26] shall be ashamed of me and

ERV margin: 1 Some ancient authorities read *Jesus Christ*   2 Or, God *have mercy on thee*   3 Or *soul*

OT references: Mt 16:27 = Psalm 62:12 and Proverbs 24:12

A The Son of man shall be delivered up into the hands of men; and they shall kill him, and the third day he shall be raised up. (§76 B = Mt 17:22-23)
A But first must he suffer many things and be rejected of this generation. (§112 D = Lk 17:25)
A Behold, we go up to Jerusalem; and the Son of man shall be delivered unto the chief priests and scribes; and they shall condemn him to death, and shall deliver him unto the Gentiles to mock, and to scourge, and to crucify: and the third day he shall be raised up. (§119 C-F = Mt 20:18-19)
A For other references to these events, compare §74 I-N and §101

A The Son of man is delivered up into the hands of men, and they shall kill him; and when he is killed, after three days he shall rise again. (§76 B = Mk 9:31)
A Behold, we go up to Jerusalem; and the Son of man shall be delivered unto the chief priests and the scribes; and they shall condemn him to death, and shall deliver him unto the Gentiles: and they shall mock him, and shall spit upon him, and shall scourge him, and shall kill him; and after three days he shall rise again. (§119 C-F = Mk 10:33-34)

A Let these words sink into your ears: for the Son of man shall be delivered up into the hands of men. (§76 B = Lk 9:44)
A Behold, we go up to Jerusalem, and all the things that are written by the prophets shall be accomplished unto the Son of man. For he shall be delivered up unto the Gentiles, and shall be mocked, and shamefully entreated, and spit upon: and they shall scourge and kill him: and the third day he shall rise again. (§119 C-F = Lk 18:31-33)

A And he that doth not take his cross and follow after me, is not worthy of me.
B   He that findeth his life shall lose it; and he that loseth his life for my sake shall find it. (§57 NO = Mt 10:38-39)
C But whosoever shall deny me before men, him will I also deny before my Father which is in heaven. (§57 K = Mt 10:33)

A Whosoever doth not bear his own cross, and come after me, cannot be my disciple. (§104 C = Lk 14:27)
B Whosoever shall seek to gain his life shall lose it: but whosoever shall lose *his life* shall preserve it. (§112 J = Lk 17:33)
C But he that denieth me in the presence of men shall be denied in the presence of the angels of God. (§91 G = Lk 12:9)

MATT 16	MARK 8	LUKE 9
Father with his angels; and then shall he render unto every man according to his ¹deeds.	words in this adulterous and sinful generation, the Son of man also shall be ashamed of him, when he cometh in the glory of his Father with the holy angels.	of my words, of him shall the Son of man be ashamed, when he cometh in his own glory, and *the glory* of the Father, and of the holy angels.
D Verily I say unto you,²⁸ There be some of them that stand here, which shall in no wise taste of death, till they see the Son of man coming in his kingdom.	D And he said 9: unto them, Verily I say unto ¹ you, There be some here of them that stand *by*, which shall in no wise taste of death, till they see the kingdom of God come with power.	D But²⁷ I tell you of a truth, There be some of them that stand here, which shall in no wise taste of death, till they see the kingdom of God.

§ 74   THE TRANSFIGURATION OF JESUS

MATT 17:1–13	MARK 9:2–13	LUKE 9:28–36
A And after six days Jesus ¹ taketh with him Peter, and James, and John his brother, and bringeth them up into a high mountain apart:	A And after six days Jesus ² taketh with him Peter, and James, and John, and bringeth them up into a high mountain apart by themselves:	A And it came to pass about²⁸ eight days after these sayings, he took with him Peter and John and James, and went up into the mountain to pray.
B and he ² was transfigured before them: and his face did shine as the sun, and his garments became white as the light.	B and he was transfigured before them: and his gar- ³ ments became glistering, exceeding white; so as no fuller on earth can whiten them.	B And as he was praying, the²⁹ fashion of his countenance was altered, and his raiment *became* white *and* dazzling.
C And be- ³ hold, there appeared unto them Moses and Elijah talking with him.	C And there appeared unto ⁴ them Elijah with Moses: and they were talking with Jesus.	C And behold, there talked³⁰ with him two men, which were Moses and Elijah; who³¹ appeared in glory, and spake of his ²decease which he was about to accomplish at Jerusalem. Now Peter and they³² that were with him were heavy with sleep: but ³when they were fully awake, they saw his glory, and the two men that stood with him.
D And Peter ⁴ answered, and said unto Jesus, Lord, it is good for us to be here: if thou wilt, I will make here three ⁴tabernacles; one for thee, and one for Moses, and one for Elijah.	D And Peter answereth and ⁵ saith to Jesus, Rabbi, it is good for us to be here: and let us make three ⁴tabernacles; one for thee, and one for Moses, and one for Elijah. For he wist not what to ⁶ answer; for they became sore afraid.	D And it came to pass, as³³ they were parting from him, Peter said unto Jesus, Master, it is good for us to be here: and let us make three ⁴tabernacles; one for thee, and one for Moses, and one for Elijah: not knowing what he said.
Eᴱ While he was yet speaking, ⁵ behold, a bright cloud overshadowed them: and behold, a voice out of the cloud, saying, This is my beloved Son, in whom I am well pleased; hear ye him.	Eᴱ And there came a ⁷ cloud overshadowing them: and there came a voice out of the cloud, This is my beloved Son: hear ye him.	Eᴱ And while he said these³⁴ things, there came a cloud, and overshadowed them: and they feared as they entered into the cloud. And a voice³⁵ came out of the cloud, saying, This is ⁵my Son, my chosen: hear ye him.
F And when the ⁶ disciples heard it, they fell on their face, and were sore afraid. And Jesus came and ⁷		

ERV margin: ¹ Greek *doing*   ² Or *departure*   ³ Or *having remained awake*   ⁴ Or *booths*   ⁵ Many ancient authorities read *my beloved son:* see Matt 17:5 and Mark 9:7

OT references: Mt 17:5 and Mk 9:7 and Lk 9:35 = Deuteronomy 18:15 and Isaiah 42:1

ᴱ Compare §18 portion ᴅ

MATT 17	MARK 9	LUKE 9
touched them and said, Arise, and be not afraid. G　　　　　And lift-8 ing up their eyes, they saw no one, save Jesus only.	G　　　　　And sud-8 denly looking round about, they saw no one any more, save Jesus only with themselves. H　*Compare portion J below*	G　　　And when the36 voice [1]came, Jesus was found alone. H　　　And they held their peace, and told no man in those days any of the things which they had seen.
I[1]　And as they were coming 9 down from the mountain, Jesus commanded them, saying, Tell the vision to no man, until the Son of man be risen from the dead.	I[1]　And as they were coming 9 down from the mountain, he charged them that they should tell no man what things they had seen, save when the Son of man should have risen again from the dead. J　　　And they kept the10 saying, questioning among themselves what the rising again from the dead should mean.	J　*Compare portion H above*
K　　　　And his dis-10 ciples asked him, saying, Why then say the scribes that Elijah must first come? And11 he answered and said, Elijah indeed cometh, and shall restore all things: L[L]　*Compare portion N below*	K　　　And they asked him,11 saying, [2]The scribes say that Elijah must first come. And12 he said unto them, Elijah indeed cometh first, and restoreth all things: L[L]　　　　and how is it written of the Son of man, that he should suffer many things and be set at nought?	
M[M]　　　　but I say12 unto you, that Elijah is come already, and they knew him not, but did unto him whatsoever they listed. N[N]　　　　Even so shall the Son of man also suffer of them. O　　　Then under-13 stood the disciples that he spake unto them of John the Baptist.	M[M]　　But I say unto you,13 that Elijah is come, and they have also done unto him whatsoever they listed, even as it is written of him. N[N]　*Compare portion L above*	

§ 75　THE YOUTH WITH THE DUMB SPIRIT

MATT 17:14-20	MARK 9:14-29	LUKE 9:37-43[a]
A　And when they were come14 to the multitude,	A　And when they came to14 the disciples, they saw a great multitude about them, and scribes questioning with them. And straightway all the mul-15 titude, when they saw him, were greatly amazed, and running to him saluted him.	A　And it came to pass, on the37 next day, when they were come down from the mountain, a great multitude met him.

ERV margin:　1 Or *was past*　　2 Or, How is it *that the scribes say . . . come?*

OT references:　Mt 17:10-11 and Mk 9:11-12 = Malachi 4:5-6　　Mt 17:12 and Mk 9:13 = 1 Kings 19:2, 10

I-N　For accounts of the forecast of suffering and death, compare §72 A and attached references
L　Compare §119 portion D
M　For another record of the identification of John the Baptist with Elijah by Jesus, compare §41 G

MATT 17	MARK 9	LUKE 9
	And he asked them,[16] What question ye with them?	
B there came to him a man, kneeling to him, and saying, Lord, have[15] mercy on my son: for he is epileptic, and suffereth grievously: for oft-times he falleth into the fire, and oft-times into the water. And I[16] brought him to thy disciples, and they could not cure him.	B And one of the multitude[17] answered him, [1]Master, I brought unto thee my son, which hath a dumb spirit; and[18] wheresoever it taketh him, it [2]dasheth him down: and he foameth, and grindeth his teeth, and pineth away: and I spake to thy disciples that they should cast it out; and they were not able.	B And behold, a man[38] from the multitude cried, saying, [1]Master, I beseech thee to look upon my son; for he is mine only child: and be-[39] hold, a spirit taketh him, and he suddenly crieth out; and it [3]teareth him that he foameth, and he hardly departeth from him, bruising him sorely. And I besought thy disciples[40] to cast it out; and they could not.
C And Jesus answered and[17] said, O faithless and perverse generation, how long shall I be with you? how long shall I bear with you? bring him hither to me.	C And he[19] answereth them and saith, O faithless generation, how long shall I be with you? how long shall I bear with you? bring him unto me.	C And Jesus answered[41] and said, O faithless and perverse generation, how long shall I be with you, and bear with you? bring hither thy son.
	D And they[20] brought him unto him: and when he saw him, straightway the spirit [6]tare him grievously; and he fell on the ground, and wallowed foaming. And he asked his[21] father, How long time is it since this hath come unto him? And he said, From a child. And oft-times it hath[22] cast him both into the fire and into the waters, to destroy him: but if thou canst do anything, have compassion on us, and help us. And[23] Jesus said unto him, If thou canst! All things are possible to him that believeth. Straightway the father of the[24] child cried out, and said,[7] I believe; help thou mine unbelief.	D And as he was yet a[42] coming, the [4]devil [5]dashed him down, and [6]tare *him* grievously.
E And Jesus re-[18] buked him; and the [4]devil went out from him: and the boy was cured from that hour.	E And when Jesus saw[25] that a multitude came running together, he rebuked the unclean spirit, saying unto him, Thou dumb and deaf spirit, I command thee, come out of him, and enter no more into him. And having cried[26] out, and [6]torn him much, he came out: and *the child* became as one dead; insomuch that the more part said, He is dead. But Jesus took him[27] by the hand, and raised him up; and he arose.	E But Jesus rebuked the unclean spirit, and healed the boy, and gave him back to his father.
		F And they[43a] were all astonished at the majesty of God.
G Then came the disciples to[19] Jesus apart, and said, Why	G And when[28] he was come into the house,	

ERV margin: 1 Or *Teacher*   2 Or *rendeth him*   3 Or *convulseth*   4 Greek *demon*   5 Or *rent him*   6 Or *convulsed*   7 Many ancient authorities add *with tears*

MATT 17	MARK 9	LUKE
could not we cast it out? And he saith unto them,[20] Because of your little faith:	his disciples asked him privately, [1]*saying*, We could not cast it out. And he said unto[29] them, This kind can come out by nothing, save by prayer.[2]	
H[H] for verily I say unto you, If ye have faith as a grain of mustard seed, ye shall say unto this mountain, Remove hence to yonder place; and it shall remove; I and nothing shall be impossible unto you.[3]		H[H] *And the Lord said, If ye*[17:] *have faith as a grain of mus-*[6] *tard seed, ye would say unto this sycamine tree, Be thou rooted up, and be thou planted in the sea; and it would have obeyed you.* (§109 F)

§ 76   JESUS REPEATS HIS FORECAST OF EVENTS

MATT 17:22–23	MARK 9:30–32	LUKE 9:43[b]–45
A And while they [4]abode in[22] Galilee, Jesus said unto them,	A And they went forth from[30] thence, and passed through Galilee; and he would not that any man should know it. For he taught his disciples,[31] and said unto them,	A But while all were mar-[43b] velling at all the things which he did, he said unto his disciples,
B[B] The Son of man shall be delivered up into the hands of men; and they shall kill him,[23] and the third day he shall be raised up.	B[B] The Son of man is delivered up into the hands of men, and they shall kill him; and when he is killed, after three days he shall rise again.	B[B] Let these words sink[44] into your ears: for the Son of man shall be delivered up into the hands of men.
C And they were exceeding sorry.	C But they under-[32] stood not the saying, and were afraid to ask him.	C But[45] they understood not this saying, and it was concealed from them, that they should not perceive it: and they were afraid to ask him about this saying.

§ 77   THE PROBLEM OF TRIBUTE PAYMENT

MATT 17:24–27

A   And when they were come to Capernaum,[24] they that received the [5]half-shekel came to Peter, and said, Doth not your [6]master pay the [5]half-shekel? He saith, Yea. And when[25] he came into the house, Jesus spake first to him, saying, What thinkest thou, Simon? the kings of the earth, from whom do they receive toll or tribute? from their sons, or from strangers? And when he said, From strangers, Jesus said[26] unto him, Therefore the sons are free.

B   But,[27] lest we cause them to stumble, go thou to the sea, and cast a hook, and take up the fish that

---

ERV margin: 1 Or, How is it *that we could not cast it out?*   2 Many ancient authorities add *and fasting*
3 Many authorities, some ancient, insert verse 21: *But this kind goeth not out save by prayer and fasting:* see Mark 9:29   4 Some ancient authorities read *were gathering themselves together*   5 Greek *didrachma*   6 Or *teacher*

OT references: Mt 17:24 = Exodus 30:11-15

H Verily I say unto you, If ye have faith, and doubt not, ye shall not only do what is done to the fig tree, but even if ye shall say unto this mountain, Be thou taken up and cast into the sea, it shall be done. (§127 C = Mt 21:21)	H Have faith in God. Verily I say unto you, Whosoever shall say unto this mountain, Be thou taken up and cast into the sea; and shall not doubt in his heart, but shall believe that what he saith cometh to pass; he shall have it. (§127 C = Mk 11:22-23)

B   For other records of these forecasts, compare §72 A and attached references

MATT 17

first cometh up; and when thou hast opened
his mouth, thou shalt find a ¹shekel: that take,
and give unto them for me and thee.

§ 78 DISCOURSE ON STANDARDS OF GREATNESS

MATT 18:1–35	MARK 9:33–50	LUKE 9:46–50
A In that hour came the dis- ¹ ciples unto Jesus, saying, Who then is ²greatest in the kingdom of heaven?	A And they came to Caper-33 naum: and when he was in the house he asked them, What were ye reasoning in the way? But they held their34 peace: for they had disputed one with another in the way, who *was* the ²greatest.	A And there arose a reason-46 ing among them, which of them should be ²greatest.
Bᴮ *Compare portion E below*	Bᴮ And35 he sat down, and called the twelve; and he saith unto them, If any man would be first, he shall be last of all, and minister of all.	Bᴮ *Compare portion H below*
C And he ² called to him a little child, and set him in the midst of them, and said, 3	C And he36 took a little child, and set him in the midst of them: and taking him in his arms, he said unto them,	C But when Jesus saw the rea-47 soning of their heart, he took a little child, and set him by his side, and said unto them,48
D Verily I say unto you, Except ye turn, and become as little children, ye shall in no wise enter into the kingdom of heaven.	D *Verily I say unto you,*10: *Whosoever shall not receive the*15 *kingdom of God as a little child, he shall in no wise enter therein.* (§116 C)	D *Verily I say unto you,*18: *Whosoever shall not receive the*17 *kingdom of God as a little child, he shall in no wise enter therein.* (§116 C)
E Whosoever therefore shall 4 humble himself as this little child, the same is the ²great- est in the kingdom of heaven.	E *Compare portion B above*	E *Compare portion H below*
F And whoso shall receive one 5 such little child in my name receiveth me:	F Whosoever37 shall receive one of such little children in my name, receiv- eth me:	F Whosoever shall receive this little child in my name receiv- eth me:
Gᴳ *He that receiveth you re-*10: *ceiveth me, and he that re-*40 *ceiveth me receiveth him that sent me.* (§57 P)	Gᴳ and whosoever re- ceiveth me, receiveth not me, but him that sent me.	Gᴳ and whosoever shall receive me receiveth him that sent me:
H *Compare portion E above*	H *Compare portion B above*	H for he that is ³least among you all, the same is great.
	I¹ John said unto him, ⁴Mas-38 ter, we saw one casting out ⁵devils in thy name: and we forbade him, because he fol- lowed not us. But Jesus said,39 Forbid him not: for there is no man which shall do a ⁶mighty work in my name, and be able quickly to speak	I¹ And John answered and49 said, Master, we saw one cast- ing out ⁵devils in thy name; and we forbade him, because he followeth not with us. But Jesus said unto him, For-50 bid *him* not: for he that is not against you is for you.

ERV margin: 1 Greek *stater*   2 Greek *greater*   3 Greek *lesser*   4 Or *Teacher*   5 Greek *demons*   6 Greek
power

B Not so shall it be among you: but whosoever would become great among you shall be your minister; and whosoever would be first among you shall be your servant. (§120 J = Mt 20:26–27)
·B But he that is greatest among you shall be your servant. (§132 G = Mt 23:11)

B But it is not so among you: but whosoever would become great among you, shall be your minis- ter: and whosoever would be first among you, shall be servant of all. (§120 J = Mk 10:43–44)

B But ye *shall* not *be* so: but he that is the greater among you, let him become as the younger; and he that is chief, as he that doth serve. (§138 M = Lk 22:26)

G He that heareth you heareth me; and he that rejecteth you rejecteth me; and he that rejecteth me rejecteth him **that** sent me. (§82 Q = Lk 10:16)
I With the last verse of this portion, compare §45 H and §86 H

93

MATT 18	MARK 9	LUKE

MARK 9: evil of me. For he that is[40] not against us is for us.

J *And whosoever shall give to*[10]: *drink unto one of these little*[42] *ones a cup of cold water only, in the name of a disciple, verily I say unto you, he shall in no wise lose his reward.* (§57 Q)

MARK J For[41] whosoever shall give you a cup of water to drink, [2]because ye are Christ's, verily I say unto you, he shall in no wise lose his reward.

K but whoso shall [6] cause one of these little ones which believe on me to stumble, it is profitable for him that [3]a great millstone should be hanged about his neck, and *that* he should be sunk in the depth of the sea.

MARK K And[42] whosoever shall cause one of these little ones that believe [2]on me to stumble, it were better for him if [3]a great millstone were hanged about his neck, and he were cast into the sea.

LUKE K *It were well for him if a*[17]: *millstone were hanged about* [2] *his neck, and he were thrown into the sea, rather than that he should cause one of these little ones to stumble.* (§109 B)

L Woe unto [7] the world because of occasions of stumbling! for it must needs be that the occasions come; but woe to that man through whom the occasion cometh!

LUKE L *It is impossible but that*[17]: *occasions of stumbling should* [1] *come: but woe unto him, through whom they come!* (§109 A)

M[M] And if thy hand or [8] thy foot causeth thee to stumble, cut it off, and cast it from thee: it is good for thee to enter into life maimed or halt, rather than having two hands or two feet to be cast into the eternal fire. And if thine [9] eye causeth thee to stumble, pluck it out, and cast it from thee: it is good for thee to enter into life with one eye, rather than having two eyes to be cast into the [6]hell of fire.

MARK M[M] And if thy hand[43] cause thee to stumble, cut it off: it is good for thee to enter into life maimed, rather than having thy two hands to go into [4]hell, into the unquenchable fire.[5] And if thy foot[45] cause thee to stumble, cut it off: it is good for thee to enter into life halt, rather than having thy two feet to be cast into [4]hell.[5] And if thine eye cause[47] thee to stumble, cast it out: it is good for thee to enter into the kingdom of God with one eye, rather than having two eyes to be cast into [4]hell;

N where their worm dieth not,[48] and the fire is not quenched. For every one shall be salted[49] with fire.[7]

O *Ye are the salt of the earth:* [5]: *but if the salt have lost its*[13] *savour, wherewith shall it be salted? it is thenceforth good for nothing, but to be cast out and trodden under foot of men.* (§36 KL)

MARK O Salt is good: but[50] if the salt have lost its saltness, wherewith will ye season it? Have salt in yourselves, and be at peace one with another.

LUKE O *Salt therefore is good: but*[14]: *if even the salt have lost its*[34] *savour, wherewith shall it be seasoned? It is fit neither*[35] *for the land nor for the dunghill: men cast it out.* (§104 E)

P See that ye despise not one[10] of these little ones; for I say unto you, that in heaven their angels do always behold the face of my Father which is in heaven.[8]

ERV margin: [1] Greek *in name that ye are*   [2] Many ancient authorities omit *on me*   [3] Greek *a millstone turned by an ass*   [4] Greek *Gehenna*   [5] Verses 44 and 46 (which are identical with verse 48) are omitted by the best ancient authorities   [6] Greek *Gehenna of fire*   [7] Many ancient authorities add *and every sacrifice shall be salted with salt*: see Leviticus 2:13   [8] Many authorities, some ancient, insert verse 11: *For the Son of man came to save that which was lost*: see Luke 19:10

OT references: Mk 9:48 = Isaiah 66:24   Mk 9:49 = Leviticus 2:13

M And if thy right eye causeth thee to stumble, pluck it out, and cast it from thee: for it is profitable for thee that one of thy members should perish, and not thy whole body be cast into hell. And if thy right hand causeth thee to stumble, cut it off, and cast it from thee: for it is profitable for thee that one of thy members should perish, and not thy whole body go into hell. (§37 c = Mt 5:29-30)

MATT 18

Q How think ye? if[12] any man have a hundred sheep, and one of them be gone astray, doth he not leave the ninety and nine, and go unto the mountains, and seek that which goeth astray? And if so be that he find it,[13] verily I say unto you, he rejoiceth over it more than over the ninety and nine which have not gone astray. Even[14] so it is not [1]the will of [2]your Father which is in heaven, that one of these little ones should perish.

R And if thy brother sin[15] [3]against thee, go, shew him his fault between thee and him alone: if he hear thee, thou hast gained thy brother.
S But[16] if he hear *thee* not, take with thee one or two more, that at the mouth of two witnesses or three every word may be established. And if he refuse[17] to hear them, tell it unto the [4]church: and if he refuse to hear the [4]church also, let him be unto thee as the Gentile and the publican.
T[T] Verily I[18] say unto you, What things soever ye shall bind on earth shall be bound in heaven: and what things soever ye shall loose on earth shall be loosed in heaven.
U Again I say unto[19] you, that if two of you shall agree on earth as touching anything that they shall ask, it shall be done for them of my Father which is in heaven. For where two or three are[20] gathered together in my name, there am I in the midst of them.
V Then came Peter, and said[21] to him, Lord, how oft shall my brother sin against me, and I forgive him? until seven times? Jesus saith unto him,[22] I say not unto thee, Until seven times; but, Until [5]seventy times seven.

LUKE

Q *What man of you, having a*[15:] *hundred sheep, and having lost 4 one of them, doth not leave the ninety and nine in the wilderness, and go after that which is lost, until he find it? And 5 when he hath found it, he layeth it on his shoulders, rejoicing. And when he cometh home, he 6 calleth together his friends and his neighbours, saying unto them, Rejoice with me, for I have found my sheep which was lost. I say unto you, that even 7 so there shall be joy in heaven over one sinner that repenteth, more than over ninety and nine righteous persons, which need no repentance.* (§105 B)
R *Take heed to yourselves: if*[17:] *thy brother sin, rebuke him; 3 and if he repent, forgive him.*

V *And if he sin against thee*[2] *seven times in the day, and seven times turn again to thee, saying, I repent; thou shalt forgive him.* (§109 CD)

ERV margin: 1 Greek *a thing willed before your Father* 2 Some ancient authorities read *my* 3 Some ancient authorities omit *against thee* 4 Or *congregation* 5 Or *seventy times and seven*

OT references: Mt 18:16 = Deuteronomy 19:15

T I will give unto thee the keys of the kingdom of heaven: and whatsoever thou shalt bind on earth shall be bound in heaven: and whatsoever thou shalt loose on earth shall be loosed in heaven. (§71 F = Mt 16:19)

MATT 18

w   There-²³
fore is the kingdom of heaven
likened unto a certain king,
which would make a reckoning with his ¹servants.   And²⁴
when he had begun to reckon,
one was brought unto him,
which owed him ten thousand
²talents.   But forasmuch as he²⁵
had not *wherewith* to pay, his
lord commanded him to be
sold, and his wife, and children, and all that he had, and
payment to be made.   The²⁶
³servant   therefore fell down
and worshipped him, saying,
Lord, have patience with me,
and I will pay thee all.   And²⁷
the lord of that ³servant, being moved with compassion,
released him, and forgave him
the ⁴debt.   But that ³serv-²⁸
ant went out, and found one
of his fellow-servants, which
owed him a hundred ⁵pence:
and he laid hold on him, and
took *him* by the throat, saying, Pay what thou owest.
So his fellow-servant fell down²⁹
and besought him, saying,
Have patience with me, and
I will pay thee. And he³⁰
would not: but went and cast
him into prison, till he should
pay that which was due.   So³¹
when his fellow-servants saw
what was done, they were
exceeding sorry, and came and
told unto their lord all that
was done.   Then his lord³²
called him unto him, and saith
to him, Thou wicked ³servant, I forgave thee all that
debt, because thou besought-
est me: shouldest not thou³³
also have had mercy on thy
fellow-servant, even as I had
mercy on thee? And his³⁴
lord was wroth, and delivered
him to the tormentors, till he
should pay all that was due.

x˟ So shall also my heavenly³⁵
Father do unto you, if ye forgive not every one his brother
from your hearts.

ERV margin: 1 Greek *bondservants*   2 This talent was probably worth about £ 240   3 Greek *bondservant*
4 Greek *loan*   5 The word in the Greek denotes a coin worth about eight pence halfpenny

x   But if ye forgive not men their trespasses, neither will your Father forgive your trespasses.   (§37 x = Mt 6:15)
x   And whensoever ye stand praying, forgive, if ye have aught against any one; that your Father also which is in
heaven may forgive you your trespasses.   (§127 E = Mk 11:25)

CHAPTER XIII

DEPARTURE FROM GALILEE FOR JERUSALEM

§ 79 GENERAL STATEMENT OF JOURNEY

MATT 19:1–2

And it came to pass when Jesus had finished these words, he departed from Galilee, and came into the borders of Judæa beyond Jordan; and great multitudes followed him; and he healed them there.

MARK 10:1

And he arose from thence, and cometh into the borders of Judæa and beyond Jordan: and multitudes come together unto him again; and, as he was wont, he taught them again.

LUKE 9:51

And it came to pass, when the days were well-nigh come that he should be received up, he stedfastly set his face to go to Jerusalem.

§ 80 ATTITUDE OF SAMARITANS TOWARD JESUS

LUKE 9:52–56

And he sent messengers before his face: and they went, and entered into a village of the Samaritans, to make ready for him. And they did not receive him, because his face was *as though he were* going to Jerusalem. And when his disciples James and John saw *this*, they said, Lord, wilt thou that we bid fire to come down from heaven, and consume them?[2] But he turned, and rebuked them.[3] And they went to another village.

§ 81 SOME TESTS OF DISCIPLESHIP

MATT 8:19–22

A *And there came [4]a scribe, and said unto him, [5]Master, I will follow thee whithersoever thou goest. And Jesus saith unto him, The foxes have holes, and the birds of the heaven have [6]nests; but the Son of man hath not where to lay his head.*

B *And another of the disciples said unto him, Lord, suffer me first to go and bury my father. But Jesus saith unto him, Follow me; and leave the dead to bury their own dead. (§50 B)*

LUKE 9:57–62

A And as they went in the way, a certain man said unto him, I will follow thee whithersoever thou goest. And Jesus said unto him, The foxes have holes, and the birds of the heaven *have* [6]nests; but the Son of man hath not where to lay his head.

B And he said unto another, Follow me. But he said, Lord, suffer me first to go and bury my father. But he said unto him, Leave the dead to bury their own dead; but go thou and publish abroad the kingdom of God.

C And another also said, I will follow thee, Lord; but first suffer me to bid farewell to them that are at my house. But Jesus said unto him, No man, having put his hand to the plough, and looking back, is fit for the kingdom of God.

ERV margin: 1 Greek *were being fulfilled*   2 Many ancient authorities add *even as Elijah did*   3 Some ancient authorities add *and said, Ye know not what manner of spirit ye are of:* some, but fewer, add also *For the Son of man came not to destroy men's lives, but to save them*   4 Greek *one scribe*   5 Or *Teacher*   6 Greek *lodging-places*

OT references: Lk 9:54 = 2 Kings 1:10–12

97

§ 82 THE MISSION OF THE DISCIPLES

MATTHEW

A   *Compare §56 portion C*

B   *Then saith he unto his disciples, The harvest* 9:
truly is plenteous, but the labourers are few. 37
Pray ye therefore the Lord of the harvest, that 38
he send forth labourers into his harvest. (§56 B)

C^C *And as ye go, preach, saying, The kingdom* 10:
of heaven is at hand. Heal the sick, raise the 7
dead, cleanse the lepers, cast out 2*devils: freely ye* 8
received, freely give.
D   *Compare portion M below*

E^E   *Get you no gold, nor silver,* 9
nor brass in your 3*purses; no wallet for your* 10
journey, neither two coats, nor shoes, nor staff:
F^F *for the labourer is worthy of his food. And* 11
*into whatsoever city or village ye shall enter, search
out who in it is worthy; and there abide till ye go
forth.*
G   *And as ye enter into the house, salute it.* 12
And if the house be worthy, let your peace come 13
*upon it: but if it be not worthy, let your peace
return to you.*

H   *Compare portion F above*

I   *Compare portion C above*

J^J   *And whosoever shall not receive* 14
*you, nor hear your words, as ye go forth out of
that house or that city, shake off the dust of your
feet.*

K   *Compare portion C above*

L^L   *Verily I say unto you, It shall be more* 15
*tolerable for the land of Sodom and Gomorrah in
the day of judgement, than for that city.*
     Compare portion P below

LUKE 10:1-24

A   Now after these things the Lord appointed 1
seventy[1] others, and sent them two and two
before his face into every city and place, whither
he himself was about to come.
B   And he said 2
unto them, The harvest is plenteous, but the
labourers are few: pray ye therefore the Lord
of the harvest, that he send forth labourers into
his harvest.
C^C   *Compare portion I below*
      Compare portion K below

D   Go your ways: behold, I send 3
you forth as lambs in the midst of wolves.
E^E Carry no purse, no wallet, no shoes: and 4
salute no man on the way.

F^F   *Compare portion H below*

G   And into whatso- 5
ever house ye shall 4enter, first say, Peace be to
this house. And if a son of peace be there, 6
your peace shall rest upon 5him: but if not, it
shall turn to you again.
H   And in that same 7
house remain, eating and drinking such things
as they give: for the labourer is worthy of his
hire. Go not from house to house. And into 8
whatsoever city ye enter, and they receive you,
eat such things as are set before you:
I   and heal 9
the sick that are therein, and say unto them,
The kingdom of God is come nigh unto you.
J^J But into whatsoever city ye shall enter, and 10
they receive you not, go out into the streets
thereof and say, Even the dust from your city, 11
that cleaveth to our feet, we do wipe off against
you:
K   howbeit know this, that the kingdom of
God is come nigh.
L^L   I say unto you, It shall be 12
more tolerable in that day for Sodom, than for
that city.

ERV margin: 1 Many ancient authorities add *and two:* and so in verse 17   2 Greek *demons*   3 Greek *girdles*
4 Or *enter first, say*   5 Or *it*

c   *Matt parallel shown above under C*

E   *Matt parallel shown above under E*

F   *Matt parallel shown above under F*

J   *Matt parallel shown above under J*

L   **Compare** portion P below

E And he charged them that they
should take nothing for *their* journey,
save a staff only; no bread, no wallet,
no money in their purse; but *to go*
shod with sandals: and, *said he,* put
not on two coats.
F   And he said unto
them, Wheresoever ye enter into a
house, there abide till ye depart
thence.
J   And whatsoever place shall
not receive you, and they hear you
not, as ye go forth thence, shake off
the dust that is under your feet for
a testimony unto them. (§56 G–K =
Mk 6:8–11)

c   And he sent them forth to preach
the kingdom of God, and to heal the
sick.
E   And he said unto them, Take
nothing for your journey, neither
staff, nor wallet, nor bread, nor
money; neither have two coats.

F And into whatsoever house ye
enter, there abide, and thence
depart.

J   And as many as receive you
not, when ye depart from that city,
shake off the dust from your feet for
a testimony against them. (§56 F–
K = Lk 9:2–5)

MATTHEW

M *Behold, I send you forth as sheep in the[16] midst of wolves: be ye therefore wise as serpents, and [1]harmless as doves.* (§56 F–M)

N *Woe unto thee, Chorazin! woe unto thee,[11]: Bethsaida! for if the [2]mighty works had been[21] done in Tyre and Sidon which were done in you, they would have repented long ago in sackcloth and ashes. Howbeit I say unto you, it shall be[22] more tolerable for Tyre and Sidon in the day of judgement, than for you. And thou, Capernaum,[23] shalt thou be exalted unto heaven? thou shalt [3]go down unto Hades.*

O *for if the [2]mighty works had been done in Sodom which were done in thee, it would have remained until this day.*

P[P] *Howbeit[24] I say unto you, that it shall be more tolerable for the land of Sodom in the day of judgement, than for thee.* (§41 L–O)

Q[Q] *He that receiveth you receiveth me, and he[10]: that receiveth me receiveth him that sent me.[40]* (§57 P)

S *At that season Jesus answered and said, I[11]: [6]thank thee, O Father, Lord of heaven and earth,[25] that thou didst hide these things from the wise and understanding, and didst reveal them unto babes: yea, Father, [7]for so it was well-pleasing in thy[26] sight.*

T[T] *All things have been delivered unto me of[27] my Father: and no one knoweth the Son, save the Father; neither doth any know the Father, save the Son, and he to whomsoever the Son willeth to reveal him.* (§41 PQ)

U *But blessed are your eyes, for they see; and[13]: your ears, for they hear. For verily I say unto[16] you, that many prophets and righteous men desired to see the things which ye see, and saw them not; and to hear the things which ye hear, and heard them not.* (§47 K)

LUKE 10

M *Compare portion D above*

N Woe unto thee, Chorazin! woe unto thee,[13] Bethsaida! for if the [2]mighty works had been done in Tyre and Sidon, which were done in you, they would have repented long ago, sitting in sackcloth and ashes. Howbeit it shall be[14] more tolerable for Tyre and Sidon in the judgement, than for you. And thou, Capernaum,[15] shalt thou be exalted unto heaven? thou shalt be brought down unto Hades.

P[P] *Compare portion L above*

Q[Q] He that heareth[16] you heareth me; and he that rejecteth you rejecteth me; and he that rejecteth me rejecteth him that sent me.

R[R] And the seventy returned with joy, saying,[17] Lord, even the [4]devils are subject unto us in thy name. And he said unto them, I beheld[18] Satan fallen as lightning from heaven. Behold, I have given you authority to tread upon serpents and scorpions, and over all the power of the enemy: and nothing shall in any wise hurt you. Howbeit in this rejoice not, that[20] the spirits are subject unto you; but rejoice that your names are written in heaven.

S In that same hour he rejoiced [5]in the Holy[21] Spirit, and said, I [6]thank thee, O Father, Lord of heaven and earth, that thou didst hide these things from the wise and understanding, and didst reveal them unto babes: yea, Father; [7]for so it was well-pleasing in thy sight.

T[T] All things have been delivered unto me[22] of my Father: and no one knoweth who the Son is, save the Father; and who the Father is, save the Son, and he to whomsoever the Son willeth to reveal *him.*

U And turning to the dis-[23] ciples, he said privately, Blessed *are* the eyes which see the things that ye see: for I say unto[24] you, that many prophets and kings desired to see the things which ye see, and saw them not; and to hear the things which ye hear, and heard them not.

ERV margin: 1 Or *simple*   2 Greek *powers*   3 Many ancient authorities read *be brought down*   4 Greek *demons*   5 Or *by*   6 Or *praise*   7 Or *that*

OT references: Mt 11:23ᵃ and Lk 10:15 = Isaiah 14:13–15   Mt 11:23ᵇ–24 and Lk 10:12 = Genesis 19:24

P Compare portion L above

Q And whoso shall receive one such little child in my name receiveth me. (§78 F = Mt 18:5)

Q Whosoever shall receive one of such little children in my name, receiveth me: and whosoever receiveth me, receiveth not me, but him that sent me. (§78 FG = Mk 9:37)

Q Whosoever shall receive this little child in my name receiveth me: and whosoever shall receive me receiveth him that sent me. (§78 FG = Lk 9:48)

R For another record of a report on a Tour, compare §59

R And these signs shall follow them that believe: in my name shall they cast out devils; they shall speak with new tongues; they shall take up serpents, and if they drink any deadly thing, it shall in no wise hurt them; they shall lay hands on the sick, and they shall recover. (§150 footnote E)

T All authority hath been given unto me in heaven and on earth. (§151 B = Mt 28:18)

§ 83　THE WAY OF ETERNAL LIFE

LUKE 10:25-37

A *For an account in Matt-Mark of somewhat similar general content, compare §130 L-N*

A And behold, a certain lawyer stood up and[25] tempted him, saying, [1]Master, what shall I do to inherit eternal life? And he said unto[26] him, What is written in the law? how readest thou? And he answering said, Thou shalt love[27] the Lord thy God [2]with all thy heart, and with all thy soul, and with all thy strength, and with all thy mind; and thy neighbour as thyself. And he said unto him, Thou hast[28] answered right: this do, and thou shalt live.

B But he, desiring to justify himself, said unto[29] Jesus, And who is my neighbour? Jesus made[30] answer and said,

C A certain man was going down from Jerusalem to Jericho; and he fell among robbers, which both stripped him and beat him, and departed, leaving him half dead. And by chance a certain priest was going down[31] that way: and when he saw him, he passed by on the other side. And in like manner a Levite[32] also, when he came to the place, and saw him, passed by on the other side. But a certain[33] Samaritan, as he journeyed, came where he was: and when he saw him, he was moved with compassion, and came to him,[34] and bound up his wounds, pouring on *them* oil and wine; and he set him on his own beast, and brought him to an inn, and took care of him. And on the morrow he took out two[35] [3]pence, and gave them to the host, and said, Take care of him; and whatsoever thou spendest more, I, when I come back again, will repay thee.

D Which of these three, thinkest thou,[36] proved neighbour unto him that fell among the robbers? And he said, He that shewed mercy[37] on him. And Jesus said unto him, Go, and do thou likewise.

§ 84　MANY THINGS *vs* ONE THING

LUKE 10:38-42

Now as they went on their way, he entered[38] into a certain village: and a certain woman named Martha received him into her house. And she had a sister called Mary, which also[39] sat at the Lord's feet, and heard his word. But[40] Martha was [4]cumbered about much serving; and she came up to him, and said, Lord, dost thou not care that my sister did leave me to serve alone? bid her therefore that she help me. But the Lord answered and said unto her,[41] [5]Martha, Martha, thou art anxious and troubled about many things: [6]but one thing[42] is needful: for Mary hath chosen the good part, which shall not be taken away from her.

ERV margin:　1 Or *Teacher*　2 Greek *from*　3 The word in the Greek denotes a coin worth about eight pence halfpenny　4 Greek *distracted*　5 A few ancient authorities read *Martha, Martha, thou art troubled: Mary hath chosen etc.*　6 Many ancient authorities read *but few things are needful, or one*

OT references:　Lk 10:27 = Deuteronomy 6:5 and Leviticus 19:18　Lk 10:28 = Leviticus 18:5

§ 85 ELEMENTS OF PREVAILING PRAYER

MATTHEW

LUKE 11:1–13

A And it came to pass, as he was praying in [1] a certain place, that when he ceased, one of his disciples said unto him, Lord, teach us to pray, even as John also taught his disciples.

B *After this manner therefore pray ye: Our* [6]: *Father which art in heaven, Hallowed be thy* [9] *name. Thy kingdom come. Thy will be*[10] *done, as in heaven, so on earth. Give us this*[11] *day* [3]*our daily bread. And forgive us our*[12] *debts, as we also have forgiven our debtors. And*[13] *bring us not into temptation, but deliver us from* [5]*the evil* one.[6] (§37 W)

B And he [2] said unto them, When ye pray, say, [1]Father, Hallowed be thy name. Thy kingdom come.[2] Give us day by day [3]our daily bread. And [3] forgive us our sins; for we ourselves also for- [4] give every one that is indebted to us. And bring us not into temptation.[4]

c And he said unto them, Which of you shall [5] have a friend, and shall go unto him at mid- night, and say to him, Friend, lend me three loaves; for a friend of mine is come to me from [6] a journey, and I have nothing to set before him; and he from within shall answer and say, [7] Trouble me not: the door is now shut, and my children are with me in bed; I cannot rise and give thee? I say unto you, Though he will [8] not rise and give him, because he is his friend, yet because of his importunity he will arise and give him [7]as many as he needeth.

D *Ask, and it shall be given you; seek, and ye* [7]: *shall find; knock, and it shall be opened unto* 7 *you: for every one that asketh receiveth; and he* [8] *that seeketh findeth; and to him that knocketh it shall be opened. Or what man is there of you,* 9 *who, if his son shall ask him for a loaf, will give him a stone; or if he shall ask for a fish,*10 *will give him a serpent? If ye then, being evil,*11 *know how to give good gifts unto your children, how much more shall your Father which is in heaven give good things to them that ask him?* (§38 K)

D And I say [9] unto you, Ask, and it shall be given you; seek, and ye shall find; knock, and it shall be opened unto you. For every one that asketh re-[10] ceiveth; and he that seeketh findeth; and to him that knocketh it shall be opened. And[11] of which of you that is a father shall his son ask [8]a loaf, and he give him a stone? or a fish, and he for a fish give him a serpent? Or *if he*[12] shall ask an egg, will he give him a scorpion? If ye then, being evil, know how to give good[13] gifts unto your children, how much more shall *your* heavenly Father give the Holy Spirit to them that ask him?

§ 86 A CHARGE OF ALLIANCE WITH SATAN

MATTHEW 12

LUKE 11:14–26

A[A] *Then was brought unto him* [9]*one possessed*22 *with a devil, blind and dumb: and he healed him, insomuch that the dumb man spake and saw.*

A[A] And he was casting out a [10]devil *which was*14 dumb. And it came to pass, when the [10]devil was gone out, the dumb man spake;

B[B] *And all the multitudes were amazed, and*23 *said, Is this the son of David?*

B[B] and the multitudes marvelled.

C[O] *But when the*24 *Pharisees heard it, they said, This man doth not cast out* [11]*devils, but* [12]*by Beelzebub the prince of the* [11]*devils.*

C[O] But some of them [15] said, [13]By Beelzebub the prince of the [11]devils casteth he out [11]devils.

D *Compare §45Q and attached references*

D And others, tempting[16] *him,* sought of him a sign from heaven.

ERV margin: [1] Many ancient authorities read *Our Father, which art in heaven:* see Matt 6:9 [2] Many ancient authorities add *Thy will be done, as in heaven, so on earth:* see Matt 6:10 [3] Greek *our bread for the coming day* [4] Many ancient authorities add *but deliver us from the evil* one (or *from evil*): see Matt 6:13 [5] Or *evil* [6] Many authorities, some ancient, but with variations, add *For thine is the kingdom, and the power, and the glory, for ever. Amen* [7] Or *whatsoever things* [8] Some ancient authorities omit *a loaf, and he give him a stone?* or [9] Or *a demoniac* [10] Greek *demon* [11] Greek *demons* [12] Or *in* [13] Or *In*

ABC For another Matthew account covering portions ABC, compare §53 B

c *Matt parallel shown above under C*   c And the scribes which came down from Jerusalem said, He hath Beelzebub, and, By the prince of the devils casteth he out the devils. (§45 C=Mk 3:22)

MATT 12

E[E]   *And knowing their thoughts he said[25] unto them, Every kingdom divided against itself is brought to desolation; and every city or house divided against itself shall not stand: and if[26] Satan casteth out Satan, he is divided against himself; how then shall his kingdom stand?*

F *And if I [3]by Beelzebub cast out [2]devils, [3]by[27] whom do your sons cast them out? therefore shall they be your judges. But if I [3]by the Spirit of[28] God cast out [2]devils, then is the kingdom of God come upon you.*

G[G]   *Or how can one enter into the[29] house of the strong* man, *and spoil his goods, except he first bind the strong* man? *and then he will spoil his house.*

H[H]   *He that is not with me is[30] against me; and he that gathereth not with me scattereth.* (§45 A-H)

I *But the unclean spirit, when [4]he is gone out[43] of the man, passeth through waterless places, seeking rest, and findeth it not. Then [4]he saith,[44] I will return into my house whence I came out; and when [4]he is come, [4]he findeth it empty, swept, and garnished. Then goeth [4]he, and taketh with[45] [5]himself seven other spirits more evil than [5]himself, and they enter in and dwell there: and the last state of that man becometh worse than the first.* (§45 W)

LUKE 11

E[E]   But[17] he, knowing their thoughts, said unto them, Every kingdom divided against itself is brought to desolation; [1]and a house *divided* against a house falleth. And if Satan also is divided[18] against himself, how shall his kingdom stand? because ye say that I cast out [2]devils [3]by Beelzebub.

F   And if I [3]by Beelzebub cast out[19] [2]devils, by whom do your sons cast them out? therefore shall they be your judges. But if I[20] by the finger of God cast out [2]devils, then is the kingdom of God come upon you.

G[G]   When[21] the strong *man* fully armed guardeth his own court, his goods are in peace: but when a[22] stronger than he shall come upon him, and overcome him, he taketh from him his whole armour wherein he trusted, and divideth his spoils.

H[H]   He that is not with me is against me;[23] and he that gathereth not with me scattereth.

I The unclean spirit when [4]he is gone out of the[24] man, passeth through waterless places, seeking rest; and finding none, [4]he saith, I will turn back unto my house whence I came out. And[25] when [4]he is come, [4]he findeth it swept and garnished. Then goeth [4]he, and taketh *to him*[26] seven other spirits more evil than [5]himself; and they enter in and dwell there: and the last state of that man becometh worse than the first.

§ 87   BASIS OF REAL RELATIONSHIP TO JESUS

For an account in Matt-Mark-Luke of similar general content, compare §46

LUKE 11:27-28

And it came to pass, as he said these things,[27] a certain woman out of the multitude lifted up her voice, and said unto him, Blessed is the womb that bare thee, and the breasts which thou didst suck. But he said, Yea rather,[28] blessed are they that hear the word of God, and keep it.

ERV margin: 1 Or *and house falleth upon house*   2 Greek *demons*   3 Or *in*   4 Or *it*   5 Or *itself*

E   *Matt parallel shown above under E*   E And he called them unto him, and said unto them in parables, How can Satan cast out Satan? And if a kingdom be divided against itself, that kingdom cannot stand. **And** if a house be divided against itself, that house will not be able to stand. And if Satan hath risen up against himself, and is divided, he cannot stand, but hath an end.

G   *Matt parallel shown above under G*   G   But no one can enter into the house of the strong *man*, and spoil his goods, except he first bind the strong *man;* and then he will spoil his house. (§45 E-G = Mk 3:23-27)

H   With the first half of this saying, compare the last verse of §78 portion I

CHAPTER XIV

CONDEMNATION FOR OPPONENTS AND CONCERN FOR DISCIPLES

§ 88 PHARISEES DEMAND SIGNS FROM JESUS

MATT 12:38-42

A^A *Then certain of the scribes and Pharisees*38 *answered him, saying, ¹Master, we would see a sign from thee.*
B^B   *But he answered and said unto*39 *them, An evil and adulterous generation seeketh after a sign; and there shall no sign be given to it but the sign of Jonah the prophet:*

C   *for as Jonah*40 *was three days and three nights in the belly of the ²whale; so shall the Son of man be three days and three nights in the heart of the earth.*
D   *Compare portion F below*

E   *The men*41 *of Nineveh shall stand up in the judgement with this generation, and shall condemn it: for they repented at the preaching of Jonah; and behold, ³a greater than Jonah is here.*
F   *The queen of the*42 *south shall rise up in the judgement with this generation, and shall condemn it: for she came from the ends of the earth to hear the wisdom of Solomon; and behold, ³a greater than Solomon is here.* (§45 Q–V)

LUKE 11:29-32

A^A   *Compare §86 portion D*

B^B And when the multitudes were gathering²9 together unto him, he began to say, This generation is an evil generation: it seeketh after a sign; and there shall no sign be given to it but the sign of Jonah.

C   For even as Jonah became3⁰ a sign unto the Ninevites, so shall also the Son of man be to this generation.

D   The queen of3¹ the south shall rise up in the judgement with the men of this generation, and shall condemn them: for she came from the ends of the earth to hear the wisdom of Solomon; and behold, ³a greater than Solomon is here.

E   The men of3² Nineveh shall stand up in the judgement with this generation, and shall condemn it: for they repented at the preaching of Jonah; and behold, ³a greater than Jonah is here.
F   *Compare portion D above*

§ 89 THE USE AND TEST OF TRUTH

MATTHEW

A^A *Neither do* men *light a lamp, and put it* 5: *under the bushel, but on the stand; and it shineth*15 *unto all that are in the house.* (§36 N)

LUKE 11:33-36

A^A No man, when he hath lighted a lamp,33 putteth it in a cellar, neither under the bushel, but on the stand, that they which enter in may see the light.

ERV margin:	1 Or *Teacher*	2 Greek *sea-monster*	3 Greek *more than*

OT references:	Mt 12:39 and Lk 11:29=Jonah 3:1-4	Mt 12:40=Jonah 1:17	Mt 12:42 and Lk 11:31=
1 Kings 10:1-3	Mt 12:41 and Lk 11:32=Jonah 3:5-10		

A And the Pharisees and Sadducees came, and tempting him asked him to shew them a sign from heaven.

B But he answered and said unto them, ... An evil and adulterous generation seeketh after a sign; and there shall no sign be given unto it, but the sign of Jonah. And he left them, and departed. (§68 A–D=Mt 16:1-4)

A And the Pharisees came forth, and began to question with him, seeking of him a sign from heaven, tempting him.
B   And he sighed deeply in his spirit, and saith, Why doth this generation seek a sign? verily I say unto you, There shall no sign be given unto this generation. And he left them, and again entering into *the boat* departed to the other side. (§68 A–D=Mk 8:11-13)

A Is the lamp brought to be put under the bushel, or under the bed, *and* not to be put on the stand? (§47 Q=Mk 4:21)

A And no man, when he hath lighted a lamp, covereth it with a vessel, or putteth it under a bed; but putteth it on a stand, that they which enter in may see the light. (§47 Q=Lk 8:16)

MATTHEW

B *The lamp of the body is the eye: if therefore* 6:
thine eye be single, thy whole body shall be full of 22
light. But if thine eye be evil, thy whole body 23
shall be full of darkness.
C   *If therefore the light
that is in thee be darkness, how great is the darkness!* (§38 B)

LUKE 11

B   The lamp of thy body is thine 34
eye: when thine eye is single, thy whole body
also is full of light; but when it is evil, thy body
also is full of darkness.
C   Look therefore whether 35
the light that is in thee be not darkness.

D   If 36
therefore thy whole body be full of light,
having no part dark, it shall be wholly full of
light, as when the lamp with its bright shining
doth give thee light.

§ 90 DISCOURSE ON THE SCRIBES AND PHARISEES

MATTHEW 23

A *Compare §63 portions ABC*

B *Woe unto you, scribes and Pharisees, hypo-* 25
*crites! for ye cleanse the outside of the cup and of
the platter, but within they are full from extortion
and excess. Thou blind Pharisee, cleanse first* 26
*the inside of the cup and of the platter, that the
outside thereof may become clean also.* (§132 M)

C *Woe unto you, scribes and Pharisees, hypo-* 23
crites! for ye tithe mint and ³*anise and cummin,
and have left undone the weightier matters of the
law, judgement, and mercy, and faith: but these
ye ought to have done, and not to have left the other
undone. Ye blind guides, which strain out the* 24
gnat, and swallow the camel. (§132 L)

D^D *But all their works they do for to be seen of* 5
*men: for they make broad their phylacteries, and
enlarge the borders* of *their garments, and love* 6
*the chief place at feasts, and the chief seats in the
synagogues, and the salutations in the market-* 7
places, and to be called of men, Rabbi. (§132 D)

E *Woe unto you, scribes and Pharisees, hypo-* 27
*crites! for ye are like unto whited sepulchres,
which outwardly appear beautiful, but inwardly
are full of dead men's bones, and of all uncleanness. Even so ye also outwardly appear right-* 28
*eous unto men, but inwardly ye are full of hypoc-
risy and iniquity.* (§132 N)

G *Yea, they bind heavy burdens* ⁵*and grievous* 4
*to be borne, and lay them on men's shoulders;
but they themselves will not move them with their
finger.* (§132 C)

LUKE 11:37-54

A Now as he spake, a Pharisee asketh him to 37
¹dine with him: and he went in, and sat down
to meat. And when the Pharisee saw it, he 38
marvelled that he had not first washed before
¹dinner. And the Lord said unto him,   39
B   Now do
ye Pharisees cleanse the outside of the cup and
of the platter; but your inward part is full of
extortion and wickedness. Ye foolish ones, 40
did not he that made the outside make the
inside also? Howbeit give for alms those 41
things which ²are within; and behold, all things
are clean unto you.
C But woe unto you Pharisees! for ye tithe 42
mint and rue and every herb, and pass over
judgement and the love of God: but these
ought ye to have done, and not to leave the
other undone.

D^D   Woe unto you Pharisees! for 43
ye love the chief seats in the synagogues, and
the salutations in the marketplaces.

E   Woe unto 44
you! for ye are as the tombs which appear not,
and the men that walk over *them* know it not.

F And one of the lawyers answering saith unto 45
him, ⁴Master, in saying this thou reproachest
us also. And he said,   46
G   Woe unto you lawyers
also! for ye lade men with burdens grievous
to be borne, and ye yourselves touch not the
burdens with one of your fingers.

ERV margin: 1 Greek *breakfast*   2 Or *ye can*   3 Or *dill*   4 Or *Teacher*   5 Many ancient authorities omit
and grievous to be borne

OT references: Mt 23:5 = Exodus 13:9 and Numbers 15:38-39 and Deuteronomy 6:8 and 11:18   Mt 23:23
and Lk 11:42 = Leviticus 27:30 and Micah 6:8

D *Matt parallel shown above under D*

D Beware of the scribes, which desire to walk in long robes, and *to
have* salutations in the marketplaces,
and chief seats in the synagogues,
and chief places at feasts. (§132 D =
Mk 12:38-39)

D Beware of the scribes, which desire to walk in long robes, and love
salutations in the marketplaces, and
chief seats in the synagogues, and
chief places at feasts. (§132 D = Lk
20:46)

MATT 23	LUKE 11
H *Woe unto you, scribes and Pharisees, hypo-*29 *crites! for ye build the sepulchres of the prophets, and garnish the tombs of the righteous, and say,*30 *If we had been in the days of our fathers, we should not have been partakers with them in the blood of the prophets. Wherefore ye witness to*31 *yourselves, that ye are sons of them that slew the prophets.* (§*132* O)	H Woe unto47 you! for ye build the tombs of the prophets, and your fathers killed them. So ye are wit-48 nesses and consent unto the works of your fathers: for they killed them, and ye build *their* tombs.
I *Therefore, behold, I send unto you prophets,*34 *and wise men, and scribes: some of them shall ye kill and crucify; and some of them shall ye scourge in your synagogues, and persecute from city to city: that upon you may come all the*35 *righteous blood shed on the earth, from the blood of Abel the righteous unto the blood of Zachariah son of Barachiah, whom ye slew between the sanctuary and the altar. Verily I say unto you, All these*36 *things shall come upon this generation.* (§*132* Q)	I Therefore also said the wisdom of God, I49 will send unto them prophets and apostles; and *some* of them they shall kill and persecute; that50 the blood of all the prophets, which was shed from the foundation of the world, may be required of this generation; from the blood of51 Abel unto the blood of Zachariah, who perished between the altar and the ¹sanctuary: yea, I say unto you, it shall be required of this generation.
J *But woe unto you, scribes and Pharisees,*13 *hypocrites! because ye shut the kingdom of heaven* ²*against men: for ye enter not in yourselves, neither suffer ye them that are entering in to enter.*³ (§*132* I)	J Woe unto you lawyers! for ye took away52 the key of knowledge: ye entered not in yourselves, and them that were entering in ye hindered.
	K And when he was come out from thence,53 the scribes and the Pharisees began to ⁴press upon *him* vehemently, and to provoke him to speak of ⁵many things; laying wait for him, to54 catch something out of his mouth.

§91 INJUNCTIONS FOR THE FUTURE OF THE DISCIPLES

MATTHEW	LUKE 12:1-12
	A In the mean time, when ⁶the many thou- I sands of the multitude were gathered together, insomuch that they trode one upon another, he began to ⁷say unto his disciples first of all,
B^B *But beware of the leaven of the Pharisees*16: *and Sadducees.* (§ *69* D) 11	B^B Beware ye of the leaven of the Pharisees, which is hypocrisy.
C^C *For there is nothing covered, that shall not be*10: *revealed; and hid, that shall not be known.*26	C^C But there is nothing 2 covered up, that shall not be revealed: and hid, that shall not be known.
D *What I tell you in the darkness, speak ye in the*27 *light: and what ye hear in the ear, proclaim upon the housetops.*	D Wherefore what- 3 soever ye have said in the darkness shall be heard in the light; and what ye have spoken in the ear in the inner chambers shall be proclaimed upon the housetops.
E *And be not afraid of them which*28 *kill the body, but are not able to kill the soul: but rather fear him which is able to destroy both soul and body in* ⁹*hell.*	E And I say unto 4 you my friends, Be not afraid of them which kill the body, and after that have no more that they can dò. But I will warn you whom ye 5 shall fear: Fear him, which after he hath killed hath ⁸power to cast into ⁹hell; yea, I say unto you, Fear him.

ERV margin: 1 Greek *house* 2 Greek *before* 3 Some authorities insert here, or after verse 12, verse 14: *Woe unto you, scribes and Pharisees, hypocrites! for ye devour widows' houses, even while for a pretence ye make long prayers: therefore ye shall receive greater condemnation:* see Mark 12:40 and Luke 20:47 4 Or *set themselves vehemently against him* 5 Or *more* 6 Greek *the myriads of* 7 Or *say unto his disciples, First of all beware ye* 8 Or *authority* 9 Greek *Gehenna*

OT references: Mt 23:35 and Lk 11:50-51 = Genesis 4:8 and 2 Chronicles 24:20-21

B Take heed and beware of the leaven of the Pharisees and Sadducees. (§69 A = Mt 16:6)	B Take heed, beware of the leaven of the Pharisees and the leaven of Herod. (§69 A = Mk 8:15) c For there is nothing hid, save that it should be manifested; neither was *anything* made secret, but that it should come to light. (§47 R = Mk 4:22)	c For nothing is hid, that shall not be made manifest; nor *anything* secret, that shall not be known and come to light. (§47 R = Lk 8:17)

MATTHEW

F^F *Are not two sparrows sold for²⁹ a farthing? and not one of them shall fall on the ground without your Father: but the very hairs³⁰ of your head are all numbered. Fear not there-³¹ fore; ye are of more value than many sparrows.*

G^G *Every one therefore who shall confess ¹me³² before men, ²him will I also confess before my Father which is in heaven. But whosoever shall³³ deny me before men, him will I also deny before my Father which is in heaven.* (§57 H–K)

H^H *And whosoever shall speak a word against¹²: the Son of man, it shall be forgiven him; but³² whosoever shall speak against the Holy Spirit, it shall not be forgiven him.* (§45 J)

I^I *But when they deliver you up, be not anxious¹⁰: how or what ye shall speak: for it shall be given¹⁹ you in that hour what ye shall speak. For it is²⁰ not ye that speak, but the Spirit of your Father that speaketh in you.* (§57 C)

LUKE 12

F^F Are not five sparrows ⁶ sold for two farthings? and not one of them is forgotten in the sight of God. But the very ⁷ hairs of your head are all numbered. Fear not: ye are of more value than many sparrows.

G^G And I say unto you, Every one who shall ⁸ confess ¹me before men, ²him shall the Son of man also confess before the angels of God: but ⁹ he that denieth me in the presence of men shall be denied in the presence of the angels of God.

H^H And every one who shall speak a word¹⁰ against the Son of man, it shall be forgiven him: but unto him that blasphemeth against the Holy Spirit it shall not be forgiven.

I^I And¹¹ when they bring you before the synagogues, and the rulers, and the authorities, be not anxious how or what ye shall answer, or what ye shall say: for the Holy Spirit shall teach¹² you in that very hour what ye ought to say.

§92   TEACHINGS AGAINST CONCERN ABOUT WEALTH

LUKE 12:13–21

A And one out of the multitude said unto him,¹³ ³Master, bid my brother divide the inheritance with me. But he said unto him, Man, who¹⁴ made me a judge or a divider over you? And¹⁵ he said unto them, Take heed, and keep yourselves from all covetousness: ⁴for a man's life consisteth not in the abundance of the things which he possesseth.

B And he spake a parable¹⁶ unto them, saying, The ground of a certain rich man brought forth plentifully: and he¹⁷ reasoned within himself, saying, What shall I do, because I have not where to bestow my fruits? And he said, This will I do: I will pull¹⁸ down my barns, and build greater; and there will I bestow all my corn and my goods. And¹⁹ I will say to my ⁵soul, ⁵Soul, thou hast much goods laid up for many years; take thine ease, eat, drink, be merry. But God said unto him,²⁰

ERV margin: 1 Greek *in me*   2 Greek *in him*   3 Or *Teacher*   4 Greek *for not in a man's abundance consisteth his life, from the things which he possesseth*   5 Or *life*

F And not a hair of your head shall perish. (§134 M=Lk 21:18)

G For the Son of man shall come in the glory of his Father with his angels; and then shall he render unto every man according to his deeds. (§73 C=Mt 16:27)

H Therefore I say unto you, Every sin and blasphemy shall be forgiven unto men; but the blasphemy against the Spirit shall not be forgiven. . . . . neither in this world, nor in that which is to come. (§45 I–K=Mt 12:31–32)

G For whosoever shall be ashamed of me and of my words in this adulterous and sinful generation, the Son of man also shall be ashamed of him, when he cometh in the glory of his Father with the holy angels. (§73 C=Mk 8:38)

H Verily I say unto you, All their sins shall be forgiven unto the sons of men, and their blasphemies wherewith soever they shall blaspheme: but whosoever shall blaspheme against the Holy Spirit hath never forgiveness, but is guilty of an eternal sin. (§45 I–K=Mk 3:28–30)

I And when they lead you *to judgement,* and deliver you up, be not anxious beforehand what ye shall speak: but whatsoever shall be given you in that hour, that speak ye: for it is not ye that speak, but the Holy Ghost. (§134 I=Mk 13:11)

G For whosoever shall be ashamed of me and of my words, of him shall the Son of man be ashamed, when he cometh in his own glory, and *the glory* of the Father, and of the holy angels. (§73 C=Lk 9:26)

I Settle it therefore in your hearts, not to meditate beforehand how to answer: for I will give you a mouth and wisdom, which all your adversaries shall not be able to withstand or to gainsay. (§134 I= Lk 21:14–15)

LUKE 12

Thou foolish one, this night [1]is thy [2]soul required of thee; and the things which thou hast
prepared, whose shall they be?
C   So is he that[21]
layeth up treasure for himself, and is not rich
toward God.

§93 TEACHINGS AGAINST ANXIETY ABOUT FOOD AND CLOTHING

MATTHEW 6

B *Therefore I say unto you, Be not anxious for[25]
your life, what ye shall eat, or what ye shall drink;
nor yet for your body, what ye shall put on. Is
not the life more than the food, and the body than
the raiment?*

C   *Behold the birds of the heaven,[26]
that they sow not, neither do they reap, nor gather
into barns; and your heavenly Father feedeth
them. Are not ye of much more value than they?*

D *And which of you by being anxious can add[27]
one cubit unto his [4]stature? And why are ye[28]
anxious concerning raiment?*

E   *Consider the lilies
of the field, how they grow; they toil not, neither
do they spin: yet I say unto you, that even Solo-[29]
mon in all his glory was not arrayed like one of
these. But if God doth so clothe the grass of the[30]
field, which to-day is, and to-morrow is cast into the
oven, shall he not much more clothe you, O ye of
little faith?*

F[F]   *Be not therefore anxious, saying,[31]
What shall we eat? or, What shall we drink? or,
Wherewithal shall we be clothed? For after all[32]
these things do the Gentiles seek; for your heavenly
Father knoweth that ye have need of all these
things.*

G   *But seek ye first his kingdom, and his[33]
righteousness; and all these things shall be added
unto you.*

H   *Be not therefore anxious for the mor-[34]
row: for the morrow will be anxious for itself.
Sufficient unto the day is the evil thereof.* (§38 DE)

I *Lay not up for yourselves treasures upon the[19]
earth, where moth and rust doth consume, and
where thieves [6]break through and steal:*

J   *but lay up[20]
for yourselves treasures in heaven, where neither
moth nor rust doth consume, and where thieves
do not [6]break through nor steal:*

K   *for where thy[21]
treasure is, there will thy heart be also.* (§38 A)

LUKE 12:22–34

A And he said unto his disciples,   22

B   Therefore I
say unto you, Be not anxious for *your* [3]life,
what ye shall eat; nor yet for your body, what
ye shall put on. For the [3]life is more than the[23]
food, and the body than the raiment.

C   Con-[24]
sider the ravens, that they sow not, neither
reap; which have no store-chamber nor barn;
and God feedeth them: of how much more
value are ye than the birds!

D   And which of you[25]
by being anxious can add a cubit unto his
[4]stature? If then ye are not able to do even[26]
that which is least, why are ye anxious concerning the rest?

E   Consider the lilies, how they[27]
grow: they toil not, neither do they spin; yet
I say unto you, Even Solomon in all his glory
was not arrayed like one of these. But if God[28]
doth so clothe the grass in the field, which to-
day is, and to-morrow is cast into the oven;
how much more *shall he clothe* you, O ye of little
faith?

F[F]   And seek not ye what ye shall eat, and[29]
what ye shall drink, neither be ye of doubtful
mind. For all these things do the nations of[30]
the world seek after: but your Father knoweth
that ye have need of these things.

G   Howbeit[31]
seek ye [5]his kingdom, and these things shall be
added unto you.

H   Fear not, little flock; for it[32]
is your Father's good pleasure to give you the
kingdom.

I   Sell that ye have, and give alms;[33]

J make for yourselves purses which wax not
old, a treasure in the heavens that faileth not,
where no thief draweth near, neither moth
destroyeth.

K   For where your treasure is, there[34]
will your heart be also.

§94 TEACHINGS ABOUT THE FUTURE

MATT 24:43–51

A *Compare the parable recorded in §136 portion
E = Matt 25:1–10*

LUKE 12:35–48

A Let your loins be girded about, and your[35]
lamps burning; and be ye yourselves like unto[36]

ERV margin: 1 Greek *they require thy soul* 2 Or *life* 3 Or *soul* 4 Or *age* 5 Many ancient authorities read *the kingdom of God* 6 Greek *dig through*

F Be not therefore like unto them: for your Father knoweth what things ye have need of, before ye ask him. (§37 V =
Mt 6:8)

MATT 24   LUKE 12

men looking for their lord, when he shall return
from the marriage feast; that, when he cometh
and knocketh, they may straightway open unto
him.   Blessed are those [1]servants, whom the lord[37]
when he cometh shall find watching: verily I say
unto you, that he shall gird himself, and make
them sit down to meat, and shall come and serve
them.   And if he shall come in the second[38]
watch, and if in the third, and find *them* so,
blessed are those *servants*.

B   [2]*But know this, that if the master of the house43*
had known in what watch the thief was coming,
he would have watched, and would not have
suffered his house to be [3]*broken through.*

B   [2]But know this,[39]
that if the master of the house had known in
what hour the thief was coming, he would have
watched, and not have left his house to be
[3]broken through.

C[C]   *There-44*
fore be ye also ready: for in an hour that ye think
not the Son of man cometh.

C[C]   Be ye also ready: for in an[40]
hour that ye think not the Son of man cometh.

D   And Peter said, Lord, speakest thou this[41]
parable unto us, or even unto all?   And the[42]
Lord said,

E   *Who then is the45*
faithful and wise [5]*servant, whom his lord hath*
set over his household, to give them their food in
due season?   Blessed is that [5]*servant, whom his46*
lord when he cometh shall find so doing.   Verily47
I say unto you, that he will set him over all that he
hath.   But if that evil [5]*servant shall say in his48*
heart, My lord tarrieth; and shall begin to beat49
his fellow-servants, and shall eat and drink with
the drunken; the lord of that [5]*servant shall come50*
in a day when he expecteth not, and in an hour
when he knoweth not, and shall [6]*cut him asunder,51*
and appoint his portion with the hypocrites:

E   Who then is [4]the faithful and wise
steward, whom his lord shall set over his household, to give them their portion of food in due
season?   Blessed is that [5]servant, whom his[43]
lord when he cometh shall find so doing.   Of[44]
a truth I say unto you, that he will set him over
all that he hath.   But if that [5]servant shall say[45]
in his heart, My lord delayeth his coming; and
shall begin to beat the menservants and the
maidservants, and to eat and drink, and to be
drunken; the lord of that [5]servant shall come[46]
in a day when he expecteth not, and in an hour
when he knoweth not, and shall [6]cut him
asunder, and appoint his portion with the unfaithful.

F[F]   *there shall be the weeping and gnashing of*
teeth.   (§*136 A–D*)

G   And that [5]servant, which knew his[47]
lord's will, and made not ready, nor did according to his will, shall be beaten with many
stripes; but he that knew not, and did things[48]
worthy of stripes, shall be beaten with few
stripes.

H   And to whomsoever much is given,
of him shall much be required: and to whom
they commit much, of him will they ask the
more.

ERV margin: 1 Greek *bondservants*   2 Or *But this ye know*   3 Greek *digged through*   4 Or *the faithful*
steward, the wise man *whom etc.*   5 Greek *bondservant*   6 Or *severely scourge him*

C   Compare §136 B and attached references
⁖   Compare §136 D and attached references

108

CHAPTER XV

DEEP FEELING AND DIRECT TEACHING

---

§ 95 PHASES OF THE MISSION OF JESUS

MATT 10:34-36

LUKE 12:49-53

A^A I came to cast fire upon the earth; and49 what will I, if it is already kindled? But I50 have a baptism to be baptized with; and how am I straitened till it be accomplished!

B *Think not that I came to ¹send peace on the*34 *earth: I came not to ¹send peace, but a sword.* *For I came to set a man at variance against his*35 *father, and the daughter against her mother, and the daughter in law against her mother in law: and a man's foes* shall be *they of his own house*-36 *hold.* (§57 L)

B   Think51 ye that I am come to give peace in the earth? I tell you, Nay; but rather division: for there52 shall be from henceforth five in one house divided, three against two, and two against three. They shall be divided, father against53 son, and son against father; mother against daughter, and daughter against her mother; mother in law against her daughter in law, and daughter in law against her mother in law.

---

§ 96 THE SIGNS OF THE TIMES

MATTHEW

LUKE 12:54-59

A *But he answered and said unto them,*16: ²*When it is evening, ye say,* It will be *fair weather:* 2 *for the heaven is red. And in the morning,* It 3 will be *foul weather to-day: for the heaven is red and lowring. Ye know how to discern the face of the heaven; but ye cannot* discern *the signs of the times.* (§68 B)

A And he said to the multitudes also, When54 ye see a cloud rising in the west, straightway ye say, There cometh a shower; and so it cometh to pass. And when *ye see* a south wind blow-55 ing, ye say, There will be a ³scorching heat; and it cometh to pass. Ye hypocrites, ye know56 how to ⁴interpret the face of the earth and the heaven; but how is it that ye know not how to ⁴interpret this time?

B   And why even of your-57 selves judge ye not what is right?

C *Agree with thine adversary quickly, whiles* 5: *thou art with him in the way; lest haply the*25 *adversary deliver thee to the judge, and the judge* ⁵*deliver thee to the officer, and thou be cast into prison. Verily I say unto thee, Thou shalt by*26 *no means come out thence, till thou have paid the last farthing.* (§37 B)

C   For as thou58 art going with thine adversary before the magistrate, on the way give diligence to be quit of him; lest haply he hale thee unto the judge, and the judge shall deliver thee to the ⁶officer, and the ⁶officer shall cast thee into pris-on. I say unto thee, Thou shalt by no means59 come out thence, till thou have paid the very last mite.

---

§ 97 WARNINGS OF IMPENDING FATE

LUKE 13:1-9

A Now there were some present at that very 1 season which told him of the Galilæans, whose blood Pilate had mingled with their sacrifices.

ERV margin: 1 Greek *cast*   2 The following words, to the end of verse 3, are omitted by some of the most ancient and other important authorities   3 Or *hot wind*   4 Greek *prove*   5 Some ancient authorities omit *deliver thee*   6 Greek *exactor*

OT references: Mt 10:35-36 and Lk 12:52-53 = Micah 7:6

A   Or to be baptized with the baptism that I am baptized with? (§120 D = Mk 10:38)
A   And with the baptism that I am baptized withal shall ye be baptized. (§120 F = Mk 10:39)

LUKE 13

And he answered and said unto them, Think 2
ye that these Galilæans were sinners above all
the Galilæans, because they have suffered these
things? I tell you, Nay: but, except ye 3
repent, ye shall all in like manner perish.

B   Or 4
those eighteen, upon whom the tower in Siloam
fell, and killed them, think ye that they were
¹offenders above all the men that dwell in Jerusalem? I tell you, Nay: but, except ye repent, 5
ye shall all likewise perish.

C   And he spake this parable; A certain man 6
had a fig tree planted in his vineyard; and he
came seeking fruit thereon, and found none.
And he said unto the vinedresser, Behold, these 7
three years I come seeking fruit on this fig tree,
and find none: cut it down; why doth it also
cumber the ground? And he answering saith 8
unto him, Lord, let it alone this year also, till
I shall dig about it, and dung it: and if it bear 9
fruit thenceforth, *well;* but if not, thou shalt
cut it down.

§98   JESUS CENSURED FOR SABBATH HEALING

LUKE 13:10–17

A   And he was teaching in one of the synagogues 10
on the sabbath day. And behold, a woman 11
which had a spirit of infirmity eighteen years;
and she was bowed together, and could in no
wise lift herself up. And when Jesus saw her, 12
he called her, and said to her, Woman, thou art
loosed from thine infirmity. And he laid his 13
hands upon her: and immediately she was
made straight, and glorified God.

B   And the 14
ruler of the synagogue, being moved with indignation because Jesus had healed on the sabbath, answered and said to the multitude,
There are six days in which men ought to work:
in them therefore come and be healed, and not
on the day of the sabbath.

C   But the Lord an- 15
swered him, and said, Ye hypocrites, doth not
each one of you on the sabbath loose his ox or
his ass from the ²stall, and lead him away to
watering? And ought not this woman, being 16
a daughter of Abraham, whom Satan had
bound, lo, *these* eighteen years, to have been
loosed from this bond on the day of the sabbath?

D   And as he said these things, all his 17
adversaries were put to shame: and all the multitude rejoiced for all the glorious things that
were done by him.

ERV margin: ¹ Greek *debtors*   ² Greek *manger*

OT references: Lk 13:14 = Exodus 20:8–11 and Deuteronomy 5:12–15

§ 99 PARABLES OF THE KINGDOM OF GOD

MATT 13:31–33

A^A *Another parable set he before them, saying,*[31] *The kingdom of heaven is like unto a grain of mustard seed, which a man took, and sowed in his field: which indeed is less than all seeds; but*[32] *when it is grown, it is greater than the herbs, and becometh a tree, so that the birds of the heaven come and lodge in the branches thereof.*

B *Another parable spake he unto them; The*[33] *kingdom of heaven is like unto leaven, which a woman took, and hid in three* [1]*measures of meal, till it was all leavened.* (§48 *EF*)

LUKE 13:18–21

A^A He said therefore, Unto what is the king-[18] dom of God like? and whereunto shall I liken it? It is like unto a grain of mustard seed,[19] which a man took, and cast into his own garden; and it grew, and became a tree; and the birds of the heaven lodged in the branches thereof.

B And again he said, Whereunto shall I[20] liken the kingdom of God? It is like unto[21] leaven, which a woman took and hid in three [1]measures of meal, till it was all leavened.

§ 100 LIMITS OF THE KINGDOM OF GOD

MATTHEW

C *Enter ye in by the narrow gate: for wide* [2]*is* 7: *the gate, and broad is the way, that leadeth to*[13] *destruction, and many be they that enter in thereby.* [3]*For narrow is the gate, and straitened*[14] *the way, that leadeth unto life, and few be they that find it.* (§38 M)

D *And the door was shut. Afterward come*[25]: *also the other virgins, saying, Lord, Lord, open*[11] *to us. But he answered and said, Verily I say*[12] *unto you, I know you not.* (§136 F)

E *Many will say to me in that day, Lord, Lord,* 7: *did we not prophesy by thy name, and by thy*[22] *name cast out* [5]*devils, and by thy name do many* [6]*mighty works?*

F *And then will I profess unto*[23] *them, I never knew you: depart from me, ye that work iniquity.* (§38 V)

G^G *And I say unto you, that many shall come* 8: *from the east and the west, and shall* [7]*sit down*[11]

LUKE 13:22–30

A And he went on his way through cities and[22] villages, teaching, and journeying on unto Jerusalem.

B   And one said unto him, Lord, are[23] they few that be saved? And he said unto them,

C   Strive to enter in by the narrow door:[24] for many, I say unto you, shall seek to enter in, and shall not be [4]able.

D   When once the master[25] of the house is risen up, and hath shut to the door, and ye begin to stand without, and to knock at the door, saying, Lord, open to us; and he shall answer and say to you, I know you not whence ye are;

E   then shall ye begin to say,[26] We did eat and drink in thy presence, and thou didst teach in our streets;

F   and he shall say, I[27] tell you, I know not whence ye are; depart from me, all ye workers of iniquity.

G^G   There[28] shall be the weeping and gnashing of teeth,

ERV margin: 1 The word in the Greek denotes the Hebrew seah, a measure containing nearly a peck and a half   2 Some ancient authorities omit *is the gate*   3 Many ancient authorities read *How narrow is the gate, etc.*   4 Or *able, when once*   5 Greek *demons*   6 Greek *powers*   7 Greek *recline*

OT references: Mt 13:32 and Lk 13:19=Daniel 4:10–12 and 20–22   Mt 7:23 and Lk 13:27=Psalm 6:8
Mt 8:11 and Lk 13:29=Psalm 107:3 and Isaiah 49:12

A *Matt parallel shown above under A*

A And he said, How shall we liken the kingdom of God? or in what parable shall we set it forth? It is like a grain of mustard seed, which, when it is sown upon the earth, though it be less than all the seeds that are upon the earth, yet when it is sown, groweth up, and becometh greater than all the herbs, and putteth out great branches; so that the birds of the heaven can lodge under the shadow thereof. (§48 E=Mk 4:30–32)

G And shall cast them into the furnace of fire: there shall be the weeping and gnashing of teeth. (§48 L=Mt 13:42)
G And shall cast them into the furnace of fire: there shall be the weeping and gnashing of teeth. (§48 Q=Mt 13:50)
G And cast him out into the outer darkness: there shall be the weeping and gnashing of teeth. (§129 P=Mt 22:13)

G And shall cut him asunder, and appoint his portion with the hypocrites: there shall be the weeping and gnashing of teeth. (§136 D=Mt 24:51)

G And shall cut him asunder, and appoint his portion with the unfaithful. (§94 E=Lk 12:46)

G And cast ye out the unprofitable servant into the outer darkness: there shall be the weeping and gnashing of teeth. (§136 Q=Mt 25:30)

MATTHEW	LUKE 13
with Abraham, and Isaac, and Jacob, in the kingdom of heaven: but the sons of the kingdom[12] *shall be cast forth into the outer darkness: there shall be the weeping and gnashing of teeth.* (§ *30 D*)	when ye shall see Abraham, and Isaac, and Jacob, and all the prophets, in the kingdom of God, and yourselves cast forth without. And[29] they shall come from the east and west, and from the north and south, and shall [1]sit down in the kingdom of God.
H[H] *So the last shall be first, and the first last.*[20:] (§ *118 B*) 16	H[H] And behold, there are[30] last which shall be first, and there are first which shall be last.

§ 101 FORECAST OF HIS DEATH BY JESUS

MATT 23:37–39	LUKE 13:31–35
A *For other forecasts of forthcoming events at Jerusalem, compare* §*72 A and attached references*	A In that very hour there came certain[31] Pharisees, saying to him, Get thee out, and go hence: for Herod would fain kill thee. And[32] he said unto them, Go and say to that fox, Behold, I cast out [2]devils and perform cures to-day and to-morrow, and the third *day* I am perfected. Howbeit I must go on my way[33] to-day and to-morrow and the *day* following: for it cannot be that a prophet perish out of Jerusalem.
B *O Jerusalem, Jerusalem, which killeth the*[37] *prophets, and stoneth them that are sent unto her! how often would I have gathered thy children together, even as a hen gathereth her chickens under her wings, and ye would not! Behold,*[38] *your house is left unto you* [3]*desolate. For I say*[39] *unto you, Ye shall not see me henceforth, till ye shall say, Blessed* is *he that cometh in the name of the Lord.* (§*132 R*)	B O Jerusalem, Jerusalem, which[34] killeth the prophets, and stoneth them that are sent unto her! how often would I have gathered thy children together, even as a hen *gathereth* her own brood under her wings, and ye would not! Behold, your house is left unto you *deso-*[35] *late:* and I say unto you, Ye shall not see me, until ye shall say, Blessed *is* he that cometh in the name of the Lord.

§ 102 AGAIN CENSURED FOR SABBATH HEALING

MATT 12:11–12	LUKE 14:1–6
	A And it came to pass, when he went into the [1] house of one of the rulers of the Pharisees on a sabbath to eat bread, that they were watching him. And behold, there was before him a [2] certain man which had the dropsy.
	B[B] And [3] Jesus answering spake unto the lawyers and Pharisees, saying, Is it lawful to heal on the sabbath, or not? But they held their peace. [4]
	c And he took him, and healed him, and let him go.
D *And he said unto them, What man shall there*[11] *be of you, that shall have one sheep, and if this fall into a pit on the sabbath day, will he not lay hold on it, and lift it out? How much then is a*[12] *man of more value than a sheep!* (§*33 D*)	D And he said unto them, Which of [5] you shall have [4]an ass or an ox fallen into a well, and will not straightway draw him up on a sabbath day?
	E And they could not answer again [6] unto these things.

ERV margin: 1 Greek *recline*   2 Greek *demons*   3 Some ancient authorities omit *desolate*   4 Many ancient authorities read *a son:* see Luke 13:15

OT references: Mt 23:38 and Lk 13:35[a]=Jeremiah 12:7 and 22:5   Mt 23:39 and Lk 13:35[b]=Psalm 118:26

H But many shall be last *that are* first; and first *that are* last. (§117 N=Mt 19:30)	H But many *that are* first shall be last; and the last first. (§117 N=Mk 10:31)	
B Wherefore it is lawful to do good on the sabbath day. (§33 E= Mt 12:12)	B And he saith unto them, Is it lawful on the sabbath day to do good, or to do harm? to save a life, or to kill? But they held their peace. (§33 E=Mk 3:4)	B And Jesus said unto them, I ask you, Is it lawful on the sabbath to do good, or to do harm? to save a life, or to destroy it? (§33 E= Lk 6:9)

§ 103 TEACHINGS AT THE TABLE OF A PHARISEE

MATT 22:2-10 LUKE 14:7-24

A And he spake a parable unto those which 7 were bidden, when he marked how they chose out the chief seats; saying unto them, When 8 thou art bidden of any man to a marriage feast, ¹sit not down in the chief seat; lest haply a more honourable man than thou be bidden of him, and he that bade thee and him shall come and 9 say to thee, Give this man place; and then thou shalt begin with shame to take the lowest place. But when thou art bidden, go and sit¹⁰ down in the lowest place; that when he that hath bidden thee cometh, he may say to thee, Friend, go up higher: then shalt thou have glory in the presence of all that sit at meat with thee.

Bᴮ   For every one that exalteth himself¹¹ shall be humbled; and he that humbleth himself shall be exalted.

c And he said to him also that had bidden¹² him, When thou makest a dinner or a supper, call not thy friends, nor thy brethren, nor thy kinsmen, nor rich neighbours; lest haply they also bid thee again, and a recompense be made thee. But when thou makest a feast, bid the poor,¹³ the maimed, the lame, the blind: and thou¹⁴ shalt be blessed; because they have not *wherewith* to recompense thee: for thou shalt be recompensed in the resurrection of the just.

D And when one of them that sat at meat with¹⁵ him heard these things, he said unto him, Blessed is he that shall eat bread in the kingdom of God.

E *The kingdom of heaven is likened unto a cer-² tain king, which made a marriage feast for his son, and sent forth his ²servants to call them that 3 were bidden to the marriage feast: and they would not come. Again he sent forth other ²servants, 4 saying, Tell them that are bidden, Behold, I have made ready my dinner: my oxen and my fatlings are killed, and all things are ready: come to the marriage feast.*

E   But he said unto him, A certain¹⁶ man made a great supper; and he bade many: and he sent forth his ³servant at supper time to¹⁷ say to them that were bidden, Come; for *all* things are now ready.

F   *But they made light of it, 5 and went their ways, one to his own farm, another to his merchandise: and the rest laid 6 hold on his ²servants, and entreated them shamefully, and killed them.*

F   And they all with one¹⁸ *consent* began to make excuse. The first said unto him, I have bought a field, and I must needs go out and see it: I pray thee have me excused. And another said, I have bought¹⁹ five yoke of oxen, and I go to prove them: I pray thee have me excused. And another said,²⁰ I have married a wife, and therefore I cannot come. And the ³servant came, and told his²¹ lord these things.

G   *But the king was wroth; 7 and he sent his armies, and destroyed those murderers, and burned their city.*

H   *Then saith he 8 to his ²servants, The wedding is ready, but they that were bidden were not worthy. Go ye there- 9 fore unto the partings of the highways, and as many as ye shall find, bid to the marriage feast.*

H   Then the master of the house being angry said to his ³servant, Go out quickly into the streets and lanes of the city, and bring in hither the poor and maimed and blind and lame. And the ³servant said, Lord,²²

ERV margin: 1 Greek *recline not*   2 Greek *bondservants*   3 Greek *bondservant*

B For every one that exalteth himself shall be humbled; but he that humbleth himself shall be exalted. (§114 B = Lk 18:14)
B And whosoever shall exalt himself shall be humbled; and whosoever shall humble himself shall be exalted. (§132 H = Mt 23:12)

MATT 22	LUKE 14
And those ¹servants went out into the highways,¹⁰ and gathered together all as many as they found, both bad and good: and the wedding was filled with guests. (§129 L–O)	what thou didst command is done, and yet there is room. And the lord said unto the²³ ²servant, Go out into the highways and hedges, and constrain *them* to come in, that my house may be filled. For I say unto you, that none²⁴ of those men which were bidden shall taste of my supper.

§ 104 THE COSTS OF DISCIPLESHIP

MATTHEW	LUKE 14:25–35
	A Now there went with him great multitudes:²⁵ and he turned, and said unto them,
B *He that loveth father or mother more than me*¹⁰: *is not worthy of me: and he that loveth son or*³⁷ *daughter more than me is not worthy of me.*	B If any man²⁶ cometh unto me, and hateth not his own father, and mother, and wife, and children, and brethren, and sisters, yea, and his own life also, he cannot be my disciple.
cᶜ *And he that doth not take his cross and follow*³⁸ *after me, is not worthy of me.* (§57 MN)	cᶜ Whosoever²⁷ doth not bear his own cross, and come after me, cannot be my disciple.
	D For which of you,²⁸ desiring to build a tower, doth not first sit down and count the cost, whether he have *wherewith* to complete it? Lest haply, when he hath laid²⁹ a foundation, and is not able to finish, all that behold begin to mock him, saying, This man³⁰ began to build, and was not able to finish. Or what king, as he goeth to encounter another³¹ king in war, will not sit down first and take counsel whether he is able with ten thousand to meet him that cometh against him with twenty thousand? Or else, while the other is³² yet a great way off, he sendeth an ambassage, and asketh conditions of peace. So therefore³³ whosoever he be of you that renounceth not all that he hath, he cannot be my disciple.
Eᴱ *Ye are the salt of the earth: but if the salt* 5: *have lost its savour, wherewith shall it be salted?*¹³ *it is thenceforth good for nothing, but to be cast out and trodden under foot of men.* (§36 KL)	Eᴱ Salt³⁴ therefore is good: but if even the salt have lost its savour, wherewith shall it be seasoned? I.³⁵ is fit neither for the land nor for the dunghill: *men* cast it out.
Fᶠ *He that hath ears ³to hear, let him hear.*¹¹: (§41 H) 15	Fᶠ He that hath ears to hear, let him hear.

ERV margin:　　1 Greek *bondservants*　　2 Greek *bondservant*　　3 Some ancient authorities omit *to hear*

c If any man would come after me, let him deny himself, and take up his cross, and follow me. (§73 A = Mt 16:24)

c If any man would come after me, let him deny himself, and take up his cross, and follow me. (§73 A = Mk 8:34)

c If any man would come after me, let him deny himself, and take up his cross daily, and follow me. (§73 A = Lk 9:23)

E Salt is good: but if the salt have lost its saltness, wherewith will ye season it? Have salt in yourselves, and be at peace one with another. (§78 O = Mk 9:50)

F He that hath ears, let him hear. (§47 F = Mt 13:9)

F Who hath ears to hear, let him hear. (§47 F = Mk 4:9)

F He that hath ears to hear, let him hear. (§47 F = Lk 8:8)

F If any man hath ears to hear, let him hear. (§47 S = Mk 4:23)

ᴅ He that hath ears, let him hear. (§48 M = Mt 13:43)

CHAPTER XVI

MANY TRUTHS TAUGHT IN PARABLES

§ 105 PARABLES ON THE WORTH OF SINNERS

MATT 18:12-14

LUKE 15:1-32

A Now all the publicans and sinners were 1 drawing near unto him for to hear him. And 2 both the Pharisees and the scribes murmured, saying, This man receiveth sinners, and eateth with them.

And he spake unto them this parable, saying, 3

B What man of you, having a hundred sheep, 4 and having lost one of them, doth not leave the ninety and nine in the wilderness, and go after that which is lost, until he find it? And 5 when he hath found it, he layeth it on his shoulders, rejoicing. And when he cometh 6 home, he calleth together his friends and his neighbours, saying unto them, Rejoice with me, for I have found my sheep which was lost. I say unto you, that even so there shall be joy 7 in heaven over one sinner that repenteth, *more* than over ninety and nine righteous persons, which need no repentance.

C Or what woman having ten 3pieces of silver, 8 if she lose one piece, doth not light a lamp, and sweep the house, and seek diligently until she find it? And when she hath found it, she 9 calleth together her friends and neighbours, saying, Rejoice with me, for I have found the piece which I had lost. Even so, I say unto 10 you, there is joy in the presence of the angels of God over one sinner that repenteth.

D And he said, A certain man had two sons: 11 and the younger of them said to his father, 12 Father, give me the portion of 4thy substance that falleth to me. And he divided unto them his living. And not many days after the 13 younger son gathered all together, and took his journey into a far country; and there he wasted his substance with riotous living. And 14 when he had spent all, there arose a mighty famine in that country; and he began to be in want. And he went and joined himself to one 15 of the citizens of that country; and he sent him into his fields to feed swine. And he would 16 fain have been filled with 5the husks that the swine did eat: and no man gave unto him. But when he came to himself he said, How 17 many hired servants of my father's have bread enough and to spare, and I perish here with hunger! I will arise and go to my father, and 18 will say unto him, Father, I have sinned against heaven, and in thy sight: I am no more worthy 19 to be called thy son: make me as one of thy hired servants. And he arose, and came to 20

How think ye? if any man have a hundred 12 *sheep, and one of them be gone astray, doth he not leave the ninety and nine, and go unto the mountains, and seek that which goeth astray? And if so be that he find it, verily I say unto you,* 13 *he rejoiceth over it more than over the ninety and nine which have not gone astray. Even so* 14 *it is not* 1*the will of* 2*your Father which is in heaven, that one of these little ones should perish.* (§78 Q)

ERV margin: 1 Greek *a thing willed before your Father* 2 Some ancient authorities read *my* 3 Greek *drachma*, a coin worth about eight pence 4 Greek *the* 5 Greek *the pods of the carob tree*

115

LUKE 15

his father. But while he was yet afar off, his father saw him, and was moved with compassion, and ran, and fell on his neck, and [1]kissed him. And the son said unto him, Father, I[21] have sinned against heaven, and in thy sight: I am no more worthy to be called thy son.[2] But the father said to his [3]servants, Bring forth[22] quickly the best robe, and put it on him; and put a ring on his hand, and shoes on his feet: and bring the fatted calf, *and* kill it, and let us[23] eat, and make merry: for this my son was[24] dead, and is alive again; he was lost, and is found. And they began to be merry. Now[25] his elder son was in the field: and as he came and drew nigh to the house, he heard music and dancing. And he called to him one of the[26] [3]servants, and inquired what these things might be. And he said unto him, Thy brother is[27] come; and thy father hath killed the fatted calf, because he hath received him safe and sound. But he was angry, and would not go[28] in: and his father came out, and intreated him. But he answered and said to his father, Lo,[29] these many years do I serve thee, and I never transgressed a commandment of thine: and *yet* thou never gavest me a kid, that I might make merry with my friends: but when this[30] thy son came, which hath devoured thy living with harlots, thou killedst for him the fatted calf. And he said unto him, [4]Son, thou art[31] ever with me, and all that is mine is thine. But it was meet to make merry and be glad:[32] for this thy brother was dead, and is alive *again;* and *was* lost, and is found.

§ 106 PARABLE OF THE STEWARD

LUKE 16:1-12

And he said also unto the disciples, There was [1] a certain rich man, which had a steward; and the same was accused unto him that he was wasting his goods. And he called him, and [2] said unto him, What is this that I hear of thee? render the account of thy stewardship; for thou canst be no longer steward. And the steward [3] said within himself, What shall I do, seeing that my lord taketh away the stewardship from me? I have not strength to dig; to beg I am ashamed. I am resolved what to do, that, [4] when I am put out of the stewardship, they may receive me into their houses. And calling to [5] him each one of his lord's debtors, he said to the first, How much owest thou unto my lord? And he said, A hundred [5]measures of oil. And [6] he said unto him, Take thy [6]bond, and sit down quickly and write fifty. Then said he to [7] another, And how much owest thou? And he said, A hundred [7]measures of wheat. He saith unto him, Take thy [6]bond, and write fourscore. And his lord commended [8]the unright- [8] eous steward because he had done wisely: for the sons of this [9]world are for their own generation

LUKE 16

wiser than the sons of the light. And I say 9 unto you, Make to yourselves friends ¹by means of the mammon of unrighteousness; that, when it shall fail, they may receive you into the eternal tabernacles. He that is faithful in a¹⁰ very little is faithful also in much: and he that is unrighteous in a very little is unrighteous also in much. If therefore ye have not been faith-¹¹ ful in the unrighteous mammon, who will commit to your trust the true *riches?* And if¹² ye have not been faithful in that which is another's, who will give you that which is ²your own?

§ 107 SEVERAL SAYINGS OF JESUS

MATTHEW

A *No man can serve two masters: for either he* 6: *will hate the one, and love the other; or else he*²⁴ *will hold to one, and despise the other. Ye can-* *not serve God and mammon. (§38 C)*

C *And from the days of John the Baptist until*¹¹: *now the kingdom of heaven suffereth violence, and*¹² *men of violence take it by force. For all the*¹³ *prophets and the law prophesied until John.* *(§41 F)*

D *For verily I say unto you, Till heaven and* 5: *earth pass away, one jot or one tittle shall in no*¹⁸ *wise pass away from the law, till all things be* *accomplished. (§36 Q)*

Eᴱ *But I say unto you, that every one that* 5: *putteth away his wife, saving for the cause of*³² *fornication, maketh her an adulteress: and who-* *soever shall marry her when she is put away* *committeth adultery. (§37 E)*

LUKE 16:13-18

A No ³servant can serve two masters: for¹³ either he will hate the one, and love the other; or else he will hold to one, and despise the other. Ye cannot serve God and mammon.
B And the Pharisees, who were lovers of¹⁴ money, heard all these things; and they scoffed at him. And he said unto them, Ye are they¹⁵ that justify yourselves in the sight of men; but God knoweth your hearts: for that which is exalted among men is an abomination in the sight of God.
C   The law and the prophets were¹⁶ until John: from that time the gospel of the kingdom of God is preached, and every man entereth violently into it.

D   But it is easier for¹⁷ heaven and earth to pass away, than for one tittle of the law to fall.

Eᴱ   Every one that putteth¹⁸ away his wife, and marrieth another, committeth adultery: and he that marrieth one that is put away from a husband committeth adultery.

§ 108 PARABLE OF THE RICH MAN AND THE BEGGAR

LUKE 16:19-31

Now there was a certain rich man, and he¹⁹ was clothed in purple and fine linen, ⁴faring sumptuously every day: and a certain beggar²⁰ named Lazarus was laid at his gate, full of sores, and desiring to be fed with the *crumbs* that fell²¹ from the rich man's table; yea, even the dogs came and licked his sores. And it came to pass,²² that the beggar died, and that he was carried away by the angels into Abraham's bosom: and the rich man also died, and was buried. And²³ in Hades he lifted up his eyes, being in tor-

---

ERV margin: 1 Greek *out of living in mirth and splendour every day*   2 Some ancient authorities read *our own*   3 Greek *household-servant*   4 Or

E And I say unto you, Whosoever shall put away his wife, except for fornication, and shall marry another, committeth adultery: and he that marrieth her when she is put away committeth adultery. (§115 F = Mt 19:9)

E And he saith unto them, Whosoever shall put away his wife, and marry another, committeth adultery against her: and if she herself shall put away her husband, and marry another, she committeth adultery. (§115 F = Mk 10:11-12)

LUKE 16

ments, and seeth Abraham afar off, and Lazarus in his bosom. And he cried and said,[24]
Father Abraham, have mercy on me, and send
Lazarus, that he may dip the tip of his finger
in water, and cool my tongue; for I am in
anguish in this flame. But Abraham said,[25]
[1]Son, remember that thou in thy lifetime re-
ceivedst thy good things, and Lazarus in like
manner evil things: but now here he is comforted, and thou art in anguish. And [2]beside[26]
all this, between us and you there is a great
gulf fixed, that they which would pass from
hence to you may not be able, and that none
may cross over from thence to us. And he said,[27]
I pray thee therefore, father, that thou wouldest send him to my father's house; for I have[28]
five brethren; that he may testify unto them,
lest they also come into this place of torment.
But Abraham saith, They have Moses and the[29]
prophets; let them hear them. And he said,[30]
Nay, father Abraham: but if one go to them
from the dead, they will repent. And he said[31]
unto him, If they hear not Moses and the
prophets, neither will they be persuaded, if one
rise from the dead.

§ 109 SEVERAL SAYINGS OF JESUS

MATTHEW 18	LUKE 17:1-6
A *Woe unto the world because of occasions of* [7] *stumbling! for it must needs be that the occasions come; but woe to that man through whom the occasion cometh!* (§78 L)	A And he said unto his disciples, It is impos-[1] sible but that occasions of stumbling should come: but woe unto him, through whom they come!
B[B] *But whoso shall cause one of these little ones* [6] *which believe on me to stumble, it is profitable for him that* [3]*a great millstone should be hanged about his neck, and* that *he should be sunk in the depth of the sea.* (§78 K)	B[B] It were well for him if a millstone were [2] hanged about his neck, and he were thrown into the sea, rather than that he should cause one of these little ones to stumble.
C *And if thy brother sin* [4]*against thee, go, shew*[15] *him his fault between thee and him alone: if he hear thee, thou hast gained thy brother.* (§78 R)	C Take heed [3] to yourselves: if thy brother sin, rebuke him; and if he repent, forgive him.
D *Then came Peter, and said to him, Lord, how*[21] *oft shall my brother sin against me, and I forgive him? until seven times? Jesus saith unto him,*[22] *I say not unto thee, Until seven times; but, Until* [5]*seventy times seven.* (§78 V)	D And if he sin [4] against thee seven times in the day, and seven times turn again to thee, saying, I repent; thou shalt forgive him.
	E And the apostles said unto the Lord, In-[5] crease our faith.
F[F] *For verily I say unto you, If ye have faith*[17]: *as a grain of mustard seed, ye shall say unto this*[20] *mountain, Remove hence to yonder place; and it shall remove.* (§75 H)	F[F] And the Lord said, If ye have [6] faith as a grain of mustard seed, ye would say unto this sycamine tree, Be thou rooted up, and be thou planted in the sea; and it would have obeyed you.

ERV margin: 1 Greek *Child*   2 Or *in all these things*   3 Greek *a millstone turned by an ass*   4 Some ancient
authorities omit *against thee*   5 Or *seventy times and seven*

B *Matt parallel shown above under B*	B And whosoever shall cause one of these little ones that believe on me to stumble, it were better for him if a great millstone were hanged about his neck, and he were cast into the sea. (§78 K = Mk 9:42)
F Verily I say unto you, If ye have faith, and doubt not, ye shall not only do what is done to the fig tree, but even if ye shall say unto this mountain, Be thou taken up and cast into the sea, it shall be done. (§127 C = Mt 21:21)	F Have faith in God. Verily I say unto you, Whosoever shall say unto this mountain, Be thou taken up and cast into the sea; and shall not doubt in his heart, but shall believe that what he saith cometh to pass: he shall have it. (§127 C = Mk 11:22-23)

§ 110 PARABLE ON DUTY

LUKE 17:7-10

But who is there of you, having a [1]servant 7 plowing or keeping sheep, that will say unto him, when he is come in from the field, Come straightway and will sit down to meat; and will 8 not rather say unto him, Make ready wherewith I may sup, and gird thyself, and serve me, till I have eaten and drunken; and afterward thou shalt eat and drink? Doth he thank the 9 [1]servant because he did the things that were commanded? Even so ye also, when ye shall 10 have done all the things that are commanded you, say, We are unprofitable [2]servants; we have done that which it was our duty to do.

§ 111 THE HEALING OF THE LEPERS

LUKE 17:11-19

A And it came to pass, [3]as they were on the 11 way to Jerusalem, that he was passing [4]through the midst of Samaria and Galilee.
B And as he 12 entered into a certain village, there met him ten men that were lepers, which stood afar off: and they lifted up their voices, saying, Jesus, 13 Master, have mercy on us. And when he saw 14 them, he said unto them, Go and shew yourselves unto the priests. And it came to pass, as they went, they were cleansed. And one of 15 them, when he saw that he was healed, turned back, with a loud voice glorifying God; and 16 he fell upon his face at his feet, giving him thanks: and he was a Samaritan. And Jesus 17 answering said, Were not the ten cleansed? but where are the nine? [5]Were there none 18 found that returned to give glory to God, save this [6]stranger? And he said unto him, Arise, 19 and go thy way: thy faith hath [7]made thee whole.

§ 112 THE DAY OF THE SON OF MAN

MATTHEW 24

LUKE 17:20-37

A And being asked by the Pharisees, when 20 the kingdom of God cometh, he answered them and said, The kingdom of God cometh not with observation: neither shall they say, Lo, here! 21 or, There! for lo, the kingdom of God is [8]within you.
B And he said unto the disciples, The days 22 will come, when ye shall desire to see one of the days of the Son of man, and ye shall not see it.

c[c] *If therefore they shall say unto you, Behold,* [26] *he is in the wilderness; go not forth: Behold, he is in the inner chambers; believe* [9]*it not. For as* [27]

c[c] And they shall say to you, Lo, there! Lo, [23] here! go not away, nor follow after *them:* for [24] as the lightning, when it lighteneth out of the

---

ERV margin: 1 Greek *bondservant* 2 Greek *bondservants* 3 Or *as he was* 4 Or *between* 5 Or *There were none found . . . save this stranger* 6 Or *alien* 7 Or *saved thee* 8 Or *in the midst of you* 9 Or, *them*

OT references: Lk 17:12=Leviticus 13:45-46 Lk 17:14=Leviticus 13:49 and 14:1-3

c Compare §134 portion D

c Then if any man shall say unto you, Lo, here is the Christ, or, Here; believe *it* not. (§135 A=Mt 24:23)

c And then if any man shall say unto you, Lo, here is the Christ; or, Lo, there; believe *it* not. (§135 A= Mk 13:21)

MATT 24	LUKE 17

the lightning cometh forth from the east, and is seen even unto the west; so shall be the ¹coming of the Son of man. (§135 CD)

one part under the heaven, shineth unto the other part under heaven; so shall the Son of man be ²in his day.

D^D   Compare §72 A and attached references

D^D   But first must he suffer²⁵ many things and be rejected of this generation.

E *And as* were *the days of Noah, so shall be the*³⁷ ¹*coming of the Son of man. For as in those days*³⁸ *which were before the flood they were eating and drinking, marrying and giving in marriage, until the day that Noah entered into the ark, and*³⁹ *they knew not until the flood came, and took them all away;*

E And as it came to pass in the days of Noah,²⁶ even so shall it be also in the days of the Son of man. They ate, they drank, they married,²⁷ they were given in marriage, until the day that Noah entered into the ark, and the flood came, and destroyed them all.

F   Likewise even as it²⁸ came to pass in the days of Lot: they ate, they drank, they bought, they sold, they planted, they builded; but in the day that Lot went out²⁹ from Sodom it rained fire and brimstone from heaven, and destroyed them all:

G   *so shall be the* ¹*coming of the Son of man.* (§135 LM)

G   after the same³⁰ manner shall it be in the day that the Son of man is revealed.

H^H   Compare with portions P and Q of §134

H^H   In that day, he which shall³¹ be on the housetop, and his goods in the house, let him not go down to take them away: and let him that is in the field likewise not return back.

                              I   Remember Lot's wife.   ³²

J^J *He that* ³*findeth his* ⁴*life shall lose it; and*¹⁰: *he that* ⁵*loseth his* ⁴*life for my sake shall find it.*³⁹ (§57 O)

J^J   Whosoever shall³³ seek to gain his ⁴life shall lose it: but whosoever shall lose *his* ⁴life shall ⁶preserve it.

K *Then shall two men be in the field; one is*²⁴: *taken, and one is left: two women* shall be *grind*⁴⁰ *ing at the mill; one is taken, and one is left.*⁴¹ (§135 N)

K   I say unto³⁴ you, In that night there shall be two men on one bed; the one shall be taken, and the other shall be left. There shall be two women grind-³⁵ ing together; the one shall be taken, and the other shall be left.⁷

L   And they answering say³⁷ unto him, Where, Lord?

M *Wheresoever the carcase is, there will the*²⁸ ⁸*eagles be gathered together.* (§135 E)

M   And he said unto them, Where the body *is*, thither will the ⁸eagles also be gathered together.

§ 113   PARABLE OF THE WIDOW AND THE JUDGE

LUKE 18:1–8

A And he spake a parable unto them to the ¹ end that they ought always to pray, and not to faint; saying, There was in a city a judge, ² which feared not God, and regarded not man: and there was a widow in that city; and she ³ came oft unto him, saying, ⁹Avenge me of mine adversary. And he would not for a while: but ⁴ afterward he said within himself, Though I fear not God, nor regard man; yet because ⁵

ERV margin: 1 Greek *presence*   2 Some ancient authorities omit *in his day*   3 Or *found*   4 Or *soul*   5 Or *lost*   6 Greek *save it alive*   7 Some ancient authorities add verse 36: *There shall be two men in the field; the one shall be taken, and the other shall be left*   8 Or *vultures*   9 Or *Do me justice of:* and so in verses 5, 7 and 8

OT references: Mt 24:37–39 and Lk 17:26–27 = Genesis 6:11–13 and 7:7, 21–23   Lk 17:28 = Genesis 18:20–22
Lk 17:29 = Genesis 19:24–25   Lk 17:32 = Genesis 19:26

D   Compare §72 A and attached references
H   Compare with portions P and Q of §134

J For whosoever would save his life shall lose it: and whosoever shall lose his life for my sake shall find it. (§73 B = Mt 16:25)	J For whosoever would save his life shall lose it; and whosoever shall lose his life for my sake and the gospel's shall save it. (§73 B = Mk 8:35)	J For whosoever would save his life shall lose it; but whosoever shall lose his life for my sake, the same shall save it. (§73 B = Lk 9:24)

LUKE 18

this widow troubleth me, I will avenge her, lest she ¹wear me out by her continual coming.

B And the Lord said, Hear what ²the unright- 6 eous judge saith. And shall not God avenge 7 his elect, which cry to him day and night, and he is longsuffering over them? I say unto 8 you, that he will avenge them speedily. Howbeit when the Son of man cometh, shall he find ³faith on the earth?

§ 114 PARABLE OF THE PUBLICAN AND THE PHARISEE

LUKE 18:9–14

A   And he spake also this parable unto certain 9 which trusted in themselves that they were righteous, and set ⁴all others at nought: Two 10 men went up into the temple to pray; the one a Pharisee, and the other a publican. The 11 Pharisee stood and prayed thus with himself, God, I thank thee, that I am not as the rest of men, extortioners, unjust, adulterers, or even as this publican; I fast twice in the week; I 12 give tithes of all that I get. But the publican, 13 standing afar off, would not lift up so much as his eyes unto heaven, but smote his breast, saying, God, ⁵be merciful to me ⁶a sinner. I 14 say unto you, This man went down to his house justified rather than the other:
B^B   for every one that exalteth himself shall be humbled; but he that humbleth himself shall be exalted.

ERV margin: 1 Greek *bruise*   2 Greek *the judge of unrighteousness*   3 Or *the faith*   4 Greek *the rest*   5 Or *be propitiated*   6 Or *the sinner*

B   For every one that exalteth himself shall be humbled; and he that humbleth himself shall be exalted. (§103 B=Lk 14:11)
B   And whosoever shall exalt himself shall be humbled; and whosoever shall humble himself shall be exalted. (§132 H =Mt 23:12)

121

CHAPTER XVII

TEACHING AND JOURNEYING ON TO JERUSALEM

§ 115   TEACHINGS ABOUT DIVORCE

MATT 19:3–12	MARK 10:2–12
A And there came unto him 3 [1]Pharisees, tempting him, and saying, Is it lawful *for a man* to put away his wife for every cause?	A And there came unto him 2 Pharisees, and asked him, Is it lawful for a man to put away *his* wife? tempting him.
B And he answered and 4 said,	B And 3 he answered and said unto them,
C *Compare portion E below*	C What did Moses command you? And they said, 4 Moses suffered to write a bill of divorcement, and to put her away. But Jesus said 5 unto them, For your hardness of heart he wrote you this commandment.
D Have ye not read, that he which [2]made *them* from the beginning made them male and female, and said, For this 5 cause shall a man leave his father and mother, and shall cleave to his wife; and the twain shall become one flesh? So that they are no more 6 twain, but one flesh. What therefore God hath joined together, let not man put asunder.	D But from the 6 beginning of the creation, Male and female made he them. For this cause shall 7 a man leave his father and mother, [3]and shall cleave to his wife; and the twain shall 8 become one flesh: so that they are no more twain, but one flesh. What therefore God 9 hath joined together, let not man put asunder.
E They say unto him, Why 7 then did Moses command to give a bill of divorcement, and to put *her* away? He 8 saith unto them, Moses for your hardness of heart suffered you to put away your wives: but from the beginning it hath not been so.	E *Compare portion C above*
FF And 9 I say unto you, Whosoever shall put away his wife, [4]except for fornication, and shall marry another, committeth adultery: [5]and he that mar-	FF And in the 10 house the disciples asked him again of this matter. And he 11 saith unto them, Whosoever shall put away his wife, and marry another, committeth

---

ERV margin: 1 Many authorities, some ancient, insert *the*   2 Some ancient authorities read *created*   3 Some ancient authorities omit *and shall cleave to his wife*   4 Some ancient authorities read *saving for the cause of fornication*, *maketh her an adulteress:* as in Matt 5:32   5 The following words, to the end of the verse, are omitted by some ancient authorities

---

OT references: Mt 19:4 and Mk 10:6 = Genesis 1:27   Mt 19:5 and Mk 10:7–8 = Genesis 2:24   Mt 19:7 and Mk 10:4 = Deuteronomy 24:1

F   But I say unto you, that every one that putteth away his wife, saving for the cause of fornication, maketh her an adulteress: and whosoever shall marry her when she is put away committeth adultery. (§37 E = Mt 5:32)

F   Every one that putteth away his wife, and marrieth another, committeth adultery: and he that marrieth one that is put away from a husband committeth adultery. (§107 E = Lk 16:18)

MATT 19

rieth her when she is put away committeth adultery.

G   The dis-[10] ciples say unto him, If the case of the man is so with his wife, it is not expedient to marry. But he said unto[11] them, All men cannot receive this saying, but they to whom it is given. For there are[12] eunuchs, which were so born from their mother's womb: and there are eunuchs, which were made eunuchs by men: and there are eunuchs, which made themselves eunuchs for the kingdom of heaven's sake. He that is able to receive it, let him receive it.

MARK 10

adultery against her: and if[12] she herself shall put away her husband, and marry another, she committeth adultery.

§ 116   ATTITUDE OF JESUS TOWARD CHILDREN

MATT 19:13-15

A   Then were there brought[13] unto him little children, that he should lay his hands on them, and pray: and the disciples rebuked them.
B   But Je-[14] sus said, Suffer the little children, and forbid them not, to come unto me: for of such is the kingdom of heaven.

c   *Verily I say unto you, Ex-*[18:] *cept ye turn, and become as lit-* [3] *tle children, ye shall in no wise enter into the kingdom of heaven.* (§78 D)
D   And[15] he laid his hands on them, and departed thence.

MARK 10:13-16

A   And they brought unto[13] him little children, that he should touch them: and the disciples rebuked them.
B   But[14] when Jesus saw it, he was moved with indignation, and said unto them, Suffer the little children to come unto me; forbid them not: for of such is the kingdom of God.

c   Verily I say unto you, Who-[15] soever shall not receive the kingdom of God as a little child, he shall in no wise enter therein.
D   And he took them[16] in his arms, and blessed them, laying his hands upon them.

LUKE 18:15-17

A   And they brought unto[15] him also their babes, that he should touch them: but when the disciples saw it, they rebuked them.
B   But Jesus called[16] them unto him, saying, Suffer the little children to come unto me, and forbid them not: for of such is the kingdom of God.

c   Verily I say unto you,[17] Whosoever shall not receive the kingdom of God as a little child, he shall in no wise enter therein.

§ 117   RELATION OF RICHES TO ETERNAL LIFE

MATT 19:16-30

A   And behold, one came to[16] him and said, [1,2]Master, what good thing shall I do, that I may have eternal life?

B   And[17] he said unto him, [4]Why askest thou me concerning that which is good? One there is who is good:

MARK 10:17-31

A   And as he was going forth[17] [3]into the way, there ran one to him, and kneeled to him, and asked him, Good [1]Master, what shall I do that I may inherit eternal life?
B   And Jesus[18] said unto him, Why callest thou me good? none is good save one, *even* God.

LUKE 18:18-30

A   And a certain ruler asked[18] him, saying, Good [1]Master, what shall I do to inherit eternal life?

B   And Jesus said unto[19] him, Why callest thou me good? none is good, save one, *even* God.

ERV margin: 1 Or *Teacher*   2 Some ancient authorities read *Good Master:* see Mark 10:17 and Luke 18:18   3 Or *on his way*   4 Some ancient authorities read *Why callest thou me good? None is good save one,* even *God:* see Mark 10:18 and Luke 18:19

MATT 19

c but if thou wouldest enter into life, keep the commandments. He saith unto[18] him, Which? And Jesus said, Thou shalt not kill, Thou shalt not commit adultery, Thou shalt not steal, Thou shalt not bear false witness, Honour thy father and thy[19] mother: and, Thou shalt love thy neighbour as thyself.

D The[20] young man saith unto him, All these things have I observed: what lack I yet?

E Jesus said unto him, If thou[21] wouldest be perfect, go, sell that thou hast, and give to the poor, and thou shalt have treasure in heaven: and come, follow me.

F But when the[22] young man heard the saying, he went away sorrowful: for he was one that had great possessions.

G And Jesus said unto his[23] disciples, Verily I say unto you, It is hard for a rich man to enter into the kingdom of heaven.

I And again I say unto[24] you, It is easier for a camel to go through a needle's eye, than for a rich man to enter into the kingdom of God.

J And[25] when the disciples heard it, they were astonished exceedingly, saying, Who then can be saved? And Jesus looking[26] upon *them* said to them, With men this is impossible; but with God all things are possible.

K Then answered Peter[27] and said unto him, Lo, we have left all, and followed thee; what then shall we have?

L And Jesus said unto[28] them, Verily I say unto you,

MARK 10

c Thou[19] knowest the commandments, Do not kill, Do not commit adultery, Do not steal, Do not bear false witness, Do not defraud, Honour thy father and mother.

D And he said unto[20] him, [1]Master, all these things have I observed from my youth.

E And Jesus looking[21] upon him loved him, and said unto him, One thing thou lackest: go, sell whatsoever thou hast, and give to the poor, and thou shalt have treasure in heaven: and come, follow me.

F But his counte-[22] nance fell at the saying, and he went away sorrowful: for he was one that had great possessions.

G And Jesus looked round[23] about, and saith unto his disciples, How hardly shall they that have riches enter into the kingdom of God!

H And the dis-[24] ciples were amazed at his words. But Jesus answereth again, and saith unto them, Children, how hard is it [2]for them that trust in riches to enter into the kingdom of God!

I It is easier for a camel to go[25] through a needle's eye, than for a rich man to enter into the kingdom of God.

J And they[26] were astonished exceedingly, saying [3]unto him, Then who can be saved? Jesus looking[27] upon them saith, With men it is impossible, but not with God: for all things are possible with God.

K Peter began[28] to say unto him, Lo, we have left all, and have followed thee.

LUKE 18

c Thou knowest the[20] commandments, Do not commit adultery, Do not kill, Do not steal, Do not bear false witness, Honour thy father and mother.

D And he said, All[21] these things have I observed from my youth up.

E And when[22] Jesus heard it, he said unto him, One thing thou lackest yet: sell all that thou hast, and distribute unto the poor, and thou shalt have treasure in heaven: and come, follow me.

F But when he heard these[23] things, he became exceeding sorrowful; for he was very rich.

G And Jesus seeing him[24] said, How hardly shall they that have riches enter into the kingdom of God!

I For it is[25] easier for a camel to enter in through a needle's eye, than for a rich man to enter into the kingdom of God.

J And they[26] that heard it said, Then who can be saved? But he said,[27] The things which are impossible with men are possible with God.

K And Peter said, Lo,[28] we have left [4]our own, and followed thee.

L *But ye are they which have*[22:] *continued with me in my temp-*[28]

ERV margin: 1 Or *Teacher* 2 Some ancient authorities omit *for them that trust in riches* 3 Many ancient authorities read *among themselves* 4 Or *our own* homes

OT references: Mt 19:18–19[a] and Mk 10:19 and Lk 18:20 = Exodus 20:12–16 and Deuteronomy 5:16–20 Mt 19:19[b] = Leviticus 19:18 Mt 19:26 and Mk 10:27 and Lk 18:27 = Genesis 18:14 and Job 42:2

MATT 19	MARK 10	LUKE 18
that ye which have followed me, in the regeneration when the Son of man shall sit on the throne of his glory, ye also shall sit upon twelve thrones, judging the twelve tribes of Israel.		*tations; and [1]I appoint unto[29] you a kingdom, even as my Father appointed unto me, that[30] ye may eat and drink at my table in my kingdom; and ye shall sit on thrones judging the twelve tribes of Israel.* (§*138 N*)
M And every one that[29] hath left houses, or brethren, or sisters, or father, or mother,[2] or children, or lands, for my name's sake, shall receive [3]a hundredfold, and shall inherit eternal life.	M Jesus said, Verily I say[29] unto you, There is no man that hath left house, or brethren, or sisters, or mother, or father, or children, or lands, for my sake, and for the gospel's sake, but he shall receive[30] a hundredfold now in this time, houses, and brethren, and sisters, and mothers, and children, and lands, with persecutions; and in the [4]world to come eternal life.	M And he said[29] unto them, Verily I say unto you, There is no man ·that hath left house, or wife, or brethren, or parents, or children, for the kingdom of God's sake, who shall not receive[30] manifold more in this time, and in the [4]world to come eternal life.
N[N] But many[30] shall be last *that are* first; and first *that are* last.	N[N] But many[31] *that are* first shall be last; and the last first.	

§ 118 PARABLE OF THE HOUSEHOLDER AND THE LABOURERS

MATT 20:1–16	LUKE
A For the kingdom of heaven is like unto a [1] man that is a householder, which went out early in the morning to hire labourers into his vineyard. And when he had agreed with the [2] labourers for a [5]penny a day, he sent them into his vineyard. And he went out about [3] the third hour, and saw others standing in the marketplace idle; and to them he said, Go ye [4] also into the vineyard, and whatsoever is right I will give you. And they went their way. Again he went out about the sixth and the [5] ninth hour, and did likewise. And about the [6] eleventh *hour* he went out, and found others standing; and he saith unto them, Why stand ye here all the day idle? They say unto him, [7] Because no man hath hired us. He saith unto them, Go ye also into the vineyard. And [8] when even was come, the lord of the vineyard saith unto his steward, Call the labourers, and pay them their hire, beginning from the last unto the first. And when they came that *were* [9] *hired* about the eleventh hour, they received every man a [5]penny. And when the first came,[10] they supposed that they would receive more; and they likewise received every man a [5]penny. And when they received it, they murmured[11] against the householder, saying, These last[12] have spent *but* one hour, and thou hast made them equal unto us, which have borne the burden of the day and the [6]scorching heat. But he[13] answered and said to one of them, Friend, I do thee no wrong: didst not thou agree with me for a [5]penny? Take up that which is thine,[14] and go thy way; it is my will to give unto this	

ERV margin: [1] Or *I appoint unto you, even as my Father appointed unto me a kingdom, that ye may eat and drink, etc.*   [2] Many ancient authorities add *or wife*: as in Luke 18:29   [3] Some ancient authorities read *manifold*   [4] Or *age*   [5] The word in the Greek denotes a coin worth about eight pence halfpenny   [6] Or *hot wind*

N   So the last shall be first, and the first last. (§118 B = Mt 20:16)

N   And behold, there are last which shall be first, and there are first which shall be last. (§100 H = Lk 13:30)

MATT 20	LUKE 13
last, even as unto thee. Is it not lawful for me[15] to do what I will with mine own? or is thine eye evil, because I am good?	
B[B] So the last shall[16] be first, and the first last.	B[B] *And behold, there are last which shall be first,*[30] *and there are first which shall be last.* (§100 H)

§ 119   JESUS FORECASTS EVENTS AT JERUSALEM

MATT 20:17–19	MARK 10:32–34	LUKE 18:31–34
A And as Jesus was going up[17] to Jerusalem,	A And they were in the way,[32] going up to Jerusalem; and Jesus was going before them: and they were amazed; [1]and they that followed were afraid.	
B he took the twelve disciples apart, and in the way he said unto them,	B And he took again the twelve, and began to tell them the things that were to happen unto him, *saying,* 33	B And he took unto him the[31] twelve, and said unto them,
C[C] Behold, we go up to Jeru-[18] salem;	C[C] Behold, we go up to Jerusalem;	C[C] Behold, we go up to Jerusalem, D[D] and all the things that are written [2]by the prophets shall be accomplished unto the Son of man.
E[E] and the Son of man shall be delivered unto the chief priests and scribes; and they shall condemn him to death,	E[E] and the Son of man shall be delivered unto the chief priests and the scribes; and they shall condemn him to death,	
F[F] and shall deliver him[19] unto the Gentiles to mock, and to scourge, and to crucify: and the third day he shall be raised up.	F[F] and shall deliver him unto the Gentiles: and they shall[34] mock him, and shall spit upon him, and shall scourge him, and shall kill him; and after three days he shall rise again.	F[F] For he shall be[32] delivered up unto the Gentiles, and shall be mocked, and shamefully entreated, and spit upon: and they shall[33] scourge and kill him: and the third day he shall rise again. G And they understood none[34] of these things; and this saying was hid from them, and they perceived not the things that were said.

§ 120   TEACHING ON STANDARDS OF GREATNESS

MATT 20:20–28	MARK 10:35–45	LUKE 22:24–27
A Then came to him the[20] mother of the sons of Zebedee with her sons, worshipping *him*, and asking a certain thing of him.	A And there come near unto[35] him James and John, the sons of Zebedee, saying unto him, [3]Master, we would that thou shouldest do for us whatsoever we shall ask of thee.	
B And he said[21] unto her, What wouldest thou? She saith unto him, Command that these my two sons may sit, one on thy right hand, and one on thy left hand, in thy kingdom.	B And[36] he said unto them, What would ye that I should do for you? And they said unto him, Grant[37] unto us that we may sit, one on thy right hand, and one on *thy* left hand, in thy glory.	B *And there arose also a con-*[24] *tention among them, which of them is accounted to be* [4]*greatest.*

ERV margin: 1 Or *but some as they followed were afraid*   2 Or *through*   3 Or *Teacher*   4 Greek *greater*

B But many shall be last *that are* first; and first *that are* last. (§117 N = Mt 19:30)

B But many *that are* first shall be last; and the last first. (§117 N = Mk 10:31)

CEF   For other records of these forecasts, compare §72 A and attached references
D   Compare §74 portion L

MATT 20	MARK 10	LUKE 22

c   But[22] Jesus answered and said, Ye know not what ye ask. Are ye able to drink the cup that I am about to drink?

c But Jesus said unto them,[38] Ye know not what ye ask. Are ye able to drink the cup that I drink?

D[D]   or to be baptized with the baptism that I am baptized with?

E   They say unto him, We are able. He saith unto them, My cup[23] indeed ye shall drink:

E   And they[3] said unto him, We are able. And Jesus said unto them, The cup that I drink ye shall drink;
F[F]   and with the baptism that I am baptized withal shall ye be baptized:

G   but to sit on my right hand, and on *my* left hand, is not mine to give, but *it is for them* for whom it hath been prepared of my Father.

G   but to[40] sit on my right hand or on *my* left hand is not mine to give: but *it is for them* for whom it hath been prepared.

H   And when the[24] ten heard it, they were moved with indignation concerning the two brethren.

H   And[41] when the ten heard it, they began to be moved with indignation concerning James and John.

I   But Jesus[25] called them unto him, and said, Ye know that the rulers of the Gentiles lord it over them, and their great ones exercise authority over them.

I   And Jesus called[42] them to him, and saith unto them, Ye know that they which are accounted to rule over the Gentiles lord it over them; and their great ones exercise authority over them.

I   *And he said unto them,*[25] *The kings of the Gentiles have lordship over them; and they that have authority over them are called Benefactors.*

J[J] Not so shall it be among[26] you: but whosoever would become great among you shall be your ¹minister; and who-[27] soever would be first among you shall be your ²servant:

J[J] But it is not so among you:[43] but whosoever would become great among you, shall be your ¹minister: and whoso-[44] ever would be first among you, shall be ²servant of all.

J[J]   But[26] ye shall *not* be *so: but he that is the greater among you, let him become as the younger; and he that is chief, as he that doth serve.*

K even as the Son of man[28] came not to be ministered unto, but to minister, and to give his life a ransom for many.

K For verily the Son of man[45] came not to be ministered unto, but to minister, and to give his life a ransom for many.

K   *For whether is*[27] *greater, he that* ³*sitteth at meat, or he that serveth? is not he that* ³*sitteth at meat? but I am in the midst of you as he that serveth.* (§*138 LM*)

§ 121   THE BLIND BEGGAR OF JERICHO

MATT 20:29-34*	MARK 10:46-52	LUKE 18:35-43

A And as they went out from[29] Jericho, a great multitude followed him. And behold, two[30] blind men sitting by the way side,

A And they come to Jericho:[46] and as he went out from Jericho, with his disciples and a great multitude, the son of Timæus, Bartimæus, a blind

A And it came to pass, as he[35] drew nigh unto Jericho, a certain blind man sat by the way side begging:

ERV margin: ¹ Or *servant*   ² Greek *bondservant*   ³ Greek *reclineth*

D I came to cast fire upon the earth; and what will I, if it is already kindled? But I have a baptism to be baptized with; and how am I straitened till it be accomplished! (§95 A=Lk 12:49-50)
D Compare also portion F below
F Compare portion D above and attached references

J Whosoever therefore shall humble himself as this little child, the same is the greatest in the kingdom of heaven. (§78 E=Mt 18:4)

J If any man would be first, he shall be last of all, and minister of all. (§78 B=Mk 9:35)

J For he that is least among you all, the same is great. (§78 H=Lk 9:48)

J But he that is greatest among you shall be your servant. (§132 G=Mt 23:11)

---

*For another Matthew account of similar general content, compare §53 A

MATT 20	MARK 10	LUKE 18
	beggar, was sitting by the way side.	
B when they heard that Jesus was passing by, cried out, saying, Lord, have mercy on us, thou son of David.	B And when he heard that[47] it was Jesus of Nazareth, he began to cry out, and say, Jesus, thou son of David, have mercy on me.	B and hearing a[36] multitude going by, he inquired what this meant. And[37] they told him, that Jesus of Nazareth passeth by. And[38] he cried, saying, Jesus, thou son of David, have mercy on me.
C And[31] the multitude rebuked them, that they should hold their peace: but they cried out the more, saying, Lord, have mercy on us, thou son of David.	C And many re-[48] buked him, that he should hold his peace: but he cried out the more a great deal, Thou son of David, have mercy on me.	C And they that went be-[39] fore rebuked him, that he should hold his peace: but he cried out the more a great deal, Thou son of David, have mercy on me.
D And Jesus stood still,[32] and called them, and said, What will ye that I should do unto you?	D And Jesus stood[49] still, and said, Call ye him. And they call the blind man, saying unto him, Be of good cheer: rise, he calleth thee. And he, casting away his gar-[50] ment, sprang up, and came to Jesus. And Jesus answered[51] him, and said, What wilt thou that I should do unto thee?	D And Jesus[40] stood, and commanded him to be brought unto him: and when he was come near, he asked him, What wilt thou[41] that I should do unto thee?
E They say unto[33] him, Lord, that our eyes may be opened. And Jesus, being[34] moved with compassion, touched their eyes:	E And the blind man said unto him, [1]Rabboni, that I may receive my sight. And Jesus[52] said unto him, Go thy way; thy faith hath [2]made thee whole.	E And he said, Lord, that I may receive my sight. And[42] Jesus said unto him, Receive thy sight: thy faith hath [2]made thee whole.
F and straightway they received their sight, and followed him.	F And straightway he received his sight, and followed him in the way.	F And imme-[43] diately he received his sight, and followed him, glorifying God: G and all the people, when they saw it, gave praise unto God.

§ 122 THE RICH PUBLICAN OF JERICHO

LUKE 19:1-10

And he entered and was passing through [1] Jericho. And behold, a man called by name [2] Zacchæus; and he was a chief publican, and he was rich. And he sought to see Jesus who he [3] was; and could not for the crowd, because he was little of stature. And he ran on before, [4] and climbed up into a sycamore tree to see him: . for he was to pass that way. And when Jesus [5] came to the place, he looked up, and said unto him, Zacchæus, make haste, and come down; for to-day I must abide at thy house. And [6] he made haste, and came down, and received him joyfully. And when they saw it, they all [7] murmured, saying, He is gone in to lodge with a man that is a sinner. And Zacchæus stood, [8] and said unto the Lord, Behold, Lord, the half of my goods I give to the poor; and if I have wrongfully exacted aught of any man, I restore fourfold. And Jesus said unto him, To-day is [9]

ERV margin: [1] See John 20:16 [2] Or *saved thee*

OT references: Lk 19:8 = Exodus 22:1 and Numbers 5:6-7

LUKE 19

salvation come to this house, forasmuch as he also is a son of Abraham. For the Son of man[10] came to seek and to save that which was lost.

§ 123 APPEARANCE OF THE KINGDOM OF GOD

MATT 25:14–30   LUKE 19:11–28

A And as they heard these things, he added[11] and spake a parable, because he was nigh to Jerusalem, and *because* they supposed that the kingdom of God was immediately to appear.

B *For* it is *as* when *a man, going into another*[14] *country, called his own* [1]*servants, and delivered unto them his goods. And unto one he gave five*[15] *talents, to another two, to another one; to each according to his several ability; and he went on his journey.*

B He said therefore, A certain nobleman went[12] into a far country, to receive for himself a kingdom, and to return. And he called ten [1]serv-[13] ants of his, and gave them ten [2]pounds, and said unto them, Trade ye *herewith* till I come.

C   But[14] his citizens hated him, and sent an ambassage after him, saying, We will not that this man reign over us.

D   *Straightway he that received the five*[16] *talents went and traded with them, and made other five talents. In like manner he also that*[17] *received the two gained other two. But he that*[18] *received the one went away and digged in the earth, and hid his lord's money.*
E   *Now after a*[19] *long time the lord of those* [1]*servants cometh, and maketh a reckoning with them.*

E   And it came to pass, when he[15] was come back again, having received the kingdom, that he commanded these [1]servants, unto whom he had given the money, to be called to him, that he might know what they had gained by trading.
F   And the first came before him,[16] saying, Lord, thy pound hath made ten pounds more. And he said unto him, Well done, thou[17] good [3]servant: because thou wast found faithful in a very little, have thou authority over ten cities.

F   *And he that re-*[20] *ceived the five talents came and brought other five talents, saying, Lord, thou deliveredst unto me five talents: lo, I have gained other five talents. His lord said unto him, Well done, good and*[21] *faithful* [3]*servant: thou hast been faithful over a few things, I will set thee over many things: enter thou into the joy of thy lord.*
G   *And he also that*[22] *received the two talents came and said, Lord, thou deliveredst unto me two talents: lo, I have gained other two talents. His lord said unto him,*[23] *Well done, good and faithful* [3]*servant; thou hast been faithful over a few things, I will set thee over many things: enter thou into the joy of thy lord.*
H   *And he also that had received the one talent*[24] *came and said, Lord, I knew thee that thou art a hard man, reaping where thou didst not sow, and gathering where thou didst not scatter: and I was*[25] *afraid, and went away and hid thy talent in the earth: lo, thou hast thine own.*
I   *But his lord an-*[26] *swered and said unto him, Thou wicked and slothful* [3]*servant, thou knewest that I reap where I sowed not, and gather where I did not scatter; thou oughtest therefore to have put my money to the*[27] *bankers, and at my coming I should have received*

G   And the second came, saying, Thy[18] pound, Lord, hath made five pounds. And he[19] said unto him also, Be thou also over five cities.

H And [4]another came, saying, Lord, behold,[20] *here is* thy pound, which I kept laid up in a napkin: for I feared thee, because thou art an[21] austere man: thou takest up that thou layedst not down, and reapest that thou didst not sow.
I He saith unto him, Out of thine own mouth[22] will I judge thee, thou wicked [3]servant. Thou knewest that I am an austere man, taking up that I laid not down, and reaping that I did not sow; then wherefore gavest thou not my[23] money into the bank, and [5]I at my coming

---

ERV margin: 1 Greek *bondservants*   2 *Mina,* here translated a pound, is equal to one hundred drachmas: a drachma is a coin worth about eight pence   3 Greek *bondservant*   4 Greek *the other*   5 Or *I should have gone and required*

OT references: Lk 19:10 = Ezekiel 34:16

MATT 25	LUKE 19

back mine own with interest. Take ye away[28] *therefore the talent from him, and give it unto him that hath the ten talents.*

J^J   *For unto every one*[29] *that hath shall be given, and he shall have abundance: but from him that hath not, even that which he hath shall be taken away.*

K^K   *And cast ye out*[30] *the unprofitable* ¹*servant into the outer darkness: there shall be the weeping and gnashing of teeth.* (§*136 H–Q*)

should have required it with interest ? And he[24] said unto them that stood by, Take away from him the pound, and give it unto him that hath the ten pounds.   And they said unto him, Lord,[25] he hath ten pounds.

J^J   I say unto you, that unto[26] every one that hath shall be given; but from him that hath not, even that which he hath shall be taken away from him.

L   Howbeit these[27] mine enemies, which would not that I should reign over them, bring hither, and slay them before me.

M   And when he had thus spoken, he went on[28] before, going up to Jerusalem.

ERV margin: ¹ Greek *bondservant*

J For whosoever hath, to him shall be given, and he shall have abundance: but from him that hath not, from him shall be taken away even that which he hath. (§47 H = Mt 13:12)

J For he that hath, to him shall be given: and he that hath not, from him shall be taken away even that which he hath. (§47 V = Mk 4:25)

J For whosoever hath, to him shall be given; and whosoever hath not, from him shall be taken away even that which he thinketh he hath. (§47 V = Lk 8:18)

K And I say unto you, that many shall come from the east and the west, and shall sit down with Abraham, and Isaac, and Jacob, in the kingdom of heaven: but the sons of the kingdom shall be cast forth into the outer darkness: there shall be the weeping and gnashing of teeth. (§39 D = Mt 8:11–12)

K There shall be the weeping and gnashing of teeth, when ye shall see Abraham, and Isaac, and Jacob, and all the prophets, in the kingdom of God, and yourselves cast forth without. And they shall come from the east and west, and from the north and south, and shall sit down in the kingdom of God. (§100 G = Lk 13:28–29)

K And shall cast them into the furnace of fire: there shall be the weeping and gnashing of teeth. (§48 L = Mt 13:42)

K And shall cast them into the furnace of fire: there shall be the weeping and gnashing of teeth. (§48 Q = Mt 13:50)

K And cast him out into the outer darkness; there shall be the weeping and gnashing of teeth. (§129 P = Mt 22:13)

K And shall cut him asunder, and appoint his portion with the hypocrites: there shall be the weeping and gnashing of teeth. (§136 D = Mt 24:51)

K And shall cut him asunder, and appoint his portion with the unfaithful. (§94 E = Lk 12:46)

CHAPTER XVIII

CHALLENGE OF THE JERUSALEM LEADERS BY JESUS

§ 124 JESUS ENTERS JERUSALEM AS A POPULAR LEADER

MATT 21:1–11	MARK 11:1–11	LUKE 19:29–44
A And when they drew nigh 1 unto Jerusalem, and came unto Bethphage, unto the mount of Olives, then Jesus sent two disciples, saying unto 2 them,	A And when they draw nigh 1 unto Jerusalem, unto Bethphage and Bethany, at the mount of Olives, he sendeth two of his disciples, and saith 2 unto them,	A And it came to pass, when 29 he drew nigh unto Bethphage and Bethany, at the mount that is called the mount of Olives, he sent two of the disciples, saying, 30
B Go into the village that is over against you, and straightway ye shall find an ass tied, and a colt with her: loose *them*, and bring *them* unto me. And if any one say 3 aught unto you, ye shall say, The Lord hath need of them; and straightway he will send them.	B Go your way into the village that is over against you: and straightway as ye enter into it, ye shall find a colt tied, whereon no man ever yet sat; loose him, and bring him. And if any one say 3 unto you, Why do ye this? say ye, The Lord hath need of him; and straightway he 1will send him 2back hither.	B Go your way into the village over against *you;* in the which as ye enter ye shall find a colt tied, whereon no man ever yet sat: loose him, and bring him. And if 31 any one ask you, Why do ye loose him? thus shall ye say, The Lord hath need of him.
C Now this is come to 4 pass, that it might be fulfilled which was spoken 3by the prophet, saying,		
Tell ye the daughter of Zion, 5 Behold, thy King cometh unto thee, Meek, and riding upon an ass, And upon a colt the foal of an ass.		
D And the disciples went, and 6 did even as Jesus appointed them,	D And 4 they went away, and found a colt tied at the door without in the open street; and they loose him. And certain of 5 them that stood there said unto them, What do ye, loosing the colt? And they said 6 unto them even as Jesus had said: and they let them go.	D And they that were sent 32 went away, and found even as he had said unto them. And 33 as they were loosing the colt, the owners thereof said unto them, Why loose ye the colt? And they said, The Lord 34 hath need of him.
E and brought the ass, 7 and the colt, and put on them their garments; and he sat thereon.	E And they bring the colt 7 unto Jesus, and cast on him their garments; and he sat upon him.	E And they 35 brought him to Jesus: and they threw their garments upon the colt, and set Jesus thereon.
F And the most part 8 of the multitude spread their garments in the way; and others cut branches from the trees, and spread them in the way.	F And many spread 8 their garments upon the way; and others 4branches, which they had cut from the fields.	F And as he went, 36 they spread their garments in the way.
G And the multitudes 9 that went before him, and	G And they that went before, 9 and they that followed, cried,	G And as he was now 37 drawing nigh, *even* at the de-

---

ERV margin: 1 Greek *sendeth*   2 Or *again*   3 Or *through*   4 Greek *layers of leaves*

OT references: Mt 21:5 = Isaiah 62:11 and Zechariah 9:9

MATT 21	MARK 11	LUKE 19
that followed, cried, saying, Hosanna to the son of David: Blessed *is* he that cometh in the name of the Lord; Hosanna in the highest.	Hosanna; Blessed *is* he that cometh in the name of the Lord: Blessed *is* the kingdom[10] that cometh, *the kingdom* of our father David: Hosanna in the highest.	scent of the mount of Olives, the whole multitude of the disciples began to rejoice and praise God with a loud voice for all the [1]mighty works which they had seen; saying,[38] Blessed *is* the King that cometh in the name of the Lord: peace in heaven, and glory in the highest.

H   *Compare §126 portions GH*

LUKE (continued):

H   And some[39] of the Pharisees from the multitude said unto him, [2]Master, rebuke thy disciples. And he answered and said, I[40] tell you that, if these shall hold their peace, the stones will cry out.

1   And when he drew nigh, he[41] saw the city and wept over it, saying, [3]If thou hadst known[42] in this day, even thou, the things which belong unto peace! but now they are hid from thine eyes. For the days[43] shall come upon thee, when thine enemies shall cast up a [4]bank about thee, and compass thee round, and keep thee in on every side, and[44] shall dash thee to the ground, and thy children within thee; and they shall not leave in thee one stone upon another; because thou knewest not the time of thy visitation.

J   And when[10] he was come into Jerusalem, all the city was stirred, saying, Who is this? And the multi-[11]tudes said, This is the prophet, Jesus, from Nazareth of Galilee.

K   And he entered into Jeru-[11]salem, into the temple; and when he had looked round about upon all things, it being now eventide, he went out unto Bethany with the twelve.

§ 125   JESUS RETURNS TO JERUSALEM

MATT 21:18–19	MARK 11:12–14
Now in the morning as he re-[18] turned to the city, he hungered. And seeing [5]a fig tree by the[19] way side, he came to it, and found nothing thereon, but leaves only; and he saith unto it, Let there be no fruit from thee henceforward for ever. (§127 A)	And on the morrow, when[12] they were come out from Bethany, he hungered. And[13] seeing a fig tree afar off having leaves, he came, if haply he might find anything thereon: and when he came to it, he found nothing but leaves; for it was not the season of figs. And he answered and said[14]

ERV margin: 1 Greek *powers*   2 Or *Teacher*   3 Or *O that thou hadst known*   4 Greek *palisade*   5 Or *a single*

OT references: Mt 21:9 and Mk 11:9–10 and Lk 19:38 = Psalm 118:25–26   Lk 19:44 = Psalm 137:9

MARK 11

unto it, No man eat fruit from
thee henceforward for ever.
And his disciples heard it.

§ 126 JESUS CASTS COMMERCE FROM THE TEMPLE

MATT 21:12–17

A And Jesus entered into the[12] temple [1]of God, and cast out all them that sold and bought in the temple, and overthrew the tables of the money-changers, and the seats of them that sold the doves;

C   and[13] he saith unto them, It is writ-ten, My house shall be called a house of prayer: but ye make it a den of robbers.

E *Compare §130 portion I*

F   And[14] the blind and the lame came to him in the temple: and he healed them.
G   But when the[15] chief priests and the scribes saw the wonderful things that he did, and the children that were crying in the temple and saying, Hosanna to the son of David; they were moved with indignation, and said[16] unto him, Hearest thou what these are saying?
H   And Jesus saith unto them, Yea: did ye never read, Out of the mouth of babes and sucklings thou hast perfected praise?
I   And[17] he left them, and went forth out of the city to Bethany, and lodged there.

MARK 11:15–19

A And they come to Jerusa-[15] lem: and he entered into the temple, and began to cast out them that sold and them that bought in the temple, and overthrew the tables of the money-changers, and the seats of them that sold the doves;
B and he would not suffer that[16] any man should carry a vessel through the temple.
C   And he[17] taught, and said unto them, Is it not written, My house shall be called a house of prayer for all the nations? but ye have made it a den of robbers.

E   And the chief priests[18] and the scribes heard it, and sought how they might destroy him: for they feared him, for all the multitude was astonished at his teaching.

I And [2]every evening [3]he[19] went forth out of the city.

LUKE 19:45–48

A And he entered into the[45] temple, and began to cast out them that sold,

C   saying unto[46] them, It is written, And my house shall be a house of prayer: but ye have made it a den of robbers.

D And he was teaching daily[47] in the temple.
E   But the chief priests and the scribes and the principal men of the people sought to destroy him: and[48] they could not find what they might do; for the people all hung upon him, listening.

G *Compare §124 portion H*

H *Compare §124 portion H*

I *And every day he was teach-[21]: ing in the temple; and every[37] night he went out, and lodged in the mount that is called the mount of Olives. And all the[38] people came early in the morning to him in the temple, to hear him. (§135 R)*

ERV margin: 1 Many ancient authorities omit *of God*   2 Greek *whenever evening came*   3 Some ancient authorities read *they*

OT references: Mt 21:13 and Mk 11:17 and Lk 19:46 = Isaiah 56:7 and Jeremiah 7:11   Mt 21:16 = Psalm 8:2

§ 127   FAITH AS A POWER

MATT 21:18-22

A   Now in the morning as he[18] returned to the city, he hungered. And seeing [1]a fig tree[19] by the way side, he came to it, and found nothing thereon, but leaves only; and he saith unto it, Let there be no fruit from thee henceforward for ever.

B   And immediately the fig tree withered away. And[20] when the disciples saw it, they marvelled, saying, How did the fig tree immediately wither away?

C[C]   And Jesus an-[21] swered and said unto them, Verily I say unto you, If ye have faith, and doubt not, ye shall not only do what is done to the fig tree, but even if ye shall say unto this mountain, Be thou taken up and cast into the sea, it shall be done.
D   And all things, what-[22] soever ye shall ask in prayer, believing, ye shall receive.

E[E]   *For if ye forgive men their* [6]: *trespasses, your heavenly Father*[14] *will also forgive you. But if*[15] *ye forgive not men their trespasses, neither will your Father forgive your trespasses.* (§37 X)

MARK 11:20-25

A   *And on the morrow, when*[11]: *they were come out from Beth-*[12] *any, he hungered. And seeing*[13] *a fig tree afar off having leaves, he came, if haply he might find anything thereon: and when he came to it, he found nothing but leaves; for it was not the season of figs. And he answered*[14] *and said unto it, No man eat fruit from thee henceforward for ever. And his disciples heard it.* (§125)
B   And as they passed by in[20] the morning, they saw the fig tree withered away from the roots. And Peter calling to[21] remembrance saith unto him, Rabbi, behold, the fig tree which thou cursedst is withered away.

C[C]   And Jesus answer-[22] ing saith unto them, Have faith in God. Verily I say[23] unto you, Whosoever shall say unto this mountain, Be thou taken up and cast into the sea; and shall not doubt in his heart, but shall believe that what he saith cometh to pass; he shall have it.
D   There-[24] fore I say unto you, All things whatsoever ye pray and ask for, believe that ye have received them, and ye shall have them.
E[E]   And whensoever[25] ye stand praying, forgive, if ye have aught against any one; that your Father also which is in heaven may forgive you your trespasses.[2]

ERV margin: 1 Or *a single*   2 Many ancient authorities add verse 26: *But if ye do not forgive, neither will your Father which is in heaven forgive your trespasses*

c   And he saith unto them, Because of your little faith: for verily I say unto you, If ye have faith as a grain of mustard seed, ye shall say unto this mountain, Remove hence to yonder place; and it shall remove. (§75 GH = Mt 17:20)
E   So shall also my heavenly Father do unto you, if ye forgive not every one his brother from your hearts. (§78 x = Mt 18:35)

c   And the Lord said, If ye have faith as a grain of mustard seed, ye would say unto this sycamine tree, Be thou rooted up, and be thou planted in the sea; and it would have obeyed you. (§109 F = Lk 17:6)

CHAPTER XIX

FINAL CONTEST OF JESUS WITH THE JEWISH RULERS

§ 128   JEWISH RULERS CHALLENGE THE AUTHORITY OF JESUS

MATT 21:23-27	MARK 11:27-33	LUKE 20:1-8
A And when he was come²³ into the temple, the chief priests and the elders of the people came unto him as he was teaching, and said, By what authority doest thou these things? and who gave thee this authority?	A And they come again to²⁷ Jerusalem: and as he was walking in the temple, there come to him the chief priests, and the scribes, and the elders; and they said unto him, By²⁸ what authority doest thou these things? or who gave thee this authority to do these things?	A And it came to pass, on ¹ one of the days, as he was teaching the people in the temple, and preaching the gospel, there came upon him the chief priests and the scribes with the elders; and ² they spake, saying unto him, Tell us: By what authority doest thou these things? or who is he that gave thee this authority?
B And Jesus²⁴ answered and said unto them, I also will ask you one ¹question, which if ye tell me, I likewise will tell you by what authority I do these things. The baptism of John, whence²⁵ was it? from heaven or from men?	B And Jesus said unto²⁹ them, I will ask of you one ¹question, and answer me, and I will tell you by what author-ity I do these things. The³⁰ baptism of John, was it from heaven, or from men? answer me.	B And he answered ³ and said unto them, I also will ask you a ¹question; and tell me: The baptism of John, was ⁴ it from heaven, or from men?
c And they reasoned with themselves, saying, If we shall say, From heaven; he will say unto us, Why then did ye not believe him? But if we shall²⁶ say, From men; we fear the multitude; for all hold John as a prophet.	c And they reasoned with³¹ themselves, saying, If we shall say, From heaven; he will say, Why then did ye not be-lieve him? ²But should we³² say, From men—they feared the people: ³for all verily held John to be a prophet.	c And they reasoned with ⁵ themselves, saying, If we shall say, From heaven; he will say, Why did ye not believe him? But if we shall say, From ⁶ men; all the people will stone us: for they be persuaded that John was a prophet.
D And they an-²⁷ swered Jesus, and said, We know not. He also said unto them, Neither tell I you by what authority I do these things.	D And³³ they answered Jesus and say, We know not. And Jesus saith unto them, Neither tell I you by what authority I do these things.	D And they ⁷ answered, that they knew not whence *it was*. And Jesus ⁸ said unto them, Neither tell I you by what authority I do these things.

§ 129   PARABLES IN CONDEMNATION OF JEWISH LEADERS

MATT 21:28—22:14	MARK 12:1-12	LUKE 20:9-19
A But what think ye? A²⁸ man had two sons; and he came to the first, and said, ⁴Son, go work to-day in the vineyard. And he answered²⁹ and said, I will not: but after-ward he repented himself, and went. And he came to the³⁰ second, and said likewise. And he answered and said, I *go*, sir: and went not. Whether of the twain did³¹		

ERV margin: ¹ Greek *word*   ² Or *But shall we say, From men?*   ³ Or *for all held John to be a prophet indeed*
⁴ Greek *Child*

137

MATT 21

the will of his father? They say, The first.

B   Jesus saith unto them, Verily I say unto you, that the publicans and the harlots go into the kingdom of God before you. For John 32 came unto you in the way of righteousness, and ye believed him not: but the publicans and the harlots believed him: and ye, when ye saw it, did not even repent yourselves afterward, that ye might believe him.

MARK 12

LUKE 20

B *And all the people when* 7 *they heard, and the publicans,* 29 *justified God,* 1*being baptized with the baptism of John. But* 30 *the Pharisees and the lawyers rejected for themselves the counsel of God,* 2*being not baptized of him.* (§41 I)

C Hear another parable: 33 There was a man that was a householder, which planted a vineyard, and set a hedge about it, and digged a winepress in it, and built a tower, and let it out to husbandmen, and went into another country.

D   And when the season of 34 the fruits drew near, he sent his 3servants to the husbandmen, to receive 5his fruits. And the husbandmen took his 35 3servants, and beat one, and killed another, and stoned another.

E   Again, he sent other 36 3servants more than the first: and they did unto them in like manner.

C And he began to speak 1 unto them in parables. A man planted a vineyard, and set a hedge about it, and digged a pit for the winepress, and built a tower, and let it out to husbandmen, and went into another country.

D   And at 2 the season he sent to the husbandmen a 4servant, that he might receive from the husbandmen of the fruits of the vineyard. And they took 3 him, and beat him, and sent him away empty.

E   And again 4 he sent unto them another 4servant; and him they wounded in the head, and handled shamefully. And he 5 sent another; and him they killed: and many others; beating some, and killing some.

C And he began to speak 9 unto the people this parable: A man planted a vineyard, and let it out to husbandmen, and went into another country for a long time.

D   And at 10 the season he sent unto the husbandmen a 4servant, that they should give him of the fruit of the vineyard: but the husbandmen beat him, and sent him away empty.

E   And 11 he sent yet another 4servant: and him also they beat, and handled him shamefully, and sent him away empty. And 12 he sent yet a third: and him also they wounded, and cast him forth.

F   But afterward he 37 sent unto them his son, saying, They will reverence my son. But the husbandmen, 38 when they saw the son, said among themselves, This is the heir; come, let us kill him, and take his inheritance. And 39 they took him, and cast him forth out of the vineyard, and killed him.

F He had yet one, a beloved 6 son: he sent him last unto them, saying, They will reverence my son. But those hus- 7 bandmen said among themselves, This is the heir; come, let us kill him, and the inheritance shall be ours. And they 8 took him, and killed him, and cast him forth out of the vineyard.

F   And the lord of the 13 vineyard said, What shall I do? I will send my beloved son: it may be they will reverence him. But when the 14 husbandmen saw him, they reasoned one with another, saying, This is the heir: let us kill him, that the inheritance may be ours. And they cast 15 him forth out of the vineyard, and killed him.

G   When therefore 40 the lord of the vineyard shall come, what will he do unto those husbandmen? They say 41 unto him, He will miserably destroy those miserable men, and will let out the vineyard

G   What therefore will 9 the lord of the vineyard do? he will come and destroy the husbandmen, and will give the vineyard unto others.

G   What therefore will the lord of the vineyard do unto them? He will 16 come and destroy these husbandmen, and will give the vineyard unto others.

ERV margin: 1 Or *having been*   2 Or *not having been*   3 Greek *bondservants*   4 Greek *bondservant*   5 Or *the fruits of it*

OT references: Mt 21:33 and Mk 12:1 and Lk 20:9 = Isaiah 5:1-2

MATT 21-22	MARK 12	LUKE 20
unto other husbandmen, which shall render him the fruits in their seasons.		
H Jesus[42] saith unto them, Did ye never read in the scriptures,	H Have[10] ye not read even this scripture;	H And when they heard it, they said, [1]God forbid. But he looked[17] upon them, and said, What then is this that is written,

MATT 21-22	MARK 12	LUKE 20
The stone which the builders rejected, The same was made the head of the corner: This was from the Lord, And it is marvellous in our eyes?	The stone which the builders rejected, The same was made the head of the corner: This was from the Lord, 11 And it is marvellous in our eyes?	The stone which the builders rejected, The same was made the head of the corner?

MATT 21-22	MARK 12	LUKE 20
I Therefore say I unto you,[43] The kingdom of God shall be taken away from you, and shall be given to a nation bringing forth the fruits thereof.		
J [2]And he that falleth on[44] this stone shall be broken to pieces: but on whomsoever it shall fall, it will scatter him as dust.		J Every one that falleth on[18] that stone shall be broken to pieces; but on whomsoever it shall fall, it will scatter him as dust.
K And when the chief[45] priests and the Pharisees heard his parables, they perceived that he spake of them. And when they sought to lay[46] hold on him, they feared the multitudes, because they took him for a prophet.	K And they sought to lay hold[12] on him; and they feared the multitude; for they perceived that he spake the parable against them: and they left him, and went away.	K And the scribes and the[19] chief priests sought to lay hands on him in that very hour; and they feared the people: for they perceived that he spake this parable against them.

MATT 21-22	MARK 12	LUKE 20
L And Jesus answered and[22]: spake again in parables unto 1 them, saying, The kingdom of 2 heaven is likened unto a certain king, which made a marriage feast for his son, and 3 sent forth his [3]servants to call them that were bidden to the marriage feast: and they would not come. Again he 4 sent forth other [3]servants, saying, Tell them that are bidden, Behold, I have made ready my dinner: my oxen and my fatlings are killed, and all things are ready: come to the marriage feast.		L *But he said unto him, A cer-*[14]: *tain man made a great supper;*[16] *and he bade many: and he sent*[17] *forth his* [4]*servant at supper time to say to them that were bidden, Come; for all* things are now ready.
M But they 5 made light of it, and went their ways, one to his own farm, another to his merchandise: and the rest laid hold on 6 his [3]servants, and entreated them shamefully, and killed them.		M *And they all with one*[18] *consent began to make excuse. The first said unto him, I have bought a field, and I must needs go out and see it: I pray thee have me excused. And another*[19] *said, I have bought five yoke of oxen, and I go to prove them: I*

ERV margin: 1 Greek *Be it not so*   2 Some ancient authorities omit verse 44   3 Greek *bondservants*   4 Greek *bondservant*

OT references: Mt 21:42 and Mk 12:10-11 and Lk 20:17 = Psalm 118:22-23   Mt 21:44 and Lk 20:18 = Isaiah 8:14-15

MATT 22

LUKE

pray thee have me excused.
*And another said, I have mar-*20
ried a wife, and therefore I can-
not come. And the 2*servant*21
came, and told his lord these
things.

N   But the king was 7
wroth; and he sent his armies,
and destroyed those mur-
derers, and burned their city.
o Then saith he to his 1serv- 8
ants, The wedding is ready,
but they that were bidden
were not worthy. Go ye 9
therefore unto the partings
of the highways, and as many
as ye shall find, bid to the
marriage feast. And those10
1servants went out into the
highways, and gathered together all as many as they
found, both bad and good:
and the wedding was filled
with guests.

o   *Then the master of the*
house being angry said to his
2*servant, Go out quickly into*
the streets and lanes of the city,
and bring in hither the poor
and maimed and blind and
lame. And the 2*servant said,*22
Lord, what thou didst com-
mand is done, and yet there is
*room. And the lord said unto*23
the 2*servant, Go out into the*
highways and hedges, and con-
strain them to come in, that
*my house may be filled. For*24
I say unto you, that none of
those men which were bidden
shall taste of my supper.
(§ *103 E-H*)

PP   But when the11
king came in to behold the
guests, he saw there a man
which had not on a wedding-
garment: and he saith unto12
him, Friend, how camest thou
in hither not having a wedding-
garment? And he was speech-
less. Then the king said to13
the 3servants, Bind him hand
and foot, and cast him out into
the outer darkness; there
shall be the weeping and
gnashing of teeth. For many14
are called, but few chosen.

§ 130 EFFORTS TO ACCUMULATE EVIDENCE AGAINST JESUS

MATT 22:15-40   MARK 12:13-34   LUKE 20:20-40

A Then went the Pharisees,15
and took counsel how they
might ensnare him in *his* talk.
And they send to him their16
disciples, with the Herodians,

A And they send unto him13
certain of the Pharisees and
of the Herodians, that they
might catch him in talk.

A And they watched him,20
and sent forth spies, which
feigned themselves to be
righteous, that they might
take hold of his speech, so as

ERV margin: 1 Greek *bondservants*   2 Greek *bondservant*   3 Or *ministers*

P And I say unto you, that many shall come from the
east and the west, and shall sit down with Abraham, and
Isaac, and Jacob, in the kingdom of heaven: but the
sons of the kingdom shall be cast forth into the outer
darkness: there shall be the weeping and gnashing of
teeth. (§39 D = Mt 8:11-12)

P There shall be the weeping and gnashing of teeth,
when ye shall see Abraham, and Isaac, and Jacob, and
all the prophets, in the kingdom of God, and yourselves
cast forth without. And they shall come from the east
and west, and from the north and south, and shall sit
down in the kingdom of God. (§100 G = Lk 13:28-29)

P And shall cast them into the furnace of fire: there shall be the weeping and gnashing of teeth. (§48 L = Mt 13:42)
P And shall cast them into the furnace of fire: there shall be the weeping and gnashing of teeth. (§48 Q = Mt 13:50)

P And shall cut him asunder, and appoint his portion
with the hypocrites: there shall be the weeping and
gnashing of teeth. (§136 D = Mt 24:51)

P And shall cut him asunder, and appoint his portion
with the unfaithful. (§94 E = Lk 12:46)

P And cast ye out the unprofitable servant into the outer darkness: there shall be the weeping and gnashing of teeth.
(§136 Q = Mt 25:30)

MATT 22

B saying, ¹Master, we know that thou art true, and teachest the way of God in truth, and carest not for any one: for thou regardest not the person of men. Tell us there-¹⁷ fore, What thinkest thou? Is it lawful to give tribute unto Cæsar, or not?

c But Jesus per-¹⁸ ceived their wickedness, and said, Why tempt ye me, ye hypocrites? Shew me the¹⁹ tribute money. And they brought unto him a ²penny. And he saith unto them,²⁰ Whose is this image and superscription? They say unto²¹ him, Cæsar's. Then saith he unto them, Render therefore unto Cæsar the things that are Cæsar's; and unto God the things that are God's.

D And²² when they heard it, they marvelled, and left him, and went their way.

E On that day there came to²³ him Sadducees, ³which say that there is no resurrection: and they asked him, saying,²⁴

F ¹Master, Moses said, If a man die, having no children his brother ⁴shall marry his wife, and raise up seed unto his brother. Now there were²⁵ with us seven brethren: and the first married and deceased, and having no seed left his wife unto his brother; in like²⁶ manner the second also, and the third, unto the ⁵seventh. And after them all the woman²⁷ died. In the resurrection²⁸ therefore whose wife shall she be of the seven? for they all had her.

G But Jesus answered²⁹ and said unto them, Ye do err,

MARK 12

B And¹⁴ when they were come, they say unto him, ¹Master, we know that thou art true, and carest not for any one: for thou regardest not the person of men, but of a truth teachest the way of God: Is it lawful to give tribute unto Cæsar, or not? Shall we give, or¹⁵ shall we not give?

c But he, knowing their hypocrisy, said unto them, Why tempt ye me? bring me a ²penny, that I may see it. And they¹⁶ brought it. And he saith unto them, Whose is this image and superscription? And they said unto him, Cæsar's. And Jesus said unto¹⁷ them, Render unto Cæsar the things that are Cæsar's, and unto God the things that are God's.

D And they marvelled greatly at him.

E And there come unto him¹⁸ Sadducees, which say that there is no resurrection; and they asked him, saying,

F ¹Mas-¹⁹ ter, Moses wrote unto us, If a man's brother die, and leave a wife behind him, and leave no child, that his brother should take his wife, and raise up seed unto his brother. There were seven brethren:²⁰ and the first took a wife, and dying left no seed; and the²¹ second took her, and died, leaving no seed behind him; and the third likewise: and²² the seven left no seed. Last of all the woman also died. In the resurrection whose wife²³ shall she be of them? for the seven had her to wife.

G Jesus²⁴ said unto them, Is it not for

LUKE 20

to deliver him up to the rule and to the authority of the governor.

B And they asked²¹ him, saying, ¹Master, we know that thou sayest and teachest rightly, and acceptest not the person of any, but of a truth teachest the way of God: Is it lawful for us to give²² tribute unto Cæsar, or not?

c But he perceived their²³ craftiness, and said unto them, Shew me a ²penny. Whose²⁴ image and superscription hath it? And they said, Cæsar's. And he said unto them, Then²⁵ render unto Cæsar the things that are Cæsar's, and unto God the things that are God's.

D And they were not able to²⁶ take hold of the saying before the people: and they marvelled at his answer, and held their peace.

E And there came to him²⁷ certain of the Sadducees, they which say that there is no resurrection; and they asked²⁸ him, saying, ¹Master, Moses wrote unto us, that if a man's brother die, having a wife, and he be childless, his brother should take the wife, and raise up seed unto his brother. There were therefore seven²⁹ brethren: and the first took a wife, and died childless; and³⁰ the second; and the third³¹ took her; and likewise the seven also left no children, and died. Afterward the woman³² also died. In the resurrection³³ therefore whose wife of them shall she be? for the seven had her to wife.

G And Jesus³⁴ said unto them, The sons of

ERV margin: 1 Or *Teacher* 2 The word in the Greek denotes a coin worth about eight pence halfpenny 3 Greek *saying* 4 Greek *shall perform the duty of a husband's brother to his wife*: compare Deuteronomy 25:5 5 Greek *seven*

OT references: Mt 22:24 and Mk 12:19 and Lk 20:28 = Deuteronomy 25:5-6 (compare Genesis 38:8)

MATT 22	MARK 12	LUKE 20
not knowing the scriptures, nor the power of God. For in30 the resurrection they neither marry, nor are given in marriage, but are as angels[2] in heaven.	this cause that ye err, that ye know not the scriptures, nor the power of God? For when25 they shall rise from the dead, they neither marry, nor are given in marriage; but are as angels in heaven.	this [1]world marry, and are given in marriage: but they35 that are accounted worthy to attain to that [1]world, and the resurrection from the dead, neither marry, nor are given in marriage: for neither can36 they die any more: for they are equal unto the angels; and are sons of God, being sons of the resurrection.
H But as touching the31 resurrection of the dead, have ye not read that which was spoken unto you by God, saying, I am the God of Abra-32 ham, and the God of Isaac, and the God of Jacob? God is not *the God* of the dead, but of the living.	H But as26 touching the dead, that they are raised; have ye not read in the book of Moses, in *the place concerning* the Bush, how God spake unto him, saying, I *am* the God of Abraham, and the God of Isaac, and the God of Jacob? He is not the27 God of the dead, but of the living: ye do greatly err.	H But37 that the dead are raised, even Moses shewed, in *the place concerning* the Bush, when he calleth the Lord the God of Abraham, and the God of Isaac, and the God of Jacob. Now he is not the God of the38 dead, but of the living: for all live unto him.
I And when the33 multitudes heard it, they were astonished at his teaching.	I *Compare §126 portion E*	I *Compare §126 portion E*
	J *Compare portion O below*	J And certain39 of the scribes answering said, [3]Master, thou hast well said.
K *Compare §131 portion D*	K *Compare portion Q below*	K For they durst not any more40 ask him any question.
L But the Pharisees, when34 they heard that he had put the Sadducees to silence, gathered themselves together. And one of them, a lawyer,35 asked him a question, tempting him, [3]Master, which is36 the great commandment in the law?	L And one of the scribes28 came, and heard them questioning together, and knowing that he had answered them well, asked him, What commandment is the first of all?	L *And behold, a certain law-10: yer stood up and tempted him,*25 *saying,* [3]*Master, what shall I do to inherit eternal life? And he said unto him, What is*26 *written in the law? how readest thou?*
M And he said unto37 him, Thou shalt love the Lord thy God with all thy heart, and with all thy soul, and with all thy mind. This is the38 great and first commandment. [4]And a second like *unto it* is39 this, Thou shalt love thy neighbour as thyself.	M Jesus answered, The first is,29 Hear, O Israel; [5]The Lord our God, the Lord is one: and30 thou shalt love the Lord thy God [6]with all thy heart, and [6]with all thy soul, and [6]with all thy mind, and [6]with all thy strength. The second31 is this, Thou shalt love thy neighbour as thyself.	M *And he answering said,*27 *Thou shalt love the Lord thy God* [6]*with all thy heart, and with all thy soul, and with all thy strength, and with all thy mind; and thy neighbour as thyself.*
NN On these40 two commandments hangeth the whole law, and the prophets.	NN There is none other commandment greater than these.	NN *And he said unto him,*28 *Thou hast answered right: this do, and thou shalt live.* (§83 A)
	O And the32 scribe said unto him, Of a truth, [3]Master, thou hast well	O *Compare portion J above*

ERV margin: 1 Or *age*   2 Many ancient authorities add *of God*   3 Or *Teacher*   4 Or *And a second is like unto it, Thou shalt love* etc.   5 Or *The Lord* is *our God; the Lord is one*   6 Greek *from*

OT references: Mt 22:32 and Mk 12:26 and Lk 20:37 = Exodus 3:6   Mk 12:29 = Deuteronomy 6:4 Mt 22:37 and Mk 12:30 and Lk 10:27 = Deuteronomy 6:5   Mt 22:39 and Mk 12:31 and Lk 10:27 = Leviticus 19:18 Lk 10:28 = Leviticus 18:5   Mk 12:32 = Deuteronomy 6:4 and 4:35

N For this is the law and the prophets. (§38 L = Mt 7:12)

MATT 22	MARK 12	LUKE 20
	said that he is one; and there is none other but he: and to33 love him with all the heart, and with all the understanding, and with all the strength, and to love his neighbour as himself, is much more than all whole burnt offerings and sacrifices. P And when Jesus34 saw that he answered discreetly, he said unto him, Thou art not far from the kingdom of God.	
Q *Compare §131 portion D*	Q And no man after that durst ask him any question.	Q *Compare portion K above*

§ 131   THE PROBLEM OF THE CHRIST

MATT 22:41-46	MARK 12:35-37	LUKE 20:41-44
A Now while the Pharisees41 were gathered together, Jesus asked them a question, saying,42 What think ye of the Christ? whose son is he? They say unto him, *The son* of David.	A And Jesus answered and35 said, as he taught in the temple, How say the scribes that the Christ is the son of David?	A And he said unto them,41 How say they that the Christ is David's son?
B He saith unto them, How43 then doth David in the Spirit call him Lord, saying, The Lord said unto my44 Lord, Sit thou on my right hand, Till I put thine enemies underneath thy feet? If David then calleth him45 Lord, how is he his son?	B David himself said in the36 Holy Spirit, The Lord said unto my Lord, Sit thou on my right hand, Till I make thine enemies ¹the footstool of thy feet. David himself calleth him37 Lord; and whence is he his son? C And ²the common people heard him gladly.	B For David42 himself saith in the book of Psalms, The Lord said unto my Lord, Sit thou on my right hand, Till I make thine enemies43 the footstool of thy feet. David therefore calleth him44 Lord, and how is he his son?
D And46 no one was able to answer him a word, neither durst any man from that day forth ask him any more questions.	D *Compare §130 portion Q*	D *Compare §130 portion K*

ERV margin: ı Some ancient authorities read *underneath thy feet*   2 Or *the great multitude*

OT references: Mk 12:33=Deuteronomy 6:5 and Leviticus 19:18 and 1 Samuel 15:22   Mt 22:44 and Mk 12:36 and Lk 20:42-43=Psalm 110:1

§ 132 DISCOURSE IN CONDEMNATION OF SCRIBES AND PHARISEES

MATT 23:1-39	MARK 12:38-40	LUKE 20:45-47
A Then spake Jesus to the 1 multitudes and to his disciples, saying, 2	A And in his teaching he38 said,	A And in the hearing of all45 the people he said unto his disciples,
B The scribes and the Pharisees sit on Moses' seat: all things therefore 3 whatsoever they bid you, *these* do and observe: but do not ye after their works; for they say, and do not.		
C Yea, they 4 bind heavy burdens 1and grievous to be borne, and lay them on men's shoulders; but they themselves will not move them with their finger.		C *Woe unto you lawyers also!*11: *for ye lade men with burdens*46 *grievous to be borne, and ye yourselves touch not the burdens with one of your fingers.* (§90 G)
D But 5 all their works they do for to be seen of men: for they make broad their phylacteries, and enlarge the borders *of their garments*, and love the chief 6 place at feasts, and the chief seats in the synagogues, and 7 the salutations in the marketplaces, and to be called of men, Rabbi.	D Beware of the scribes, which desire to walk in long robes, and *to have* salutations in the marketplaces, and chief39 seats in the synagogues, and chief places at feasts:	D Beware of the scribes,46 which desire to walk in long robes, and love salutations in the marketplaces, and chief seats in the synagogues, and chief places at feasts; *Woe unto you Pharisees! for*11: *ye love the chief seats in the*43 *synagogues, and the salutations in the marketplaces.* (§90 D)
	E they40 which devour widows' houses, 2and for a pretence make long prayers; these shall receive greater condemnation.	E which47 devour widows' houses, and for a pretence make long prayers: these shall receive greater condemnation.
F But be not ye 8 called Rabbi: for one is your teacher, and all ye are brethren. And call no man your 9 father on the earth: for one is your Father, 3which is in heaven. Neither be ye called10 masters: for one is your master, *even* the Christ. GG But he11 that is 4greatest among you shall be your 5servant.		

ERV margin: 1 Many ancient authorities omit *and grievous to be borne*   2 Or *even while for a pretence they make* 3 Greek *the heavenly*   4 Greek *greater*   5 Or *minister*

OT references: Mt 23:5 = Exodus 13:9 and Numbers 15:38-39 and Deuteronomy 6:8 and 11:18

G Whosoever therefore shall humble himself as this little child, the same is the greatest in the kingdom of heaven. (§78 E = Mt 18:4)	G If any man would be first, he shall be last of all, and minister of all. (§78 B = Mk 9:35)	G For he that is least among you all, the same is great. (§78 H = Lk 9:48)
G Not so shall it be among you: but whosoever would become great among you shall be your minister; and whosoever would be first among you shall be your servant. (§120 J = Mt 20:26-27)	G But it is not so among you: but whosoever would become great among you, shall be your minister: and whosoever would be first among you, shall be servant of all. (§120 J = Mk 10:43-44)	G But ye *shall* not *be* so: but he that is the greater among you, let him become as the younger; and he that is chief, as he that doth serve. (§138 M = Lk 22:26)

MATT 23

H[H]   And[12] whosoever shall exalt himself shall be humbled; and whosoever shall humble himself shall be exalted.

I But woe unto you, scribes[13] and Pharisees, hypocrites! because ye shut the kingdom of heaven [1]against men: for ye enter not in yourselves, neither suffer ye them that are entering in to enter.[2]

J Woe unto you, scribes and[15] Pharisees, hypocrites! for ye compass sea and land to make one proselyte; and when he is become so, ye make him twofold more a son of [3]hell than yourselves.

K Woe unto you, ye blind[16] guides, which say, Whosoever shall swear by the [4]temple, it is nothing; but whosoever shall swear by the gold of the [4]temple, he is [5]a debtor. Ye fools and blind:[17] for whether is greater, the gold, or the [4]temple that hath sanctified the gold? And,[18] Whosoever shall swear by the altar, it is nothing; but whosoever shall swear by the gift that is upon it, he is [5]a debtor. Ye blind: for whether is[19] greater, the gift, or the altar that sanctifieth the gift? He[20] therefore that sweareth by the altar, sweareth by it, and by all things thereon. And he[21] that sweareth by the [4]temple, sweareth by it, and by him that dwelleth therein. And[22] he that sweareth by the heaven, sweareth by the throne of God, and by him that sitteth thereon.

L Woe unto you, scribes and[23] Pharisees, hypocrites! for ye tithe mint and [6]anise and cummin, and have left undone the weightier matters of the law, judgement, and mercy, and faith: but these ye ought to have done, and not to have left the other undone. Ye blind[24] guides, which strain out the gnat, and swallow the camel.

LUKE II

I *Woe unto you lawyers! for[5] ye took away the key of knowledge: ye entered not in yourselves, and them that were entering in ye hindered.* (§90 J)

L *But woe unto you Phari-[42] sees! for ye tithe mint and rue and every herb, and pass over judgement and the love of God: but these ought ye to have done, and not to leave the other undone.* (§90 C)

ERV margin: 1 Greek *before*   2 Some authorities insert here, or after verse 12, verse 14: *Woe unto you, scribes and Pharisees, hypocrites! for ye devour widows' houses, even while for a pretence ye make long prayers: therefore ye shall receive greater condemnation:* see Mark 12:40 and Luke 20:47   3 Greek *Gehenna*   4 Or *sanctuary:* as in verse 35   ; Or *bound* by his oath   6 Or *dill*

OT references: Mt 23:23 and Lk 11:42 = Leviticus 27:30 and Micah 6:8

H For every one that exalteth himself shall be humbled; and he that humbleth himself shall be exalted. (§103 P = Lk 14:11)
H For every one that exalteth himself shall be humbled; but he that humbleth himself shall be exalted. (§114 B = Lk 18:14)

MATT 23

1 Woe unto you, scribes and[25] Pharisees, hypocrites! for ye cleanse the outside of the cup and of the platter, but within they are full from extortion and excess. Thou blind Pharisee,[26] cleanse first the inside of the cup and of the platter, that the outside thereof may become clean also.

Woe unto you, scribes and[27] Pharisees, hypocrites! for ye are like unto whited sepulchres, which outwardly appear beautiful, but inwardly are full of dead men's bones, and of all uncleanness. Even[28] so ye also outwardly appear righteous unto men, but inwardly ye are full of hypocrisy and iniquity.

Woe unto you, scribes and[29] Pharisees, hypocrites! for ye build the sepulchres of the prophets, and garnish the tombs of the righteous, and[30] say, If we had been in the days of our fathers, we should not have been partakers with them in the blood of the prophets. Wherefore ye wit-[31] ness to yourselves, that ye are sons of them that slew the prophets.

P Fill ye up then the[32] measure of your fathers. Ye[33] serpents, ye offspring of vipers, how shall ye escape the judgement of [2]hell?

Therefore, be-[34] hold, I send unto you prophets, and wise men, and scribes: some of them shall ye kill and crucify; and some of them shall ye scourge in your synagogues, and persecute from city to city: that upon you[35] may come all the righteous blood shed on the earth, from the blood of Abel the righteous unto the blood of Zachariah son of Barachiah, whom ye slew between the sanctuary and the altar. Verily I say[36] unto you, All these things shall come upon this generation.

R O Jerusalem, Jerusalem,[37] which killeth the prophets, and stoneth them that are sent unto her! how often

LUKE 11

M *Now do ye Pharisees[39] cleanse the outside of the cup and of the platter; but your inward part is full of extortion and wickedness. Ye foolish[40] ones, did not he that made the outside make the inside also? Howbeit give for alms those[41] things which [1]are within; and behold, all things are clean unto you.* (§90 B)
N *Woe unto you! for ye are[44] as the tombs which appear not, and the men that walk over them know it not.* (§90 E)

O *Woe unto you! for ye build[47] the tombs of the prophets, and your fathers killed them. So[48] ye are witnesses and consent unto the works of your fathers: for they killed them, and ye build their tombs.* (§90 H)

Q *Therefore also said the wis-[49] dom of God, I will send unto them prophets and apostles; and some of them they shall kill and persecute; that the[50] blood of all the prophets, which was shed from the foundation of the world, may be required of this generation; from the[51] blood of Abel unto the blood of Zachariah, who perished between the altar and the [3]sanctuary: yea, I say unto you, it shall be required of this generation.* (§90 I)

R *O Jerusalem, Jerusalem,[13:] which killeth the prophets, and[34] stoneth them that are sent unto her! how often would I have*

ERV margin: 1 Or *ye can*   2 Greek *Gehenna*   3 Greek *house*

OT references: Mt 23:35 and Lk 11:50-51 = Genesis 4:8 and 2 Chronicles 24:20-21

For the record of a saying by John the Baptist somewhat similar to verse 33, compare §17 M. The saying is recorded of Jesus in §45 N

MATT 23

would I have gathered thy children together, even as a hen gathereth her chickens under her wings, and ye would not! Behold, your house is[38] left unto you [1]desolate. For[39] I say unto you, Ye shall not see me henceforth, till ye shall say, Blessed *is* he that cometh in the name of the Lord.

LUKE

gathered thy children together, even as a hen gathereth *her own brood under her wings, and ye would not! Behold, your*[3][1] *house is left unto you* desolate: *and I say unto you, Ye shall not see me, until ye shall say, Blessed* is *he that cometh in the name of the Lord.* (§*101 B*)

§ 133   THE TRUE TEST OF GIVING

MARK 12:41-44

A And he sat down over[41] against the treasury, and beheld how the multitude cast [2]money into the treasury: and many that were rich cast in much. And there came [3]a[42] poor widow, and she cast in two mites, which make a farthing.

B   And he called unto him[43] his disciples, and said unto them, Verily I say unto you, This poor widow cast in more than all they which are casting into the treasury: for they[44] all did cast in of their superfluity; but she of her want did cast in all that she had, *even* all her living.

LUKE 21:1-4

A And he looked up, [4]and[1] saw the rich men that were casting their gifts into the treasury. And he saw a cer-[2] tain poor widow casting in thither two mites.

B   And he[3] said, Of a truth I say unto you, This poor widow cast in more than they all: for all[4] these did of their superfluity cast in unto the gifts: but she of her want did cast in all the living that she had.

ERV margin: 1 Some ancient authorities omit *desolate*   2 Greek *brass*   3 Greek *one*   4 Or *and saw them that . . . treasury, and they were rich*

OT references: Mt 23:38 and Lk 13:35ª = Jeremiah 12:7 and 22:5   Mt 23:39 and Lk 13:35ᵇ = Psalm 118:26

CHAPTER XXI

DISCOURSE ON EVENTS OF THE FUTURE

§ 134 DISCOURSE ON EVENTS OF THE FUTURE

MATT 24:1—25:46	MARK 13:1-37	LUKE 21:5-38
A And Jesus went out from 1 the temple, and was going on his way; and his disciples came to him to shew him the buildings of the temple.	A And as he went forth out 1 of the temple, one of his disciples saith unto him, ¹Master, behold, what manner of stones and what manner of buildings!	A And as some spake of the 5 temple, how it was adorned with goodly stones and offerings,
B But 2 he answered and said unto them, See ye not all these things? verily I say unto you, There shall not be left here one stone upon another, that shall not be thrown down.	B And Jesus said unto 2 him, Seest thou these great buildings? there shall not be left here one stone upon another, which shall not be thrown down.	B he said, As for these 6 things which ye behold, the days will come, in which there shall not be left here one stone upon another, that shall not be thrown down.
C And as he sat on the mount 3 of Olives, the disciples came unto him privately, saying, Tell us, when shall these things be? and what *shall be* the sign of thy ²coming, and of ³the end of the world?	C And as he sat on the mount 3 of Olives over against the temple, Peter and James and John and Andrew asked him privately, Tell us, when shall 4 these things be? and what *shall be* the sign when these things are all about to be accomplished?	C And they 7 asked him, saying, ¹Master, when therefore shall these things be? and what *shall be* the sign when these things are about to come to pass?
DD And 4 Jesus answered and said unto them, Take heed that no man lead you astray. For many 5 shall come in my name, saying, I am the Christ; and shall lead many astray.	DD And Jesus began 5 to say unto them, Take heed that no man lead you astray. Many shall come in my name, 6 saying, I am *he;* and shall lead many astray.	DD And 8 he said, Take heed that ye be not led astray: for many shall come in my name, saying, I am *he;* and, The time is at hand: go ye not after them.
E And ye 6 shall hear of wars and rumours of wars: see that ye be not troubled: for *these things* must needs come to pass; but the end is not yet.	E And when 7 ye shall hear of wars and rumours of wars, be not troubled: *these things* must needs come to pass; but the end is not yet.	E And when ye shall hear of 9 wars and tumults, be not terrified: for these things must needs come to pass first; but the end is not immediately.
F For nation 7 shall rise against nation, and kingdom against kingdom: and there shall be famines and earthquakes in divers places. But all these things 8 are the beginning of travail.	F For nation 8 shall rise against nation, and kingdom against kingdom: there shall be earthquakes in divers places; there shall be famines: these things are the beginning of travail.	F Then said he unto them,10 Nation shall rise against nation, and kingdom against kingdom: and there shall be11 great earthquakes, and in divers places famines and pestilences; and there shall be terrors and great signs from heaven.
G *But beware of men: for they*10: *will deliver you up to councils,*17 *and in their synagogues they will scourge you; yea and be-*18 *fore governors and kings shall*	G But take ye heed to your- 9 selves: for they shall deliver you up to councils; and in synagogues shall ye be beaten; and before governors and	G But before all these12 things, they shall lay their hands on you, and shall persecute you, delivering you up to the synagogues and prisons,

ERV margin: 1 Or *Teacher*   2 Greek *presence*   3 Or *the consummation of the age*

OT references: Mt 24:7 and Mk 13:8 and Lk 21:10 = Isaiah 19:2

D Compare §135 portions ABC

MATT 24

ye be brought for my sake, for a testimony to them and to the Gentiles.
Then shall they deliver you [9a] up unto tribulation,

H   *Compare portion N below*
    Compare §57 portion F

I[1]   *But when they deliver* [19] *you up, be not anxious how or what ye shall speak: for it shall be given you in that hour what ye shall speak. For it is not ye* [20] *that speak, but the Spirit of your Father that speaketh in you.*

J   *And brother shall deliver* [21] *up brother to death, and the father his child: and children shall rise up against parents, and* [2]*cause them to be put to death.*   and shall [9b] kill you:

K   *And ye shall be hated of* [22a] *all men for my name's sake:*
    and ye shall be hated [9c] of all the nations for my name's sake.

L   And then shall [10] many stumble, and shall deliver up one another, and shall hate one another. And many [11] false prophets shall arise, and shall lead many astray. And [12] because iniquity shall be multiplied, the love of the many shall wax cold.

M *but he that endureth to the* [22b] *end, the same shall be saved.*
(§57 A–E)   But he that [13] endureth to the end, the same shall be saved.

N   And [5]this gos- [14] pel of the kingdom shall be preached in the whole [6]world for a testimony unto all the nations; and then shall the end come.

O   When therefore ye see the [15] abomination of desolation, which was spoken of [7]by Daniel the prophet, standing in [8]the holy place (let him that readeth understand), then let them that be in [16] Judæa flee unto the mountains:

MARK 13

kings shall ye stand for my sake, for a testimony unto them.

H   And the gospel must [10] first be preached unto all the nations.

I[1]   And when they lead [11] you *to judgement*, and deliver you up, be not anxious beforehand what ye shall speak: but whatsoever shall be given you in that hour, that speak ye: for it is not ye that speak, but the Holy Ghost.

J   And brother [12] shall deliver up brother to death, and the father his child; and children shall rise up against parents, and [2]cause them to be put to death.

K   And [13] ye shall be hated of all men for my name's sake:

M   but he that endureth to the end, the same shall be saved.

N   *Compare portion H above*

O   But when ye see the abomi- [14] nation of desolation standing where he ought not (let him that readeth understand), then let them that are in Judæa flee unto the mountains:

LUKE 21

[1]bringing you before kings and governors for my name's sake. It shall turn unto you for a [13] testimony.

I[1]   Settle it therefore [14] in your hearts, not to meditate beforehand how to answer: for I will give you a mouth [15] and wisdom, which all your adversaries shall not be able to withstand or to gainsay.

J   But [16] ye shall be delivered up even by parents, and brethren, and kinsfolk, and friends; and *some* of you [3]shall they cause to be put to death.

K   And ye [17] shall be hated of all 'men for my name's sake.

M[M]   And not a [18] hair of your head shall perish. In your patience ye shall win [19] your [4]souls.

O   But when ye see Jerusalem [20] compassed with armies, then know that her desolation is at hand. Then let them that [21] are in Judæa flee unto the mountains;

ERV margin: 1 Greek, *you being brought*   2 Or *put them to death*   3 Or *shall they put to death*   4 Or *lives*
5 Or *these good tidings*   6 Greek *inhabited earth*   7 Or *through*   8 Or *a holy place*

OT references: Mt 10:21 and Mk 13:12 and Lk 21:16 = Micah 7:6   Mt 24:15 and Mk 13:14 = Daniel 11:31
and 12:11

1 And when they bring you before the synagogues, and the rulers, and the authorities, be not anxious how or what ye shall answer, or what ye shall say: for the Holy Spirit shall teach you in that very hour what ye ought to say. (§91 I = Lk 12:11–12)
M (Lk)   But the very hairs of your head are all numbered. (§57 J = Mt 10:30)   M (Lk)   But the very hairs of your head are all numbered. (§91 F = Lk 12:7)

MATT 24	MARK 13	LUKE 21
P *Compare portion Q below*	P *Compare portion Q below*	P and let them that are in the midst of her depart out; and let not them that are in the country enter therein. For these are days of ven-[22] geance, that all things which are written may be fulfilled.
Q let him that is on the[17] housetop not go down to take out the things that are in his house: and let him that is in[18] the field not return back to take his cloke.	Q and[15] let him that is on the house-top not go down, nor enter in, to take anything out of his house: and let him that is in[16] the field not return back to take his cloke.	Q *In that day, he which shall*[17]: *be on the housetop, and his*[31] *goods in the house, let him not go down to take them away: and let him that is in the field like-wise not return back.* (§112 H) *Compare portion P above*
R But woe unto[19] them that are with child and to them that give suck in those days! And pray ye[20] that your flight be not in the winter, neither on a sabbath: for then shall be great tribu-[21] lation, such as hath not been from the beginning of the world until now, no, nor ever shall be.	R But woe unto[17] them that are with child and to them that give suck in those days! And pray ye that[18] it be not in the winter. For[19] those days shall be tribula-tion, such as there hath not been the like from the begin-ning of the creation which God created until now, and never shall be.	R Woe[23] unto them that are with child and to them that give suck in those days! for there shall be great distress upon the [1]land, and wrath unto this people. And they shall fall by the edge[24] of the sword, and shall be led captive into all the nations: and Jerusalem shall be trod-den down of the Gentiles, until the times of the Gentiles be fulfilled.
S And except those[22] days had been shortened, no flesh would have been saved: but for the elect's sake those days shall be shortened.	S And except the Lord[20] had shortened the days, no flesh would have been saved: but for the elect's sake, whom he chose, he shortened the days.	

§ 135 DISCOURSE ON EVENTS OF THE FUTURE (*continued*)

A Then if any man shall say[23] unto you, Lo, here is the Christ, or, Here; believe [2]*it* not.	A And then if any man shall[21] say unto you, Lo, here is the Christ; or, Lo, there; believe [2]*it* not:	A *And they shall say to you,*[17]: *Lo, there! Lo, here! go not*[23] *away, nor follow after* them:
BB For there shall arise[24] false Christs, and false proph-ets, and shall shew great signs and wonders; so as to lead astray, if possible, even the elect. Behold, I have told you[25] beforehand.	BB for there shall arise[22] false Christs and false proph-ets, and shall shew signs and wonders, that they may lead astray, if possible, the elect. But take ye heed: behold, I[23] have told you all things be-forehand.	
C If therefore they[26] shall say unto you, Behold, he is in the wilderness; go not forth: Behold, he is in the inner chambers; believe [3]*it* not.		C *Compare portion A above*
D For as the lightning[27] cometh forth from the east, and is seen even unto the west; so shall be the [4]coming of the Son of man.		D *for as the lightning, when it*[24] *lighteneth out of the one part under the heaven, shineth unto the other part under heaven; so shall the Son of man be* [5]*in his day.* (§112 C)

ERV margin: 1 Or *earth*   2 Or, him   3 Or, them   4 Greek *presence*   5 Some ancient authorities omit *in his day*

OT references: Mt 24:21 and Mk 13:19 = Daniel 12:1   Mt 24:24 and Mk 13:22 = Deuteronomy 13:1

B   Compare §134 portion D

MATT 24	MARK 13	LUKE 21

E Whereso-[28] ever the carcase is, there will the [1]eagles be gathered together.

E *Where the body* is, *thither*[17] *will the* [1]*eagles also be gathered*[37] *together.* (§*112 M*)

F But immediately, after the[29] tribulation of those days, the sun shall be darkened, and the moon shall not give her light, and the stars shall fall from heaven, and the powers of the heavens shall be shaken:

F But in those days, after[24] that tribulation, the sun shall be darkened, and the moon shall not give her light, and[25] the stars shall be falling from heaven, and the powers that are in the heavens shall be shaken.

F And there shall be signs in[25] sun and moon and stars; and upon the earth distress of nations, in perplexity for the roaring of the sea and the billows; men [2]fainting for fear,[26] and for expectation of the things which are coming on [3]the world: for the powers of the heavens shall be shaken.

G and[30] then shall appear the sign of the Son of man in heaven: and then shall all the tribes of the earth mourn,

H and they shall see the Son of man coming on the clouds of heaven with power and great glory. And[31] he shall send forth his angels [4]with [5]a great sound of a trumpet, and they shall gather together his elect from the four winds, from one end of heaven to the other.

H And then shall they[26] see the Son of man coming in clouds with great power and glory. And then shall he send[27] forth the angels, and shall gather together his elect from the four winds, from the uttermost part of the earth to the uttermost part of heaven.

H And then shall they see the[27] Son of man coming in a cloud with power and great glory. But when these things begin[28] to come to pass, look up, and lift up your heads; because your redemption draweth nigh.

I Now from the fig tree learn[32] her parable: when her branch is now become tender, and putteth forth its leaves, ye know that the summer is nigh; even so ye also, when ye see[33] all these things, know ye that [6]he is nigh, *even* at the doors.

I Now from the fig tree learn[28] her parable: when her branch is now become tender, and putteth forth its leaves, ye know that the summer is nigh; even so ye also, when ye see[29] these things coming to pass, know ye that [6]he is nigh, *even* at the doors.

I And he spake to them a[29] parable: Behold the fig tree, and all the trees: when they[30] now shoot forth, ye see it and know of your own selves that the summer is now nigh. Even[31] so ye also, when ye see these things coming to pass, know ye that the kingdom of God is nigh.

J Verily I say unto you, This[34] generation shall not pass away, till all these things be accomplished. Heaven and earth[35] shall pass away, but my words shall not pass away.

J Verily I say unto[30] you, This generation shall not pass away, until all these things be accomplished. Heaven and[31] earth shall pass away: but my words shall not pass away.

J Verily I say unto you,[32] This generation shall not pass away, till all things be accomplished. Heaven and earth[33] shall pass away: but my words shall not pass away.

K But of[36] that day and hour knoweth no one, not even the angels of heaven, [7]neither the Son, but the Father only.

K But of that day or that[32] hour knoweth no one, not even the angels in heaven, neither the Son, but the Father.

L And as[37] *were* the days of Noah, so shall be the [8]coming of the Son of man. For as in those days[38] which were before the flood they were eating and drinking, marrying and giving in marriage, until the day that Noah entered into the ark,

L *And as it came to pass in*[17] *the days of Noah, even so shall*[26] *it be also in the days of the Son of man. They ate, they drank,*[27] *they married, they were given in marriage, until the day that Noah entered into the ark, and the flood came, and destroyed them all.* (§*112 E*)

ERV margin: 1 Or *vultures*   2 Or *expiring*   3 Greek *the inhabited earth*   4 Many ancient authorities read *with a great trumpet, and they shall gather, etc.*   5 Or *a trumpet of great sound*   6 Or *it*   7 Many authorities, some ancient, omit *neither the Son*   8 Greek *presence*

OT references: Mt 24:29 and Mk 13:24-25 and Lk 21:25-26 = Isaiah 13:9-10 and 34:4 and Ezekiel 32:7-8 and Joel 2:1-2, 10-11, 30-31 and Amos 8:9 and Zephaniah 1:14-16   Mt 24:30ᵃ = Zechariah 12:12   Mt 24:30ᵇ and Mk 13:26 and Lk 21:27 = Daniel 7:13-14 (LXX)   Mt 24:31 and Mk 13:27 and Lk 21:28 = Deuteronomy 30:4 (LXX) and Isaiah 27:12-13 and Zechariah 2:6 (LXX)   Mt 24:37-39 and Lk 17:26-27 = Genesis 6:11-14 and 7:7, 21-23

MATT 24 | MARK 13 | LUKE 21

MATT 24

and they knew not until the39 flood came, and took them all away;
M so shall be the 1coming of the Son of man.

N Then shall40 two men be in the field; one is taken, and one is left: two41 women *shall be* grinding at the mill; one is taken, and one is left.

O O Watch therefore: for ye42 know not on what day your Lord cometh.

P *Compare the parable recorded in §136 portions H–R*

Q Q *Compare the parable recorded in §136 portions E–G*

R *And he left them, and went21: forth out of the city to Bethany,17 and lodged there.* (§126 I)

MARK 13

O O Take33 ye heed, watch 3and pray: for ye know not when the time is.

P *It is* as *when* a man, so34 journing in another country, having left his house, and given authority to his 4servants, to each one his work, commanded also the porter to watch.

Q Q Watch therefore: for35 ye know not when the lord of the house cometh, whether at even, or at midnight, or at cockcrowing, or in the morning; lest coming suddenly he36 find you sleeping. And what37 I say unto you I say unto all, Watch.

R *And 5every evening 6he went11: forth out of the city.* (§126 I) 19

LUKE 21

M *After the same manner shall17: it be in the day that the Son of30 man is revealed.* (§112 G)
N *In that night there shall be17: two men on one bed; the one34 shall be taken, and the other shall be left. There shall be35 two women grinding together; the one shall be taken, and the other shall be left.2* (§112 K)
O O But take heed to your-34 selves,

P lest haply your hearts be overcharged with surfeiting, and drunkenness, and cares of this life, and that day come on you suddenly as a snare: for *so* shall it come35 upon all them that dwell on the face of all the earth.
Q Q But36 watch ye at every season, making supplication, that ye may prevail to escape all these things that shall come to pass, and to stand before the Son of man.

R And every day he was37 teaching in the temple; and every night he went out, and lodged in the mount that is called *the mount* of Olives. And all the people came early38 in the morning to him in the temple, to hear him.

§136 DISCOURSE ON EVENTS OF THE FUTURE (*concluded*)

MATT 24

A 7But know this, that if43 the master of the house had known in what watch the thief was coming, he would have watched, and would not have suffered his house to be 8broken through.
B B Therefore be ye also44 ready: for in an hour that ye think not the Son of man cometh.
C Who then is the45 faithful and wise 9servant, whom his lord hath set over

MARK 13

B B *Compare §135 portion O*
Compare §135 portion Q

LUKE 21

A 7But know this, that if the12: master of the house had known39 in what hour the thief was coming, he would have watched, and not have left his house to be 8broken through.
B B Be ye also40 ready: for in an hour that ye think not the Son of man cometh. (§94 BC)
C Who then is 10the faithful12: and wise steward, whom his42 lord shall set over his household,

---

ERV margin: 1 Greek *presence* 2 Some ancient authorities add verse 36: *There shall be two men in the field; the one shall be taken, and the other shall be left* 3 Some ancient authorities omit *and pray* 4 Greek *bondservants* 5 Greek *whenever evening came* 6 Some ancient authorities read *they* 7 Or *But this ye know* 8 Greek *digged through* 9 Greek *bondservant* 10 Or *the faithful steward, the wise* man *whom, etc.*

O Compare portion Q below and also §136 B and §136 G
Q Compare portion O above and also §136 B and §136 G

B Compare portion G below and also §135 O and §135 Q

MATT 24–25	MARK	LUKE

MATT 24–25

his household, to give them their food in due season? Blessed is that [1]servant, whom[46] his lord when he cometh shall find so doing. Verily I say[47] unto you, that he will set him over all that he hath. But if[48] that evil [1]servant shall say in his heart, My lord tarrieth; and shall begin to beat his[49] fellow-servants, and shall eat and drink with the drunken; the lord of that [1]servant shall[50] come in a day when he expecteth not, and in an hour when he knoweth not, and[51] shall [2]cut him asunder, and appoint his portion with the hypocrites:

D[D]   there shall be the weeping and gnashing of teeth.

E   Then shall the kingdom[25] of heaven be likened unto[1] ten virgins, which took their [3]lamps, and went forth to meet the bridegroom. And[2] five of them were foolish, and five were wise. For the fool-[3] ish, when they took their [3]lamps, took no oil with them: but the wise took oil in their[4] vessels with their [3]lamps. Now while the bridegroom[5] tarried, they all slumbered and slept. But at midnight[6] there is a cry, Behold, the bridegroom! Come ye forth to meet him. Then all those[7] virgins arose, and trimmed their [3]lamps. And the fool-[8] ish said unto the wise, Give us of your oil; for our [3]lamps are going out. But the wise[9] answered, saying, Peradventure there will not be enough for us and you: go ye rather to them that sell, and buy for yourselves. And while they[10] went away to buy, the bridegroom came; and they that were ready went in with him to the marriage feast:

F   and the door was shut. Afterward[11] come also the other virgins,

MARK

E   *Compare the parable recorded in §135 portion Q*

LUKE

to give them their portion of food in due season? Blessed is that[43] [1]servant, whom his lord when he cometh shall find so doing. Of[44] a truth I say unto you, that he will set him over all that he hath. But if that [1]servant shall say in[45] his heart, My lord delayeth his coming; and shall begin to beat the menservants and the maidservants, and to eat and drink, and to be drunken; the lord of[46] that [1]servant shall come in a day when he expecteth not, and in an hour when he knoweth not, and shall [2]cut him asunder, and appoint his portion with the unfaithful. (§94 E)

E   *Let your loins be girded[12] about, and your lamps burning;[35] and be ye yourselves like unto[36] men looking for their lord, when he shall return from the marriage feast; that, when he cometh and knocketh, they may straightway open unto him. Blessed are those [4]servants,[37] whom the lord when he cometh shall find watching: verily I say unto you, that he shall gird himself, and make them sit down to meat, and shall come and serve them. And if he[38] shall come in the second watch, and if in the third, and find them so, blessed are those servants.* (§94 A)

F   *When once the master of the[13] house is risen up, and hath[25] shut to the door, and ye begin to*

ERV margin: 1 Greek *bondservant*   2 Or *severely scourge him*   3 Or *torches*   4 Greek *bondservants*

D   And I say unto you, that many shall come from the east and the west, and shall sit down with Abraham, and Isaac, and Jacob, in the kingdom of heaven: but the sons of the kingdom shall be cast forth into the outer darkness: there shall be the weeping and gnashing of teeth. (§39 D = Mt 8 : 11–12)

D   There shall be the weeping and gnashing of teeth, when ye shall see Abraham, and Isaac, and Jacob, and all the prophets, in the kingdom of God, and yourselves cast forth without. And they shall come from the east and west, and from the north and south, and shall sit down in the kingdom of God. (§100 G = Lk 13 : 28–29)

D   And shall cast them into the furnace of fire: there shall be the weeping and gnashing of teeth. (§48 L = Mt 13 : 42)
D   And shall cast them into the furnace of fire: there shall be the weeping and gnashing of teeth. (§48 Q = Mt 13 : 50)
D   And cast him out into the outer darkness; there shall be the weeping and gnashing of teeth. (§120 P = Mt 22 : 13)
D   And cast ye out the unprofitable servant into the outer darkness: there shall be the weeping and gnashing of teeth. (§136 Q = Mt 25 : 30)

MATT 25	MARK	LUKE

MATT 25

...aying, Lord, Lord, open to ...s. But he answered and[12] ...aid, Verily I say unto you, I ...now you not.

[G] Watch there-[13] ...ore, for ye know not the day ...nor the hour.

... For *it is* as *when* a man,[14] ...going into another country, ...alled his own [1]servants, and ...delivered unto them his goods. ...And unto one he gave five[15] ...alents, to another two, to ...another one; to each accord-...ng to his several ability; and ...he went on his journey.

... Straightway he that re-[16] ...eived the five talents went ...and traded with them, and ...made other five talents. In[17] ...like manner he also that *re-*...*ceived* the two gained other ...two. But he that received[18] ...he one went away and digged ...in the earth, and hid his ...ord's money.

[K] Now after a[19] ...ong time the lord of those ...servants cometh, and maketh ...a reckoning with them.

[L] And[20] ...he that received the five tal-...ents came and brought other ...five talents, saying, Lord, ...thou deliveredst unto me five ...talents: lo, I have gained ...other five talents. His lord[21] ...said unto him, Well done, ...good and faithful [3]servant: ...thou hast been faithful over a ...few things, I will set thee over ...many things: enter thou into ...the joy of thy lord.

[M] And he[22] ...also that *received* the two tal-...ents came and said, Lord, ...thou deliveredst unto me two ...talents: lo, I have gained ...other two talents. His lord[23] ...said unto him, Well done, ...good and faithful [3]servant; ...thou hast been faithful over ...a few things, I will set thee

MARK

[GG] *Compare §135 portion O*
Compare §135 portion Q

[H] *Compare the parable re-corded in §135 portion P*

LUKE

stand without, and to knock at the door, saying, Lord, open to us; and he shall answer and say to you, I know you not whence ye are. (§100 D)

[H] *A certain nobleman went*[19] *into a far country, to receive*[12] *for himself a kingdom, and to return. And he called ten*[13] [1]*servants of his, and gave them ten* [2]*pounds, and said unto them, Trade ye herewith till I come.*

[I] *But his citizens hated*[14] *him, and sent an ambassage after him, saying, We will not that this man reign over us.*

[K] *And it came to pass, when*[15] *he was come back again, having received the kingdom, that he commanded these* [1]*servants, unto whom he had given the money, to be called to him, that he might know what they had gained by trading.*

[L] *And the first came*[16] *before him, saying, Lord, thy pound hath made ten pounds more. And he said unto him,*[17] *Well done, thou good* [3]*servant: because thou wast found faithful in a very little, have thou authority over ten cities.*

[M] *And*[18] *the second came, saying, Thy pound, Lord, hath made five pounds. And he said unto him*[19] *also, Be thou also over five cities.*

ERV margin: [1] Greek *bondservants* [2] *Mina*, here translated a pound, is equal to one hundred drachmas: a drachma is a coin worth about eight pence [3] Greek *bondservant*

[?] Compare portion B above and also §135 O and §135 Q

MATT 25

over many things: enter thou
into the joy of thy lord.

N   And[24]
he also that had received the
one talent came and said,
Lord, I knew thee that thou
art a hard man, reaping where
thou didst not sow, and gathering where thou didst not scatter: and[25] I was afraid, and
went away and hid thy talent
in the earth: lo, thou hast
thine own.

O   But his lord an-[26]
swered and said unto him,
Thou wicked and slothful
'servant, thou knewest that I
reap where I sowed not, and
gather where I did not scatter;
thou oughtest therefore to[27]
have put my money to the
bankers, and at my coming I
should have received back
mine own with interest. Take[28]
ye away therefore the talent
from him, and give it unto
him that hath the ten talents.

P^P For unto every one that[29]
hath shall be given, and he
shall have abundance: but
from him that hath not, even
that which he hath shall be
taken away.

Q^Q   And cast ye out[30]
the unprofitable 'servant into
the outer darkness: there
shall be the weeping and
gnashing of teeth.

S   But when the Son of man[31]
shall come in his glory, and
all the angels with him, then
shall he sit on the throne of
his glory: and before him shall[32]
be gathered all the nations:
and he shall separate them
one from another, as the shepherd separateth the sheep from
the 4goats: and he shall set[33]
the sheep on his right hand,
but the 4goats on the left.
Then shall the King say unto[34]
them on his right hand, Come,

LUKE

N *And* 2*another came, saying,*[20]
Lord, behold, here is thy pound,
which I kept laid up in a nap-
kin: for I feared thee, because[21]
thou art an austere man: thou
takest up that thou layedst not
down, and reapest that thou
didst not sow.

O   *He saith unto*[22]
him, Out of thine own mouth
will I judge thee, thou wicked
1*servant. Thou knewest that I*
am an austere man, taking up
that I laid not down, and reap-
ing that I did not sow; then[23]
wherefore gavest thou not my
money into the bank, and 3*I at*
my coming should have required
it with interest? And he said[24]
unto them that stood by, Take
away from him the pound, and
give it unto him that hath the ten
pounds. And they said unto[25]
him, Lord, he hath ten pounds.

P^P *I say unto you, that unto*[26]
every one that hath shall be
given; but from him that hath
not, even that which he hath
shall be taken away from him.

R *Howbeit these mine enemies,*[27]
which would not that I should
reign over them, bring hither,
and slay them before me.
(§123 B-L)

ERV margin: 1 Greek *bondservant*   2 Greek *the other*   3 Or *I should have gone and required*   4 Greek *kids*

OT references: Mt 25:31 = Zechariah 14:5^b

P For whosoever hath, to him shall
be given, and he shall have abundance: but whosoever hath not, from
him shall be taken away even that
which he hath.   (§47 H = Mt 13:12)

P For he that hath, to him shall
be given: and he that hath not, from
him shall be taken away even that
which he hath.   (§47 V = Mk 4:25)

P For whosoever hath, to him shall
be given; and whosoever hath not,
from him shall be taken away even
that which he thinketh he hath.
(§47 V = Lk 8:18)

Q Compare portion D above and attached references

MATT 25

ye blessed of my Father, inherit the kingdom prepared for you from the foundation of the world: for I was an[35] hungred, and ye gave me meat: I was thirsty, and ye gave me drink: I was a stranger, and ye took me in; naked, and ye clothed me:[36] I was sick, and ye visited me: I was in prison, and ye came unto me. Then shall the[37] righteous answer him, saying, Lord, when saw we thee an hungred, and fed thee? or athirst, and gave thee drink? And when saw we thee a[38] stranger, and took thee in? or naked, and clothed thee? And when saw we thee sick,[39] or in prison, and came unto thee? And the King shall[40] answer and say unto them, Verily I say unto you, Inasmuch as ye did it unto one of these my brethren, *even* these least, ye did it unto me. Then[41] shall he say also unto them on the left hand, [1]Depart from me, ye cursed, into the eternal fire which is prepared for the devil and his angels: for I was[42] an hungred, and ye gave me no meat: I was thirsty, and ye gave me no drink: I was a[43] stranger, and ye took me not in; naked, and ye clothed me not; sick, and in prison, and ye visited me not. Then shall[44] they also answer, saying, Lord, when saw we thee an hungred, or athirst, or a stranger, or naked, or sick, or in prison, and did not minister unto thee? Then shall he answer[45] them, saying, Verily I say unto you, Inasmuch as ye did it not unto one of these least, ye did it not unto me. And[46] these shall go away into eternal punishment: but the righteous into eternal life.

§ 137 CONSPIRACY FOR THE ARREST OF JESUS

MATT 26:1-16	MARK 14:1-11	LUKE 22:1-6
A And it came to pass, when [1] Jesus had finished all these words, he said unto his disciples, Ye know that after two [2] days the passover cometh, and	A Now after two days was [1] *the feast of* the passover and the unleavened bread: and the chief priests and the scribes sought how they might	A Now the feast of un- [1] leavened bread drew nigh, which is called the Passover. And the chief priests and the [2] scribes sought how they might

---

ERV margin: [1] Or *Depart from me under a curse*

OT references: Mt 25:46 = Daniel 12:2

MATT 26

the Son of man is delivered up to be crucified. Then were 3 gathered together the chief priests, and the elders of the people, unto the court of the high priest, who was called Caiaphas; and they took 4 counsel together that they might take Jesus by subtilty, and kill him. But they said, 5 Not during the feast, lest a tumult arise among the people.

B Now when Jesus was in 6 Bethany, in the house of Simon the leper, there came 7 unto him a woman having [1]an alabaster cruse of exceeding precious ointment, and she poured it upon his head, as he sat at meat.

C   But when the 8 disciples saw it, they had indignation, saying, To what purpose is this waste? For 9 this *ointment* might have been sold for much, and given to the poor.

D   But Jesus perceiv-10 ing it said unto them, Why trouble ye the woman? for she hath wrought a good work upon me. For ye have the[11] poor always with you; but me ye have not always. For in[12] that she [4]poured this ointment upon my body, she did it to prepare me for burial.

E   Verily[13] I say unto you, Wheresoever [5]this gospel shall be preached in the whole world, that also which this woman hath done shall be spoken of for a memorial of her.

F Then one of the twelve,[14] who was called Judas Iscariot, went unto the chief priests, and said, What are ye willing[15] to give me, and I will deliver him unto you? And they weighed unto him thirty pieces of silver. And from[16] that time he sought opportunity to deliver him *unto them.*

MARK 14

take him with subtilty, and kill him: for they said, Not 2 during the feast, lest haply there shall be a tumult of the people.

B And while he was in Beth- 3 any in the house of Simon the leper, as he sat at meat, there came a woman having [1]an alabaster cruse of ointment of [2]spikenard very costly; *and* she brake the cruse, and poured it over his head.

C   But there were some 4 that had indignation among themselves, *saying,* To what purpose hath this waste of the ointment been made? For 5 this ointment might have been sold for above three hundred [3]pence, and given to the poor. And they murmured against her.

D   But Jesus said, 6 Let her alone; why trouble ye her? she hath wrought a good work on me. For ye have the 7 poor always with you, and whensoever ye will ye can do them good: but me ye have not always. She hath done 8 what she could: she hath anointed my body aforehand for the burying.

E   And verily I 9 say unto you, Wheresoever the gospel shall be preached throughout the whole world, that also which this woman hath done shall be spoken of for a memorial of her.

F And Judas Iscariot, [6]he[10] that was one of the twelve, went away unto the chief priests, that he might deliver him unto them. And they,[11] when they heard it, were glad, and promised to give him money. And he sought how he might conveniently deliver him *unto them.*

LUKE 22

put him to death; for they feared the people.

B *Compare §42 portion A*

F And Satan entered into 3 Judas who was called Iscariot, being of the number of the twelve. And he went away, 4 and communed with the chief priests and captains, how he might deliver him unto them. And they were glad, and cove- 5 nanted to give him money. And he consented, and sought 6 opportunity to deliver him unto them [7]in the absence of the multitude.

ERV margin: 1 Or *a flask*   2 Greek *pistic nard*, pistic being perhaps a local name: others take it to mean *genuine;* others, *liquid*   3 The word in the Greek denotes a coin worth about eight pence halfpenny   4 Greek *cast*   5 Or *these good tidings*   6 Greek *the one of the twelve*   7 Or *without tumult*

OT references: Mt 26:15 = Zechariah 11:12

CHAPTER XXII

FINAL HOURS OF JESUS WITH HIS DISCIPLES

§ 138 THE PASSOVER WITH THE DISCIPLES

MATT 26:17-29	MARK 14:12-25	LUKE 22:7-30
A Now on the first *day* of[17] unleavened bread the disciples came to Jesus, saying, Where wilt thou that we make ready for thee to eat the passover?	A And on the first day of un-[12] leavened bread, when they sacrificed the passover, his disciples say unto him, Where wilt thou that we go and make ready that thou mayest eat the passover?	A And the day of unleavened [7] bread came, on which the passover must be sacrificed. And he sent Peter and John, [8] saying, Go and make ready for us the passover, that we may eat. And they said unto him, [9] Where wilt thou that we make ready?
B And he said, Go into[18] the city to such a man, and say unto him, The [1]Master saith, My time is at hand; I keep the passover at thy house with my disciples.	B And he sendeth[13] two of his disciples, and saith unto them, Go into the city, and there shall meet you a man bearing a pitcher of water: follow him; and where-[14] soever he shall enter in, say to the goodman of the house, The [1]Master saith, Where is my guest-chamber, where I shall eat the passover with my disciples? And he will him-[15] self shew you a large upper room furnished *and* ready: and there make ready for us.	B And he said unto[10] them, Behold, when ye are entered into the city, there shall meet you a man bearing a pitcher of water; follow him into the house whereinto he goeth. And ye shall say unto[11] the goodman of the house, The [1]Master saith unto thee, Where is the guest-chamber, where I shall eat the passover with my disciples? And he[12] will shew you a large upper room furnished: there make ready.
C And the dis-[19] ciples did as Jesus appointed them; and they made ready the passover.	C And the disciples went[16] forth, and came into the city, and found as he had said unto them: and they made ready the passover.	C And they went, and[13] found as he had said unto them: and they made ready the passover.
D Now when even[20] was come, he was sitting at meat with the twelve [2]disciples; and as they were eat-[21] ing, he said,	D And when it was evening[17] he cometh with the twelve. And as they [3]sat and were eat-[18] ing, Jesus said,	D And when the hour was[14] come, he sat down, and the apostles with him. And he[15] said unto them,
E Verily I say unto you, that one of you shall betray me. And they were[22] exceeding sorrowful, and began to say unto him every one, Is it I, Lord? And he an-[23] swered and said, He that dipped his hand with me in the dish, the same shall betray me. The Son of man goeth,[24] even as it is written of him: but woe unto that man through whom the Son of man is betrayed! good were it [4]for that man if he had not been born.	E Verily I say unto you, One of you shall betray me, *even* he that eateth with me. They began to be[19] sorrowful, and to say unto him one by one, Is it I? And[20] he said unto them, *It is* one of the twelve, he that dippeth with me in the dish. For the[21] Son of man goeth, even as it is written of him: but woe unto that man through whom the Son of man is betrayed! good were it [4]for that man if he had not been born.	E *Compare portion K below*

ERV margin: [1] Or *Teacher* [2] Many authorities, some ancient, omit *disciples* [3] Greek *reclined* [4] Greek *for him if that man*

OT references: Mt 26:17 and Mk 14:12 and Lk 22:7 = Exodus 12:17-20 Mk 14:18 = Psalm 41:9

MATT 26	MARK 14	LUKE 22
F And Judas, which be-[25] trayed him, answered and said, Is it I, Rabbi? He saith unto him, Thou hast said.		
		G With desire I have desired to eat this passover with you before I suffer: for I say unto you, I will not[16] eat it, until it be fulfilled in the kingdom of God.
H *Compare portion J below*	H *Compare portion J below*	H And he[17] received a cup, and when he had given thanks, he said, Take this, and divide it among yourselves: for I say unto[18] you, I will not drink from henceforth of the fruit of the vine, until the kingdom of God shall come.
I And as they were eating,[26] Jesus took [1]bread, and blessed, and brake it; and he gave to the disciples, and said, Take, eat; this is my body.	I And as they were eating,[22] he took [1]bread, and when he had blessed, he brake it, and gave to them, and said, Take ye: this is my body.	I[1] And he took[19] [1]bread, and when he had given thanks, he brake it, and gave to them, saying, This is my body [2]which is given for you: this do in remembrance of me.
J And he[27] took [3]a cup, and gave thanks, and gave to them, saying, Drink ye all of it; for this is[28] my blood of [4]the [5]covenant, which is shed for many unto remission of sins. But I say[29] unto you, I will not drink henceforth of this fruit of the vine, until that day when I drink it new with you in my Father's kingdom.	J And he took[23] a cup, and when he had given thanks, he gave to them: and they all drank of it. And he[24] said unto them, This is my blood of [4]the [6]covenant, which is shed for many. Verily I[25] say unto you, I will no more drink of the fruit of the vine, until that day when I drink it new in the kingdom of God.	J[1] And the cup in like manner[20] after supper, saying, This cup is the new [7]covenant in my blood, *even* that which is poured out for you. *Compare portion H above*
K *Compare portion E above*	K *Compare portion E above*	K But be-[21] hold, the hand of him that betrayeth me is with me on the table. For the Son of[22] man indeed goeth, as it hath been determined: but woe unto that man through whom he is betrayed! And they[23] began to question among themselves, which of them it was that should do this thing.
		L[L] And there arose also a con-[24] tention among them, which of them is accounted to be [8]greatest.

ERV margin: 1 Or *a loaf*   2 Some ancient authorities omit *which is given for you . . . which is poured out for you*   3 Some ancient authorities read *the cup*   4 Or *the testament*   5 Many ancient authorities insert *new*   6 Some ancient authorities insert *new*   7 Or *testament*   8 Greek *greater*

OT references: Mt 26:28 and Mk 14:24 and Lk 22:20 = Exodus 24:8 and Zechariah 9:11 and Jeremiah 31:31 and Leviticus 4:18–20

I J (Lk)   The Lord Jesus in the night in which he was betrayed took bread; and when he had given thanks, he brake it, and said, This is my body, which is for you: this do in remembrance of me. In like manner also the cup, after supper, saying, This cup is the new covenant in my blood: this do, as oft as ye drink *it*, in remembrance of me. (1 Corinthians 11:23–25)

| L In that hour came the disciples unto Jesus, saying, Who then is greatest in the kingdom of heaven? (§78 A = Mt 18:1) | L And they came to Capernaum: and when he was in the house he asked them, What were ye reasoning in the way? But they held their peace: for they had disputed one with another in the way, who *was* the greatest. (§78 A = Mk 9:33–34) | L And there arose a reasoning among them, which of them should be greatest. (§78 A = Lk 9:46) |

MATT	MARK	LUKE 22
M[M] *Ye know that the rulers of*[20]: *the Gentiles lord it over them,*[25] *and their great ones exercise authority over them. Not so*[26] *shall it be among you: but whosoever would become great among you shall be your* [1]*minister; and whosoever would be*[27] *first among you shall be your* [2]*servant: even as the Son of*[28] *man came not to be ministered unto, but to minister, and to give his life a ransom for many.* (§*120 I–K*)	M[M] *Ye know that they which*[10]: *are accounted to rule over the*[42] *Gentiles lord it over them; and their great ones exercise authority over them. But it is not so*[43] *among you: but whosoever would become great among you, shall be your* [1]*minister: and*[44] *whosoever would be first among you, shall be* [2]*servant of all. For verily the Son of man*[45] *came not to be ministered unto, but to minister, and to give his life a ransom for many.* (§*120 I–K*)	M[M] And he said unto[25] them, The kings of the Gentiles have lordship over them; and they that have authority over them are called Benefactors. But ye *shall* not be[26] so: but he that is the greater among you, let him become as the younger; and he that is chief, as he that doth serve. For whether is greater, he[27] that [3]sitteth at meat, or he that serveth? is not he that [3]sitteth at meat? but I am in the midst of you as he that serveth.
N *And Jesus said unto them,*[19]: *Verily I say unto you, that ye*[28] *which have followed me, in the regeneration when the Son of man shall sit on the throne of his glory, ye also shall sit upon twelve thrones, judging the twelve tribes of Israel.* (§*117 L*)		N But ye are they[28] which have continued with me in my temptations; and[29] [4]I appoint unto you a kingdom, even as my Father appointed unto me, that ye may[30] eat and drink at my table in my kingdom; and ye shall sit on thrones judging the twelve tribes of Israel.

§ 139 WITHDRAWAL TO THE MOUNT OF OLIVES

MATT 26:30–35	MARK 14:26–31	LUKE 22:31–38
A And when they had sung[30] a hymn, they went out unto the mount of Olives.	A And when they had sung a[26] hymn, they went out unto the mount of Olives.	A *And he came out, and went,*[22]: *as his custom was, unto the*[39] *mount of Olives; and the disciples also followed him.* (§*140 A*)
B Then saith Jesus unto[31] them, All ye shall be [5]offended in me this night: for it is written, I will smite the shepherd, and the sheep of the flock shall be scattered abroad.	B And Jesus saith unto them,[27] All ye shall be [5]offended: for it is written, I will smite the shepherd, and the sheep shall be scattered abroad.	B Simon, Simon, behold,[31] Satan [6]asked to have you, that he might sift you as wheat: but I made supplication for[32] thee, that thy faith fail not: and do thou, when once thou hast turned again, stablish thy brethren.
C But after[32] I am raised up, I will go before you into Galilee.	C Howbeit,[28] after I am raised up, I will go before you into Galilee.	
D But Peter[33] answered and said unto him, If all shall be [5]offended in thee, I will never be [5]offended. Jesus said unto him, Verily I[34] say unto thee, that this night, before the cock crow, thou shalt deny me thrice. Peter[35] saith unto him, Even if I must die with thee, *yet* will I not	D But[29] Peter said unto him, Although all shall be [5]offended, yet will not I. And Jesus saith unto[30] him, Verily I say unto thee, that thou to-day, *even* this night, before the cock crow twice, shalt deny me thrice. But he spake exceeding vehe-[31] mently, If I must die with	D And he said unto[33] him, Lord, with thee I am ready to go both to prison and to death. And he said,[34] I tell thee, Peter, the cock shall not crow this day, until thou shalt thrice deny that thou knowest me.

ERV margin: 1 Or *servant*   2 Greek *bondservant*   3 Greek *reclineth*   4 Or *I appoint unto you, even as my Father appointed unto me a kingdom, that ye may eat and drink, etc.*   5 Greek *caused to stumble*   6 Or *obtained you by asking*

OT references: Mt 26:31 and Mk 14:27 = Zechariah 13:7

M Whosoever therefore shall humble himself as this little child, the same is the greatest in the kingdom of heaven. (§78 E = Mt 18:4)

M And he sat down, and called the twelve; and he saith unto them, If any man would be first, he shall be last of all, and minister of all. (§78 B = Mk 9:35)

M For he that is least among you all, the same is great. (§78 H = Lk 9:48)

M But he that is greatest among you shall be your servant. (§132 G = Mt 23:11)

MATT 26	MARK 14	LUKE 22
deny thee. Likewise also said all the disciples.	thee, I will not deny thee. And in like manner also said they all.	

E And he said unto them,35 When I sent you forth without purse, and wallet, and shoes, lacked ye anything? And they said, Nothing. And36 he said unto them, But now, he that hath a purse, let him take it, and likewise a wallet: 1and he that hath none, let him sell his cloke, and buy a sword. For I say unto you,37 that this which is written must be fulfilled in me, And he was reckoned with transgressors: for that which concerneth me hath 2fulfilment. And they said, Lord, behold,38 here are two swords. And he said unto them, It is enough.

§ 140 AT THE PLACE NAMED GETHSEMANE

MATT 26:36–46

A *And when they had sung26: a hymn, they went out unto30 the mount of Olives.* (§139A)

B Then cometh Jesus with36 them unto3 a place called Gethsemane, and saith unto his disciples, Sit ye here, while I go yonder and pray. And37 he took with him Peter and the two sons of Zebedee, and began to be sorrowful and sore troubled. Then saith he unto38 them, My soul is exceeding sorrowful, even unto death: abide ye here, and watch with me.

C And he went forward a39 little, and fell on his face, and prayed, saying, O my Father, if it be possible, let this cup pass away from me: nevertheless, not as I will, but as thou wilt.

MARK 14:32–42

A *And when they had sung a14: hymn, they went out unto the26 mount of Olives.* (§139A)

B And they come unto 3a32 place which was named Gethsemane: and he saith unto his disciples, Sit ye here, while I pray. And he taketh with33 him Peter and James and John, and began to be greatly amazed, and sore troubled. And he saith unto them, My34 soul is exceeding sorrowful even unto death: abide ye here, and watch.

C And he went35 forward a little, and fell on the ground, and prayed that, if it were possible, the hour might pass away from him. And he36 said, Abba, Father, all things are possible unto thee; remove this cup from me: howbeit not what I will, but what thou wilt.

LUKE 22:39–46

A And he came out, and39 went, as his custom was, unto the mount of Olives; and the disciples also followed him. B And when he was at the40 place, he said unto them, Pray that ye enter not into temptation.

C And he was parted from41 them about a stone's cast; and he kneeled down and prayed, saying, Father, if thou be42 willing, remove this cup from me: nevertheless not my will, but thine, be done.

D 4And there43 appeared unto him an angel from heaven, strengthening him. And being in an agony44 he prayed more earnestly: and his sweat became as it were great drops of blood falling down upon the ground.

ERV margin: 1 Or *and he that hath no sword, let him sell his cloke, and buy one*   2 Greek *end*   3 Greek *an enclosed piece of ground*   4 Many ancient authorities omit verses 43 and 44

OT references: Lk 22:37 = Isaiah 53:12   Mt 26:38 and Mk 14:34 = Psalm 42:6

MATT 26

E   And he cometh unto40 the disciples, and findeth them sleeping, and saith unto Peter, What, could ye not watch with me one hour? [1]Watch and41 pray, that ye enter not into temptation: the spirit indeed is willing, but the flesh is weak.

F   Again a second time42 he went away, and prayed, saying, O my Father, if this cannot pass away, except I drink it, thy will be done. And he came again and found43 them sleeping, for their eyes were heavy.

G   And he left them44 again, and went away, and prayed a third time, saying again the same words. Then45 cometh he to the disciples, and saith unto them, Sleep on now, and take your rest: behold, the hour is at hand, and the Son of man is betrayed unto the hands of sinners. Arise, let us be going: behold,46 he is at hand that betrayeth me.

MARK 14

E   And he cometh,37 and findeth them sleeping, and saith unto Peter, Simon, sleepest thou? couldest thou not watch one hour? [1]Watch38 and pray, that ye enter not into temptation: the spirit indeed is willing, but the flesh is weak.

F   And again he went39 away, and prayed, saying the same words. And again he40 came, and found them sleeping, for their eyes were very heavy; and they wist not what to answer him.

G   And he41 cometh the third time, and saith unto them, Sleep on now, and take your rest: it is enough; the hour is come; behold, the Son of man is betrayed into the hands of sinners. Arise, let us be going:42 behold, he that betrayeth me is at hand.

LUKE 22

E   And45 when he rose up from his prayer, he came unto the disciples, and found them sleeping for sorrow, and said unto46 them, Why sleep ye? rise and pray, that ye enter not into temptation.

§ 141 THE BETRAYAL AND ARREST OF JESUS

MATT 26:47-56

A   And while he yet spake,47 lo, Judas, one of the twelve, came, and with him a great multitude with swords and staves, from the chief priests and elders of the people.

B   Now48 he that betrayed him gave them a sign, saying, Whomsoever I shall kiss, that is he: take him. And straightway49 he came to Jesus, and said, Hail, Rabbi; and [2]kissed him. And Jesus said unto him,50 Friend, *do* that for which thou art come. Then they came and laid hands on Jesus, and took him.

D   And behold, one51 of them that were with Jesus stretched out his hand, and drew his sword, and smote the [3]servant of the high priest, and struck off his ear.

MARK 14:43-52

A   And straightway, while he43 yet spake, cometh Judas, one of the twelve, and with him a multitude with swords and staves, from the chief priests and the scribes and the elders.

B   Now he that betrayed him44 had given them a token, saying, Whomsoever I shall kiss, that is he; take him, and lead him away safely. And when45 he was come, straightway he came to him, and saith, Rabbi; and [2]kissed him. And they laid hands on him,46 and took him.

D   But a certain47 one of them that stood by drew his sword, and smote the [3]servant of the high priest, and struck off his ear.

LUKE 22:47-53

A   While he yet spake, be-47 hold, a multitude, and he that was called Judas, one of the twelve, went before them;

B   and he drew near unto Jesus to kiss him. But Jesus said48 unto him, Judas, betrayest thou the Son of man with a kiss?

C   And when they that49 were about him saw what would follow, they said, Lord, shall we smite with the sword?

D   And a certain one of them50 smote the [3]servant of the high priest, and struck off his right ear.

E   But Jesus answered and51 said, Suffer ye thus far. And

ERV margin: 1 Or *Watch ye, and pray that ye enter not*   2 Greek *kissed him much*   3 Greek *bondservant*

MATT 26	MARK 14	LUKE 22

LUKE 22

he touched his ear, and healed him.

MATT 26

F   Then[52] saith Jesus unto him, Put up again thy sword into its place: for all they that take the sword shall perish with the sword. Or thinkest thou that[53] I cannot beseech my Father, and he shall even now send me more than twelve legions of angels? How then should[54] the scriptures be fulfilled, that thus it must be?

G   In that hour[55] said Jesus to the multitudes, Are ye come out as against a robber with swords and staves to seize me? I sat daily in the temple teaching, and ye **took me not.**

H   But all this is[56] come to pass, that the scriptures of the prophets might be fulfilled.

I   Then all the disciples left him, and fled.

MARK 14

G   And[48] Jesus answered and said unto them, Are ye come out, as against a robber, with swords and staves to seize me? I[49] was daily with you in the temple teaching, and ye took me not:

H   but *this is done* that the scriptures might be fulfilled.

I   And they all left him,[50] and fled.

J And a certain young man[51] followed with him, having a linen cloth cast about him, over *his* naked *body:* and they lay hold on him; but[52] he left the linen cloth, and fled naked.

LUKE 22

G   And Jesus said unto[52] the chief priests, and captains of the temple, and elders, which were come against him, Are ye come out, as against a robber, with swords and staves? When I was[53] daily with you in the temple, ye stretched not forth your hands against me:

H   but this is your hour, and the power of darkness.

CHAPTER XXIII

JUDICIAL TRIALS AND CRUCIFIXION OF JESUS

§ 142   THE TRIAL BEFORE THE JEWISH AUTHORITIES

MATT 26:57-75

A And they that had taken57 Jesus led him away to *the house of* Caiaphas the high priest, where the scribes and the elders were gathered together.

B   But Peter followed58 him afar off, unto the court of the high priest, and entered in, and sat with the officers, to see the end.

C   Now the chief59 priests and the whole council sought false witness against Jesus, that they might put him to death; and they found60 it not, though many false witnesses came. But afterward came two, and said, This man61 said, I am able to destroy the ¹temple of God, and to build it in three days.

D   And the high62 priest stood up, and said unto him, Answerest thou nothing? what is it which these witness against thee? But Jesus held63 his peace.

E   And the high priest said unto him, I adjure thee by the living God, that thou tell us whether thou be the Christ, the Son of God. Jesus64 saith unto him, Thou hast said: nevertheless I say unto you, Henceforth ye shall see the Son of man sitting at the right hand of power, and coming on the clouds of heaven.

F Then the high priest rent65 his garments, saying, He hath spoken blasphemy: what fur-

MARK 14:53-72

A And they led Jesus away53 to the high priest: and there come together with him all the chief priests and the elders and the scribes.

B   And54 Peter had followed him afar off, even within, into the court of the high priest; and he was sitting with the officers, and warming himself in the light *of the fire.*

C   Now the55 chief priests and the whole council sought witness against Jesus to put him to death; and found it not. For many56 bare false witness against him, and their witness agreed not together. And there stood57 up certain, and bare false witness against him, saying, We58 heard him say, I will destroy this ²temple that is made with hands, and in three days I will build another made without hands. And not even so59 did their witness agree together.

D   And the high priest60 stood up in the midst, and asked Jesus, saying, Answerest thou nothing? what is it which these witness against thee? But he held his peace,61 and answered nothing.

E   Again the high priest asked him, and saith unto him, Art thou the Christ, the Son of the Blessed? And Jesus said, I am: and ye62 shall see the Son of man sitting at the right hand of power, and coming with the clouds of heaven.

F   And the63 high priest rent his clothes, and saith, What further need

LUKE 22:54-71

A And they seized him, and54 led him *away,* and brought him into the high priest's house.

B   But Peter followed afar off. And when they had kin-55 dled a fire in the midst of the court, and had sat down together, Peter sat in the midst of them.

C *Compare portion M below*

E *Compare portion N below*

F *Compare portion O below*

ERV margin: ₁ Or *sanctuary:* as in Matt 23:35 and 27:5   2 Or *sanctuary*

OT references: Mt 26:64 and Mk 14:62 and Lk 22:69 = Psalm 110:1 and Daniel 7:13

MATT 26	MARK 14	LUKE 22

ther need have we of wit-nesses? behold, now ye have heard the blasphemy: what[66] think ye? They answered and said, He is [1]worthy of death.

G   Then did they spit in[67] his face and buffet him: and some smote him [2]with the palms of their hands, saying,[68] Prophesy unto us, thou Christ: who is he that struck thee?

H Now Peter was sitting[69] without in the court: and a maid came unto him, saying, Thou also wast with Jesus the Galilæan. But he denied be-[70]fore them all, saying, I know not what thou sayest.

I   And[71] when he was gone out into the porch, another *maid* saw him, and saith unto them that were there, This man also was with Jesus the Nazarene. And[72] again he denied with an oath, I know not the man.

J   And[73] after a little while they that stood by came and said to Peter, Of a truth thou also art *one* of them; for thy speech bewrayeth thee. Then began[74] he to curse and to swear, I know not the man.

K   And straightway the cock crew. And Peter remembered the[75] word which Jesus had said, Before the cock crow, thou shalt deny me thrice. And he went out, and wept bitterly.

L *Compare portion G above*

M *Compare portion C above*
    Compare §143 portion A

---

have we of witnesses? Ye[64] have heard the blasphemy: what think ye? And they all condemned him to be [1]worthy of death.

G   And some began to[65] spit on him, and to cover his face, and to buffet him, and to say unto him, Prophesy: and the officers received him with [3]blows of their hands.

H And as Peter was beneath[66] in the court, there cometh one of the maids of the high priest; and seeing Peter warming[67] himself, she looked upon him, and saith, Thou also wast with the Nazarene, *even* Jesus. But he denied, saying, [4]I[68] neither know, nor understand what thou sayest:

I   and he went out into the [5]porch; [6]and the cock crew. And the maid[69] saw him, and began again to say to them that stood by, This is *one* of them. But he[70] again denied it.

J   And after a little while again they that stood by said to Peter, Of a truth thou art *one* of them; for thou art a Galilæan. But[71] he began to curse, and to swear, I know not this man of whom ye speak.

K   And straight-[72]way the second time the cock crew. And Peter called to mind the word, how that Jesus said unto him, Before the cock crow twice, thou shalt deny me thrice. [7]And when he thought thereon, he wept.

L *Compare portion G above*

M *Compare portion C above*
    Compare §143 portion A

G *Compare portion L below*

H   And a certain maid[56] seeing him as he sat in the light *of the fire*, and looking stedfastly upon him, said, This man also was with him. But[57] he denied, saying, Woman, I know him not.

I   And after a[58] little while another saw him, and said, Thou also art *one* of them. But Peter said, Man, I am not.

J   And after the[59] space of about one hour another confidently affirmed, saying, Of a truth this man also was with him: for he is a Galilæan. But Peter[60] said, Man, I know not what thou sayest.

K   And immediately, while he yet spake, the cock crew. And the Lord turned,[61] and looked upon Peter. And Peter remembered the word of the Lord, how that he said unto him, Before the cock crow this day, thou shalt deny me thrice. And he went[62] out, and wept bitterly.

L And the men that held[63] [8]*Jesus* mocked him, and beat him. And they blindfolded[64] him, and asked him, saying, Prophesy: who is he that struck thee? And many other[65] things spake they against him, reviling him.

M And as soon as it was day,[66] the assembly of the elders of the people was gathered to-gether, both chief priests and

---

ERV margin: 1 Greek *liable to*   2 Or *with rods*   3 Or *strokes of rods*   4 Or *I neither know, nor understand: thou,*
what sayest thou?   5 Greek *forecourt*   6 Many ancient authorities omit *and the cock crew*   7 Or *And he began to weep*
8 Greek *him*

OT references: Mt 26:65–66 and Mk 14:63–64 = Leviticus 24:16

MATT 26	MARK 14	LUKE 22
		scribes; and they led him away into their council,
N *Compare portion E above*	N *Compare portion E above*	N saying, If thou art the Christ, tell us.[67] But he said unto them, If I tell you, ye will not believe: and if I ask *you*, ye will not[68] answer. But from henceforth[69] shall the Son of man be seated at the right hand of the power of God.
o *Compare portion F above*	o *Compare portion F above*	o And they all said,[70] Art thou then the Son of God? And he said unto them, [1]Ye say that I am. And they said, What further[71] need have we of witness? for we ourselves have heard from his own mouth.

§ 143 THE TRIAL BEFORE THE ROMAN AUTHORITIES

MATT 27:1–31	MARK 15:1–20	LUKE 23:1–25
A Now when morning was [1] come, all the chief priests and the elders of the people took counsel against Jesus to put him to death: and they bound [2] him, and led him away, and delivered him up to Pilate the governor.	A And straightway in the [1] morning the chief priests with the elders and scribes, and the whole council, held a consultation, and bound Jesus, and carried him away, and delivered him up to Pilate.	A *Compare §142 portion M* And the whole company of [1] them rose up, and brought him before Pilate.
B Then Judas, which be-[3] trayed him, when he saw that he was condemned, repented himself, and brought back the thirty pieces of silver to the chief priests and elders, say-[4] ing, I have sinned in that I betrayed [2]innocent blood. But they said, What is that to us? see thou *to it*. And he cast [5] down the pieces of silver into the sanctuary, and departed; and he went away and hanged himself. And the chief priests [6] took the pieces of silver, and said, It is not lawful to put them into the [3]treasury, since it is the price of blood. And [7] they took counsel, and bought with them the potter's field, to bury strangers in. Where-[8] fore that field was called, The field of blood, unto this day. Then was fulfilled that which [9] was spoken [4]by Jeremiah the prophet, saying, And [5]they took the thirty pieces of silver, the price of him that was priced, [6]whom *certain* of the children of Israel did price;		

ERV margin: 1 Or *Ye say it, because I am*   2 Many ancient authorities read *righteous*   3 Greek *corbanas*, that is, *sacred treasury:* compare Mark 7:11   4 Or *through*   5 Or *I took*   6 Or *whom they priced on the part of the Sons of Israel*

OT references: Lk 22:69=Psalm 110:1 and Daniel 7:13   Mt 27:6=Deuteronomy 23:18   Mt 27:9-10= Zechariah 11:12-13 and Jeremiah 32:6-15 and 18:1-4

MATT 27   MARK 15   LUKE 23

and [1]they gave them for the[10] potter's field, as the Lord appointed me.

c   And they [2] began to accuse him, saying, We found this man perverting our nation, and forbidding to give tribute to Cæsar, and saying that he himself is [2]Christ a king.

D Now Jesus stood before[11] the governor: and the governor asked him, saying, Art thou the King of the Jews? And Jesus said unto him, Thou sayest.

D   And [2] Pilate asked him, Art thou the King of the Jews? And he answering saith unto him, Thou sayest.

D   And Pilate [3] asked him, saying, Art thou the King of the Jews? And he answered him and said, Thou sayest.

E   And when he[12] was accused by the chief priests and elders, he answered nothing. Then saith Pilate[13] unto him, Hearest thou not how many things they witness against thee? And he gave[14] him no answer, not even to one word: insomuch that the governor marvelled greatly.

E   And the chief [3] priests accused him of many things. And Pilate again [4] asked him, saying, Answerest thou nothing? behold how many things they accuse thee of. But Jesus no more answered anything; insomuch that Pilate marvelled. [5]

F   And Pilate said [4] unto the chief priests and the multitudes, I find no fault in this man. But they were the [5] more urgent, saying, He stirreth up the people, teaching throughout all Judæa, and beginning from Galilee even unto this place. But when Pilate [6] heard it, he asked whether the man were a Galilæan. And [7] when he knew that he was of Herod's jurisdiction, he sent him unto Herod, who himself also was at Jerusalem in these days.

G Now when Herod saw [8] Jesus, he was exceeding glad: for he was of a long time desirous to see him, because he had heard concerning him; and he hoped to see some [3]miracle done by him. And [9] he questioned him in many words; but he answered him nothing. And the chief priests[10] and the scribes stood, vehemently accusing him. And[11] Herod with his soldiers set him at nought, and mocked him, and arraying him in gorgeous apparel sent him back to Pilate. And Herod[12] and Pilate became friends with each other that very day: for before they were at enmity between themselves.

H And Pilate called together[13] the chief priests and the rulers

ERV margin: 1 Some ancient authorities read *I gave*   2 Or *an anointed king*   3 Greek *sign*

MATT 27   MARK 15   LUKE 23

and the people, and said unto[14] them, Ye brought unto me this man, as one that perverteth the people: and behold, I, having examined him before you, found no fault in this man touching those things whereof ye accuse him: no,[15] nor yet Herod: for he sent him back unto us; and behold, nothing worthy of death hath been done by him.

1 Now at [1]the feast the gover-[15] nor was wont to release unto the multitude one prisoner, whom they would. And they[16] had then a notable prisoner, called Barabbas. When[17] therefore they were gathered together, Pilate said unto them, Whom will ye that I release unto you? Barabbas, or Jesus which is called Christ? For he knew that[18] for envy they had delivered him up.

1 Now at [1]the feast he used 6 to release unto them one prisoner, whom they asked of him. And there was one 7 called Barabbas, *lying* bound with them that had made insurrection, men who in the insurrection had committed murder. And the multitude 8 went up and began to ask him *to do* as he was wont to do unto them. And Pilate an- 9 swered them, saying, Will ye that I release unto you the King of the Jews? For he[10] perceived that for envy the chief priests had delivered him up.

1   I will[16] therefore chastise him, and release him.[2] But they cried[18] out all together, saying, Away with this man, and release unto us Barabbas: one who[1c] for a certain insurrection made in the city, and for murder, was cast into prison.

J   And while he was[19] sitting on the judgement-seat, his wife sent unto him, saying, Have thou nothing to do with that righteous man: for I have suffered many things this day in a dream because of him.

K   Now the chief priests[20] and the elders persuaded the multitudes that they should ask for Barabbas, and destroy Jesus. But the governor an-[21] swered and said unto them, Whether of the twain will ye that I release unto you? And they said, Barabbas. Pilate[22] saith unto them, What then shall I do unto Jesus which is called Christ? They all say, Let him be crucified. And he said, Why, what evil[23] hath he done? But they cried out exceedingly, saying, Let him be crucified.

K   But the chief priests[11] stirred up the multitude, that he should rather release Barabbas unto them. And Pilate[12] again answered and said unto them, What then shall I do unto him whom ye call the King of the Jews? And they[13] cried out again, Crucify him. And Pilate said unto them,[14] Why, what evil hath he done? But they cried out exceedingly, Crucify him.

K   And Pi-[20] late spake unto them again, desiring to release Jesus; but[21] they shouted, saying, Crucify, crucify him. And he said unto[22] them the third time, Why, what evil hath this man done? I have found no cause of death in him: I will therefore chastise him and release him. But they were instant with[23] loud voices, asking that he might be crucified.

L   So[24] when Pilate saw that he prevailed nothing, but rather that a tumult was arising, he took water, and washed his hands before the multitude, saying, I am innocent [3]of the

---

ERV margin: 1 Or *a feast*   2 Many ancient authorities insert verse 17: *Now he must needs release unto them at the feast one* prisoner: others add the same words after verse 19   3 Some ancient authorities read *of this blood: see ye, etc.*

OT references: Mt 27:24 = Deuteronomy 21:6–9

MATT 27	MARK 15	LUKE 23
blood of this righteous man: see ye *to it*. And all the[25] people answered and said, His blood *be* on us, and on our children. M Then released he unto[26] them Barabbas: but Jesus he scourged and delivered to be crucified.	M And Pilate,[15] wishing to content the multitude, released unto them Barabbas, and delivered Jesus, when he had scourged him, to be crucified.	M And their voices prevailed. And Pilate[24] gave sentence that what they asked for should be done. And he released him that for[25] insurrection and murder had been cast into prison, whom they asked for; but Jesus he delivered up to their will.
N Then the soldiers of the[27] governor took Jesus into the ¹palace, and gathered unto him the whole ²band. And[28] they ³stripped him, and put on him a scarlet robe. And they[29] plaited a crown of thorns and put it upon his head, and a reed in his right hand; and they kneeled down before him, and mocked him, saying, Hail, King of the Jews! And they[30] spat upon him, and took the reed and smote him on the head. And when they had[31] mocked him, they took off from him the robe, and put on him his garments, and led him away to crucify him.	N And the soldiers led him[16] away within the court, which is the ⁴Prætorium; and they call together the whole ²band. And they clothe him with pur-[17] ple, and plaiting a crown of thorns, they put it on him; and they began to salute him,[18] Hail, King of the Jews! And[19] they smote his head with a reed, and did spit upon him, and bowing their knees worshipped him. And when they[20] had mocked him, they took off from him the purple, and put on him his garments. And they lead him out to crucify him.	N *Compare verse 11 of portion G above*

§ 144   THE CRUCIFIXION OF JESUS

MATT 27:32–56	MARK 15:21–41	LUKE 23:26–49
A And as they came out,[32] they found a man of Cyrene, Simon by name: him they ⁵compelled to go *with them*, that he might bear his cross.	A And they ⁶compel one pas-[21] sing by, Simon of Cyrene, coming from the country, the father of Alexander and Rufus, to go *with them*, that he might bear his cross.	A And when they led him[26] away, they laid hold upon one Simon of Cyrene, coming from the country, and laid on him the cross, to bear it after Jesus.
		B And there followed him a[27] great multitude of the people, and of women who bewailed and lamented him. But Je-[28] sus turning unto them said, Daughters of Jerusalem, weep not for me, but weep for yourselves, and for your children. For behold, the days are com-[29] ing, in which they shall say, Blessed are the barren, and the wombs that never bare, and the breasts that never gave suck. Then shall they[30] begin to say to the mountains, Fall on us; and to the hills, Cover us. For if they[31] do these things in the green tree, what shall be done in the dry ?

ERV margin: 1 Greek *Prætorium:* see Mark 15:16   2 Or *cohort*   3 Some ancient authorities read *clothed*
4 Or *palace*   5 Greek *impressed*   6 Greek *impress*

OT references: Lk 23:30 = Hosea 10:8

MATT 27

c And when they were come[33] unto a place called Golgotha, that is to say, The place of a skull, they gave him wine to[34] drink mingled with gall: and when he had tasted it, he would not drink. And when[35] they had crucified him, they parted his garments among them, casting lots: and they[36] sat and watched him there. And they set up over his head[37] his accusation written, THIS IS JESUS THE KING OF THE JEWS. Then are there[38] crucified with him two robbers, one on the right hand, and one on the left.

D And they[39] that passed by railed on him, wagging their heads, and say-[40]ing, Thou that destroyest the [4]temple, and buildest it in three days, save thyself: if thou art the Son of God, come down from the cross. In like[41] manner also the chief priests mocking *him*, with the scribes and elders, said, He saved[42] others; [5]himself he cannot save. He is the King of Israel; let him now come down from the cross, and we will believe on him. He[43] trusteth on God; let him deliver him now, if he desireth him: for he said, I am the Son of God.

E And the robbers[44] also that were crucified with him cast upon him the same reproach.

MARK 15

c And[22] they bring him unto the place Golgotha, which is, being interpreted, The place of a skull. And they offered him wine[23] mingled with myrrh: but he received it not. And they[24] crucify him, and part his garments among them, casting lots upon them, what each should take. And it was the[25] third hour, and they crucified him. And the superscription[26] of his accusation was written over, THE KING OF THE JEWS. And with him they[27] crucify two robbers; one on his right hand, and one on his left.[3]

D And they that passed by[29] railed on him, wagging their heads, and saying, Ha! thou that destroyest the [4]temple, and buildest it in three days, save thyself, and come down[30] from the cross. In like manner also the chief priests mocking *him* among themselves with the scribes said, He saved others; [5]himself he cannot save. Let the Christ, the[32] King of Israel, now come down from the cross, that we may see and believe.

E And they[33] that were crucified with him reproached him.

LUKE 23

c And there were also two[32] others, malefactors, led with him to be put to death. And when they came unto[33] the place which is called [1]The skull, there they crucified him, and the malefactors, one on the right hand and the other on the left. [2]And Jesus said,[34] Father, forgive them; for they know not what they do. And parting his garments among them, they cast lots.

Compare verse 38 of portion D below

D And the[35] people stood beholding. And the rulers also scoffed at him, saying, He saved others; let him save himself, if this is the Christ of God, his chosen. And the soldiers also mocked[36] him, coming to him, offering him vinegar, and saying, If[37] thou art the King of the Jews, save thyself. And there was[38] also a superscription over him, THIS IS THE KING OF THE JEWS.

E And one of the malefactors[39] which were hanged railed on him, saying, Art not thou the Christ? save thyself and us. But the other answered, and[40] rebuking him said, Dost thou not even fear God, seeing thou art in the same condemnation? And we indeed justly;[41] for we receive the due reward of our deeds: but this man hath done nothing amiss. And he said, Jesus, remember[42] me when thou comest [6]in thy kingdom. And he said unto[43] him, Verily I say unto thee, To-day shalt thou be with me in Paradise.

ERV margin: 1 According to the Latin, *Calvary,* which has the same meaning   2 Some ancient authorities omit *And Jesus said, Father, forgive them; for they know not what they do*   3 Many ancient authorities insert verse 28: *And the scripture was fulfilled, which saith, And he was reckoned with transgressors:* see Luke 22:37   4 Or *sanctuary* 5 Or *can he not save himself?*   6 Some ancient authorities read *into thy kingdom*

OT references: Mt 27:34 and Mk 15:23 and Lk 23:36=Psalm 69:21   Mt 27:35 and Mk 15:24 and Lk 23:34= Psalm 22:18   Mt 27:39 and Mk 15:29 and Lk 23:35=Psalm 22:7   Mt 27:43=Psalm 22:8

MATT 27	MARK 15	LUKE 23
F Now from the sixth hour[45] there was darkness over all the ¹land until the ninth hour.	F And when the sixth hour[33] was come, there was darkness over the whole ¹land until the ninth hour.	F And it was now about the[44] sixth hour, and a darkness came over the whole ¹land until the ninth hour, ²the[45] sun's light failing:
G And about the ninth hour[46] Jesus cried with a loud voice, saying, Eli, Eli, lama sabach-thani? that is, My God, my God, ³why hast thou forsaken me? And some of them that[47] stood there, when they heard it, said, This man calleth Eli-jah. And straightway one of[48] them ran, and took a sponge, and filled it with vinegar, and put it on a reed, and gave him to drink. And the rest said,[49] Let be; let us see whether Elijah cometh to save him.⁴	G And at the ninth[34] hour Jesus cried with a loud voice, Eloi, Eloi, lama sabach-thani? which is, being inter-preted, My God, my God, ³why hast thou forsaken me? And some of them that stood[35] by, when they heard it, said, Behold, he calleth Elijah. And one ran, and filling a[36] sponge full of vinegar, put it on a reed, and gave him to drink, saying, Let be; let us see whether Elijah cometh to take him down.	G *Compare verse 36 of por-tion D above*
H And Jesus cried again with[50] a loud voice, and yielded up his spirit. And behold, the[51] veil of the ⁵temple was rent in twain from the top to the bottom;	H And Jesus ut-[37] tered a loud voice, and gave up the ghost. And the veil of[38] the ⁵temple was rent in twain from the top to the bottom.	H and the veil of the ⁵temple was rent in the midst. ⁶And when Jesus had[46] cried with a loud voice, he said, Father, into thy hands I commend my spirit: and having said this, he gave up the ghost.
I and the earth did quake; and the rocks were rent; and the tombs were[52] opened; and many bodies of the saints that had fallen asleep were raised; and com-[53] ing forth out of the tombs after his resurrection they entered into the holy city and appeared unto many.		
J Now the[54] centurion, and they that were with him watching Jesus, when they saw the earthquake, and the things that were done, feared exceedingly, saying, Truly this was ⁸the Son of God.	J And when the centurion,[39] which stood by over against him, saw that he ⁷so gave up the ghost, he said, Truly this man was ⁸the Son of God.	J And when the cen-[47] turion saw what was done, he glorified God, saying, Cer-tainly this was a righteous man.
		K And all the multitudes[48] that came together to this sight, when they beheld the things that were done, re-turned smiting their breasts.
L And many women were[55] there beholding from afar, which had followed Jesus from Galilee, ministering unto him: among whom was Mary[56] Magdalene, and Mary the mother of James and Joses, and the mother of the sons of Zebedee.	L And[40] there were also women be-holding from afar: among whom *were* both Mary Mag-dalene, and Mary the mother of James the ⁹less and of Joses, and Salome; who, when he[41] was in Galilee, followed him, and ministered unto him; and	L And all his acquaintance,[49] and the women that followed with him from Galilee, stood afar off, seeing these things.

ERV margin: 1 Or *earth*   2 Greek *the sun failing*   3 Or *why didst thou forsake me?*   4 Many ancient author-ities add *And another took a spear and pierced his side, and there came out water and blood:* see John 19:34   5 Or *sanctu-ary*   6 Or *And Jesus, crying with a loud voice, said*   7 Many ancient authorities read *so cried out, and gave up the ghost* 8 Or *a son of God*   9 Greek *little*

OT references: Mt 27:46 and Mk 15:34 = Psalm 22:1   Mt 27:48 and Mk 15:36 and Lk 23:36 = Psalm 69:21 Lk 23:46 = Psalm 31:5

MARK 15

many other women which came up with him unto Jerusalem.

§ 145 THE BURIAL OF JESUS

MATT 27:57-61	MARK 15:42-47	LUKE 23:50-55
A And when even was come,57	A And when even was now42 come, because it was the Preparation, that is, the day before the sabbath,	A *Compare portion E below*
B there came a rich man from Arimathæa, named Joseph, who also himself was Jesus' disciple: this man went to58 Pilate, and asked for the body of Jesus.	B there came43 Joseph of Arimathæa, a councillor of honourable estate, who also himself was looking for the kingdom of God; and he boldly went in unto Pilate, and asked for the body of Jesus.	B And behold, a man named50 Joseph, who was a councillor, a good man and a righteous (he had not consented to their51 counsel and deed), *a man* of Arimathæa, a city of the Jews, who was looking for the kingdom of God: this man went52 to Pilate, and asked for the body of Jesus.
C Then Pilate commanded it to be given up.	C And Pilate marvelled44 if he were already dead: and calling unto him the centurion, he asked him whether he ¹had been any while dead. And45 when he learned it of the centurion, he granted the corpse to Joseph.	
D And Joseph took the body,59 and wrapped it in a clean linen cloth, and laid it in his60 own new tomb, which he had hewn out in the rock: and he rolled a great stone to the door of the tomb, and departed.	D And he bought a46 linen cloth, and taking him down, wound him in the linen cloth, and laid him in a tomb which had been hewn out of a rock; and he rolled a stone against the door of the tomb.	D And he took53 it down, and wrapped it in a linen cloth, and laid him in a tomb that was hewn in stone, where never man had yet lain.
E *Compare portion A above*	E *Compare portion A above*	E And it was the day54 of the Preparation, and the sabbath ²drew on.
F And Mary Magdalene was61 there, and the other Mary, sitting over against the sepulchre.	F And Mary Magdalene and47 Mary the *mother* of Joses beheld where he was laid.	F And the55 women, which had come with him out of Galilee, followed after, and beheld the tomb, and how his body was laid.

ERV margin: ¹ Many ancient authorities read *were already dead* ² Greek *began to dawn*

OT references: Mt 27:57-60 and Mk 15:42-46 and Lk 23:50-54 = Deuteronomy 21:22-23

CHAPTER XXIV

EVENTS SUBSEQUENT TO THE DEATH OF JESUS

§ 146 THE GUARD FOR THE SEPULCHRE

MATT 27:62–66

Now on the morrow, which is *the day* after[62] the Preparation, the chief priests and the Pharisees were gathered together unto Pilate, saying,[63] Sir, we remember that that deceiver said, while he was yet alive, After three days I rise again. Command therefore that the sepulchre be[64] made sure until the third day, lest haply his disciples come and steal him away, and say unto the people, He is risen from the dead: and the last error will be worse than the first.   Pilate[65] said unto them, [1]Ye have a guard: go your way, [2]make it *as* sure as ye can.   So they went,[66] and made the sepulchre sure, sealing the stone, the guard being with them.

§ 147 THE VISIT TO THE SEPULCHRE

MATT 28:1–10	MARK 16:1–8	LUKE 23:56—24:12
	A And when the sabbath was [1] past, Mary Magdalene, and Mary the *mother* of James, and Salome, bought spices, that they might come and anoint him.	A And they returned, and[56] prepared spices and ointments. And on the sabbath they rested according to the commandment.
B Now late on the sabbath [1] day, as it began to dawn toward the first *day* of the week, came Mary Magdalene and the other Mary to see the sepulchre.	B And very early [2] on the first day of the week, they come to the tomb when the sun was risen.	B But on the first[24:] day of the week, at early [1] dawn, they came unto the tomb, bringing the spices which they had prepared.
c And behold, there [2] was a great earthquake; for an angel of the Lord descended from heaven, and came and rolled away the stone, and sat upon it.	c And they [3] were saying among themselves, Who shall roll us away the stone from the door of the tomb? and looking up, they [4] see that the stone is rolled back: for it was exceeding great.	c And [2] they found the stone rolled away from the tomb. And [3] they entered in, and found not the body [3]of the Lord Jesus.
D His ap- [3] pearance was as lightning, and his raiment white as snow: and [4] for fear of him the watchers did quake, and became as dead men. And the angel [5] answered and said unto the women, Fear not ye: for I know that ye seek Jesus, which hath been crucified. He is not here; for he is risen, [6]	D And entering into the [5] tomb, they saw a young man sitting on the right side, arrayed in a white robe; and [6] they were amazed. And [6] he saith unto them, Be not amazed: ye seek Jesus, the Nazarene, which hath been crucified: he is risen; he is not here: behold, the place where they laid him!	D And it came to pass, while [4] they were perplexed thereabout, behold, two men stood by them in dazzling apparel: and as they were affrighted, [5] and bowed down their faces to the earth, they said unto them, Why seek ye [4]the living among the dead? [5]He is not [6] here, but is risen:

ERV margin: [1] Or *Take a guard*   [2] Greek *make it sure, as ye know*   [3] Some ancient authorities omit *of the Lord Jesus*   [4] Greek *him that liveth*   [5] Some ancient authorities omit *He is not here, but is risen*

OT references: Lk 23:56 = Exodus 12:16 and 20:8–11 and Deuteronomy 5:12–15

MATT 28   MARK 16   LUKE 24

even as he said. Come, see the place [1]where the Lord lay.

E   remember how he spake unto you when he was yet in Galilee, saying 7 that the Son of man must be delivered up into the hands of sinful men, and be crucified, and the third day rise again.

F And go quickly, and tell his 7 disciples, He is risen from the dead; and lo, he goeth before you into Galilee; there shall ye see him: lo, I have told you. G And they departed quickly 8 from the tomb with fear and great joy, and ran to bring his disciples word.

F   But go, 7 tell his disciples and Peter, He goeth before you into Galilee: there shall ye see him, as he said unto you. G   And 8 they went out, and fled from the tomb; for trembling and astonishment had come upon them: and they said nothing to any one; for they were afraid.*

G And they remembered his 8 words, and returned [2]from the 9 tomb, and told all these things to the eleven, and to all the rest.

[H]   And behold, 9 Jesus met them, saying, All hail. And they came and took hold of his feet, and worshipped him. Then saith 10 Jesus unto them, Fear not: go tell my brethren that they depart into Galilee, and there shall they see me.

I[1] Now they were Mary Mag-10 dalene, and Joanna, and Mary the *mother* of James: and the other women with them told these things unto the apostles. And these words appeared in 11 their sight as idle talk; and they disbelieved them. J   [3]But 12 Peter arose, and ran unto the tomb; and stooping and looking in, he seeth the linen cloths by themselves; and he [4]departed to his home, wondering at that which was come to pass.

§ 148 THE GUARD AND THE AUTHORITIES

MATT 28:11-15

Now while they were going, behold, some of 11 the guard came into the city, and told unto the chief priests all the things that were come to pass. And when they were assembled with 12 the elders, and had taken counsel, they gave

---

ERV margin: 1 Many ancient authorities read *where he lay*   2 Some ancient authorities omit *from the tomb* 3 Some ancient authorities omit verse 12   4 Or *departed, wondering with himself*   5 Greek *demons*

---

* About the ending of the record of Mark, both ERV and ARV have the marginal statement: *The two oldest Greek manuscripts, and some other authorities, omit from verse 9 to the end. Some other authorities have a different ending to the Gospel.* From 16:9 to the end is therefore not placed in full parallelism, but is set forth in footnote form:

[H] 9 Now when he was risen early on the first day of the week, he appeared first to Mary Magdalene, from whom he had cast out seven [5]devils.

I   10 She went and told them that had been with him, as they mourned and wept. 11 And they, when they heard that he was alive, and had been seen of her, disbelieved. (Mark 16:9-11)

MATT 28

large money unto the soldiers, saying, Say ye,13
His disciples came by night, and stole him away
while we slept. And if this ¹come to the14
governor's ears, we will persuade him, and rid
you of care. So they took the money, and did15
as they were taught: and this saying was spread
abroad among the Jews, *and continueth* until
this day.

§ 149 WITH THE DISCIPLES IN THE COUNTRY

LUKE 24:13-32

A^A^ And behold, two of them were going that13
very day to a village named Emmaus, which
was threescore furlongs from Jerusalem. And14
they communed with each other of all these
things which had happened. And it came to15
pass, while they communed and questioned together, that Jesus himself drew near, and went
with them. But their eyes were holden that they16
should not know him.

B   And he said unto them,17
²What communications are these that ye have
one with another, as ye walk? And they stood
still, looking sad. And one of them, named18
Cleopas, answering said unto him, ³Dost thou
alone sojourn in Jerusalem and not know the
things which are come to pass there in these
days? And he said unto them, What things?19
And they said unto him, The things concerning Jesus of Nazareth, which was a prophet
mighty in deed and word before God and all the
people: and how the chief priests and our rulers20
delivered him up to be condemned to death,
and crucified him. But we hoped that it was21
he which should redeem Israel.

C   Yea and beside all this, it is now the third day since these
things came to pass. Moreover certain women22
of our company amazed us, having been early
at the tomb; and when they found not his body,23
they came, saying, that they had also seen a
vision of angels, which said that he was alive.

D And certain of them that were with us went24
to the tomb, and found it even so as the women
had said: but him they saw not.

E   And he said25
unto them, O foolish men, and slow of heart to
believe ⁴in all that the prophets have spoken!
Behoved it not the Christ to suffer these things,26
and to enter into his glory? And beginning27
from Moses and from all the prophets, he interpreted to them in all the scriptures the things
concerning himself.

F   And they drew nigh unto28
the village, whither they were going: and he
made as though he would go further. And29
they constrained him, saying, Abide with us:
for it is toward evening, and the day is now
far spent. And he went in to abide with them.
And it came to pass, when he had sat down30
with them to meat, he took the ⁵bread, and

ERV margin: 1 Or *come to a hearing before the governor* 2 Greek *What words are these that ye exchange one with another* 3 Or *Dost thou sojourn alone in Jerusalem, and knowest thou not the things* 4 Or *after* 5 Or *loaf*

12 And after these things he was manifested in another form unto two of them, as they walked, on their way into the country. (Mark 16:12)

LUKE 24

blessed it, and brake, and gave to them. And[31] their eyes were opened, and they knew him; and he vanished out of their sight. And they[32] said one to another, Was not our heart burning within us, while he spake to us in the way, while he opened to us the scriptures?

§ 150   WITH THE DISCIPLES IN JERUSALEM

MATT 28:19-20   LUKE 24:33-53

A^A   And they rose up that very hour, and re-[33] turned to Jerusalem, and found the eleven gathered together, and them that were with them, saying, The Lord is risen indeed, and[34] hath appeared to Simon. And they rehearsed[35] the things *that happened* in the way, and how he was known of them in the breaking of the bread.

B^B   And as they spake these things, he himself[36] stood in the midst of them, [1]and saith unto them, Peace *be* unto you. But they were terri-[37] fied and affrighted, and supposed that they beheld a spirit. And he said unto them, Why[38] are ye troubled? and wherefore do reasonings arise in your heart? See my hands and my[39] feet, that it is I myself: handle me, and see; for a spirit hath not flesh and bones, as ye behold me having. [2]And when he had said this,[40] he shewed them his hands and his feet.

C   And[41] while they still disbelieved for joy, and wondered, he said unto them, Have ye here anything to eat? And they gave him a piece of a[42] broiled fish.[3] And he took it, and did eat[43] before them.

D   And he said unto them, These are my words[44] which I spake unto you, while I was yet with you, how that all things must needs be fulfilled, which are written in the law of Moses, and the prophets, and the psalms, concerning me. Then opened he their mind, that they might[45] understand the scriptures; and he said unto[46] them, Thus it is written, that the Christ should suffer, and rise again from the dead the third day;

E^E   *Go ye therefore, and make disciples of all the*[19] *nations, baptizing them into the name of the Father and of the Son and of the Holy Ghost: teaching them to observe all things whatsoever I*[20] *commanded you: and lo, I am with you* [6]*alway, even unto* [7]*the end of the world.* (§*151 C*)

E^E   and that repentance [4]and remission of sins[47] should be preached in his name unto all the [5]nations, beginning from Jerusalem. Ye are[48] witnesses of these things. And behold, I send[49] forth the promise of my Father upon you: but tarry ye in the city, until ye be clothed with power from on high.

ERV margin: 1 Some ancient authorities omit *and saith unto them, Peace* be *unto you*   2 Some ancient authorities omit verse 40   3 Many ancient authorities add *and a honeycomb*   4 Some ancient authorities read *unto*   5 Or *nations. Beginning from Jerusalem, ye are witnesses*   6 Greek *all the days*   7 Or *the consummation of the age*   8 Greek *demons*   9 Some ancient authorities omit *new*

OT references: Lk 24:46 = Hosea 6:2

A   13 And they went away and told it unto the rest: neither believed they them.

B   14 And afterward he was manifested unto the eleven themselves as they sat at meat; and he upbraided them with their unbelief and hardness of heart, because they believed not them which had seen him after he was risen.

E   15 And he said unto them, Go ye into all the world, and preach the gospel to the whole creation. 16 He that believeth and is baptized shall be saved; but he that disbelieveth shall be condemned. 17 And these signs shall follow them that believe: in my name shall they cast out [8]devils; they shall speak with [9]new tongues; 18 they shall take up serpents, and if they drink any deadly thing, it shall in no wise hurt them; they shall lay hands on the sick, and they shall recover. (Mark 16:13-18)

LUKE 24

FF   And he led them out until *they were* over50 against Bethany: and he lifted up his hands, and blessed them.   And it came to pass, while51 he blessed them, he parted from them, ¹and was carried up into heaven.   And they ²worshipped52 him, and returned to Jerusalem with great joy; and were continually in the temple, blessing53 God.

§ 151   WITH THE DISCIPLES IN GALILEE

MATT 28:16-20	LUKE 24:47-49
A But the eleven disciples went into Galilee,16 unto the mountain where Jesus had appointed them. And when they saw him, they wor-17 shipped *him:* but some doubted.	
BB And Jesus18 came to them and spake unto them, saying, All authority hath been given unto me in heaven and on earth.	
cC Go ye therefore, and19 make disciples of all the nations, baptizing them into the name of the Father and of the Son and of the Holy Ghost: teaching them20 to observe all things whatsoever I commanded you: and lo, I am with you ³alway, even unto ⁴the end of the world.	cC *And that repentance* ⁵*and remission of sins*47 *should be preached in his name unto all the* ⁶*nations, beginning from Jerusalem. Ye are*48 *witnesses of these things. And behold, I send*49 *forth the promise of my Father upon you: but tarry ye in the city, until ye be clothed with power from on high.* (§150 E)

ERV margin: 1 Some ancient authorities omit *and was carried up into heaven*   2 Some ancient authorities omit *worshipped him, and*   3 Greek *all the days*   4 Or *the consummation of the age*   5 Some ancient authorities read *unto*   6 Or *nations.   Beginning from Jerusalem, ye are witnesses*

OT references: Mk 16:19 = Psalm 110:1

F   19 So then the Lord Jesus, after he had spoken unto them, was received up into heaven, and sat down at the right hand of God.   20 And they went forth, and preached everywhere, the Lord working with them, and confirming the word by the signs that followed.   Amen.   (Mark 16:19-20)

B   All things have been delivered unto me of my Father.   (§41 Q = Mt 11:27) | B   All things have been delivered unto me of my Father. (§82 T = Lk 10:22)

C   Compare the reference attached to §150 portion E

BOOK II

THE RECORD OF JOHN

RECORDS OF THE LIFE OF JESUS

BOOK II

THE RECORD OF JOHN

CHAPTER I

PROLOGUE TO THE RECORD OF JOHN

§ 152 PROLOGUE TO THE RECORD OF JOHN

JOHN I: 1–18   MT-MK-LK

A 1 In the beginning was the Word, and the Word was with God, and the Word was God. 2 The same was in the beginning with God. 3 All things were made ¹by him; and without him ²was not anything made that hath been made. 4 In him was life; and the life was the light of men. 5 And the light shineth in the darkness; and the darkness ³apprehended it not.

B   6 There came a man,

B *The Mt-Mk-Lk account of the activity of John is recorded in §17*

sent from God, whose name was John. 7 The same came for witness, that he might bear witness of the light, that all might believe through him. 8 He was not the light, but *came* that he might bear witness of the light. 9 ⁴There was the true light, *even the light* which lighteth ⁵every man, coming into the world.

C   10 He

was in the world, and the world was made ¹by him, and the world knew him not. 11 He came unto ⁶his own, and they that were his own received him not. 12 But as many as received him, to them gave he the right to become children of God, *even* to them that believe on his name: 13 which were ⁷born, not of ⁸blood, nor of the will of the flesh, nor of the will of man, but of God.

D   14 And

D *For the Mt-Mk-Lk reference to a beholding of the glory of Jesus, compare §74C(Lk)*

the Word became flesh, and ⁹dwelt among us (and we beheld his glory, glory as of ¹⁰the only begotten from the Father), full of grace and truth.

Eᴱ   15 John beareth witness of him, and crieth, say-

E *Compare §17 portion P*

ing, ¹¹This was he of whom I said, He that cometh after me is become before me: for he was ¹²before me.

F   16 For of his fulness we

all received, and grace for grace. 17 For the law was given ¹by Moses; grace and truth came ¹by Jesus Christ. 18 No man hath seen God at any time; ¹³the only begotten Son, which is in the bosom of the Father, he hath declared *him*.

ERV margin: 1 Or *through*   2 Or *was not anything made. That which hath been made was life in him; and the life, etc.*   3 Or *overcame:* see John 12:35 (Greek)   4 Or *The true light, which lighteth every man, was coming* 5 Or *every man as he cometh* 6 Greek *his own things*   7 Or *begotten*   8 Greek *bloods*   9 Greek *tabernacled*   10 Or *an only begotten from a father*   11 Some ancient authorities read (*this was he that said*)   12 Greek *first in regard of me* 13 Many very ancient authorities read *God only begotten*

E Compare §154 portion A

CHAPTER II

IN BETHANY BEYOND JORDAN

§ 153 PURPOSE OF THE PREACHING OF JOHN

JOHN 1: 19–28

A 19 And this is the witness of John, when the Jews sent unto him from Jerusalem priests and Levites to ask him, Who art thou? 20 And he confessed, and denied not; and he confessed, I am not the Christ.
B 21 And they asked him, What then? Art thou Elijah? And he saith, I am not. Art thou the prophet? And he answered, No. 22 They said therefore unto him, Who art thou? that we may give an answer to them that sent us. What sayest thou of thyself?

C 23 He said, I am the voice of one crying in the wilderness, Make straight the way of the Lord, as said Isaiah the prophet.
D 24 ¹And they had been sent from the Pharisees. 25 And they asked him, and said unto him, Why then baptizest thou, if thou art not the Christ, neither Elijah, neither the prophet?
E 26 John answered them, saying, I baptize ²with water: in the midst of you standeth one whom ye know not, 27 *even* he that cometh after me, the latchet of whose shoe I am not worthy to unloose.
F 28 These things were done in ³Bethany beyond Jordan, where John was baptizing.

MT-MK-LK

A *Compare §17 portion O*

B *For records of the identification of John as Elijah or the prophet, compare §41G and §74M. For records of the identification of Jesus as Elijah or the prophet, compare §58BC and §71C*
C *Compare §17 portions D-F Compare §41 portion E*

E *Compare §17 portion P*

§ 154 PURPOSE OF THE BAPTISM BY JOHN

JOHN 1: 29–34

Aᴬ 29 On the morrow he seeth Jesus coming unto him, and saith, Behold, the Lamb of God, which ⁴taketh away the sin of the world! 30 This is he of whom I said, After me cometh a man which is become before me: for he was ⁵before me.
B 31 And I knew him not; but that he should be made manifest to Israel, for this cause came I baptizing ²with water.
C 32 And John bare witness, saying, I have beheld the Spirit descending as a dove out of heaven; and it abode upon him.
D 33 And I knew him not: but he that sent me to baptize ²with water, he said unto me, Upon whomsoever thou shalt see the Spirit descending, and abiding upon him, the same is he that baptizeth ²with the Holy Spirit. 34 And I have seen, and have borne witness that this is the Son of God.

A *Compare §17 portion P*

B *Compare §18 portion B*

C *Compare §18 portion C*

D *Compare §18 portion B Compare §18 portion C*

ERV margin: 1 Or *And* certain *had been sent from among the Pharisees* 2 Or *in* 3 Many ancient authorities read *Bethabarah,* some *Betharabah* 4 Or *beareth the sin* 5 Greek *first in regard of me*

OT references: John 1: 23 = Isaiah 40: 3

A Compare §152 portion **E**

§ 155 TRANSITION OF DISCIPLES FROM JOHN TO JESUS

Mt-Mk-Lk

A *For the Mt-Mk-Lk record of the relation of Andrew and Simon Peter to Jesus, compare §23 and §27*

JOHN 1:35-42

A 35 Again on the morrow John was standing, and two of his disciples; 36 and he looked upon Jesus as he walked, and saith, Behold, the Lamb of God! 37 And the two disciples heard him speak, and they followed Jesus. 38 And Jesus turned, and beheld them following, and saith unto them, What seek ye? And they said unto him, Rabbi (which is to say, being interpreted, [1]Master), where abidest thou? 39 He saith unto them, Come, and ye shall see. They came therefore and saw where he abode; and they abode with him that day: it was about the tenth hour. 40 One of the two that heard John *speak*, and followed him, was Andrew, Simon Peter's brother. 41 He findeth first his own brother Simon, and saith unto him, We have found the Messiah (which is, being interpreted, [2]Christ). 42 He brought him unto Jesus.

B *In connection with the double name of Simon Peter, compare §35C, §56D, and §71E*

B   Jesus looked upon him, and said, Thou art Simon the son of [3]John: thou shalt be called Cephas (which is by interpretation, [4]Peter).

§ 156 JESUS WINS EARLY FOLLOWERS

A *For the complete list of the close associates of Jesus, compare §35C and §56D*

JOHN 1:43-51

A 43 On the morrow he was minded to go forth into Galilee, and he findeth Philip: and Jesus saith unto him, Follow me. 44 Now Philip was from Bethsaida, of the city of Andrew and Peter. 45 Philip findeth Nathanael, and saith unto him, We have found him, of whom Moses in the law, and the prophets, did write, Jesus of Nazareth, the son of Joseph. 46 And Nathanael said unto him, Can any good thing come out of Nazareth? Philip saith unto him, Come and see. 47 Jesus saw Nathanael coming to him, and saith of him, Behold, an Israelite indeed, in whom is no guile! 48 Nathanael saith unto him, Whence knowest thou me? Jesus answered and said unto him, Before Philip called thee, when thou wast under the fig tree, I saw thee. 49 Nathanael answered him, Rabbi, thou art the Son of God; thou art King of Israel. 50 Jesus answered and said unto him, Because I said unto thee, I saw thee underneath the fig tree, believest thou? thou shalt see greater things than these.

B *On the ministry of angels to Jesus, compare §20G and §140D*

B   51 And he saith unto him, Verily, verily, I say unto you, Ye shall see the heaven opened, and the angels of God ascending and descending upon the Son of man.

ERV margin: 1 Or *Teacher*   2 That is *Anointed*   3 Greek *Joanes:* called in Matthew 16:17, *Jonah*
4 That is *Rock* or *Stone*

OT references: John 1:51 = Genesis 28:12

CHAPTER III

IN THE PROVINCE OF GALILEE

§ 157 IN CANA OF GALILEE

JOHN 2:1–11   MT-MK-LK

A   1 And the third day there was a marriage in Cana of Galilee; and the mother of Jesus was there: 2 and Jesus also was bidden, and his disciples, to the marriage.   3 And when the wine failed, the mother of Jesus saith unto him, They have no wine.   4 And Jesus saith unto her, Woman, what have I to do with thee? mine hour is not yet come.   5 His mother saith unto the servants, Whatsoever he saith unto you, do it.

B   6 Now there were six waterpots of stone set there after the Jews' manner of purifying, containing two or three firkins apiece.   7 Jesus saith unto them, Fill the waterpots with water.   And they filled them up to the brim.   8 And he saith unto them, Draw out now, and bear unto the ¹ruler of the feast.   And they bare it.   9 And when the ruler of the feast tasted the water ²now become wine, and knew not whence it was (but the servants which had drawn the water knew), the ruler of the feast calleth the bridegroom, 10 and saith unto him, Every man setteth on first the good wine; and when *men* have drunk freely, *then* that which is worse: thou hast kept the good wine until now.

Cᶜ   11 This beginning of his signs did Jesus in Cana of Galilee, and manifested his glory;   and his disciples believed on him.

§ 158 AT CAPERNAUM IN GALILEE

JOHN 2:12

12 After this he went down to Capernaum, he, and his mother,   *Compare §21 portion B*
and *his* brethren, and his disciples: and there they abode not   *Compare §24 portion A*
many days.

ERV margin: 1 Or *steward*   2 Or *that it had become*

c   Compare §173 portion c

187

CHAPTER IV

IN JERUSALEM AT THE PASSOVER

§ 159 JESUS CASTS COMMERCE FROM THE TEMPLE

JOHN 2:13-22   MT-MK-LK

A 13 And the passover of the Jews was at hand, and Jesus went up to Jerusalem.   **A** *Compare §137 portion A*

B 14 And he found in the temple those that sold oxen and sheep and doves, and the changers of money sitting: 15 and he made a scourge of cords, and he cast all out of the temple, both the sheep and the oxen; and he poured out the changers' money, and overthrew their tables;   **B** *Compare §126 portion A*

C 16 and to them that sold the doves he said, Take these things hence; make not my Father's house a house of merchandise.   **C** *Compare §126 portion C*

D 17 His disciples remembered that it was written, The zeal of thine house shall eat me up.

E 18 The Jews therefore answered and said unto him, What sign shewest thou unto us, seeing that thou doest these things?   **E** *Compare §128 portion A*

F 19 Jesus answered and said unto them, Destroy this ¹temple, and in three days I will raise it up.   **F** *Compare §142 portion C*
 Compare §144 portion D

G 20 The Jews therefore said, Forty and six years was this ¹temple in building, and wilt thou raise it up in three days? 21 But he spake of the ¹temple of his body. 22 When therefore he was raised from the dead, his disciples remembered that he spake this; and they believed the scripture, and the word which Jesus had said.

§ 160 ATTITUDE IN JERUSALEM TOWARD JESUS

JOHN 2:23-25

23 Now when he was in Jerusalem at the passover, during the feast, many believed on his name, beholding his signs which he did. 24 But Jesus did not trust himself unto them, for that he knew all men, 25 and because he needed not that any one should bear witness concerning ²man; for he himself knew what was in man.

§ 161 DISCOURSE WITH A JEWISH TEACHER

JOHN 3:1-12

Aᴬ 1 Now there was a man of the Pharisees, named Nicodemus, a ruler of the Jews: 2 the same came unto him by night, and said to him,

B Rabbi, we know that thou art a teacher come from God: for no man can do these signs that thou doest, except God be with him.   **B** *Compare §130 portion B*

C 3 Jesus answered and said unto him, Verily, verily, I say unto thee, Except a man be born ³anew, he cannot see the kingdom of God.   **C** *Compare §78 portion D*
 Compare §116 portion C

D 4 Nicodemus saith unto him, How can a man be born when he is old? can he enter a second time into his mother's

---

ERV margin: 1 Or *sanctuary*   2 Or *a man; for . . . the man*   3 Or *from above*

OT references: John 2:17 = Psalm 69:9

▲ For other references to Nicodemus, compare §189 H and §218 E

MT–MK–LK   JOHN 3

womb, and be born? 5 Jesus answered, Verily, verily, I say unto
thee, Except a man be born of water and the Spirit, he cannot
enter into the kingdom of God.
E   6 That which is born of the flesh
is flesh; and that which is born of the Spirit is spirit. 7 Marvel
not that I said unto thee, Ye must be born ¹anew. 8 ²The wind
bloweth where it listeth, and thou hearest the voice thereof, but
knowest not whence it cometh, and whither it goeth: so is every
one that is born of the Spirit.
F   9 Nicodemus answered and said
unto him, How can these things be? 10 Jesus answered and said
unto him, Art thou the teacher of Israel, and understandest not
these things?
G^G   11 Verily, verily, I say unto thee, We speak that
we do know, and bear witness of that we have seen; and ye
receive not our witness. 12 If I told you earthly things, and ye
believe not, how shall ye believe, if I tell you heavenly things?

§ 162   MISSION OF THE SON OF MAN AND SON OF GOD

JOHN 3:13–21

A   13 And no man hath ascended into heaven, but he that descended out of heaven, *even* the Son of man, ³which is in heaven.
14 And as Moses lifted up the serpent in the wilderness, even so
must the Son of man be lifted up: 15 that whosoever ⁴believeth
may in him have eternal life.
B^B   16 For God so loved the world, that he gave his only begotten
Son, that whosoever believeth on him should not perish, but have
eternal life. 17 For God sent not the Son into the world to judge
the world; but that the world should be saved through him.
18 He that believeth on him is not judged: he that believeth not
hath been judged already, because he hath not believed on the
name of the only begotten Son of God.
C   19 And this is the judgement, that the light is come into the world, and men loved the
darkness rather than the light; for their works were evil. 20 For
every one that ⁵doeth ill hateth the light, and cometh not to the
light, lest his works should be ⁶reproved. 21 But he that doeth
the truth cometh to the light, that his works may be made manifest, ⁷that they have been wrought in God.

ERV margin: 1 Or *from above*   2 Or *The Spirit breatheth*   3 Many ancient authorities omit *which is in heaven*
4 Or *believeth in him may have*   5 Or *practiseth*   6 Or *convicted*   7 Or *because*

G   Compare §166 portion A

B   Compare §166 portion C

CHAPTER V

IN THE LAND OF JUDÆA

§ 163 BAPTISM OF THE DISCIPLES OF JESUS

JOHN 3:22   MT-MK-LK

22 After these things came Jesus and his disciples into the land
of Judæa; and there he tarried with them, and baptized.*

§ 164 BAPTISM OF DISCIPLES BY JOHN

JOHN 3:23-24

23 And John also was baptizing in Ænon near to Salim, because   *For the Mt-Mk-Lk account*
there ¹was much water there: and they came, and were baptized.   *of the imprisonment of John,*
24 For John was not yet cast into prison.   *compare §17 R and §58 D*

§ 165 RELATION OF JOHN TO JESUS

JOHN 3:25-30

A 25 There arose therefore a questioning on the part of John's
disciples with a Jew about purifying. 26 And they came unto
John, and said to him, Rabbi, he that was with thee beyond
Jordan, to whom thou hast borne witness, behold, the same baptizeth, and all men come to him. 27 John answered and said, A
man can receive nothing, except it have been given him from
heaven.
BB   28 Ye yourselves bear me witness, that I said, I am not
the Christ, but, that I am sent before him.
c   29 He that hath the
bride is the bridegroom: but the friend of the bridegroom, which
standeth and heareth him, rejoiceth greatly because of the bridegroom's voice: this my joy therefore is fulfilled. 30 He must
increase, but I must decrease.

§ 166 RELATION OF TRUTH TO SOURCE

JOHN 3:31-36

AA   31 He that cometh from above is above all: he that is of the
earth is of the earth, and of the earth he speaketh: ²he that
cometh from heaven is above all. 32 What he hath seen and
heard, of that he beareth witness; and no man receiveth his
witness. 33 He that hath received his witness hath set his seal
to *this*, that God is true. 34 For he whom God hath sent speaketh
the words of God: for he giveth not the Spirit by measure.
B 35 The Father loveth the Son, and hath given all things into his   B *Compare §41 Q and §82 T*
hand.   *Compare §151 portion B*
cc   36 He that believeth on the Son hath eternal life; but he
that ³obeyeth not the Son shall not see life, but the wrath of God
abideth on him.

ERV margin: 1 Greek *were many waters*   2 Some ancient authorities read *he that cometh from heaven beareth*
witness of what he hath seen and heard   3 Or *believeth not*

---

* Compare §167
B Compare §153

A   Compare §161 portion G
c   Compare §162 portion B

§ 167 DEPARTURE FROM JUDÆA FOR GALILEE

Mt-Mk-Lk

Compare §21 portion A

John 4:1-3

1 When therefore the Lord knew how that the Pharisees had heard that Jesus was making and baptizing more disciples than John 2 (although Jesus himself baptized not, but his disciples), 3 he left Judæa, and departed again into Galilee.

CHAPTER VI

IN THE PROVINCE OF SAMARIA

§ 168   JESUS JOURNEYS TO SYCHAR OF SAMARIA

JOHN 4:4-6

MT-MK-LK

4 And he must needs pass through Samaria. 5 So he cometh to
a city of Samaria, called Sychar, near to the parcel of ground that
Jacob gave to his son Joseph: 6 and Jacob's ¹well was there.
Jesus therefore, being wearied with his journey, sat ²thus by the
¹well.   It was about the sixth hour.

§ 169   DISCOURSE WITH A WOMAN OF SAMARIA

JOHN 4:7-26

A   7 There cometh a woman of Samaria to draw water: Jesus saith
unto her, Give me to drink. 8 For his disciples were gone away
into the city to buy food. 9 The Samaritan woman therefore
saith unto him, How is it that thou, being a Jew, askest drink of
me, which am a Samaritan woman? (³For Jews have no dealings
with Samaritans.)

B   10 Jesus answered and said unto her, If thou
knewest the gift of God, and who it is that saith to thee, Give me
to drink; thou wouldest have asked of him, and he would have
given thee living water. 11 The woman saith unto him, ⁴Sir,
thou hast nothing to draw with, and the well is deep: from
whence then hast thou that living water? 12 Art thou greater
than our father Jacob, which gave us the well, and drank thereof
himself, and his sons, and his cattle?

C   13 Jesus answered and said
unto her, Every one that drinketh of this water shall thirst again:
14 but whosoever drinketh of the water that I shall give him shall
never thirst; but the water that I shall give him shall become in
him a well of water springing up unto eternal life. 15 The woman
saith unto him, ⁴Sir, give me this water, that I thirst not, neither
come all the way hither to draw.

D   16 Jesus saith unto her, Go, call
thy husband, and come hither. 17 The woman answered and
said unto him, I have no husband. Jesus saith unto her, Thou
saidst well, I have no husband: 18 for thou hast had five husbands;
and he whom thou now hast is not thy husband: this hast thou said
truly.

E   19 The woman saith unto him, ⁴Sir, I perceive that thou
art a prophet. 20 Our fathers worshipped in this mountain; and
ye say, that in Jerusalem is the place where men ought to worship.
21 Jesus saith unto her, Woman, believe me, the hour cometh,
when neither in this mountain, nor in Jerusalem, shall ye worship
the Father. 22 Ye worship that which ye know not: we worship that which we know: for salvation is from the Jews. 23 But
the hour cometh, and now is, when the true worshippers shall
worship the Father in spirit and truth: ⁵for such doth the Father
seek to be his worshippers. 24 ⁶God is a Spirit: and they that
worship him must worship in spirit and truth.

F   25 The woman
saith unto him, I know that Messiah cometh (which is called
Christ): when he is come, he will declare unto us all things.
26 Jesus saith unto her, I that speak unto thee am *he*.

ERV margin: 1 Greek *spring:* and so in verse 14; but not in verses 11 and ⁻2   2 Or *as he was*   3 Some
ancient authorities omit *For Jews have no dealings with Samaritans*   4 Or *Lord*   5 Or *for such the Father also seeketh*
6 Or *God is spirit*

§ 170   DISCOURSE WITH THE DISCIPLES

Mt-Mk-Lk

JOHN 4:27–38

A   27 And upon this came his disciples; and they marvelled that he was speaking with a woman; yet no man said, What seekest thou? or, Why speakest thou with her?

B   28 So the woman left her waterpot, and went away into the city, and saith to the men, 29 Come, see a man, which told me all things that *ever* I did: can this be the Christ? 30 They went out of the city, and were coming to him.

C   31 In the mean while the disciples prayed him, saying, Rabbi, eat. 32 But he said unto them, I have meat to eat that ye know not. 33 The disciples therefore said one to another, Hath any man brought him *aught* to eat? 34 Jesus saith unto them, My meat is to do the will of him that sent me, and to accomplish his work.

D   *Compare §56 portion B*   **D**   35 Say not ye, There are yet four months, and
     Compare §82 portion B   *then* cometh the harvest? behold, I say unto you, Lift up your eyes, and look on the fields, that they are [1]white already unto harvest.

E   36 He that reapeth receiveth wages, and gathereth fruit unto life eternal; that he that soweth and he that reapeth may rejoice together. 37 For herein is the saying true, One soweth, and another reapeth. 38 I sent you to reap that whereon ye have not laboured: others have laboured, and ye are entered into their labour.

§ 171   STAY OF JESUS IN SAMARIA

JOHN 4:39–42

39 And from that city many of the Samaritans believed on him because of the word of the woman, who testified, He told me all things that *ever* I did. 40 So when the Samaritans came unto him, they besought him to abide with them: and he abode there two days. 41 And many more believed because of his word; 42 and they said to the woman, Now we believe, not because of thy speaking: for we have heard for ourselves, and know that this is indeed the Saviour of the world.

ERV margin: 1 Or *white unto harvest. Already he that reapeth etc.*

CHAPTER VII

IN THE PROVINCE OF GALILEE

§ 172 ATTITUDE OF GALILÆANS TOWARD JESUS

JOHN 4:43–45

MT-MK-LK

A 43 And after the two days he went forth from thence into Galilee.

A *Compare §21 portion A*

B 44 For Jesus himself testified, that a prophet hath no honour in his own country.

B *Compare §22 portion H*
Compare §54 portion H

C 45 So when he came into Galilee, the Galilæans received him, having seen all the things that he did in Jerusalem at the feast: for they also went unto the feast.

§ 173 IN CANA OF GALILEE

JOHN 4:46–54

AA 46 He came therefore again unto Cana of Galilee, where he made the water wine.

B And there was a certain ¹nobleman, whose son was sick at Capernaum. 47 When he heard that Jesus was come out of Judæa into Galilee, he went unto him, and besought *him* that he would come down, and heal his son; for he was at the point of death. 48 Jesus therefore said unto him, Except ye see signs and wonders, ye will in no wise believe. 49 The ¹nobleman saith unto him, ²Sir, come down ere my child die. 50 Jesus saith unto him, Go thy way; thy son liveth. The man believed the word that Jesus spake unto him, and he went his way. 51 And as he was now going down, his ³servants met him, saying, that his son lived. 52 So he inquired of them the hour when he began to amend. They said therefore unto him, Yesterday at the seventh hour the fever left him. 53 So the father knew that *it was* at that hour in which Jesus said unto him, Thy son liveth: and himself believed, and his whole house.

B *For an account in Mt-Lk of somewhat similar general content, compare §39*

CC 54 This is again the second sign that Jesus did, having come out of Judæa into Galilee.

ERV margin: ¹ Or *king's officer*   ² Or *Lord*   ³ Greek *bondservants*

A   Compare §157 portions AB
C   Compare §157 portion C

CHAPTER VIII

IN JERUSALEM AT A FEAST

§ 174 AT THE POOL OF BETHESDA

JOHN 5:1–9ᵃ

MT-MK-LK

A 1 After these things there was ¹a feast of the Jews; and Jesus
went up to Jerusalem.
B 2 Now there is in Jerusalem by the sheep *gate* a pool, which is
called in Hebrew ²Bethesda, having five porches. 3 In these lay
a multitude of them that were sick, blind, halt, withered.³ 5 And
a certain man was there, which had been thirty and eight years in
his infirmity. 6 When Jesus saw him lying, and knew that he had
been now a long time *in that case*, he saith unto him, Wouldest
thou be made whole? 7 The sick man answered him, ⁴Sir, I have
no man, when the water is troubled, to put me into the pool: but
while I am coming, another steppeth down before me.
c   8 Jesus
saith unto him, Arise, take up thy bed, and walk. 9 And straightway the man was made whole, and took up his bed and walked.

c *Compare §29 portions GH*

§ 175 CRITICISM FOR ACTIVITY ON THE SABBATH

JOHN 5:9ᵇ–18

A 9 Now it was the sabbath on that day. 10 So the Jews said
unto him that was cured, It is the sabbath, and it is not lawful
for thee to take up thy bed.
B   11 But he answered them, He that
made me whole, the same said unto me, Take up thy bed, and
walk. 12 They asked him, Who is the man that said unto thee,
Take up *thy bed*, and walk? 13 But he that was healed wist not
who it was: for Jesus had conveyed himself away, a multitude
being in the place. 14 Afterward Jesus findeth him in the temple,
and said unto him, Behold, thou art made whole: sin no more, lest
a worse thing befall thee. 15 The man went away, and told the
Jews that it was Jesus which had made him whole.
cᶜ   16 And for
this cause did the Jews persecute Jesus, because he did these
things on the sabbath. 17 But Jesus answered them, My Father
worketh even until now, and I work. 18 For this cause therefore
the Jews sought the more to kill him, because he not only brake
the sabbath, but also called God his own Father, making himself
equal with God.

A *Compare §32 portion B*

c *Compare §33 portion G*

§ 176 DISCOURSE ON JUDGMENT AND LIFE

JOHN 5:19–29

A 19 Jesus therefore answered and said unto them,
  Verily, verily, I say unto you, The Son can do nothing of himself, but what he seeth the Father doing: for what things soever
he doeth, these the Son also doeth in like manner. 20 For the
Father loveth the Son, and sheweth him all things that himself
doeth:

ERV margin: 1 Many ancient authorities read *the feast* 2 Some ancient authorities read *Bethsaida* others
Bethzatha 3 Many ancient authorities insert, wholly or in part, *waiting for the moving of the water: 4 for an angel of the
Lord went down at certain seasons into the pool, and troubled the water: whosoever then first after the troubling of the water
stepped in was made whole, with whatsoever disease he was holden* 4 Or *Lord*

OT references: John 5:10 = Exodus 20:10 and Deuteronomy 5:14

c Compare §188 portion B and §195 portion B

MT-MK-LK	JOHN 5

B *With verse 23b compare*
§57 P and §78 G and §82 Q

B   and greater works than these will he shew him, that ye may marvel. 21 For as the Father raiseth the dead and quickeneth them, even so the Son also quickeneth whom he will. 22 For neither doth the Father judge any man, but he hath given all judgement unto the Son; 23 that all may honour the Son, even as they honour the Father. He that honoureth not the Son honoureth not the Father which sent him. 24 Verily, verily, I say unto you, He that heareth my word, and believeth him that sent me, hath eternal life, and cometh not into judgement, but hath passed out of death into life.

C   25 Verily, verily, I say unto you, The hour cometh, and now is, when the dead shall hear the voice of the Son of God; and they that hear shall live. 26 For as the Father hath life in himself, even so gave he to the Son also to have life in himself: 27 and he gave him authority to execute judgement, because he is ¹the Son of man.

D *Compare verse 46 of §136 portion S*

D   28 Marvel not at this: for the hour cometh, in which all that are in the tombs shall hear his voice, 29 and shall come forth; they that have done good, unto the resurrection of life; and they that have ²done ill, unto the resurrection of judgement.

§ 177   WITNESSES TO THE TRUTH OF JESUS

JOHN 5:30–47

A 30 I can of myself do nothing: as I hear, I judge: and my judgement is righteous; because I seek not mine own will, but the will of him that sent me. 31 If I bear witness of myself, my witness is not true. 32 It is another that beareth witness of me; and I know that the witness which he witnesseth of me is true.

B   33 Ye have sent unto John, and he hath borne witness unto the truth. 34 But the witness which I receive is not from man: howbeit I say these things, that ye may be saved. 35 He was the lamp that burneth and shineth: and ye were willing to rejoice for a season in his light.

C   36 But the witness which I have is greater than *that of* John: for the works which the Father hath given me to accomplish, the very works that I do, bear witness of me, that the Father hath sent me.

D   37 And the Father which sent me, he hath borne witness of me. Ye have neither heard his voice at any time, nor seen his form. 38 And ye have not his word abiding in you: for whom he sent, him ye believe not.

E   39 ³Ye search the scriptures, because ye think that in them ye have eternal life; and these are they which bear witness of me; 40 and ye will not come to me, that ye may have life.

F   41 I receive not glory from men. 42 But I know you, that ye have not the love of God in yourselves. 43 I am come in my Father's name, and ye receive me not: if another shall come in his own name, him ye will receive. 44 How can ye believe, which receive glory one of another, and the glory that *cometh* from ⁴the only God ye seek not?

G *Compare §149 portion E*
Compare §150 portion D

G   45 Think not that I will accuse you to the Father: there is one that accuseth you, *even* Moses, on whom ye have set your hope. 46 For if ye believed Moses, ye would believe me; for he wrote of me. 47 But if ye believe not his writings, how shall ye believe my words?

ERV margin: 1 Or *a son of man*   2 Or *practised*   3 Or *Search the scriptures*   4 Some ancient authorities read *the only one*

CHAPTER IX

ABOUT THE SEA OF GALILEE

§ 178 TEACHING AND FEEDING THE MULTITUDE

JOHN 6:1-13	MT-MK-LK
A 1 After these things Jesus went away to the other side of the sea of Galilee, which is *the sea* of Tiberias. 2 And a great multitude followed him, because they beheld the signs which he did on them that were sick.	**A** *Compare §60 portion A* *Compare §65*
B 3 And Jesus went up into the mountain, and there he sat with his disciples. 4 Now the passover, the feast of the Jews, was at hand. 5 Jesus therefore lifting up his eyes, and seeing that a great multitude cometh unto him,	**B** *Compare §67 portion A* *Compare §60 portion B*
C saith unto Philip, Whence are we to buy ¹bread, that these may eat? 6 And this he said to prove him: for he himself knew what he would do.	**C** *Compare §67 portion C* *Compare §60 portion C*
D 7 Philip answered him, Two hundred ²pennyworth of ¹bread is not sufficient for them, that every one may take a little. 8 One of his disciples, Andrew, Simon Peter's brother, saith unto him, 9 There is a lad here, which hath five barley loaves, and two fishes: but what are these among so many?	**D** *Compare §60 portion D* *Compare §67 portion D*
E 10 Jesus said, Make the people sit down. Now there was much grass in the place.	**E** *Compare §60 portion F* *Compare §67 portion E*
F So the men sat down, in number about five thousand.	**F** *Compare §60 portion I* *Compare §67 portion I*
G 11 Jesus therefore took the loaves; and having given thanks, he distributed to them that were set down; likewise also of the fishes as much as they would.	**G** *Compare §60 portion G* *Compare §67 portion F*
H 12 And when they were filled, he saith unto his disciples, Gather up the broken pieces which remain over, that nothing be lost. 13 So they gathered them up, and filled twelve baskets with broken pieces from the five barley loaves, which remained over unto them that had eaten.	**H** *Compare §60 portion H* *Compare §67 portion H*

§ 179 POPULAR ATTITUDE TOWARD JESUS

JOHN 6:14-15	
A 14 When therefore the people saw the ³sign which he did, they said, This is of a truth the prophet that cometh into the world.	
B 15 Jesus therefore perceiving that they were about to come and take him by force, to make him king, withdrew again into the mountain himself alone.	**B** *Compare §60 portion K* *Compare §71 portion A*

§ 180 ACROSS THE SEA OF GALILEE

JOHN 6:16-21	
A 16 And when evening came, his disciples went down unto the sea; 17 and they entered into a boat, and were going over the sea unto Capernaum.	**A** *Compare §60 portion J* *Compare §67 portion J*
B And it was now dark, and Jesus had not yet come to them. 18 And the sea was rising by reason of a great wind that blew. 19 When therefore they had rowed about five and twenty or thirty furlongs, they behold Jesus walking on the sea, and drawing nigh unto the boat:	**B** *Compare §61 portion A*

ERV margin: 1 Greek *loaves*   2 The word in the Greek denotes a coin worth about eight pence halfpenny   3 Some ancient authorities read *signs*

199

MT-MK-LK	JOHN 6

<table>
<tr><td>C</td><td>*Compare §61 portion B*</td></tr>
</table>

C   and they were afraid,
20 But he saith unto them, It is I; be not afraid.

<table>
<tr><td>D</td><td>*Compare §61 portion D*
Compare §62 portion A</td></tr>
</table>

D   21 They were
willing therefore to receive him into the boat: and straightway
the boat was at the land whither they were going.

§ 181   THE MULTITUDE IN CAPERNAUM

JOHN 6:22–26

22 On the morrow the multitude which stood on the other side
of the sea saw that there was none other [1]boat there, save one,
and that Jesus entered not with his disciples into the boat, but
that his disciples went away alone 23 (howbeit there came [2]boats
from Tiberias nigh unto the place where they ate the bread after
the Lord had given thanks): 24 when the multitude therefore
saw that Jesus was not there, neither his disciples, they themselves
got into the [2]boats, and came to Capernaum, seeking Jesus.
25 And when they found him on the other side of the sea, they
said unto him, Rabbi, when camest thou hither? 26 Jesus
answered them and said, Verily, verily, I say unto you, Ye seek
me, not because ye saw signs, but because ye ate of the loaves, and
were filled.

§ 182   DISCOURSE ON THE BREAD OF LIFE

JOHN 6:27–59

A   27 Work not for the meat which perisheth, but for the meat
which abideth unto eternal life, which the Son of man shall give
unto you: for him the Father, *even* God, hath sealed.   28 They
said therefore unto him, What must we do, that we may work the
works of God?   29 Jesus answered and said unto them, This is
the work of God, that ye believe on him whom [3]he hath sent.

B *Compare §45 portion Q*
Compare §68 portion A
Compare §86 portion D

B 30 They said therefore unto him, What then doest thou for a
sign, that we may see, and believe thee? what workest thou?
31 Our fathers ate the manna in the wilderness; as it is written,
He gave them bread out of heaven to eat.
C   32 Jesus therefore said
unto them, Verily, verily, I say unto you, It was not Moses that
gave you the bread out of heaven; but my Father giveth you the
true bread out of heaven.   33 For the bread of God is that which
cometh down out of heaven, and giveth life unto the world.
34 They said therefore unto him, Lord, evermore give us this
bread.   35 Jesus said unto them, I am the bread of life: he that
cometh to me shall not hunger, and he that believeth on me shall
never thirst.
D   36 But I said unto you, that ye have seen me, and
yet believe not.
E   37 All that which the Father giveth me shall
come unto me; and him that cometh to me I will in no wise cast
out.   38 For I am come down from heaven, not to do mine own
will, but the will of him that sent me.   39 And this is the will of
him that sent me, that of all that which he hath given me I should
lose nothing, but should raise it up at the last day.   40 For this
is the will of my Father, that every one that beholdeth the Son,
and believeth on him, should have eternal life; and [4]I will raise
him up at the last day.

F *Compare §22 portion D*
Compare §54 portion D

F 41 The Jews therefore murmured concerning him, because he
said, I am the bread which came down out of heaven.   42 And
they said, Is not this Jesus, the son of Joseph, whose father and
mother we know? how doth he now say, I am come down out of
heaven?

ERV margin: 1 Greek *little boat*   2 Greek *little boats*   3 Or *he sent*   4 Or *that I should raise him up*

OT references: John 6:31 = Exodus 16:4, 15 and Psalm 78:24 and Nehemiah 9:15

JOHN 6	MT-MK-LK

G   43 Jesus answered and said unto them, Murmur not among yourselves. 44 No man can come to me, except the Father which sent me draw him: and I will raise him up in the last day. 45 It is written in the prophets, And they shall all be taught of God. Every one that hath heard from the Father, and hath learned, cometh unto me.

H   46 Not that any man hath seen the Father, save he which is from God, he hath seen the Father.

H *Compare §41 portion Q*
 Compare §82 portion T

I 47 Verily, verily, I say unto you, He that believeth hath eternal life. 48 I am the bread of life. 49 Your fathers did eat the manna in the wilderness, and they died. 50 This is the bread which cometh down out of heaven, that a man may eat thereof, and not die. 51 I am the living bread which came down out of heaven: if any man eat of this bread, he shall live for ever: yea and the bread which I will give is my flesh, for the life of the world.

J 52 The Jews therefore strove one with another, saying, How can this man give us his flesh to eat? 53 Jesus therefore said unto them, Verily, verily, I say unto you, Except ye eat the flesh of the Son of man and drink his blood, ye have not life in yourselves. 54 He that eateth my flesh and drinketh my blood hath eternal life; and I will raise him up at the last day. 55 For my flesh is ¹meat indeed, and my blood is ²drink indeed. 56 He that eateth my flesh and drinketh my blood abideth in me, and I in him. 57 As the living Father sent me, and I live because of the Father; so he that eateth me, he also shall live because of me. 58 This is the bread which came down out of heaven: not as the fathers did eat, and died: he that eateth this bread shall live for ever.

K   59 These things said he in ³the synagogue, as he taught in Capernaum.

§ 183 EFFECT OF THE DISCOURSE ON DISCIPLES

JOHN 6:60-71

A 60 Many therefore of his disciples, when they heard *this*, said, This is a hard saying; who can hear ⁴it? 61 But Jesus knowing in himself that his disciples murmured at this, said unto them, Doth this cause you to stumble? 62 *What* then if ye should behold the Son of man ascending where he was before? 63 It is the spirit that quickeneth; the flesh profiteth nothing: the words that I have spoken unto you are spirit, and are life.

A *In connection with the question recorded in verse 62, compare §150 portion F*

B   64 But there are some of you that believe not. For Jesus knew from the beginning who they were that believed not, and who it was that should betray him. 65 And he said, For this cause have I said unto you, that no man can come unto me, except it be given unto him of the Father.

B *Compare §138 portion E*

c 66 Upon this many of his disciples went back, and walked no more with him. 67 Jesus said therefore unto the twelve, Would ye also go away? 68 Simon Peter answered him, Lord, to whom shall we go? thou ⁵hast the words of eternal life. 69 And we have believed and know that thou art the Holy One of God.

c *Compare §71 portion D*

Dᴰ   70 Jesus answered them, Did not I choose you the twelve, and one of you is a devil? 71 Now he spake of Judas *the son* of Simon Iscariot, for he it was that should betray him, *being* one of the twelve.

D *Compare §35 portion B*
 Compare §137 portion F
 Compare §138 portion F

§ 184 JESUS IN GALILEE

JOHN 7:1

1 And after these things Jesus walked in Galilee: for he would not walk in Judæa, because the Jews sought to kill him.

 Compare §76 portion A

ERV margin:	1 Greek *true meat*	2 Greek *true drink*	3 Or *a synagogue*	4 Or *him*	5 Or *hast words*

OT references: John 6:45 = Isaiah 54:13

D Compare §209 portions c (verse 11) and F and H

CHAPTER X

AT THE FEAST OF TABERNACLES

§ 185 OPINIONS OF THE BRETHREN OF JESUS

JOHN 7:2–9   MT-MK-LK

A 2 Now the feast of the Jews, the feast of tabernacles, was at hand. 3 His brethren therefore said unto him, Depart hence, and go into Judæa, that thy disciples also may behold thy works which thou doest. 4 For no man doeth anything in secret, ¹and himself seeketh to be known openly. If thou doest these things, manifest thyself to the world.

B   5 For even his brethren did not believe on him.   B *Compare §44*
                                                 Compare §54 portion J

C   6 Jesus therefore saith unto them, My time is not yet come; but your time is alway ready. 7 The world cannot hate you; but me it hateth, because I testify of it, that its works are evil. 8 Go ye up unto the feast: I go not up ²yet unto this feast; because my time is not yet fulfilled. 9 And having said these things unto them, he abode *still* in Galilee.

§ 186 POPULAR OPINIONS ABOUT JESUS

JOHN 7:10–13

10 But when his brethren were gone up unto the feast, then went he also up, not publicly, but as it were in secret. 11 The Jews therefore sought him at the feast, and said, Where is he? 12 And there was much murmuring among the multitudes concerning him: some said, He is a good man; others said, Not so, but he leadeth the multitude astray. 13 Howbeit no man spake openly of him for fear of the Jews.

§ 187 SOURCE OF THE TEACHING OF JESUS

JOHN 7:14–18

A 14 But when it was now the midst of the feast Jesus went up into the temple, and taught. 15 The Jews therefore marvelled, saying, How knoweth this man letters, having never learned?   A *Compare §22 portion C*
                                             Compare §54 portion C

B 16 Jesus therefore answered them, and said, My teaching is not mine, but his that sent me. 17 If any man willeth to do his will, he shall know of the teaching, whether it be of God, or *whether* I speak from myself. 18 He that speaketh from himself seeketh his own glory: but he that seeketh the glory of him that sent him, the same is true, and no unrighteousness is in him.

§ 188 CONCERNING HEALING ON THE SABBATH

JOHN 7:19–24

A 19 Did not Moses give you the law, and *yet* none of you doeth the law? Why seek ye to kill me? 20 The multitude answered, Thou hast a ³devil: who seeketh to kill thee?   A *On the possession of Jesus by a devil, compare §45 C and §53 B and §86 C*
BB   21 Jesus answered and said unto them, I did one work, and ye all ⁴marvel. 22 For

---

ERV margin: 1 Some ancient authorities read *and seeketh it to be known openly*   2 Many ancient authorities omit *yet*   3 Greek *demon*   4 Or *marvel because of this. Moses hath given you circumcision*

OT references: John 7:22–23 = Genesis 17:9–14 and Leviticus 12:1–3

B Compare §175 portion C and §195 portion B

Mᴛ-Mᴋ-Lᴋ   Jᴏʜɴ 7

this cause hath Moses given you circumcision (not that it is of
Moses, but of the fathers); and on the sabbath ye circumcise a
man.   23 If a man receiveth circumcision on the sabbath, that
the law of Moses may not be broken; are ye wroth with me,
because I made a man every whit whole on the sabbath?   24 Judge
not according to appearance, but judge righteous judgement.

§ 189   CONFLICTING JUDGMENTS ABOUT JESUS

Jᴏʜɴ 7:25-52

A   25 Some therefore of them of Jerusalem said, Is not this he
whom they seek to kill?   26 And lo, he speaketh openly, and they
say nothing unto him.   Can it be that the rulers indeed know that
this is the Christ?   27 Howbeit we know this man whence he is:
but when the Christ cometh, no one knoweth whence he is.

B   *With verse 29a compare*
§41 Q and §82 T

B   28 Jesus therefore cried in the temple, teaching and saying,
Ye both know me, and know whence I am; and I am not come
of myself, but he that sent me is true, whom ye know not.   29 I
know him; because I am from him, and he sent me.
C   30 They
sought therefore to take him: and no man laid his hand on him,
because his hour was not yet come.   31 But of the multitude
many believed on him; and they said, When the Christ shall come,
will he do more signs than those which this man hath done?
32 The Pharisees heard the multitude murmuring these things
concerning him; and the chief priests and the Pharisees sent
officers to take him.
Dᴰ   33 Jesus therefore said, Yet a little while
am I with you, and I go unto him that sent me.   34 Ye shall seek
me, and shall not find me: and where I am, ye cannot come.
35 The Jews therefore said among themselves, Whither will this
man go that we shall not find him? will he go unto the Disper-
sion ¹among the Greeks, and teach the Greeks?   36 What is this
word that he said, Ye shall seek me, and shall not find me: and
where I am, ye cannot come?

E   *On the promise of the Spirit*
after the death of Jesus, com-
pare §150 portion E

E   37 Now on the last day, the great *day* of the feast, Jesus stood
and cried, saying, If any man thirst, let him come unto me, and
drink.   38 He that believeth on me, as the scripture hath said,
out of his belly shall flow rivers of living water.   39 But this
spake he of the Spirit, which they that believed on him were to
receive: ²for the Spirit was not yet *given;* because Jesus was not
yet glorified.

F   *On Bethlehem as the source*
of the Christ, compare §11 por-
tion C

F   40 *Some* of the multitude therefore, when they
heard these words, said, This is of a truth the prophet.   41 Others
said, This is the Christ.   But some said, What, doth the Christ
come out of Galilee?   42 Hath not the scripture said that the
Christ cometh of the seed of David, and from Bethlehem, the
village where David was?   43 So there arose a division in the
multitude because of him.   44 And some of them would have
taken him; but no man laid hands on him.

G   *Compare §24 portion B*
Compare §24 portion E
Compare §38 portion X

G   45 The officers therefore came to the chief priests and Pharisees; and they said unto them, Why did ye not bring him?
46 The officers answered, Never man so spake.   47 The Pharisees
therefore answered them, Are ye also led astray?   48 Hath any
of the rulers believed on him, or of the Pharisees?   49 But this
multitude which knoweth not the law are accursed.
Hᴴ   50 Nicodemus saith unto them (he that came to him before, being one
of them), 51 Doth our law judge a man, except it first hear from

---

ERV margin: 1 Greek *of*   2 Some ancient authorities read *for the Holy Spirit was not yet given*

OT references: John 7:42 = 2 Samuel 7:12-17 and Micah 5:2

D   Compare §209 portion ᴍ
H   For other references to Nicodemus, compare §161 A and §218 ᴇ

himself and know what he doeth? 52 They answered and said
unto him, Art thou also of Galilee? Search, and ¹see that out of
Galilee ariseth no prophet.

§ 190 THE ADULTEROUS WOMAN AND HER ACCUSERS

JOHN 7:53—8:11

²[53 And they went every man unto his own house: 8:1 but
Jesus went unto the mount of Olives. 2 And early in the morning
he came again into the temple, and all the people came unto him;
and he sat down, and taught them. 3 And the scribes and the
Pharisees bring a woman taken in adultery; and having set her
in the midst, 4 they say unto him, ³Master, this woman hath
been taken in adultery, in the very act. 5 Now in the law Moses
commanded us to stone such: what then sayest thou of her?
6 And this they said, ⁴tempting him, that they might have
whereof to accuse him. But Jesus stooped down, and with his
finger wrote on the ground. 7 But when they continued asking
him, he lifted up himself, and said unto them, He that is without
sin among you, let him first cast a stone at her. 8 And again he
stooped down, and with his finger wrote on the ground. 9 And
they, when they heard it, went out one by one, beginning from
the eldest, *even* unto the last: and Jesus was left alone, and the
woman, where she was, in the midst. 10 And Jesus lifted up
himself, and said unto her, Woman, where are they? did no man
condemn thee? 11 And she said, No man, Lord. And Jesus
said, Neither do I condemn thee: go thy way; from henceforth
sin no more.]

§ 191 DISCOURSE ON THE LIGHT OF LIFE

JOHN 8:12–20

A   12 Again therefore Jesus spake unto them, saying, I am the
light of the world: he that followeth me shall not walk in the
darkness, but shall have the light of life.
B   13 The Pharisees therefore said unto him, Thou bearest witness of thyself; thy witness
is not true. 14 Jesus answered and said unto them, Even if I
bear witness of myself, my witness is true; for I know whence I
came, and whither I go; but ye know not whence I come, or
whither I go.
C   15 Ye judge after the flesh; I judge no man. 16 Yea
and if I judge, my judgement is true; for I am not alone, but I
and the Father that sent me.
D   17 Yea and in your law it is written,
that the witness of two men is true. 18 I am he that beareth
witness of myself, and the Father that sent me beareth witness
of me. 19 They said therefore unto him, Where is thy Father?
Jesus answered, Ye know neither me, nor my Father: if ye knew
me, ye would know my Father also.
E   20 These words spake he in
the treasury, as he taught in the temple: and no man took him;
because his hour was not yet come.

§ 192 THE IDENTITY OF JESUS

JOHN 8:21–30

A   21 He said therefore again unto them, I go away, and ye shall
seek me, and shall die in your sin: whither I go, ye cannot come.
22 The Jews therefore said, Will he kill himself, that he saith,
Whither I go, ye cannot come? 23 And he said unto them, Ye

ERV margin: 1 Or *see: for out of Galilee etc.*   2 Most of the ancient authorities omit John 7:53—8:11: those which
contain it vary much from each other   3 Or *Teacher*   4 Or *trying*

OT references: John 8:5 = Leviticus 20:10 and Deuteronomy 22:22–24   John 8:17 = Deuteronomy 17:6
and 19:15

MT-MK-LK   JOHN 8

are from beneath; I am from above: ye are of this world; I am not of this world. 24 I said therefore unto you, that ye shall die in your sins: for except ye believe that [1]I am *he*, ye shall die in your sins. 25 They said therefore unto him, Who art thou? Jesus said unto them, [2]Even that which I have also spoken unto you from the beginning.

B   26 I have many things to speak and to judge concerning you: howbeit he that sent me is true; and the things which I heard from him, these speak I [3]unto the world. 27 They perceived not that he spake to them of the Father.

C 28 Jesus therefore said, When ye have lifted up the Son of man, then shall ye know that [4]I am *he*, and *that* I do nothing of myself, but as the Father taught me, I speak these things. 29 And he that sent me is with me; he hath not left me alone; for I do always the things that are pleasing to him. 30 As he spake these things, many believed on him.

§ 193 DISCOURSE ON FREEDOM THROUGH TRUTH

JOHN 8:31-59

A 31 Jesus therefore said to those Jews which had believed him, If ye abide in my word, *then* are ye truly my disciples; 32 and ye shall know the truth, and the truth shall make you free. 33 They answered unto him, We be Abraham's seed, and have never yet been in bondage to any man: how sayest thou, Ye shall be made free? 34 Jesus answered them, Verily, verily, I say unto you, Every one that committeth sin is the bondservant of sin. 35 And the bondservant abideth not in the house for ever: the son abideth for ever. 36 If therefore the Son shall make you free, ye shall be free indeed.

B   37 I know that ye are Abraham's seed; yet ye seek to kill me, because my word [5]hath not free course in you. 38 I speak the things which I have seen with [6]*my* Father: and ye also do the things which ye heard from *your* father. 39 They answered and said unto him, Our father is Abraham. Jesus saith unto them, If ye [7]were Abraham's children, [8]ye would do the works of Abraham. 40 But now ye seek to kill me, a man that hath told you the truth, which I heard from God: this did not Abraham. 41 Ye do the works of your father.

C   They said unto him, We were not born of fornication; we have one Father, *even* God. 42 Jesus said unto them, If God were your Father, ye would love me: for I came forth and am come from God; for neither have I come of myself, but he sent me. 43 Why do ye not [9]understand my speech? *Even* because ye cannot hear my word. 44 Ye are of *your* father the devil, and the lusts of your father it is your will to do. He was a murderer from the beginning, and [10]stood not in the truth, because there is no truth in him. [11]When he speaketh a lie, he speaketh of his own: for he is a liar, and the father thereof. 45 But because I say the truth, ye believe me not. 46 Which of you convicteth me of sin? If I say truth, why do ye not believe me? 47 He that is of God heareth the words of God: for this cause ye hear *them* not, because ye are not of God.

D *On the possession of Jesus by a devil, compare §45C and §53B and §86C*

D   48 The Jews answered and said unto him, Say we not well that thou art a Samaritan, and hast a [12]devil? 49 Jesus answered, I have not a [12]devil; but I honour my Father, and ye dishonour me. 50 But I seek not mine own glory: there is one that seeketh and judgeth.

ERV margin: 1 Or *I am*   2 Or, How is it *that I even speak to you at all?*   3 Greek *into*   4 Or *I am* Or *I am he: and I do*   5 Or *hath no place in you*   6 Or *the Father: do ye also therefore the things which ye heard from the Father*   7 Greek *are*   8 Some ancient authorities read *ye do the works of Abraham*   9 Or *know*   10 Some ancient authorities read *standeth*   11 Or *When one speaketh a lie, he speaketh of his own: for his father also is a liar*   12 Greek *demon*

JOHN 8

MT-MK-LK

E   51 Verily, verily, I say unto you, If a man keep my word, he shall never see death. 52 The Jews said unto him, Now we know that thou hast a ¹devil. Abraham is dead, and the prophets; and thou sayest, If a man keep my word, he shall never taste of death. 53 Art thou greater than our father Abraham, which is dead? and the prophets are dead: whom makest thou thyself? 54 Jesus answered, If I glorify myself, my glory is nothing: it is my Father that glorifieth me; of whom ye say, that he is your God; 55 and ye have not known him: but I know him; and if I should say, I know him not, I shall be like unto you, a liar: but I know him, and keep his word.

F 56 Your father Abraham rejoiced ²to see my day; and he saw it, and was glad. 57 The Jews therefore said unto him, Thou art not yet fifty years old, and hast thou seen Abraham? 58 Jesus said unto them, Verily, verily, I say unto you, Before Abraham ³was, I am. 59 They took up stones therefore to cast at him: but Jesus ⁴hid himself, and went out of the temple.⁵

E *On verse 52a compare the references under portion D above*

ERV margin: 1 Greek *demon*   2 Or *that he should see*   3 Greek *was born*   4 Or *was hidden, and went, etc.*
5 Many ancient authorities add *and going through the midst of them went his way, and so passed by*

CHAPTER XI

AT THE FEAST OF THE DEDICATION

§ 194 THE BLIND BEGGAR OF JERUSALEM

JOHN 9:1-12   MT-MK-LK

A 1 And as he passed by, he saw a man blind from his birth.
2 And his disciples asked him, saying, Rabbi, who did sin, this
man, or his parents, that he should be born blind? 3 Jesus
answered, Neither did this man sin, nor his parents: but that the
works of God should be made manifest in him.
B   4 We must work
the works of him that sent me, while it is day: the night cometh,
when no man can work. 5 When I am in the world, I am the light
of the world.
C   6 When he had thus spoken, he spat on the ground,   C *For the Mt-Mk-Lk cases of*
and made clay of the spittle, ¹and anointed his eyes with the clay,   *the use of material means in*
7 and said unto him, Go, wash in the pool of Siloam (which is by   *healing, compare §66A and*
interpretation, Sent). He went away therefore, and washed, and   *§70A*
came seeing.
D   8 The neighbours therefore, and they which saw
him aforetime, that he was a beggar, said, Is not this he that sat
and begged? 9 Others said, It is he: others said, No, but he is
like him. He said, I am *he.* 10 They said therefore unto him,
How then were thine eyes opened? 11 He answered, The man
that is called Jesus made clay, and anointed mine eyes, and said
unto me, Go to Siloam, and wash: so I went away and washed,
and I received sight. 12 And they said unto him, Where is he?
He saith, I know not.

§ 195 CONTROVERSY ABOUT THE BEGGAR AND JESUS

JOHN 9:13-34

A 13 They bring to the Pharisees him that aforetime was blind.
14 Now it was the sabbath on the day when Jesus made the clay,
and opened his eyes. 15 Again therefore the Pharisees also
asked him how he received his sight. And he said unto them, He
put clay upon mine eyes, and I washed, and do see.
BB   16 Some   B *On the opposition to Jesus*
therefore of the Pharisees said, This man is not from God, because   *because of his attitude toward*
he keepeth not the sabbath. But others said, How can a man that   *sabbath observance, compare*
is a sinner do such signs? And there was a division among them.   *§32, §33, §98 and §102*
17 They say therefore unto the blind man again, What sayest
thou of him, in that he opened thine eyes? And he said, He is a
prophet.
C   18 The Jews therefore did not believe concerning him,
that he had been blind, and had received his sight, until they
called the parents of him that had received his sight, 19 and asked
them, saying, Is this your son, who ye say was born blind? how
then doth he now see? 20 His parents answered and said, We
know that this is our son, and that he was born blind: 21 but
how he now seeth, we know not; or who opened his eyes, we
know not: ask him; he is of age; he shall speak for himself.
22 These things said his parents, because they feared the Jews:
for the Jews had agreed already, that if any man should confess

---

ERV margin: 1 Or *and with the clay thereof anointed* his eyes

B Compare §175 and §188

MT-MK-LK   JOHN 9

him *to be* Christ, he should be put out of the synagogue. 23 Therefore said his parents, He is of age; ask him.

D   24 So they called a second time the man that was blind, and said unto him, Give glory to God: we know that this man is a sinner. 25 He therefore answered, Whether he be a sinner, I know not: one thing I know, that, whereas I was blind, now I see. 26 They said therefore unto him, What did he to thee? how opened he thine eyes? 27 He answered them, I told you even now, and ye did not hear: wherefore would ye hear it again? would ye also become his disciples? 28 And they reviled him, and said, Thou art his disciple; but we are disciples of Moses. 29 We know that God hath spoken unto Moses: but as for this man, we know not whence he is. 30 The man answered and said unto them, Why, herein is the marvel, that ye know not whence he is, and *yet* he opened mine eyes. 31 We know that God heareth not sinners: but if any man be a worshipper of God, and do his will, him he heareth. 32 Since the world began it was never heard that any one opened the eyes of a man born blind. 33 If this man were not from God, he could do nothing. 34 They answered and said unto him, Thou wast altogether born in sins, and dost thou teach us? And they cast him out.

§ 196   TRUE SIGHT AND FALSE SIGHT

JOHN 9:35-41

A   35 Jesus heard that they had cast him out; and finding him, he said, Dost thou believe on [1]the Son of God? 36 He answered and said, And who is he, Lord, that I may believe on him? 37 Jesus said unto him, Thou hast both seen him, and he it is that speaketh with thee. 38 And he said, Lord, I believe. And he worshipped him.

B   39 And Jesus said, For judgement came I into this world, that they which see not may see; and that they which see may become blind. 40 Those of the Pharisees which were with him heard these things, and said unto him, Are we also blind? 41 Jesus said unto them, If ye were blind, ye would have no sin: but now ye say, We see: your sin remaineth.

§ 197   DISCOURSE ON THE SHEEP AND THE SHEPHERD

JOHN 10:1-21

A   1 Verily, verily, I say unto you, He that entereth not by the door into the fold of the sheep, but climbeth up some other way, the same is a thief and a robber. 2 But he that entereth in by the door is [2]the shepherd of the sheep. 3 To him the porter openeth; and the sheep hear his voice: and he calleth his own sheep by name, and leadeth them out. 4 When he hath put forth all his own, he goeth before them, and the sheep follow him: for they know his voice. 5 And a stranger will they not follow, but will flee from him: for they know not the voice of strangers. 6 This [3]parable spake Jesus unto them: but they understood not what things they were which he spake unto them.

B   7 Jesus therefore said unto them again, Verily, verily, I say unto you, I am the door of the sheep. 8 All that came before me are thieves and robbers: but the sheep did not hear them. 9 I am the door: by me if any man enter in, he shall be saved, and shall go in and go out, and shall find pasture. 10 The thief cometh not, but that he may steal, and kill, and destroy: I came that they may have life, and may [4]have *it* abundantly.

C   11 I am the good shepherd: the good shepherd layeth down his life for the sheep. 12 He that is a hireling, and not a shepherd, whose own the sheep

---

ERV margin: 1 Many ancient authorities read *the Son of man*   2 Or *a shepherd*   3 Or *proverb*   4 Or *have abundance*

JOHN 10

MT-MK-LK

are not, beholdeth the wolf coming, and leaveth the sheep, and fleeth, and the wolf snatcheth them, and scattereth *them:* 13 he *fleeth* because he is a hireling, and careth not for the sheep.

D   14 I am the good shepherd; and I know mine own, and mine own know me, 15 even as the Father knoweth me, and I know the Father; and I lay down my life for the sheep.

E   16 And other sheep I have, which are not of this fold: them also I must ¹bring, and they shall hear my voice; and ²they shall become one flock, one shepherd.

F   17 Therefore doth the Father love me, because I lay down my life, that I may take it again. 18 No one ³taketh it away from me, but I lay it down of myself. I have ⁴power to lay it down, and I have ⁴power to take it again. This commandment received I from my Father.

G   19 There arose a division again among the Jews because of these words. 20 And many of them said, He hath a ⁵devil, and is mad; why hear ye him? 21 Others said, These are not the sayings of one possessed with a ⁵devil. Can a ⁵devil open the eyes of the blind?

D *With verse 15a compare* §41 Q *and* §82 T

G *On the possession of Jesus by a devil, compare* §45 C *and* §53 B *and* §86 C

§ 198 BASES OF A CHARGE OF BLASPHEMY

JOHN 10:22–39

A   22 ⁶And it was the feast of the dedication at Jerusalem: it was winter; 23 and Jesus was walking in the temple in Solomon's porch. 24 The Jews therefore came round about him, and said unto him, How long dost thou hold us in suspense? If thou art the Christ, tell us plainly. 25 Jesus answered them, I told you, and ye believe not: the works that I do in my Father's name, these bear witness of me.

B   26 But ye believe not, because ye are not of my sheep. 27 My sheep hear my voice, and I know them, and they follow me: 28 and I give unto them eternal life; and they shall never perish, and no one shall snatch them out of my hand. 29 ⁷My Father, which hath given *them* unto me, is greater than all; and no one is able to snatch ⁸*them* out of the Father's hand.

C 30 I and the Father are one. 31 The Jews took up stones again to stone him. 32 Jesus answered them, Many good works have I shewed you from the Father; for which of those works do ye stone me? 33 The Jews answered him, For a good work we stone thee not, but for blasphemy; and because that thou, being a man, makest thyself God.

D   34 Jesus answered them, Is it not written in your law, I said, Ye are gods? 35 If he called them gods, unto whom the word of God came (and the scripture cannot be broken), 36 say ye of him, whom the Father ⁹sanctified and sent into the world, Thou blasphemest; because I said, I am *the* Son of God?

E 37 If I do not the works of my Father, believe me not. 38 But if I do them, though ye believe not me, believe the works: that ye may know and understand that the Father is in me, and I in the Father. 39 They sought again to take him: and he went forth out of their hand.

ERV margin: 1 Or *lead*   2 Or *there shall be one flock*   3 Some ancient authorities read *took it away*   4 Or *right*   5 Greek *demon*   6 Some ancient authorities read *At that time was the feast*   7 Some ancient authorities read *That which my Father hath given unto me*   8 Or, *aught*   9 Or *consecrated*

OT references: John 10:16 = Ezekiel 34:23 and 37:24   John 10:34 = Psalm 82:6

CHAPTER XII

IN THE REGION OF JERUSALEM

§ 199   WITHDRAWAL TO BETHANY BEYOND JORDAN

<table>
<tr><td>JOHN 10:40-42</td><td>MT-MK-LK</td></tr>
</table>

40 And he went away again beyond Jordan into the place where John was at the first baptizing; and there he abode.   41 And many came unto him; and they said, John indeed did no sign: but all things whatsoever John spake of this man were true. 42 And many believed on him there.

§ 200   RETURN TO BETHANY NEAR JERUSALEM

JOHN 11:1-16

Aᴬ 1 Now a certain man was sick, Lazarus of Bethany, of the village of Mary and her sister Martha.   2 And it was that Mary which anointed the Lord with ointment, and wiped his feet with her hair, whose brother Lazarus was sick.   3 The sisters therefore sent unto him, saying, Lord, behold, he whom thou lovest is sick. 4 But when Jesus heard it, he said, This sickness is not unto death, but for the glory of God, that the Son of God may be glorified thereby.   5 Now Jesus loved Martha, and her sister, and Lazarus.

B 6 When therefore he heard that he was sick, he abode at that time two days in the place where he was.   7 Then after this he saith to the disciples, Let us go into Judæa again.   8 The disciples say unto him, Rabbi, the Jews were but now seeking to stone thee; and goest thou thither again?   9 Jesus answered, Are there not twelve hours in the day?   If a man walk in the day, he stumbleth not, because he seeth the light of this world.   10 But if a man walk in the night, he stumbleth, because the light is not in him.

C   11 These things spake he: and after this he saith unto them, Our friend Lazarus is fallen asleep; but I go, that I may awake him out of sleep.   12 The disciples therefore said unto him, Lord, if he is fallen asleep, he will ¹recover.   13 Now Jesus had spoken of his death: but they thought that he spake of taking rest in sleep.   14 Then Jesus therefore said unto them plainly, Lazarus is dead.   15 And I am glad for your sakes that I was not there, to the intent ye may believe; nevertheless let us go unto him.

D   16 Thomas therefore, who is called ²Didymus, said unto his fellow-disciples, Let us also go, that we may die with him.

A   *For the Mt-Mk-Lk refer-*
ence to Mary and Martha,
compare §84

§ 201   CONCERNING LAZARUS OF BETHANY

JOHN 11:17-44

A   17 So when Jesus came, he found that he had been in the tomb four days already.   18 Now Bethany was nigh unto Jerusalem, about fifteen furlongs off;   19 and many of the Jews had come to Martha and Mary, to console them concerning their brother.

B 20 Martha therefore, when she heard that Jesus was coming, went and met him: but Mary still sat in the house.   21 Martha therefore said unto Jesus, Lord, if thou hadst been here, my

---

ERV margin: 1 Greek *be saved*   2 That is *Twin*

A   On the anointing of Jesus by Mary, compare §204 portion B

MT-MK-LK   JOHN 11

brother had not died. 22 And even now I know that, whatsoever thou shalt ask of God, God will give thee. 23 Jesus saith
unto her, Thy brother shall rise again. 24 Martha saith unto him,
I know that he shall rise again in the resurrection at the last day.
25 Jesus said unto her, I am the resurrection, and the life: he
that believeth on me, though he die, yet shall he live: 26 and whosoever liveth and believeth on me shall never die. Believest thou
this? 27 She saith unto him, Yea, Lord: I have believed that
thou art the Christ, the Son of God, *even* he that cometh into the
world.

C   28 And when she had said this, she went away, and called
Mary [1]her sister secretly, saying, The [2]Master is here, and calleth
thee. 29 And she, when she heard it, arose quickly, and went
unto him. 30 (Now Jesus was not yet come into the village, but
was still in the place where Martha met him.) 31 The Jews then
which were with her in the house, and were comforting her,
when they saw Mary, that she rose up quickly and went out,
followed her, supposing that she was going unto the tomb to
[3]weep there. 32 Mary therefore, when she came where Jesus
was, and saw him, fell down at his feet, saying unto him, Lord,
if thou hadst been here, my brother had not died.

D   33 When Jesus
therefore saw her [4]weeping, and the Jews *also* [4]weeping which
came with her, he [5]groaned in the spirit, and [6]was troubled, 34 and
said, Where have ye laid him? They say unto him, Lord, come
and see. 35 Jesus wept. 36 The Jews therefore said, Behold how
he loved him! 37 But some of them said, Could not this man,
which opened the eyes of him that was blind, have caused that
this man also should not die?

E   38 Jesus therefore again [7]groaning
in himself cometh to the tomb. Now it was a cave, and a stone
lay [8]against it. 39 Jesus saith, Take ye away the stone. Martha,
the sister of him that was dead, saith unto him, Lord, by this
time he stinketh: for he hath been *dead* four days. 40 Jesus
saith unto her, Said I not unto thee, that, if thou believedst, thou
shouldest see the glory of God? 41 So they took away the stone.

F And Jesus lifted up his eyes, and said, Father, I thank thee that
thou heardest me. 42 And I knew that thou hearest me always:
but because of the multitude which standeth around I said it, that
they may believe that thou didst send me. 43 And when he had
thus spoken, he cried with a loud voice, Lazarus, come forth.
44 He that was dead came forth, bound hand and foot with [9]grave-
clothes; and his face was bound about with a napkin. Jesus
saith unto them, Loose him, and let him go.

§ 202 PLOTS FOR THE DEATH OF JESUS

JOHN 11:45-53

A 45 Many therefore of the Jews, which came to Mary and
beheld [10]that which he did, believed on him. 46 But some of
them went away to the Pharisees, and told them the things which
Jesus had done.

B *On the determination by the*   B 47 The chief priests therefore and the Pharisees gathered a
religious leaders to put Jesus to   council, and said, What do we? for this man doeth many signs.
death, compare §137 portion A   48 If we let him thus alone, all men will believe on him: and the
Romans will come and take away both our place and our nation.
C[c] 49 But a certain one of them, Caiaphas, being high priest that
year, said unto them, Ye know nothing at all, 50 nor do ye take
account that it is expedient for you that one man should die for
the people, and that the whole nation perish not.

ERV margin: 1 Or *her sister, saying secretly*   2 Or *Teacher*   3 Greek *wail*   4 Greek *wailing*   5 Or *was
moved with indignation in the spirit*   6 Greek *troubled himself*   7 Or *being moved with indignation in himself*   8 Or
upon*   9 Or *grave-bands*   10 Many ancient authorities read *the things which he did*

c Compare §215 portion A

JOHN 11	MT-MK-LK
D 51 Now this he said not of himself: but being high priest that year, he prophesied that Jesus should die for the nation; 52 and not for the nation only, but that he might also gather together into one the children of God that are scattered abroad. E 53 So from that day forth they took counsel that they might put him to death.	 E *Compare the reference under portion B above*

§ 203   WITHDRAWAL OF JESUS TO EPHRAIM

JOHN 11:54–57

A   54 Jesus therefore walked no more openly among the Jews, but departed thence into the country near to the wilderness, into a city called Ephraim; and there he tarried with the disciples.

B   55 Now the passover of the Jews was at hand: and many went up to Jerusalem out of the country before the passover, to purify themselves.   56 They sought therefore for Jesus, and spake one with another, as they stood in the temple, What think ye? That he will not come to the feast?

C   57 Now the chief priests and the Pharisees had given commandment, that, if any man knew where he was, he should shew it, that they might take him.

§ 204   THE SUPPER TO JESUS AT BETHANY

JOHN 12:1–11

A   1 Jesus therefore six days before the passover came to Bethany, where Lazarus was, whom Jesus raised from the dead.   2 So they made him a supper there: and Martha served; but Lazarus was one of them that sat at meat with him.

B   3 Mary therefore took a pound of ointment of ¹spikenard, very precious, and anointed the feet of Jesus, and wiped his feet with her hair: and the house was filled with the odour of the ointment.

C   4 But Judas Iscariot, one of his disciples, which should betray him, saith, 5 Why was not this ointment sold for three hundred ²pence, and given to the poor?

DD 6 Now this he said, not because he cared for the poor; but because he was a thief, and having the ³bag ⁴took away what was put therein.

E   7 Jesus therefore said, ⁵Suffer her to keep it against the day of my burying.   8 For the poor ye have always with you; but me ye have not always.

F   9 The common people therefore of the Jews learned that he was there: and they came, not for Jesus' sake only, but that they might see Lazarus also, whom he had raised from the dead. 10 But the chief priests took counsel that they might put Lazarus also to death; 11 because that by reason of him many of the Jews went away, and believed on Jesus.

A   *On the statement about Martha, compare §84*

B   *Compare §42 portion A*
Compare §137 portion B

C   *Compare §137 portion C*

E   *Compare §137 portion D*

ERV margin: 1 Greek *pistic nard*, pistic being perhaps a local name: others take it to mean *genuine;* others *liquid*   2 The word in the Greek denotes a coin worth about eight pence halfpenny   3 Or *box*   4 Or *carried what was put therein*   5 Or *Let her alone*: it was *that she might keep it*

D   Compare §209 portion K

CHAPTER XIII

CHALLENGE TO THE JERUSALEM LEADERS

§ 205 JESUS ENTERS JERUSALEM AS A POPULAR LEADER

JOHN 12:12-19   MT-MK-LK

A 12 On the morrow [1]a great multitude that had come to the feast, when they heard that Jesus was coming to Jerusalem, 13 took the branches of the palm trees, and went forth to meet him,

A *Compare §124 portion F*

B and cried out, Hosanna: Blessed *is* he that cometh in the name of the Lord, even the King of Israel.

B *Compare §124 portion G*

C 14 And Jesus, having found a young ass, sat thereon;

C *Compare §124 portion E*

D as it is written, 15 Fear not, daughter of Zion: behold, thy King cometh, sitting on an ass's colt. 16 These things understood not his disciples at the first: but when Jesus was glorified, then remembered they that these things were written of him, and that they had done these things unto him.

D *Compare §124 portion C*

E 17 The multitude therefore that was with him when he called Lazarus out of the tomb, and raised him from the dead, bare witness. 18 For this cause also the multitude went and met him, for that they heard that he had done this sign.

F 19 The Pharisees therefore said among themselves, [2]Behold how ye prevail nothing: lo, the world is gone after him.

§ 206 INTIMATIONS OF THE IMPENDING DEATH OF JESUS

JOHN 12:20-36[a]

A 20 Now there were certain Greeks among those that went up to worship at the feast: 21 these therefore came to Philip, which was of Bethsaida of Galilee, and asked him, saying, Sir, we would see Jesus. 22 Philip cometh and telleth Andrew: Andrew cometh, and Philip, and they tell Jesus.

B 23 And Jesus answereth them, saying, The hour is come, that the Son of man should be glorified. 24 Verily, verily, I say unto you, Except a grain of wheat fall into the earth and die, it abideth by itself alone; but if it die, it beareth much fruit.

C 25 He that loveth his [3]life loseth it; and he that hateth his [3]life in this world shall keep it unto life eternal. 26 If any man serve me, let him follow me; and where I am, there shall also my servant be: if any man serve me, him will the Father honour.

C *Compare §57 portions NO*
Compare §73 portions AB
Compare §104 portion C
Compare §112 portion J

D 27 Now is my soul troubled; and what shall I say? Father, save me from this [4]hour. But for this cause came I unto this hour. 28 Father, glorify thy name. There came therefore a voice out of heaven, *saying*, I have both glorified it, and will glorify it again. 29 The multitude therefore, that stood by, and heard it, said that it had thundered: others said, An angel hath spoken to him. 30 Jesus answered and said, This voice hath not come for my sake, but for your sakes.

D *Compare §95 portion A*
Compare §140 portions BC
In reference to an angel,
compare §140 portion D

ERV margin: 1 Some ancient authorities read *the common people*   2 Or *Ye behold*   3 Or *soul*   4 Or *hour?*

OT references: John 12:13 = Psalm 118:25-26   John 12:15 = Isaiah 62:11 and Zechariah 9:9   John 12:27 = Psalm 42:6

Mt-Mk-Lk	John 12

E   *With verse 31b compare verse 18 of §82 portion R*

E   31 Now is [1]the judgement of this world: now shall the prince of this world be cast out.   32 And I, if I be lifted up [2]from the earth, will draw all men unto myself.   33 But this he said, signifying by what manner of death he should die.   34 The multitude therefore answered him, We have heard out of the law that the Christ abideth for ever: and how sayest thou, The Son of man must be lifted up? who is this Son of man?

F   35 Jesus therefore said unto them, Yet a little while is the light [3]among you.   Walk while ye have the light, that darkness overtake you not: and he that walketh in the darkness knoweth not whither he goeth.   36 While ye have the light, believe on the light, that ye may become sons of light.

§ 207   UNBELIEF AND BELIEF IN JESUS

John 12:36b–43

A   36 These things spake Jesus, and he departed and [4]hid himself from them.   37 But though he had done so many signs before them, yet they believed not on him: 38 that the word of Isaiah the prophet might be fulfilled, which he spake,

> Lord, who hath believed our report?
> And to whom hath the arm of the Lord been revealed?

B   *Compare §47 portion J*

B 39 For this cause they could not believe, for that Isaiah said again,

> 40 He hath blinded their eyes, and he hardened their heart;
> Lest they should see with their eyes, and perceive with their heart,
> And should turn,
> And I should heal them.

41 These things said Isaiah, because he saw his glory; and he spake of him.

C   42 Nevertheless even of the rulers many believed on him; but because of the Pharisees they did not confess [5]it, lest they should be put out of the synagogue: 43 for they loved the glory of men more than the glory of God.

§ 208   THE SOURCE OF THE TRUTH IN JESUS

John 12:44–50

A   *Compare §57 portion P*
Compare §78 portion G
Compare §82 portion Q

A 44 And Jesus cried and said, He that believeth on me, believeth not on me, but on him that sent me.   45 And he that beholdeth me beholdeth him that sent me.

B   46 I am come a light into the world, that whosoever believeth on me may not abide in the darkness.

C   47 And if any man hear my sayings, and keep them not, I judge him not: for I came not to judge the world, but to save the world.   48 He that rejecteth me, and receiveth not my sayings, hath one that judgeth him: the word that I spake, the same shall judge him in the last day.

D   49 For I spake not from myself; but the Father which sent me, he hath given me a commandment, what I should say, and what I should speak.   50 And I know that his commandment is life eternal: the things therefore which I speak, even as the Father hath said unto me, so I speak.

ERV margin: 1 Or *a judgement*   2 Or *out of*   3 Or *in*   4 Or *was hidden from them*   5 Or, him

OT references: John 12:38 = Isaiah 53:1   John 12:40 = Isaiah 6:10

CHAPTER XIV

FINAL HOURS WITH DISCIPLES

---

§ 209 THE PASSOVER WITH THE DISCIPLES

JOHN 13:1–38   MT-MK-LK

A   1 Now before the feast of the passover, Jesus knowing that his hour was come that he should depart out of this world unto the Father, having loved his own which were in the world, he loved them [1]unto the end.

B   2 And during supper, the devil having already put into the heart of Judas Iscariot, Simon's *son*, to betray him, 3 *Jesus*, knowing that the Father had given all things into his hands, and that he came forth from God, and goeth unto God, 4 riseth from supper, and layeth aside his garments; and he took a towel, and girded himself. 5 Then he poureth water into the bason, and began to wash the disciples' feet, and to wipe them with the towel wherewith he was girded.

B   *With verse 2 compare Luke 22:3 in §137 portion F*
With verse 3a compare §41 Q and §82 T and §151 B
With verses 4–5 compare verse 37 in §94 A

C   6 So he cometh to Simon Peter. He saith unto him, Lord, dost thou wash my feet? 7 Jesus answered and said unto him, What I do thou knowest not now; but thou shalt understand hereafter. 8 Peter saith unto him, Thou shalt never wash my feet. Jesus answered him, If I wash thee not, thou hast no part with me. 9 Simon Peter saith unto him, Lord, not my feet only, but also my hands and my head. 10 Jesus saith to him, He that is bathed needeth not [2]save to wash his feet, but is clean every whit: and ye are clean, but not all. 11 For he knew him that should betray him; therefore said he, Ye are not all clean.

C   *With verse 11 compare §138 portion E*

D   12 So when he had washed their feet, and taken his garments, and [3]sat down again, he said unto them, Know ye what I have done to you? 13 Ye call me, [4]Master, and, Lord: and ye say well; for so I am. 14 If I then, the Lord and the [4]Master, have washed your feet, ye also ought to wash one another's feet. 15 For I have given you an example, that ye also should do as I have done to you.

D   *Compare §78 portions BEH*
Compare §120 portion J
Compare §138 portion M
Compare §132 portion G

E[E]   16 Verily, verily, I say unto you, A [5]servant is not greater than his lord; neither [6]one that is sent greater than he that sent him. 17 If ye know these things, blessed are ye if ye do them.

E   *Compare §38 portion H*
Compare §57 portion G

F   18 I speak not of you all: I know whom I [7]have chosen: but that the scripture may be fulfilled, He that eateth [8]my bread lifted up his heel against me. 19 From henceforth I tell you before it come to pass, that, when it is come to pass, ye may believe that [9]I am *he*.

F   *Compare §138 portion E*

G   20 Verily, verily, I say unto you, He that receiveth whomsoever I send receiveth me; and he that receiveth me receiveth him that sent me.

G   *Compare §57 portion P*
Compare §78 portion G
Compare §82 portion Q

H   21 When Jesus had thus said, he was troubled in the spirit, and testified, and said, Verily, verily, I say unto you, that one of you shall betray me. 22 The disciples looked one on another, doubting of whom he spake.

H   *Compare §138 portion E*
Compare §138 portion K

ERV margin: 1 Or *to the uttermost*   2 Some ancient authorities omit *save, and his feet*   3 Greek *reclined*   4 Or *Teacher*   5 Greek *bondservant*   6 Greek *an apostle*   7 Or *chose*   8 Many ancient authorities read *his bread with me* 9 Or *I am*

OT references: John 13:18 = Psalm 41:9

E   Compare §211 portion H

Mt-Mk-Lk	John 13

<table>
<tr><td>

J   *Compare §138 portion E*
Compare §138 portion F
With verse 27 compare Luke
22:3 in §137 portion F

</td><td>

I¹   23 There was at the table reclining in Jesus' bosom one of his disciples, whom Jesus loved. 24 Simon Peter therefore beckoneth to him, and saith unto him, Tell *us* who it is of whom he speaketh. 25 He leaning back, as he was, on Jesus' breast saith unto him, Lord, who is it?

J   26 Jesus therefore answereth, He it is, for whom I shall dip the sop, and give it him. So when he had dipped the sop, he taketh and giveth it to Judas, *the son* of Simon Iscariot. 27 And after the sop, then entered Satan into him.

</td></tr>
</table>

Kᴷ Jesus therefore saith unto him, That thou doest, do quickly. 28 Now no man at the table knew for what intent he spake this unto him. 29 For some thought, because Judas had the ¹bag, that Jesus said unto him, Buy what things we have need of for the feast; or, that he should give something to the poor. 30 He then having received the sop went out straightway: and it was night.

L 31 When therefore he was gone out, Jesus saith, Now ²is the Son of man glorified, and God ²is glorified in him; 32 and God shall glorify him in himself, and straightway shall he glorify him.

Mᴹ 33 Little children, yet a little while I am with you. Ye shall seek me: and as I said unto the Jews, Whither I go, ye cannot come; so now I say unto you.

Nᴺ 34 A new commandment I give unto you, that ye love one another; ³even as I have loved you, that ye also love one another. 35 By this shall all men know that ye are my disciples, if ye have love one to another.

O   *Compare §139 portion D*   **O** 36 Simon Peter saith unto him, Lord, whither goest thou? Jesus answered, Whither I go, thou canst not follow me now; but thou shalt follow afterwards. 37 Peter saith unto him, Lord, why cannot I follow thee even now? I will lay down my life for thee. 38 Jesus answereth, Wilt thou lay down thy life for me? Verily, verily, I say unto thee, The cock shall not crow, till thou hast denied me thrice.

§ 210   FAREWELL DISCOURSES OF JESUS

John 14:1-31

A 1 Let not your heart be troubled: ⁴ye believe in God, believe also in me. 2 In my Father's house are many ⁵mansions; if it were not so, I would have told you; for I go to prepare a place for you. 3 And if I go and prepare a place for you, I come again, and will receive you unto myself; that where I am, *there* ye may be also.

Bᴮ 4 ⁶And whither I go, ye know the way. 5 Thomas saith unto him, Lord, we know not whither thou goest; how know we the way? 6 Jesus saith unto him, I am the way, and the truth, and the life: no one cometh unto the Father, but ⁷by me.

C 7 If ye had known me, ye would have known my Father also: from henceforth ye know him, and have seen him. 8 Philip saith unto him, Lord, shew us the Father, and it sufficeth us. 9 Jesus saith unto him, Have I been so long time with you, and dost thou not know me, Philip? he that hath seen me hath seen the Father; how sayest thou, Shew us the Father? 10 Believest thou not that I am in the Father, and the Father in me? the words that I say unto you I speak not from myself: but the Father abiding in me

---

ERV margin: 1 Or *box*   2 Or *was*   3 Or *even as I loved you, that ye also may love one another*   4 Or *believe in God*   5 Or *abiding-places*   6 Many ancient authorities read *And whither I go ye know, and the way ye know*   7 Or *through*

I   For other references to the disciple whom Jesus loved, compare §217 E, §219 B, §222 AC and §223 A
K   Compare §204 portion D
M   Compare §189 portion D
N   Compare §211 portion E

B   Compare §211 portion L

JOHN 14   MT-MK-LK

doeth his works. 11 Believe me that I am in the Father, and the Father in me: or else believe me for the very works' sake.

D 12 Verily, verily, I say unto you, He that believeth on me, the works that I do shall he do also; and greater *works* than these shall he do; because I go unto the Father.

E   13 And whatsoever ye shall ask in my name, that will I do, that the Father may be glorified in the Son. 14 If ye shall ask ¹me anything in my name, that will I do.

> E *Compare §78 portion U*
>   *Compare §127 portion D*

F   15 If ye love me, ye will keep my commandments. 16 And I will ²pray the Father, and he shall give you another ³Comforter, that he may be with you for ever, 17 *even* the Spirit of truth: whom the world cannot receive; for it beholdeth him. not, neither knoweth him: ye know him; for he abideth with you, and shall be in you.

G   18 I will not leave you ⁴desolate: I come unto you. 19 Yet a little while, and the world beholdeth me no more; but ye behold me: because I live, ⁵ye shall live also. 20 In that day ye shall know that I am in my Father, and ye in me, and I in you.

H   21 He that hath my commandments, and keepeth them, he it is that loveth me: and he that loveth me shall be loved of my Father, and I will love him, and will manifest myself unto him. 22 Judas (not Iscariot) saith unto him, Lord, what is come to pass that thou wilt manifest thyself unto us, and not unto the world? 23 Jesus answered and said unto him, If a man love me, he will keep my word: and my Father will love him, and we will come unto him, and make our abode with him. 24 He that loveth me not keepeth not my words: and the word which ye hear is not mine, but the Father's who sent me.

> H *With verse 23b compare verse 20 in §78 portion U and verse 20b in §151 portion C*

I   25 These things have I spoken unto you, while *yet* abiding with you. 26 But the ³Comforter, *even* the Holy Spirit, whom the Father will send in my name, he shall teach you all things, and bring to your remembrance all that I said unto you.

> I *Compare §57 portion C*
>   *Compare §91 portion I*
>   *Compare §134 portion I*

J   27 Peace I leave with you; my peace I give unto you: not as the world giveth, give I unto you. Let not your heart be troubled, neither let it be fearful. 28 Ye heard how I said to you, I go away, and I come unto you. If ye loved me, ye would have rejoiced, because I go unto the Father: for the Father is greater than I.

K 29 And now I have told you before it come to pass, that, when it is come to pass, ye may believe. 30 I will no more speak much with you, for the prince of the world cometh: and he hath nothing in me; 31 but that the world may know that I love the Father, and as the Father gave me commandment, even so I do. Arise, let us go hence.

> K *With the last sentence in verse 31, compare §139 A and the last verse in §140 G*

§ 211   FAREWELL DISCOURSES OF JESUS (*concluded*)

JOHN 15:1—16:33

A 1 I am the true vine, and my Father is the husbandman. 2 Every branch in me that beareth not fruit, he taketh it away: and every *branch* that beareth fruit, he cleanseth it, that it may bear more fruit. 3 Already ye are clean because of the word which I have spoken unto you.

B   4 Abide in me, and I in you. As the branch cannot bear fruit of itself, except it abide in the vine; so neither can ye, except ye abide in me. 5 I am the vine, ye are the branches: He that abideth in me, and I in him, the same beareth much fruit: for apart from me ye can do nothing. 6 If a man abide not in me, he is cast forth as a branch, and is withered; and they gather them, and cast them into the fire, and they are burned.

ERV margin: 1 Many ancient authorities omit *me*   2 Greek *make request of*   3 Or *Advocate* Or *Helper* Greek *Paraclete*   4 Or *orphans*   5 Or *and ye shall live*

Mt-Mk-Lk

c   *Compare §78 portion U*
Compare §127 portion D

E   *With verse 14 compare*
§46 E and §49 E and §87

F   *Compare §35 portion B*
Compare the references un-
der portion C above

G   *Compare §36 portions HI*
Compare §57 E and §134 K

H   *With verse 20a compare*
§38 H and §57 G
With verses 20b–21 compare
§36 HI, §57 A and §134 G

I   *With verse 23 compare §82*
portion Q

J   *Compare §150 portion E*
Compare §151 portion C

K   *Compare §57 portion D*
Compare §134 portion J
With verses 1 and 4 compare
the last verse of §135 portion B

M   *With verse 11 compare*
verse 18 of §82 R

John 15–16

c 7 If ye abide in me, and my words abide in you, ask whatsoever ye will, and it shall be done unto you. 8 Herein ¹is my Father glorified, ²that ye bear much fruit; and *so* shall ye be my disciples.

D 9 Even as the Father hath loved me, I also have loved you: abide ye in my love. 10 If ye keep my commandments, ye shall abide in my love; even as I have kept my Father's commandments, and abide in his love. 11 These things have I spoken unto you, that my joy may be in you, and *that* your joy may be fulfilled.

E^E   12 This is my commandment, that ye love one another, even as I have loved you. 13 Greater love hath no man than this, that a man lay down his life for his friends. 14 Ye are my friends, if ye do the things which I command you. 15 No longer do I call you ³servants; for the ⁴servant knoweth not what his lord doeth: but I have called you friends; for all things that I heard from my Father I have made known unto you.

F   16 Ye did not choose me, but I chose you, and appointed you, that ye should go and bear fruit, and *that* your fruit should abide: that whatsoever ye shall ask of the Father in my name, he may give it you. 17 These things I command you, that ye may love one another.

G   18 If the world hateth you, ⁵ye know that it hath hated me before *it hated* you. 19 If ye were of the world, the world would love its own: but because ye are not of the world, but I chose you out of the world, therefore the world hateth you.

H^H   20 Remember the word that I said unto you, A ⁴servant is not greater than his lord. If they persecuted me, they will also persecute you; if they kept my word, they will keep yours also. 21 But all these things will they do unto you for my name's sake, because they know not him that sent me.

I   22 If I had not come and spoken unto them, they had not had sin: but now they have no excuse for their sin. 23 He that hateth me hateth my Father also. 24 If I had not done among them the works which none other did, they had not had sin: but now have they both seen and hated both me and my Father. 25 But *this cometh to pass*, that the word may be fulfilled that is written in their law, They hated me without a cause.

J 26 But when the ⁶Comforter is come, whom I will send unto you from the Father, *even* the Spirit of truth, which ⁷proceedeth from the Father, he shall bear witness of me: 27 ⁸and ye also bear witness, because ye have been with me from the beginning.

K 16: 1 These things have I spoken unto you, that ye should not be made to stumble. 2 They shall put you out of the synagogues: yea, the hour cometh, that whosoever killeth you shall think that he offereth service unto God. 3 And these things will they do, because they have not known the Father, nor me. 4 But these things have I spoken unto you, that when their hour is come, ye may remember them, how that I told you.

L^L   And these things I said not unto you from the beginning, because I was with you. 5 But now I go unto him that sent me; and none of you asketh me, Whither goest thou? 6 But because I have spoken these things unto you, sorrow hath filled your heart.

M   7 Nevertheless I tell you the truth; It is expedient for you that I go away: for if I go not away, the ⁶Comforter will not come unto you; but if I go, I will

---

ERV margin: 1 Or *was*   2 Many ancient authorities read *that ye bear much fruit, and be my disciples*   3 Greek *bondservants*   4 Greek *bondservant*   5 Or *know ye*   6 Or *Advocate* Or *Helper* Greek *Paraclete*   7 Or *goeth forth from*   8 Or *and bear ye also witness*

OT references: John 15:25 = Psalm 35:19 and 69:4

E   Compare §209 portion N
H   Compare §209 portion E
L   Compare §210 portion B

JOHN 16

send him unto you. 8 And he, when he is come, will convict the world in respect of sin, and of righteousness, and of judgement: 9 of sin, because they believe not on me; 10 of righteousness, because I go to the Father, and ye behold me no more; 11 of judgement, because the prince of this world hath been judged.

N 12 I have yet many things to say unto you, but ye cannot bear them now. 13 Howbeit when he, the Spirit of truth, is come, he shall guide you into all the truth: for he shall not speak from himself; but what things soever he shall hear, *these* shall he speak: and he shall declare unto you the things that are to come. 14 He shall glorify me: for he shall take of mine, and shall declare *it* unto you. 15 All things whatsoever the Father hath are mine: therefore said I, that he taketh of mine, and shall declare *it* unto you.

O 16 A little while, and ye behold me no more; and again a little while, and ye shall see me. 17 *Some* of his disciples therefore said one to another, What is this that he saith unto us, A little while, and ye behold me not; and again a little while, and ye shall see me: and, Because I go to the Father? 18 They said therefore, What is this that he saith, A little while? We know not what he saith. 19 Jesus perceived that they were desirous to ask him, and he said unto them, Do ye inquire among yourselves concerning this, that I said, A little while, and ye behold me not, and again a little while, and ye shall see me?

P 20 Verily, verily, I say unto you, that ye shall weep and lament, but the world shall rejoice: ye shall be sorrowful, but your sorrow shall be turned into joy. 21 A woman when she is in travail hath sorrow, because her hour is come: but when she is delivered of the child, she remembereth no more the anguish, for the joy that a man is born into the world. 22 And ye therefore now have sorrow: but I will see you again, and your heart shall rejoice, and your joy no one taketh away from you.

Q 23 And in that day ye shall [1]ask me nothing. Verily, verily, I say unto you, If ye shall ask anything of the Father, he will give it you in my name. 24 Hitherto have ye asked nothing in my name: ask, and ye shall receive, that your joy may be fulfilled.

R 25 These things have I spoken unto you in [2]proverbs: the hour cometh, when I shall no more speak unto you in [2]proverbs, but shall tell you plainly of the Father.

S 26 In that day ye shall ask in my name: and I say not unto you, that I will [3]pray the Father for you; 27 for the Father himself loveth you, because ye have loved me, and have believed that I came forth from the Father.

T 28 I came out from the Father, and am come into the world: again, I leave the world, and go unto the Father. 29 His disciples say, Lo, now speakest thou plainly, and speakest no [4]proverb. 30 Now know we that thou knowest all things, and needest not that any man should ask thee: by this we believe that thou camest forth from God.

U 31 Jesus answered them, Do ye now believe? 32 Behold, the hour cometh, yea, is come, that ye shall be scattered, every man to his own, and shall leave me alone: and *yet* I am not alone, because the Father is with me.

V 33 These things have I spoken unto you, that in me ye may have peace. In the world ye have tribulation: but be of good cheer; I have overcome the world.

MT-MK-LK

N *With verse 15 compare §41 Q and §82 T and §151 B*

O *Compare §139 portion C*
Compare §147 portion F

P *With verse 22 compare the references under portion O above*

Q *Compare §78 portion U*
Compare §127 portion D

U *Compare §139 portion B*

ERV margin: 1 Or *ask me no question* 2 Or *parables* 3 Greek *make request of* 4 Or *parable*

OT references: John 16:22 = Isaiah 66:14

§ 212 FAREWELL PRAYER OF JESUS

MT-MK-LK

JOHN 17:1–26

A   1 These things spake Jesus; and lifting up his eyes to heaven, he said, Father, the hour is come; glorify thy Son, that the Son may glorify thee:

B *With verse 2a compare §41 Q and §82 T and §151 B*

B   2 even as thou gavest him authority over all flesh, that whatsoever thou hast given him, to them he should give eternal life. 3 And this is life eternal, that they should know thee the only true God, and him whom thou didst send, *even* Jesus Christ.

C   4 I glorified thee on the earth, having accomplished the work which thou hast given me to do. 5 And now, O Father, glorify thou me with thine own self with the glory which I had with thee before the world was.

D   6 I manifested thy name unto the men whom thou gavest me out of the world: thine they were, and thou gavest them to me; and they have kept thy word. 7 Now they know that all things whatsoever thou hast given me are from thee: 8 for the words which thou gavest me I have given unto them; and they received *them*, and knew of a truth that I came forth from thee, and they believed that thou didst send me.

E *With verse 10a compare the references under portion B above*

E   9 I ¹pray for them: I ¹pray not for the world, but for those whom thou hast given me; for they are thine: 10 and all things that are mine are thine, and thine are mine: and I am glorified in them. 11 And I am no more in the world, and these are in the world, and I come to thee.

F   Holy Father, keep them in thy name which thou hast given me, that they may be one, even as we *are*. 12 While I was with them, I kept them in thy name which thou hast given me: and I guarded them, and not one of them perished, but the son of perdition; that the scripture might be fulfilled. 13 But now I come to thee; and these things I speak in the world, that they may have my joy fulfilled in themselves.

G   14 I have given them thy word; and the world hated them, because they are not of the world, even as I am not of the world. 15 I ¹pray not that thou shouldest take them ²from the world, but that thou shouldest keep them ²from ³the evil *one*. 16 They are not of the world, even as I am not of the world.

H *With verse 18 compare §56 C and §82 A*

H   17 ⁴Sanctify them in the truth: thy word is truth. 18 As thou didst send me into the world, even so sent I them into the world. 19 And for their sakes I ⁵sanctify myself, that they themselves also may be sanctified in truth.

I   20 Neither for these only do I ¹pray, but for them also that believe on me through their word; 21 that they may all be one; even as thou, Father, *art* in me, and I in thee, that they also may be in us: that the world may believe that thou didst send me.

J   22 And the glory which thou hast given me I have given unto them; that they may be one, even as we *are* one; 23 I in them, and thou in me, that they may be perfected into one; that the world may know that thou didst send me, and lovedst them, even as thou lovedst me.

K   24 Father, ⁶that which thou hast given me, I will that, where I am, they also may be with me; that they may behold my glory, which thou hast given me: for thou lovedst me before the foundation of the world.

L *Compare the second half of §41 Q and §82 T*

L   25 O righteous Father, the world knew thee not, but I knew thee; and these knew that thou didst send me; 26 and I made known unto them thy name, and will make it known; that the love wherewith thou lovedst me may be in them, and I in them.

ERV margin: 1 Greek *make request*   2 Greek *out of*   3 Or *evil*   4 Or *Consecrate*   5 Or *consecrate*   6 Many ancient authorities read *those whom*

OT references: John 17:12 = Psalm 41:9

§ 213 AT THE PLACE NAMED GETHSEMANE

JOHN 18:1–2

1 When Jesus had spoken these words, he went forth with his disciples over the ¹brook ²Kidron, where was a garden, into the which he entered, himself and his disciples. 2 Now Judas also, which betrayed him, knew the place: for Jesus oft-times resorted thither with his disciples.

MT-MK-LK

Compare §139 A and §140 A
Compare §140 portion B

§ 214 BETRAYAL AND ARREST OF JESUS

JOHN 18:3–11

A 3 Judas then, having received the ³band *of soldiers*, and officers from the chief priests and the Pharisees, cometh thither with lanterns and torches and weapons.

A   *Compare §141 portion A*

B   4 Jesus therefore, knowing all the things that were coming upon him, went forth, and saith unto them, Whom seek ye? 5 They answered him, Jesus of Nazareth. Jesus saith unto them, I am *he*. And Judas also, which betrayed him, was standing with them. 6 When therefore he said unto them, I am *he*, they went backward, and fell to the ground. 7 Again therefore he asked them, Whom seek ye? And they said, Jesus of Nazareth. 8 Jesus answered, I told you that I am *he:* if therefore ye seek me, let these go their way: 9 that the word might be fulfilled which he spake, Of those whom thou hast given me I lost not one.

C   10 Simon Peter therefore having a sword drew it, and struck the high priest's ⁴servant, and cut off his right ear.   Now the ⁴servant's name was Malchus.

C   *Compare §141 portion D*

D   11 Jesus therefore said unto Peter, Put up the sword into the sheath: the cup which the Father hath given me, shall I not drink it?

D   *Compare §141 portion F*
    Compare §120 portion C
    Compare §140 portion C

ERV margin: 1 Or *ravine* Greek *winter-torrent*   2 Or *of the Cedars*   3 Or *cohort*   4 Greek *bondservant*

CHAPTER XV

JUDICIAL TRIALS AND CRUCIFIXION

§ 215 TRIAL BEFORE THE JEWISH AUTHORITIES

JOHN 18:12–27   MT-MK-LK

A^A 12 So the ¹band and the ²chief captain, and the officers of   A *Compare §142 portion A*
the Jews, seized Jesus and bound him, 13 and led him to Annas
first; for he was father in law to Caiaphas, which was high priest
that year.   14 Now Caiaphas was he which gave counsel to the
Jews, that it was expedient that one man should die for the people.
B   15 And Simon Peter followed Jesus, and *so did* another disciple.
Now that disciple was known unto the high priest, and entered
in with Jesus into the court of the high priest; 16 but Peter was
standing at the door without.   So the other disciple, which was
known unto the high priest, went out and spake unto her that
kept the door, and brought in Peter.
C   17 The maid therefore that   C *Compare §142 portion H*
kept the door saith unto Peter, Art thou also *one* of this man's
disciples?   He saith, I am not.
D   18 Now the ³servants and the   D *Compare §142 portion B*
officers were standing *there*, having made ⁴a fire of coals; for it
was cold; and they were warming themselves: and Peter also was
with them, standing and warming himself.
E   19 The high priest therefore asked Jesus of his disciples, and   E *Compare §142 portion D*
of his teaching.   20 Jesus answered him, I have spoken openly to   *With verse 20 compare §141*
the world; I ever taught in ⁵synagogues, and in the temple, where   *portion G*
all the Jews come together; and in secret spake I nothing.
21 Why askest thou me? ask them that have heard *me*, what I
spake unto them: behold, these know the things which I said.
22 And when he had said this, one of the officers standing by
struck Jesus ⁶with his hand, saying, Answerest thou the high
priest so?   23 Jesus answered him, If I have spoken evil, bear
witness of the evil: but if well, why smitest thou me?
F   24 Annas   F *Compare §142 portion M*
therefore sent him bound unto Caiaphas the high priest.
G   25 Now Simon Peter was standing and warming himself.   G *Compare §142 portion I*
They said therefore unto him, Art thou also *one* of his disciples?
He denied, and said, I am not.
H   26 One of the ³servants of the   H *Compare §142 portion J*
high priest, being a kinsman of him whose ear Peter cut off, saith,   *Compare §142 portion K*
Did not I see thee in the garden with him?   27 Peter therefore
denied again: and straightway the cock crew.

§ 216 TRIAL BEFORE THE ROMAN AUTHORITIES

JOHN 18:28—19:16ª

A   28 They lead Jesus therefore from Caiaphas into the ⁷palace: A *Compare §142 portion M*
and it was early; and they themselves entered not into the   *Compare §143 portion A*
⁷palace, that they might not be defiled, but might eat the pass-
over.
B   29 Pilate therefore went out unto them, and saith, What
accusation bring ye against this man?   30 They answered and
said unto him, If this man were not an evil-doer, we should not
have delivered him up unto thee.   31 Pilate therefore said unto

---

ERV margin: 1 Or *cohort*   2 Or *military tribune* Greek *chiliarch*   3 Greek *bondservants*   4 Greek *a fire of*
charcoal   5 Greek *synagogue*   6 Or *with a rod*   7 Greek *Prætorium*

A   Compare §202 portion C

Mt-Mk-Lk   JOHN 18–19

them, Take him yourselves, and judge him according to your law. The Jews said unto him, It is not lawful for us to put any man to death: 32 that the word of Jesus might be fulfilled, which he spake, signifying by what manner of death he should die.

c *Compare §143 portion D*

C 33 Pilate therefore entered again into the ¹palace, and called Jesus, and said unto him, Art thou the King of the Jews?

D *Compare §143 portion E*

D   34 Jesus answered, Sayest thou this of thyself, or did others tell it thee concerning me? 35 Pilate answered, Am I a Jew? Thine own nation and the chief priests delivered thee unto me: what hast thou done? 36 Jesus answered, My kingdom is not of this world: if my kingdom were of this world, then would my ²servants fight, that I should not be delivered to the Jews: but now is my kingdom not from hence.

E *Compare §143 portion D*

E   37 Pilate therefore said unto him, Art thou a king then? Jesus answered, ³Thou sayest that I am a king.

F *Compare §143 portion E*

F   To this end have I been born, and to this end am I come into the world, that I should bear witness unto the truth. Every one that is of the truth heareth my voice. 38 Pilate saith unto him, What is truth?

G *Compare §143 portion F*

G And when he had said this, he went out again unto the Jews, and saith unto them, I find no crime in him.

H *Compare §143 portion I*

H   39 But ye have a custom, that I should release unto you one at the passover: will ye therefore that I release unto you the King of the Jews?

I *Compare §143 portion K*

I   40 They cried out therefore again, saying, Not this man, but Barabbas. Now Barabbas was a robber.

J *Compare §143 portion M*
K *Compare §143 portion N*
  Compare verse 11 of §143 G

J 19:1 Then Pilate therefore took Jesus, and scourged him.

K 2 And the soldiers plaited a crown of thorns, and put it on his head, and arrayed him in a purple garment; 3 and they came unto him, and said, Hail, King of the Jews! and they struck him ⁴with their hands.

L *Compare §143 portion H*

L   4 And Pilate went out again, and saith unto them, Behold, I bring him out to you, that ye may know that I find no crime in him. 5 Jesus therefore came out, wearing the crown of thorns and the purple garment.

M *Compare §143 portion K*

M   And *Pilate* saith unto them, Behold, the man! 6 When therefore the chief priests and the officers saw him, they cried out, saying. Crucify *him*, crucify *him*. Pilate saith unto them, Take him yourselves, and crucify him: for I find no crime in him.

N   7 The Jews answered him, We have a law, and by that law he ought to die, because he made himself the Son of God. 8 When Pilate therefore heard this saying, he was the more afraid; 9 and he entered into the ¹palace again, and saith unto Jesus, Whence art thou? But Jesus gave him no answer. 10 Pilate therefore saith unto him, Speakest thou not unto me? knowest thou not that I have ⁵power to release thee, and have ⁵power to crucify thee? 11 Jesus answered him, Thou wouldest have no ⁵power against me, except it were given thee from above: therefore he that delivered me unto thee hath greater sin.

o *On the charge of making himself a king, compare §143 C*
  With verse 16 compare §143 portion M

O   12 Upon this Pilate sought to release him: but the Jews cried out, saying, If thou release this man, thou art not Cæsar's friend: every one that maketh himself a king ⁶speaketh against Cæsar. 13 When Pilate therefore heard these words, he brought Jesus out, and sat down on the judgement-seat at a place called The Pavement, but in Hebrew, Gabbatha. 14 Now it was the Preparation of the passover: it was about the sixth hour. And he saith unto the Jews, Behold, your King! 15 They therefore cried out, Away with *him*, away with *him*, crucify him. Pilate saith unto them,

---

ERV margin: ¹ Greek *Prætorium*   ² Or *officers:* as in verses 3, 12, 18, 22   ³ Or *Thou sayest it, because I am a king*   ⁴ Or *with rods*   ⁵ Or *authority*   ⁶ Or *opposeth Cæsar*

JOHN 19	MT-MK-LK

Shall I crucify your King? The chief priests answered, We have no king but Cæsar. 16 Then therefore he delivered him unto them to be crucified.

§ 217   THE CRUCIFIXION OF JESUS

JOHN 19:16b–30

A   16 They took Jesus therefore: 17 and he went out, bearing the cross for himself,

B   unto the place called The place of a skull, which is called in Hebrew Golgotha: 18 where they crucified him, and with him two others, on either side one, and Jesus in the midst. 19 And Pilate wrote a title also, and put it on the cross. And there was written, JESUS OF NAZARETH, THE KING OF THE JEWS.

C   20 This title therefore read many of the Jews: ¹for the place where Jesus was crucified was nigh to the city: and it was written in Hebrew, *and* in Latin, *and* in Greek. 21 The chief priests of the Jews therefore said to Pilate, Write not, The King of the Jews; but, that he said, I am King of the Jews. 22 Pilate answered, What I have written I have written.

D   23 The soldiers therefore, when they had crucified Jesus, took his garments, and made four parts, to every soldier a part; and also the ²coat: now the ²coat was without seam, woven from the top throughout. 24 They said therefore one to another, Let us not rend it, but cast lots for it, whose it shall be: that the scripture might be fulfilled, which saith,

> They parted my garments among them,
> And upon my vesture did they cast lots.

These things therefore the soldiers did.

EE   25 But there were standing by the cross of Jesus his mother, and his mother's sister, Mary the *wife* of Clopas, and Mary Magdalene. 26 When Jesus therefore saw his mother, and the disciple standing by, whom he loved, he saith unto his mother, Woman, behold, thy son! 27 Then saith he to the disciple, Behold, thy mother! And from that hour the disciple took her unto his own *home*.

F   28 After this Jesus, knowing that all things are now finished, that the scripture might be accomplished, saith, I thirst. 29 There was set there a vessel full of vinegar: so they put a sponge full of the vinegar upon hyssop, and brought it to his mouth.

G   30 When Jesus therefore had received the vinegar, he said, It is finished: and he bowed his head, and gave up his spirit.

Right column notes:

A   *Compare §144 portion A*

B   *Compare §144 portion C*

D   *Compare §144 portion C*

E   *Compare §144 portion L*

F   *Compare §144 portion G*

G   *Compare §144 portion H*

§ 218   THE BURIAL OF JESUS

JOHN 19:31–42

A   31 The Jews therefore, because it was the Preparation, that the bodies should not remain on the cross upon the sabbath (for the day of that sabbath was a high *day*),

B   asked of Pilate that their legs might be broken, and *that* they might be taken away. 32 The soldiers therefore came, and brake the legs of the first, and of the other which was crucified with him: 33 but when they came to Jesus, and saw that he was dead already, they brake not his legs: 34 howbeit one of the soldiers with a spear pierced his side, and straightway there came out blood and water.

C   35 And he that hath seen hath borne witness, and his witness is true: and he knoweth that he saith true, that ye also may believe. 36 For

Right column note:

A   *Compare §145 portion A*

ERV margin: 1 Or *for the place of the city where Jesus was crucified was nigh at hand*   2 Or *tunic*

OT references: John 19:24 = Psalm 22:18   John 19:28–29 = Psalm 69:21   John 19:36 = Exodus 12:46 and Numbers 9:12 and Psalm 34:20

E   For other references to the disciple whom Jesus loved, compare §209 I, §219 B, §222 AC, and §223 A

Mt-Mk-Lk	John 19

       these things came to pass, that the scripture might be fulfilled, A bone of him shall not be ¹broken. 37 And again another scripture saith, They shall look on him whom they pierced.

D   *Compare §145 portion B*   D   38 And after these things Joseph of Arimathæa, being a disciple of Jesus, but secretly for fear of the Jews, asked of Pilate that he might take away the body of Jesus: and Pilate gave *him* leave. He came therefore, and took away his body.

Eᴱ   39 And there came also Nicodemus, he who at the first came to him by night, bringing a ²mixture of myrrh and aloes, about a hundred pound *weight*.

F   *Compare §145 portion D*   F   40 So they took the body of Jesus, and bound it in linen cloths with the spices, as the custom of the Jews is to bury. 41 Now in the place where he was crucified there was a garden; and in the garden a new tomb wherein was never man yet laid. 42 There then because of the Jews' Preparation (for the tomb was nigh at hand) they laid Jesus.

ERV margin: 1 Or *crushed*   2 Some ancient authorities read *roll*

OT references·   John 19:37 = Zechariah 12:10

E   For other references to Nicodemus, compare §161 A and §189 H

CHAPTER XVI

SUBSEQUENT TO THE DEATH OF JESUS

§ 219 THE VISITS TO THE SEPULCHRE

JOHN 20:1-18

MT-MK-LK

A 1 Now on the first *day* of the week cometh Mary Magdalene early, while it was yet dark, unto the tomb, and seeth the stone taken away from the tomb.

A *Compare §147 portions ABC*

B 2 She runneth therefore, and cometh to Simon Peter, and to the other disciple, whom Jesus loved, and saith unto them, They have taken away the Lord out of the tomb, and we know not where they have laid him.

B *Compare §147 portion G*
Compare §147 portion I
Compare §149 portion C

C 3 Peter therefore went forth, and the other disciple, and they went toward the tomb. 4 And they ran both together: and the other disciple outran Peter, and came first to the tomb; 5 and stooping and looking in, he seeth the linen cloths lying; yet entered he not in. 6 Simon Peter therefore also cometh, following him, and entered into the tomb; and he beholdeth the linen cloths lying, 7 and the napkin, that was upon his head, not lying with the linen cloths, but rolled up in a place by itself. 8 Then entered in therefore the other disciple also, which came first to the tomb, and he saw, and believed. 9 For as yet they knew not the scripture, that he must rise again from the dead. 10 So the disciples went away again unto their own home.

C *Compare §147 portion J*
Compare §149 portion D

D 11 But Mary was standing without at the tomb weeping: so, as she wept, she stooped and looked into the tomb; 12 and she beholdeth two angels in white sitting, one at the head, and one at the feet, where the body of Jesus had lain. 13 And they say unto her, Woman, why weepest thou? She saith unto them, Because they have taken away my Lord, and I know not where they have laid him.

D *Compare §147 portion D*
Compare §149 portion C

E 14 When she had thus said, she turned herself back, and beholdeth Jesus standing, and knew not that it was Jesus. 15 Jesus saith unto her, Woman, why weepest thou? whom seekest thou? She, supposing him to be the gardener, saith unto him, Sir, if thou hast borne him hence, tell me where thou hast laid him, and I will take him away. 16 Jesus saith unto her, Mary. She turneth herself, and saith unto him in Hebrew, Rabboni; which is to say, [1]Master. 17 Jesus saith to her, [2]Touch me not; for I am not yet ascended unto the Father: but go unto my brethren, and say to them, I ascend unto my Father and your Father, and my God and your God. 18 Mary Magdalene cometh and telleth the disciples, I have seen the Lord; and *how that* he had said these things unto her.

E *Compare §147 portion H*
For the record of the ascension here promised, compare §150 portion F

§ 220 WITH THE DISCIPLES IN JERUSALEM

JOHN 20:19-29

A 19 When therefore it was evening, on that day, the first *day* of the week, and when the doors were shut where the disciples were, for fear of the Jews, Jesus came and stood in the midst, and saith unto them, Peace *be* unto you. 20 And when he had said this, he shewed unto them his hands and his side. The disciples therefore were glad, when they saw the Lord.

A *Compare §150 portion B*

ERV margin: 1 Or *Teacher*   2 Or *Take not hold on me*

B   For other references to the disciple whom Jesus loved, compare §209 I, §217 E, §222 AC, and §223 A

Mt-Mk-Lk

B   *Compare §150 portion E*
    Compare §151 portion C

C   *Compare §71 portion F*
    Compare §78 portion T

JOHN 20

B   21 Jesus therefore said to them again, Peace *be* unto you: as the Father hath sent me, even so send I you.

C   22 And when he had said this, he breathed on them, and saith unto them, Receive ye the [1]Holy Ghost: 23 whose soever sins ye forgive, they are forgiven unto them; whose soever *sins* ye retain, they are retained.

D   24 But Thomas, one of the twelve, called [2]Didymus, was not with them when Jesus came. 25 The other disciples therefore said unto him, We have seen the Lord. But he said unto them, Except I shall see in his hands the print of the nails, and put my finger into the print of the nails, and put my hand into his side, I will not believe.

E   26 And after eight days again his disciples were within, and Thomas with them. Jesus cometh, the doors being shut, and stood in the midst, and said, Peace *be* unto you. 27 Then saith he to Thomas, Reach hither thy finger, and see my hands; and reach *hither* thy hand, and put it into my side: and be not faithless, but believing. 28 Thomas answered and said unto him, My Lord and my God. 29 Jesus saith unto him, Because thou hast seen me, [3]thou hast believed: blessed *are* they that have not seen, and *yet* have believed.

§ 221   PURPOSE OF THE RECORD OF JOHN

JOHN 20:30–31

30 Many other signs therefore did Jesus in the presence of the disciples, which are not written in this book: 31 but these are written, that ye may believe that Jesus is the Christ, the Son of God; and that believing ye may have life in his name.

§ 222   WITH THE DISCIPLES AT THE SEA OF TIBERIAS

JOHN 21:1–23

A   *For an account in the Mt-Mk-Lk record having some elements in common with this narrative, compare §27 (Luke)*

AA   1 After these things Jesus manifested himself again to the disciples at the sea of Tiberias; and he manifested *himself* on this wise. 2 There were together Simon Peter, and Thomas called [2]Didymus, and Nathanael of Cana in Galilee, and the *sons* of Zebedee, and two other of his disciples. 3 Simon Peter saith unto them, I go a fishing. They say unto him, We also come with thee. They went forth, and entered into the boat; and that night they took nothing. 4 But when day was now breaking, Jesus stood on the beach: howbeit the disciples knew not that it was Jesus. 5 Jesus therefore saith unto them, Children, have ye aught to eat? They answered him, No. 6 And he said unto them, Cast the net on the right side of the boat, and ye shall find. They cast therefore, and now they were not able to draw it for the multitude of fishes. 7 That disciple therefore whom Jesus loved saith unto Peter, It is the Lord. So when Simon Peter heard that it was the Lord, he girt his coat about him (for he was naked), and cast himself into the sea. 8 But the other disciples came in the little boat (for they were not far from the land, but about two hundred cubits off), dragging the net *full* of fishes. 9 So when they got out upon the land, they see [4]a fire of coals there, and [5]fish laid thereon, and [6]bread. 10 Jesus saith unto them, Bring of the fish which ye have now taken. 11 Simon Peter therefore went [7]up, and drew the net to land, full of great fishes, a hundred and fifty and three: and for all there were so many, the net was not rent. 12 Jesus saith unto them, Come *and* break your fast. And none of the disciples durst inquire of him, Who art thou? knowing that it was the Lord. 13 Jesus cometh, and taketh the

---

ERV margin: 1 Or *Holy Spirit*   2 That is *Twin*   3 Or *hast thou believed?*   4 Greek *a fire of charcoal*   5 Or *a fish*   6 Or *a loaf*   7 Or *aboard*

A   For other references to the disciple whom Jesus loved, compare §209 I and §217 E and §219 B

JOHN 21   MT-MK-LK

¹bread, and giveth them, and the fish likewise.   14 This is now
the third time that Jesus was manifested to the disciples, after
that he was risen from the dead.
B   15 So when they had broken their fast, Jesus saith to Simon
Peter, Simon, *son* of ²John, ³lovest thou me more than these?
He saith unto him, Yea, Lord; thou knowest that I ⁴love thee.
He saith unto him, Feed my lambs.   16 He saith to him again a
second time, Simon, *son* of ²John, ³lovest thou me?   He saith
unto him, Yea, Lord; thou knowest that I ⁴love thee.   He saith
unto him, Tend my sheep.   17 He saith unto him the third time,
Simon, *son* of ²John, ⁴lovest thou me?   Peter was grieved because
he said unto him the third time, ⁴Lovest thou me?   And he said
unto him, Lord, thou knowest all things; thou ⁵knowest that I
⁴love thee.   Jesus saith unto him, Feed my sheep.
cᶜ   18 Verily,
verily, I say unto thee, When thou wast young, thou girdedst
thyself, and walkedst whither thou wouldest: but when thou
shalt be old, thou shalt stretch forth thy hands, and another shall
gird thee, and carry thee whither thou wouldest not.   19 Now
this he spake, signifying by what manner of death he should
glorify God.   And when he had spoken this, he saith unto him,
Follow me.   20 Peter, turning about, seeth the disciple whom
Jesus loved following; which also leaned back on his breast at the
supper, and said, Lord, who is he that betrayeth thee?   21 Peter
therefore seeing him saith to Jesus, Lord, ⁶and what shall this
man do?   22 Jesus saith unto him, If I will that he tarry till I
come, what *is that* to thee?   follow thou me.   23 This saying
therefore went forth among the brethren, that that disciple should
not die: yet Jesus said not unto him, that he should not die; but,
If I will that he tarry till I come, what *is that* to thee?

§ 223   CONCLUSION OF THE RECORD OF JOHN

JOHN 21:24-25

Aᴬ   24 This is the disciple which beareth witness of these things,
and wrote these things: and we know that his witness is true.

B   25 And there are also many other things which Jesus did, the
which if they should be written every one, I suppose that even
the world itself would not contain the books that should be
written.

ERV margin: 1 Or *loaf*   2 Greek *Joanes:* called in Matthew 16:17 *Jonah*   3 4 *Love* in these places represents two different Greek words   5 Or *perceivest*   6 Greek *and this man, what?*

c   Compare § 222 A and attached references

A   Compare § 222 A and attached references

EXHIBIT OF THE RELATIONS BETWEEN THE RECORD OF MT-MK-LK AND THE RECORD OF JOHN

IN THE ORDER OF MT-MK-LK

§	§	§
§ 11 C ...... § 189 F	§ 45 Q ...... § 182 B	§ 71 E ...... § 155 B
§ 17 ...... § 152 B	§ 46 E ...... § 211 E	§ 71 F ...... § 220 C
§ 17 D–F ..... § 153 C	§ 47 J ...... § 207 B	§ 73 AB ..... § 206 C
§ 17 O ..... § 153 A	§ 49 E ...... § 211 E	§ 74 C ...... § 152 D
§ 17 P ...... § 152 E	§ 53 B ...... § 188 A	§ 74 M ...... § 153 B
§ 17 P ...... § 153 E	§ 53 B ...... § 193 D	§ 76 A ...... § 184
§ 17 P ...... § 154 A	§ 53 B ...... § 193 E	§ 78 B ...... § 209 D
§ 17 R ...... § 164	§ 53 B ...... § 197 G	§ 78 D ...... § 161 C
§ 18 B ...... § 154 B	§ 54 C ...... § 187 A	§ 78 E ...... § 209 D
§ 18 B ...... § 154 D	§ 54 D ...... § 182 F	§ 78 G ...... § 176 B
§ 18 C ...... § 154 C	§ 54 H ...... § 172 B	§ 78 G ...... § 208 A
§ 18 C ...... § 154 D	§ 54 J ...... § 185 B	§ 78 G ...... § 209 G
§ 20 G ...... § 156 B	§ 56 B ...... § 170 D	§ 78 H ...... § 209 D
§ 21 A ...... § 167	§ 56 C ...... § 212 H	§ 78 T ...... § 220 C
§ 21 A ...... § 172 A	§ 56 D ...... § 155 B	§ 78 U ...... § 210 E
§ 21 B ...... § 158	§ 56 D ...... § 156 A	§ 78 U ...... § 210 H
§ 22 C ...... § 187 A	§ 57 A ...... § 211 H	§ 78 U ...... § 211 C
§ 22 D ...... § 182 F	§ 57 C ...... § 210 I	§ 78 U ...... § 211 F
§ 22 H ...... § 172 B	§ 57 D ...... § 211 K	§ 78 U ...... § 211 Q
§ 23 ...... § 155 A	§ 57 E ...... § 211 G	§ 82 A ...... § 212 H
§ 24 A ...... § 158	§ 57 G ...... § 209 E	§ 82 B ...... § 170 D
§ 24 B ...... § 189 G	§ 57 G ...... § 211 H	§ 82 Q ...... § 176 B
§ 24 E ...... § 189 G	§ 57 NO ...... § 206 C	§ 82 Q ...... § 208 A
§ 27 ...... § 155 A	§ 57 P ...... § 176 B	§ 82 Q ...... § 209 G
§ 27 ...... § 222 A	§ 57 P ...... § 208 A	§ 82 Q ...... § 211 I
§ 29 GH ...... § 174 C	§ 57 P ...... § 209 G	§ 82 R ...... § 206 E
§ 32 ...... § 195 B	§ 58 BC ...... § 153 B	§ 82 R ...... § 211 M
§ 32 B ...... § 175 A	§ 58 D ...... § 164	§ 82 T ...... § 166 B
§ 33 ...... § 195 B	§ 60 A ...... § 178 A	§ 82 T ...... § 182 H
§ 33 G ...... § 175 C	§ 60 B ...... § 178 B	§ 82 T ...... § 189 B
§ 35 B ...... § 183 D	§ 60 C ...... § 178 C	§ 82 T ...... § 197 D
§ 35 B ...... § 211 F	§ 60 D ...... § 178 D	§ 82 T ...... § 209 B
§ 35 C ...... § 155 B	§ 60 F ...... § 178 E	§ 82 T ...... § 211 N
§ 35 C ...... § 156 A	§ 60 G ...... § 178 G	§ 82 T ...... § 212 B
§ 36 HI ...... § 211 G	§ 60 H ...... § 178 H	§ 82 T ...... § 212 E
§ 36 HI ...... § 211 H	§ 60 I ...... § 178 F	§ 82 T ...... § 212 L
§ 38 H ...... § 209 E	§ 60 J ...... § 180 A	§ 84 ...... § 200 A
§ 38 H ...... § 211 H	§ 60 K ...... § 179 B	§ 84 ...... § 204 A
§ 38 X ...... § 189 G	§ 61 A ...... § 180 B	§ 86 C ...... § 188 A
§ 39 ...... § 173 B	§ 61 B ...... § 180 C	§ 86 C ...... § 193 D
§ 41 E ...... § 153 C	§ 61 D ...... § 180 D	§ 86 C ...... § 193 E
§ 41 G ...... § 153 B	§ 62 A ...... § 180 D	§ 86 C ...... § 197 G
§ 41 Q ...... § 166 B	§ 65 ...... § 178 A	§ 86 D ...... § 182 B
§ 41 Q ...... § 182 H	§ 66 A ...... § 194 C	§ 87 ...... § 211 E
§ 41 Q ...... § 189 B	§ 67 A ...... § 178 B	§ 91 I ...... § 210 I
§ 41 Q ...... § 197 D	§ 67 C ...... § 178 C	§ 94 A ...... § 209 B
§ 41 Q ...... § 209 B	§ 67 D ...... § 178 D	§ 95 A ...... § 206 D
§ 41 Q ...... § 211 N	§ 67 E ...... § 178 E	§ 98 ...... § 195 B
§ 41 Q ...... § 212 B	§ 67 F ...... § 178 G	§ 102 ...... § 195 B
§ 41 Q ...... § 212 E	§ 67 H ...... § 178 H	§ 104 C ...... § 206 C
§ 41 Q ...... § 212 L	§ 67 I ...... § 178 F	§ 112 J ...... § 206 C
§ 42 A ...... § 204 B	§ 67 J ...... § 180 A	§ 116 C ...... § 161 C
§ 44 ...... § 185 B	§ 68 A ...... § 182 B	§ 120 C ...... § 214 D
§ 45 C ...... § 188 A	§ 70 A ...... § 194 C	§ 120 J ...... § 209 D
§ 45 C ...... § 193 D	§ 71 A ...... § 179 B	§ 124 C ...... § 205 D
§ 45 C ...... § 193 E	§ 71 C ...... § 153 B	§ 124 E ...... § 205 C
§ 45 C ...... § 197 G	§ 71 D ...... § 183 C	§ 124 F ...... § 205 A

LOCATION OF PASSAGES IN THE RECORDS